FINDING CROSS-CULTURAL
COMMON GROUND

Dignity Press
World Dignity University Press

In Finding Cross-cultural Common Ground, Michael H. Prosser (USA), Mansoureh Sharifzadeh (Iran), and Zhang Shengyong (China) have coedited a highly eclectic book, based on the www.michael-prosser.com international blog. The book's essays frequently consider critical cultural values such as human dignity, social justice, peace, human rights and gender equality. At times scholarly, sometimes semi-scholarly, often autobiographical and opinion-oriented, or presenting popular views, it includes essays, reflections, public conversations, cultural stories and book reviews. Part I emphasizes intercultural, international, and global topics; Part II stresses Asia and especially China; and Part III focuses on the Middle East and especially Iran. This book provides valuable cultural insights as the editors and included authors invite the readers to join them in seeking essential aspects of cross-cultural common ground.

FINDING CROSS-CULTURAL COMMON GROUND

Michael H. Prosser
University of Virginia,
Shanghai International Studies University

Mansoureh Sharifzadeh
Ministry of Education, Tehran, Iran

Zhang Shengyong
Dezhou University, Dezhou, China

Dignity Press
World Dignity University Press

Published by Dignity Press
16 Northview Court
Lake Oswego, OR 97035, USA
www.dignitypress.org

All photos were contributed by the authors.
Book design by Uli Spalthoff
Printed on paper from environmentally managed forestry:
www.lightningsource.com/chainofcustody

Book website: www.dignitypress.org/fcccg

ISBN 978-1-937570-25-5
Also available as EPUB: ISBN 978-1-937570-26-2
and Kindle eBook: ISBN 978-1-937570-27-9

Contents

PART II
CROSS-CULTURAL COMMON GROUND
IN CONTEMPORARY ASIA AND CHINA

Dedication

To my grandchildren: Christine Ann (1992); Elizabeth Marie (1993); Mary Catherine Rose (1996); Darya Serenity Michelle (1997); Sanders Steven Gabriel (1998); Sophia Lily Grace (2001); Conner Michael (1998); Jordan Faith (2000); and Luke Patrick (2004).

May you become world citizens!

Michael H. Prosser

To the peacemakers who solve global issues through dialogue and mutual understanding to promote correlation among nations.

Mansoureh Sharifzadeh

To the Shandong Planning Office of Philosophy And Social Science (No. 12CWJJ29). To my niece Zhang Ruihan who always brings happiness to me.

Zhang Shengyong

Preface

Michael H. Prosser

Language is the soul of culture and the metaphor is the soul of language. All humans are inherently narrative story tellers and also creators of the negative. Online, for example, in my blog www.michaelprosser.com, words as symbolic language are infinite, but in this book form there is a definite finiteness, with a greater requirement for precision and inclusion. Many posts on my blog relate to virtues and values such as dignity, peace, wisdom, and social justice, and thus a number of the essays, public conversations, travel and cultural stories, and book reviews in this book also emphasize these qualities. In this book, we are enabling many different authentic voices to be heard and we are not making judgments about their voices, even though they may be different from ours, independently or collectively. Indeed, it is reasonable to assume that the three of us do not agree on the views of some of the invited voices, nor even our co-editors' essays, but we honor the openness which comes from creating such a dialogue.

The first section of the book explores finding cross-cultural common ground in different cultural, regional, national, and international settings, including Semester at Sea around the world study tour observations related to Africa. Several book reviews highlight the scholarly activities of experts on intercultural or international topics, and the concept of righteous living. Some regional areas receive more attention than others, because of the limitations of our experiences.

The second section emphasizes contributions coming out of Asia broadly and China more specifically, as I spent about ten years teaching there, and developed cross-generational friendships with many young Chinese. There are also observations about the Semester at Sea around the world study tour related to Asia.

The third section engages the Middle East, and more specifically Iran because of an email friendship with Mansoureh Sharifzadeh of Tehran which has developed since May 2011 after the death of the second last President of Damavand College, and our mutual friend, D. Ray Heisey. Section 3 includes a number of essays by Mansoureh Sharifzadeh, public conversations, cultural stories, and a joint book review.

As I was considering turning many of the blog posts into essays for this book, and having had intercultural authorships both with Mansoureh Sharifzadeh and Zhang Shengyong, as well as having individual posts in the blog by both of them, I recognized that it would add to the book's intercultural and cross-cultural richness by inviting them as my co-editors, and thereby having more Asian and Middle Eastern perspectives than I might have alone, as well as a wider age range among us. The book is eclectic and provides both autobiographical/ academic, and observational/ opinion-oriented aspects for all three of us, and many other voices included, which we hope blend well together.

Thanks to Mansoureh Sharifzadeh and Zhang Shengyong for joining me. As almost everything in this book appeared originally in my blog, you are encouraged to visit it. We hope that the wide range of ideas in the book itself will stimulate you to consider these topics more deeply and broadly than we are able to do.

Michael H. Prosser, Ph.D.
Charlottesville, Virginia, December, 2012
www.michaelprosser.com

prossermichael@gmail.com
mansourehsharifzadeh@yahoo.com
jackyzhangshengyong@gmail.com

PART I

CONTEMPORARY CROSS-CULTURAL COMMON GROUND

A) INTRODUCTORY ESSAY: ANCIENT AND CONTEMPORARY VIEWS OF ATTITUDES AND VALUES

Michael H. Prosser
University of Virginia, Charlottesville, Virginia, USA
Shanghai International Studies University, Shanghai, China

"I am neither a citizen of Athens, nor of Greece, but of the world." (Socrates)

Introduction

When we review the many values which may have been or were considered universal at different times and in different traditions, we can see that among these major values found in the Old Testament as a pseudo history, chronicles, and poetry, for the Israelites were the sacredness of life, the covenant with God, forgiveness by God to humans and forgiveness-seeking from humans by God, as in the Psalms of David, the brotherhood of man (but often in a particularistic dimension exclusively for them as God's chosen people), dependence upon God, and a guide for righteous living among others. Basically the Old Testament was written over 1500 years, and represented for early and modern Jews as the Torah or Law and the first of the world's major religions of a monotheistic God.

The Ten Commandments given by God to Moses have become a near universal standard of conduct, at least in the Western world. It was accepted by the Christians as a part of their sacred texts along with the New Testament and later was modified somewhat as a part of the historical development of Islam as the final revelation from God through the Qur'an. The Christians saw and still see the Israelites or Jews as their fore fathers in faith, and the Muslims saw and partially see the Jews and Christians as their predecessors in faith. All three of these major monotheistic religions are Abrahamic in tradition.

The early Christian texts in the New Testament were identified as the new covenant between God and his people, but with the universalistic command "to go and teach all people." Jesus Christ claimed that he was in himself, (sui generis) "the way, the truth and the life." While accepting the Old Testament as the Law or Torah, he offered a new and more inclusive covenant and gave a new universal value to love God with one's full heart, mind, and soul, and also to love his neighbor as himself. Both Jesus and St. Paul placed major attention on the three chief virtues, faith, hope, and love (charity). Both Jesus and St. Paul identified love as the most important and enduring of all virtues, and thus clearly universal in nature. Forgiveness of others' wrong doing and mercy were central themes in his teaching. In his "Sermon on the Mount," Jesus annunciated a series of positive values and negative contrasts to these values. The Old Testament, the New Testament, the Qur'an, and the sacred writings of the polytheistic religions and philosophies, all consider prayer, fasting, and alms giving to the poor as central to the development of a good life for all.

Hinduism, and later Buddhism, accepted the concept of a divine supernatural being, just as the Jews, Christians, and Muslims did, but added other divinities as also the Greeks and Romans accepted. The Hindus, without a definite founder or time for its initiation, accepted as universal principles four broad categories based on moksha – the search for liberation from unhappiness and a past chain of lives, and samsura – one's involvement in the universe. These four broad categories included kharma– the central role in life of having a sense of doing right, but which had both positive and negative aspects, artha–the pursuit of material well- being, kama – the pleasure of the senses, and dharma – leading a right and virtuous life. These combinations, accepted at least as near universals, all have the power in Hinduism and Buddhism to lead one ultimately to happiness or linkage with Brahman or unity with the divine spirit.

Buddhism, enriched first by Sidhartha, and later living Buddhas, articulates for "all humans" "Four Noble Truths": life is suffering; all suffering is caused by ignorance of the nature of reality and craving for material well-being and attachment; suffering can be overcome by overcoming ignorance and attachment (which the Israeli psychologist Schalom Schwartz might call hedonism). Buddhism adopted the Hindu notion of life as cyclical. In Buddhism, the "Four Noble Truths" can lead to the "Eightfold Way:" which consists of right views, right intention, right speech, right action, right livelihood, right effort, right-mindedness, and right contemplation. These eight are usually divided into three categories that form the cornerstone of Buddhist faith: morality, wisdom, and samadhi, or concentration.

Confucianism, based in The Analects, provides a hierarchical system of five universal values: and proposes such concepts as ren – benevolence, kindness, filial piety, love of kind (a particularistic value), respect for authority and elders, social stability and harmony, goodness in life, courteousness in public life, diligence in relationships, and loyalty to family or superiors; jen or humaneness, li – moral propriety through established rituals which include several of the characteristics of ren; di – moral righteousness or moral power; lian – one's internalized dimension including face practices; and mianzi – one's externalized images, including also face practices, or more broadly harmony or creating a harmonious society (a major goal of the current Chinese leadership, for example). While we do not necessarily see happiness as a central factor such as Hinduism, Buddhism, and the Greeks provide in their belief systems, it certainly must be a result in Confucianism in the process of being benevolent or kind, in having moral righteousness or power, and in both the internalized and externalized images which the Confucian life-world illustrates. Despite setbacks, the Confucian world view remains a dominant philosophy in societies such as China, Japan, Korea, Vietnam, Cambodia and others. Justice (and social justice) is certainly a major value in Hinduism, Buddhism, and Confucianism and may indeed be a universal value.

For the ancient Greeks, and to an extent the ancient Romans who followed them, their perception of universal values were truth including the ultimate truth, truth-telling, wisdom, the overcoming of ignorance, goodness, justice, idealism, reality, happiness, forgiveness and reconciliation and the initiation of scientific rationalism. The goddess Athena represented both wisdom and physical power, strength and war – as contrasting drives. Early developments of individualism were encouraged by the Greeks whose young male citizens were taught and encouraged to be direct, to argue for their own rights and positions, to debate forcefully, as well as to be fully involved in civic life through the courts, the theatre, the arts, poetics, and sports, in contrast to young ancient Asians who were taught to respect authority and only to speak when they had obtained wisdom and their own respected position in society. The Greeks saw themselves as like the gods and goddesses whom they had created anthropomorphically to have all of their own human attributes and failures.

Islam is derived from the Arabic word 'Salema"; peace, purity, submission and obedience. The major values and virtues that Islam holds have been reflected in the holy book of Qur'an in its thirty chapters. The opening chapter of the Quran reads, "In the name of Allah, the beneficient, the merciful, all praise is due to Allah, the lord of the worlds, the beneficent, the merciful master of the day of judgment, thee do we serve and thee do we beseech for help, keep us on the right path, the path of those upon whom thou hast bestowed favors not (the path) of those upon whom thy wrath is brought down, nor of those who go astray."

Islam encourages the followers to seek help from the divine power that surrenders the entire existence. Islam values may be interpreted differently but avoiding sins and corruption to keep chastity are the permanent rules. Islam values are summarized in the will of God and acceptance of what comes while taking actions and pursuing one's goals. The will of Allah is the highest as Allah is the most kind and merciful.

The Middle Ages – Enlightenment

Noting that what is called the high medieval period (about 1000 to 1400 AD) and the early Renaissance (about 1400-1600 AD) in the West continued to place God at the center of their universe, at the same time, it led to the creation of great European universities as early as the thirteenth century, extraordinary art and architecture, an evolving middle class, an enriched literature, dissident thought in the development of the Protestant Revolution, and global exploration. Often considered the greatest Westerner of the second millennium, Johannes Gutenberg with his printing press had a great opportunity to promote values not just as cultural, but as truly universal, with the printing of 200 Bibles over several years. As the Renaissance, or rebirth of classical knowledge, art, literature, and architecture, began in the West (Italy), and spread widely to France, Germany, and Spain, it led to the eighteenth century as the Age of Reason. John Locke pondered the concept of the social contract and civil society and later in the writings of Thomas Jefferson, Benjamin Franklin, Alexander Hamilton, John Adams, and James Madison, we see life, liberty and the pursuit of happiness, and later private property, emerging as perceived universal rights and values in the United States Constitution and the Bill of Rights.

The 1789 French Rights of Man and of the Citizen declaration based on these ideas and certainly those of Jean Jacques Rousseau in the French Revolution in 1789: freedom, equality, and fraternity (or later called the brotherhood of man), included also universal notions of popular national sovereignty, religious tolerance, and the separation of powers as universal values and rights Other values perceived as universal in the French document included equality of all persons before the law; equitable taxation; protection against loss of property through arbitrary action by the state; freedom of religion, speech, and the press; and protection against arbitrary arrest and punishment, all which found their way into the Universal Declaration of Human Rights (1948) and the International Bill of Human Rights established by the two binding treaties in 1966 related to political and civil rights.

Modern Theories of Attitudes and Values

Milton Rokeach in his 1972 book, Beliefs, Attitudes and Values: A Theory of Organization and Change, argues that attitudes long held the central position in the scholarship of social psychology and sociology, but that the value concept should move ahead of attitudes as social psychology's and sociology's central focus:

First, value seems to be a more dynamic concept since it has a strong motivational component as well as cognitive, affective, and behavioral components. Second, while attitudes and values are both widely assumed to be determinants of social behavior, value is a determinant of attitude as well as behavior. Third, if we further assume that a person possesses considerably fewer values than attitudes, then the value concept provides us with a more economical analytical tool for describing and explaining similarities and differences between persons, groups, nations, and cultures (Rokeach, 1972, pp. 157-158).

He notes that while attitudes seem to focus in the study of social psychology and sociology, the academic nature of values crosses many more disciplines, thereby creating the possibility for interdisciplinary scholarly collaboration. Rokeach defines attitudes, which are an organization of several beliefs focused on a specific object or situation as predisposing one to respond in some preferential manner. However, he postulates that: "Values, on the other hand, have to do with modes of conduct and end-states of existence.... Once a value is internalized it becomes – consciously or unconsciously – a standard or criterion for guiding action, for developing and maintaining attitudes toward relevant objects and situations, for justifying one's own and others' actions and attitudes, for morally judging self and others, and for comparing self with others. Finally, a value is a standard employed to influence the values, attitudes, and actions of at least some others...." (pp. 159-160). He sees two types of values, instrumental – which may be centered around one or a small group of beliefs, and terminal values – which suggests: "I believe that such-and-such an end-state of existence (for example, salvation, a world at peace) is personally worth striving for" (p. 160).

Although Rokeach does not discuss human rights as values, in considering the Universal Declaration of Human Rights, we can assume that universal human rights are like terminal values, or end-states. This view of the universalism of human rights tends to be more of a Western worldview, while the cultural specificity or particularism of such rights tends to be more of an Asian, Middle Eastern and African system. Rokeach later suggests that in the polarity of values in terms of social relations as they relate to the criteria of desirability, different dimensions or modes of valuing may emphasize "equality or inequality; collectivity or individual interest; acceptance or rejection or authority; individual autonomy or interdependence; expressiveness or restraint (affectivity/neutrality); diffuseness or specificity; ascribed qualities or excellence of performance (ascription/achievement); particularistic relationship relationships or categorical memberships; personalized or universalistic standards; hostility or affection or indifference; dominance or submission" (1979).

Because values are learned culturally, a densely filled "value space" can be represented reasonably well by four factors: "(1) the extent of acceptance of authority, (2) need-determined expression or value-determined expression or value-determined restraint (3) acceptance or rejection of egalitarianism, and (4) extent of acceptance of indivi¬dualism…. The communication of common appraisals eventually builds value standards, which often become widely accepted across many social and cultural boundaries…." (1979, p. 22). Arguing that in any ideal value system, Rokeach says that if pressed to extreme limits, unexpected and undesired implications and consequences may result: "Example 1: Who does not want freedom? Who does not believe in some aspects of equality of human rights? But what happens if we demand instant and total freedom, or instant and total equality? Total freedom is chaos, and the end result always is a dictatorial order. Total substantive equality requires a tight system of social control" (1979, p. 43).

In this context, we must note that the universalism of human rights may in certain circumstances conflict with other views in the specific cultural or particularistic context, basically a contrast between Western and Eastern/Middle Eastern/African perspectives. This view, however, contrasts cultural specificity vs. the basic principles of the Universal Declaration of Human Rights as universal values, to which the document itself recommends, and to which I personally subscribe. However, I am speaking as a Westerner. Rokeach does argue in fact, noting that one reasonable patterning of values, in addition to hierarchical (i.e. Confucian orientation) ordering which may be very imperfect, and the extensiveness of adherence to particular values, is the degree of universality of application and consistency between cultures (1979, p. 18). He sees a general movement to apply "universalistic criteria and to accept humanitarian values seems evident in public policies toward ethnic and racial minorities, poor people, the physically disabled, children, women workers, and others subject to special stresses, disabilities, and discrimination" (1979, p. 37). These are clearly areas addressed by various articles of the Universal Declaration of Human Rights as universal values (for example, Article 2 – equal rights; Article 7 – equality before the law; Article 25 – adequate standard of living, Article 26 – education.

Munro S. Edmunson has stressed the most difficult cultural structural or functional views to identify values. "The common denominator of all culture is its communicative process, because it is through cultural communication that values are passed on within the culture and are shared with others in other cultural settings" (1973, p. 192-196). Pope John Paul II in speaking of values says: "I will only say that it is what costs that constitutes value. It is not, in fact, possible to be truly free without an honest and profound relationship with values" (1983). K.S. Sitaram argues that in western societies, the most important value configuration emphasizes individualism while in eastern societies, the chief value concentration revolves around the concept of responsibility (1995).

Clyde Kluckhohn defines values as "a conception, explicit or implicit, distinctive of an individual or characteristics of a group, of the desirable which influences the selection from available modes, means, and ends of action" suggesting that key words include desirable [normative], conception [values as a logical construct], and selection [ability to choose between alternatives]. Kluckhohn proposes that since all values are arrived at on an evaluative basis, often culturally fixed, the realm of value is conduct, which is culturally approved or disapproved, reinforced, supported, or challenged (1962, pp. 394-403). We could define values as something to believe in, to be devoted to, to hope in, by which to structure our morality, and something to give us rootedness within our own cultures or societies, as well as those which are universally accepted.

This might also be called an idealistic, elitist, and very broad world view, in contrast to what Kwang-Kuo Hwang calls the lifeworld or the real world in which people live, not necessarily idealistically, but in terms of reality. He believes that the worldviews of a specific cultural lifeworld opposite to the scientific microworld proposed by Western values scholars are essentially different. He proposes that cultural lifeworlds are gradually constructed by people in a given culture when they ponder on the nature of the universe and situations of human beings by "orginative" thinking in history and provides answers to four fundamental questions: "Who am I? What is my situation in life? Why do I suffer? What is my salvation" (Hwang, 2008, p. 255)? Hwang believes that the western worldview of the scientific microworld "does not answer questions about the meaning of life, which is essentially different from the worldview of our [Chinese] lifeworld" (Hwang, 2008, p. 258).

Nonetheless, though approaching values from a Western perspective, Kluckhohn sees a group's worldview or collection of values as consisting of both normative and existential postulates, both of what should be and what actually is. He not only considers the notion of values as central to cultural study, but also of value-orientations, which he describes as a generalization of nature, of the human's place in it, of his relation to other humans, and of what is desirable and nondesirable in relating as individuals to humans, their environment, and to their interhuman relations (1962, p. 409-411). "Essentially, this means that as humans we may have generalized preferences toward certain values potentially derived on a universalistic basis, because we are humans" (quoted in Prosser, 1978, p. 180).

Florence Kluckhohn and Fred Strodtbeck define value orientations as complex but definitely patterned or rank ordered principles in the human evaluative process, which include the cognitive, the affective or emotional, and the directional or motivational elements which give direction to the constant stream of human acts and thoughts as they relate to the solution of "common human" problems and occur in ranking patterns of component parts which are themselves cultural universals (1961, pp. 4-8). At the level of cultural universals, Kluckhohn and Strodtbeck formulate a set of basic assumptions in considering value-orientations based on the culturally specific premise that ordered variations exist among cultures. They assume that there is a limited number of common human and universalistic problems for which "all people at all times and in all locations must find solutions" (p. 10). Clyde Kluckhohn postulated that, "it should be possible to construct the views of a given group regarding the structure of the universe, the relation of humans to the universe, both natural and supernatural, and the relations of one human to another. These views will represent the group's own definition of the ultimate meaning of human life, including its rationalization of frustration, disappointment, and calamity" (cited in Prosser, 1978, p. 179).

Kluckhohn and Strotbeck argue that, "essentially, this means that as humans we may have generalized preferences toward certain values potentially derived on a universalistic basis because we are humans" (cited in Prosser, 1978, p. 180). They isolate five basic problems to all human groups and cultures, including the character of innate human nature (human nation orientation); humans to nature and supernature; the temporal focus of human life; the modality of activity – doing or being; and human relationships to other humans. They sum up their approach to a major research problem: (1) What is the character of innate human nature (human nature orientation)? (2) What is the relation of humans to nature and supernature (human-nature orientation)? (3) What is the temporal focus of human life (time-orientation)? (4) What is the modality of human activity (activity orientation)? (5) What is the modality of human's relationship to others (relational orientation)? They also have posed but did not test the spatial orientation. (Prosser, 1978, pp. 181–182).

John C. Condon and Fathi Yousef further expand these value orientations to twenty-five. As universal values and value orientations, they include the self (including individualism/ interdependence, age, sex, and activity), the family including relational interaction, authority, positional role behavior and mobility), the society including social reciprocity, group membership, intermediaries, formality, and property), human nature (including rationality, good and evil, happiness and pleasure, and mutability) nature (including relationships of humans and nature, ways of knowing nature, structure of nature, and the concept of time), and the supernatural including the relationship of humans and the supernatural, the meaning of life, providence, and knowledge of the cosmic order) (1975, p. 60-62). Adopting the contributions of Kluckhohn and Strodtbeck, Edward C. Stewart compares these variables between two cultures, Filipinos and North Americans. I. Perception of the self and the individual; II. Perception of the world; III. Motivation; IV. Form of relations to others; V. Form of activity (1971). Such comparisons speak as Rokeach does to the polarity of values between the East (but including also Africa) which emphasizes particularism and the West which stresses universalism (1979), and also as Sitaram does in his comparisons between Western and Eastern values (1995).

While Hwang's lifeworld speaks of a culture gradually determining its worldview or approaches to universal values and value orientations, H. L. Nieburg suggests that changes in values are precursors to political, social, and institutional changes, and that we can determine whether values such as truth and reality are universal or culturally specific by stripping away cultural rituals: "All of the forms of ritual behavior are parts or dimensions of culture; they are expressions, often nonverbal, of the values, attitudes theories, interpretations, potential actions, and expectations of individuals in a community" (Nieburg, 1973, pp. 3-30).

Shalom H. Schwartz quotes the psychologist Milton Rokeach (1973), the sociologist Robin M. Williams, Jr. (1968), and anthropologist Clyde Kluckhohn (1951) in promoting "the centrality of the value concept" and as viewing "values as the criteria people use to evaluate actions, people (including the self) and events." Agreeing with these theorists, Schwartz writes "I too view values as criteria people use, rather than as qualities inherent in objects" Schwartz identifies ten motivationally distinct value orientations, the goals that are identified by these values, and the dynamics of conflict and congruence among these values: self-direction, stimulation, hedonism, achievement, power, security, conformity, tradition, benevolence, and universalism.

He offers a unifying theory "for the field of human motivation, a way of organizing the different needs, motives, and goals proposed in other theories." He argues that to develop a coherent theory of universal values, one must address four issues: "(1) Is there a near universal set of values differentiated by motivational content? (2) Is the set of values identified by the theory comprehensive, leaving out none of the broad values to which individuals attribute at least moderate importance: (3) Do the values have similar meanings in different groups (e.g., ethnic, national, gender, etc.), thereby justifying comparison of value priorities across groups? (4) Is there a near-universal structure of dynamic relations among values?" Schwartz in his value theory, and that of Schwartz and Bilsky, notes the following five main features of all values: (1) Values are beliefs. (2) Values are a motivational construct. (3) Values transcend specific actions and situations. (4) Values guide the selection or evaluation of actions, policies, people, and events. (5) Values are ordered by importance relative to one another. The above are features of all values.

Personally, I have never considered hedonism as a universal value, but rather as a contrasting and negative drive; however as he describes hedonism "as pleasure or sensuous gratification for oneself," as a biological response, it no doubt can be considered as important as the other universal values which he identifies. Rokeach also includes gratification as a value, which should be included in broad cultural values. Additionally, I have never considered power by itself as a positive value, but also as a contrasting and negative drive: "There is a constant interplay between the drives and the values of the technological society...." Jules Henry notes that in our modern society, the society's media have led us to a feverish quality of life, already suggested by de Tocqueville in the nineteenth century. Henry argues that the technological society is a driven culture, forced by drives such as expansiveness, competitiveness, individuality, and achievement" (Henry, 1963). Prejudice, for example, can be seen as the combination of power and negative stereotypes and prejudice against other groups: "At the same time, many of us who are products of such a society believe strongly in values such as gentleness, kindliness and generosity" (Henry, 1963, pp. 23-25 in Prosser, 1978, p. 28). However, as Schwartz identifies that power and achievement values focus on social esteem, which certainly is commonly considered an important universal value, he notes that he does not include happiness as a universal value: "though it is an important value that some might associate with hedonism. Happiness can be linked to all values, because people achieve it through attaining whatever outcomes they value" (Sagiv & Schwartz, 2000)."

Shalom H. Schwartz's theory of the basic values that people in all cultures recognize identifies ten motivationally distinct value orientations and specifies the dynamics of conflict and congruence among these values which were measured by his SVS test: benevolence (clearly identified in Confucianism), universalism (established in the Universal Declaration of Human Rights, and its subsequent treaties, covenants, and conventions), self-direction (also proposed by the Kluckhohns and Strodtbeck considerations of values and value orientations and identifying all persons as independent individuals worthy of dignity and respect in the UN Charter and Universal Declaration of Human Rights), stimulation and, hedonism (seen in Greek, Hindu, and Buddhist traditions as potential contrasts to higher ideals), achievement and power (relating to physical versus moral power as found among the Confucianists, Greeks, and early Christians, and recognizing social esteem and dignity for all individuals), security (seen in developing the social contract, popular sovereignty, and national sovereignty), conformity (seen in the Universal Declaration of Human Rights in its call for all states and individuals to adhere to its principles), and tradition (the development over time of perceived universal values, rights, and later human rights versus culturally, philosophically, or religiously different traditions).

Schwartz notes that: "The values theory describes aspects of the human psychological structure that are fundamental, aspects presumably common to all humankind. Consequently, its propositions should apply across cultures." This statement certainly relates to the Universal Declaration of Human Rights and other universal values as perceived historically. There are four issues for consideration proposed by Schwartz: "(1) Is there a near universal set of values differentiated by motivational content? (2) Is the set of values identified by the theory comprehensive, leaving out none of the broad values to which individuals attribute at least moderate importance? (3) Do the values have similar meanings in different groups (e.g. ethnic, national, gender, etc.) thereby justifying comparison of value priorities across groups? (4) Is there a near universal structure of dynamic relations among values? Though it is obvious that the governments from an Eastern, Middle Eastern, and African context might disagree sharply with me as they come from a particularistic and culturally diverse framework for human rights and human values, the UN Charter, the Universal Declaration of Human Rights, and the subsequent treaties, covenants, and conventions demand a universalistic approach to human rights, and thus in my perception also to the even broader framework of universalistic human values.

While Clyde Kluckhohn, Florence Kluckhohn, and Fred Strodtbeck were not explicitly concerned in their formulation and study of universal human values and value orientations specifically with universal human rights, the connections above linking universal values and value orientations and universal human rights are at least implicit. The values and value orientations that they have accepted and studied, and those added by Condon and Yousef and others such as Geert Hofstede, Michael Harris Bond, and Shalom Schwartz later have at least implicitly offered the foundation for merging the tenets of the Universal Declaration of Human Rights and the later human rights treaties, covenants, and conventions with universal values. Rokeach clearly identifies the dimensions between universalistic and particularistic dimensions of universal values and universalistic versus particularistic or culturally diverse views of human rights

Henk Vinken's discussion about human rights coming from two different camps, universalism and particularism is very appropriate and in terms of human values, his view is supported by Shalom Schwartz' studies of universal, regional, and culturally specific values. We note that in principle the Universal Declaration of Human Rights sets an ideal standard for all of humanity, at every time, and in every place, and for every individual in society. The subsequent UN treaties, covenants, and conventions remain in contrast to the view by Asian, Middle Eastern, and African countries that certain human rights are not universal but can only be seen through the perspective of particularism or cultural diversity. A number of authors have considered the relationship between multiculturalism, cultural diversity, (leaning toward particularism), and global communication (leaning toward universalism) in Sitaram and Prosser (1998 & 1999).

Most likely, the term human rights was first fully developed in the 1815 Treaty of Vienna, when the international slave trade was abolished as a fundamental violation of the rights of those who were enslaved. However, the actual abolishment of slavery in the West did not occur until President Abraham Lincoln's Emancipation Proclamation in 1863. Unfortunately, although slavery has been identified more recently in United Nations treaties, documents, and declarations as a "crime against humanity," it still exists in many societies in the world. Universal values such as peace, national sovereignty, social justice, dignity, tolerance, and equality, all have been stressed more and more in modern times and as central to the Universal Declaration of Human Rights, and subsequent United Nations treaties, covenants, documents, and declarations.

The Hague Conventions, the League of Nations, and the United Nations all set the stage for the Universal Declaration of Human Rights, and subsequent treaties, conventions, and declarations for a broad set of universalistic principles, norms, values, and ideals to be accepted, at least theoretically, on a world-wide basis. The universal search for international peace and security, as well as the rights and values noted above, in contrast to particularistic and culturally selective values and rights have been at odds in modern societies, especially in Eastern, Middle Eastern, and African contexts. Universal values are clearly linked to universal human rights in the principles of the United Nations, although often not in the practice in individual societies.

Conclusion

Personally, I believe with Aristotle that happiness may be among the most important universal values. Self-esteem naturally should also be considered among the highest of universal values and norms. As a Christian, I accept the three major values expressed by Jesus and St. Paul, faith, hope, and love (charity). I accept the Greek concepts of truth, justice, wisdom, and the good life. I accept the Confucian virtues of benevolence, kindness, proper behavior, and harmony as part of my own lifeworld.

Selected References

Condon, J.C., & Yousef, F. (1975).An introduction to intercultural communication. Indianapolis, IN: Bobbs Merrill.

Edmunson, M. S. (193). The anthropology of values. In W.S. Taylor, J. L. Fischer, & E. Z. VogtIn (Eds.), Culture and life: Essays in memory of Clyde Kluckhohn. Carbondale, IL: Southern Illinois University Press.

Friere, P. (1992). Address. SIETAR International Congress. Montegro Bay, Jamaica.

Henry, J. (1963). Culture against man. Middlesex, England: Penguin.

Hwang, K.-K. (2007). The development of indigenous social psychology in Confucian society. In S. J. Kulich & M.H. Prosser (Eds.), Intercultural perspectives on Chinese communication. Shanghai, China: Shanghai Foreign Language Education Press.

Kluckhohn, R. (Ed). (1962). Culture and behavior: Collected essays of Clyde Kluckhohn. New York, NY: Free Press.

Kluckhohn, C., Rockwood Kluckhohn, F., & Strodbeck, F. (1961).Variations of value orientations. Evanston, IL: Row, Peterson.

Kulich, S.J. & Prosser, M.H. (in press). Values dimensions and their contextual dynamics: Intercultural research: Vol. 5. Shanghai, China: Shanghai Foreign Language Education Press.

Li, M. & Prosser, M.H. (2012). Communicating interculturally. Beijing, China: Higher Education Press.

Nieburg, H. L. (1973). Culture storm: Politics and the ritual order. New York, NY: St. Martins.

Prosser, M.H. (1978). The cultural dialogue: An introduction to intercultural communication. Boston, MA: Houghton Mifflin.

Prosser, M.H. & Sitaram, K.S. (1999). Civic discourse: Intercultural, international, and global media. Westport, CT: Ablex.

Rokeach, M. (1972). Beliefs, attitudes and values: A theory of organization and change. San Francisco, CA: Jossey Bass.

Rokeach, M. (Ed.). (1979). Understanding human values: Individual and societal. New York, NY: The Free Press.

Schwartz, S. H. (1994). Are there universal aspects in the structure and contents of human values? In S. J. Kulich & M. H. Prosser (Eds.) (2012).Values frameworks at the theoretical crossroads of culture, Intercultural research, Vol. 4. Shanghai, China: Shanghai Foreign Language Education Press.

Schwartz, S. H. (2012). Basic human values: Their content and structure across cultures, in S. J. Kulich & M. H. Prosser (Eds.), Values frameworks at the theoretical crossroads of culture, Intercultural research, Vol. 4. Shanghai, China: Shanghai Foreign Language Education Press

Sitaram, K. S. (1995). Communication and culture: A world view. New York, NY: McGraw Hill.

Sitaram, K. S. & Prosser,M. H. (Eds.). (1998). Civic discourse: Multiculturalism, cultural diversity, and global communication. Westport, CT: Ablex.

Vinken, H. (2012). The cultural fit of global values surveys in East Asia: The urgency to include East Asian-origin concepts. In S. J. Kulich & M. H. Prosser (Eds.), Values frameworks at the theoretical crossroads of culture, Intercultural research, Vol. 4. Shanghai, China: Shanghai Foreign Language Education Press.

B) SEMESTER AT SEA AROUND THE WORLD STUDY VOYAGE

The University of Virginia/Institute for Shipboard Education, Autumn, 2011

Michael H. Prosser
University of Virginia, Charlottesville, Virginia,
Shanghai International Studies University, Shanghai, China

Originally sponsored by Chapman College, then the University of Colorado, then the University of Pittsburg, and now the University of Virginia, the Semester at Sea is fifty years old in 2013 and has had 60,000 participants. For the three and a half month autumn semester 2011 voyage in our Jeffersonian "Academic Village" 28,000 nautical mile voyage, faculty and staff, dependents, 451 students and sixty-one Lifelong Learners were at sea, plus 187 crew members, mostly Filipinos, and spent 55 days at sea and 56 days in ports: Casablanca, Morocco; Tema, Ghana; Cape Town, South Africa; Port Louis, Mauritius; Chennai, India; Penang, Malaysia; Ho Chi Minh City, Viet Nam; Hong Kong and Shanghai, China; Kobe and Yoko-hama, Japan; Hilo, Hawaii; Las Palmas, Costa Rica; traversing the Panama Canal; Ruitan, Honduras; and disembarking at Fort Lauderdale, Florida. The theme of this voyage was global studies, and all participants attended the global studies class; evening explorer seminars were provided and many other shipboard activities occurred. Social justice was a major theme of the experience, and many students volunteered at an AIDs orphanage, other orphanages, hospitals, and schools, in village workshops, in a South African hunger project, in Habitat for Humanity, and at a Thanksgiving Day soup kitchen in Hilo. Many participants brought books and school supplies to give at different social justice locations.

Some interesting statistics for this Semester at Sea voyage include this profile: 451 students, 38% male, 62% female; 27% non-Caucasian, including 8% Hispanic, 5% Asian, international students 5%, and African American students 4%.

C) Semester at Sea: Africa – Social Justice, Poverty, and Human Rights

Michael H. Prosser
University of Virginia,Charlottesville, Virginia,
Shanghai International Studies University, Shanghai, China

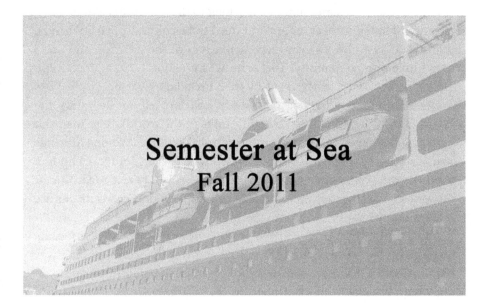

Semester at Sea
Fall 2011

Casablanca, Morocco

This afternoon, for the Lifelong Learners, a world religions professor, a professor of Islam and I provided a panel discussion on the three main monotheistic religions, Judaism, Christianity, and Islam.

This evening, we had a ship-wide cultural seminar about Morocco and Islam. The professor of Islam gave the entire shipboard community a succinct understanding of the Five Pillars of the Islamic faith: "There is only one God – Allah, and Mohammed is His prophet, Peace be upon him; prayer five times daily facing Mecca; alms for the poor; fasting from food, any form of drink, or intimate activities for the month of Ramadan, sunrise to sunset; and if possible participating in the Hage at Mecca." We will be in Morocco at the festival of Aid, for the ending of Ramadan. The Semester at Sea dean of students discussed the African concept of "Ubuntu:" the consideration that we belong to the wholeness of humanity, or unity of humans together and our need to be culturally sensitive in all that we do as active learners, representatives of the program and one's own university community. This term was a major Tanzanian concept, among others, in the early 1960s by then President Nyerre.

This morning, our shipboard professor of Islam led our visit into the Hassan II Mosque (the third largest mosque in the world). Both men and women are allowed to enter the interior of the mosque. Women Muslims worship from two balconies inside the worship space. Moroccan children from the area have kindergarten for two years of Qu'ranic learning at the Mosque, before they enter primary school. All Moroccan citizens are required to belong to the Islamic faith.

About half of the surface of the mosque lies over the Atlantic Ocean, inspired by the verse of the Qu'ran that states "the throne of Allah was built on water." King Hassan II, stated, "I want to build this mosque on the water, because God's throne is on the water. Therefore, the faithful who go there to pray, to praise the Creator on firm soil, can contemplate God's sky and ocean." Six thousand worshipers can fill the Mosque, and outside another 125 thousand can participate in Mosque activities.

We also visited Notre Dame de Lourdes Church, the only one of four Roman Catholic churches still open for foreigners. There are 20,000 foreign Catholics in Morocco. Among the stained glass windows the church has a very vivid, unusual, and large stained glass window of the devil, "diablo."

MARRAKECH, MOROCCO

Arriving in Marrakech in southern Morocco, "the red city" because of the red clay exteriors, one of the four imperial cities in Morocco and a city of more than one million residents, our group of 26 enjoyed the extraordinary square, filled with a mosque, tourists and residents, noisy drummers, snake charmers, eager trinket sellers, two-horse carriages, dancers, cafes, restaurants, clothing stalls, and souvenir shops. We explored the extensive Souk Medina's alleys, constantly filled with motor bikes and pedestrians, including many children since schools don't begin until September 15.

On the second day of our excursion, we traveled to the Ourika Valley below the Atlas Mountains, inhabited entirely by the Berber tribes, who have their own language and customs that are quite different than those in the large cities such as Casablanca, Rabat, Marrakech, and Fes. Many of the Berbers do not speak Arabic. This excursion gave us a good impression of rural Morocco, with a multitude of sheep, and the local people. Other excursions and many students independently visited the capitol Rabat, and the ancient city of Fes, with an even larger Medina than in Marrakech. Still others took a long excursion to the desert for camel trekking, and staying in tents in the desert overnight. as well as visits with the Berber tribesmen and families.

Yesterday, a group of more than thirty of us went north past Rabat to the Roman ruins near Voboublis, an area that had been penetrated during the Roman Empire by Roman Legions and buildings. By coincidence, the guide for our first excursion and the trip to the Roman ruins was a 60 year old Mohammed, who began and ended each visit "in the name of God, and with the help of our driver and his assistant, we have arrived." He was a very wise and profound Muslim who spoke individually to me at some length about his relationship to Allah, his adult children, and his times in London and Amsterdam. It was my good fortune that he was the tour guide on my second two excursions.

Morocco provided us an excellent initial introduction to Africa. Now, we have several days at sea again before reaching Tema, Ghana. Ghana is considered one of the most important countries in West Africa. In 1970, I included UN General Assembly addresses by Nkrouma, often called the

"George Washington of Africa in my two volume collection: Sow the Wind: Reap the Whirlwind: Heads of State Address the United Nations (1970).

Today's Global Studies course for the shipboard community included discussions about the Modernization Theory and the Dependency Theory of sustainable development, as well as the eight 2000 UN Millennium Goals which call for implementation by 2015. A very brief video produced by www.thegirleffect.com, showing the rise of populations in the developed and emerging worlds, plus the increase in poverty in the least developed world, and a video demonstration showing both simple baskets and digital graphs demonstrating the world population growth of 3 billion in 1960 to nearly 7 billion in 2010 were all very powerful visual images. The Semester at Sea participants are in some ways fortunate to be visiting three of the countries (Morocco, Ghana, and South Africa) which are developing more rapidly than many of the countries in the interior of Africa.

In 1990-91, I served as a Fulbright Professor initiating the communication major in the University of Swaziland. At that time, Swaziland was prospering because multinational companies such as Coca Cola were operating from there rather than in South Africa – still under the negative effects of apartheid. Then too, Zimbabwe was a model of development which sadly is no longer the case. In contrast, the economy of Zimbabwe has declined markedly under the leadership of the founding president Robert Mugabwe, now 84.

Recent political changes that have occurred this past summer in Morocco include: "2011 Constitutional reforms." On July 1, voters approved a set of political reforms that the King proposed and were voted on by the citizens on July 2, 2011 and passed by an overwhelming majority.

ENROUTE TO GHANA

September 10, 2011: The UN Millennium Goals; Sustainable Development; Slavery in the Gold Coast and in the Americas; Ghanaian Society and Culture

On board, we have had extensive information about the slave trade originating in western Africa, including Ghana, where all along the coast there are the slave castles which held captured Africans in the 17th and 18th centuries for months until the slave ships came to transport them to Brazil and the West Indies, and eventually to the United States. Many were held chained to the floor or walls, with only an hour or two daily for exercise. Slave captains, who purchased the slaves at wholesale prices, had figured out mathematically how many slaves could lie chained on different parts of the ship, how much food to provide to keep them reasonably healthy, and how many were likely to die on the passage. Africans from many different regional tribes were held so that they didn't have the ability to plan escapes or revolts together, either in the slave castles, on the ships, or after reaching the Americas. In the process of selling them, often with families separated, Brazil became the largest country with a native African population in the world outside of Africa. Slave auctions were held all over the south of the United States regularly, including at the courthouse in Charlottesville, Virginia, the home of Presidents Thomas Jefferson and James Monroe, both major slaveowners.

Recently, a 27 year old Semester at Sea alumnus from 2006, Adam Braun, and the founder of "Pencils of Promise," who came on board in Morocco with his mother, was our speaker. Inspired by his Semester at Sea experience while in Laos, he met children who had no access to education, but when he explored what they most would like, one child said "a pencil." As the child's eyes lighted up with the gift of a pencil, Adam thought "Why not build a school?" After returning to the United States, completing his degree at Brown University, and with frequent back packing trips alone in poor countries, he decided to hold a giant Halloween Party for students as a fundraiser to build a school in the Laotian village which he had visited and he raised $8,000 for building the school. Later, expanding on this idea, he held masquerade parties for students to raise more funds to build schools in Laos and Guatemala. Presently, "Pencils of Promise" has begun or completed construction of 41 schools in developing countries and has become a major nonprofit foundation, gaining respect from many corporate foundations and executives. The local native population supplies 20-30% of the cost to build the small schools and to hire a native teacher through their labor or contribution of building materials. Since we are going to Ghana, he challenged us to hold a fund-raiser to pay the costs of building a rural school in Ghana.

Two other faculty members and I offered a panel discussion for the Lifelong Learners on the United Nations and sustainable national development. The former UN Secretary General and Nobel Peace Laureate, Kofi Annan, has stressed that the two most serious human problems remain war and abject poverty. The panel discussed the eight 2000 United Nations Millennium goals to be achieved by 2015 and sustainable national development, including women's reproductive choices and rights and the elimination of environmental poverty.

The UN Millennium Development goals for 2015, including cutting poverty and hunger in half, universal primary school education, gender equality, child health, maternal health, combatting HIV/AIDs, environmental sustainability, and global partnerships for women's and girls' education have been partially met, raising 350 million out of extreme poverty. Many rural people throughout the world have been left far behind, with major migrations from the rural areas to the urban centers as now 171 cities have more than 1 million population. "Significant strides have been made towards the Millennium Development Goals, yet reaching all the goals by the 2015 deadline remains challenging, as the world's poorest are being left behind," according to the MDG Report 2011, the UN's annual progress report. "The MDGs have helped lift millions of people out of poverty, save countless children's lives and ensure that they attend school," UN Secretary-General Ban Ki-moon said. "At the same time, we still have a long way to go in empowering women and girls, promoting sustainable development, and protecting the most vulnerable." On July 11, 2011, the 7 billionth person was born, according to UN statistics, very likely to come from one of the world's most impoverished regions.

Also today, a seminar was held on the "after effects of slavery in the United States." Two major achievements in integration were cited: 1. Both WWI and WWII caused a major migration of African Americans from the south in the United States to the north, no longer allowing northerners to say that racial tensions were simply a southern problem, 2. In 1948, President Harry S. Truman made an executive order that all US military organizations were to be immediately integrated. This decision by a southern president nearly cost him the 1948 election, but it led by 1952 to the US military being the most integrated institution in the United States.

I recalled the 1993 250th anniversary of the birth of Thomas Jefferson at the University of Virginia, which he founded, and for which Mikhail Gorbachev was the main speaker on the historic lawn, that the University president allowed the request of the African American students to have a silent march of 80 African American students, blindfolded after the first one, down the lawn as a part of the ceremony, representing Jefferson's 80 slaves at his death. Jefferson died nearly penniless, and in his will, he only freed five of the most trusted slaves. The family sold the rest of the slaves to various slaveholders, breaking up the long developed families and friendships at Jefferson's Monticello. It was then a very powerful symbolic march for the thousands of participants on the lawn to remind us of Jefferson's own complex relationship with claiming to want to free the slaves at his death, while only identifying the five in his will, and his family selling the rest of the slaves.

GHANA: CHRISTIANITY AND ISLAM IN WEST AFRICA

Arriving in Teme, Ghana, on September 13, about thirty of us attended a program at Trinity Theological Seminary, near Teme, "Christianity and Islam in West Africa", where Professor J. Kwabewa Aramoah-Gyadu, a leading Protestant theologian in Ghana gave us two lectures on the role of Christianity, especially Pentecostalism, and a small amount on Islam in Ghana. The Seminary, supported jointly by the Anglican, Methodist, African Zion Methodist, African Methodist Episcopal, and the Presbyterian churches, is the largest Christian seminary in Ghana and offers a three year diploma in theology, as well as master's degrees in theology, active ministry (for lay people), and social living programs with an enrollment of 400 students. The seminary has cordial relations with the three major liturgical churches' dioceses in Accra: the Catholic Archdiocese, the Anglican Archdiocese of West Africa, and the Presiding Methodist Bishop. The Christian churches, excluding the Pentecostals and traditional organizations represent more than 60% of the Ghanaian population, and tend to consider the Pentecostals as cults, While the Christian churches are dominant in the southern part of Ghana, a recent census notes 15% as Muslims, a figure disputed by the Muslims who claim to include 30% of the population in Ghana, mostly in the North.

Professor Asamoah-Gyadu discussed the "catch-up" role of the traditional churches in promoting their faith, comparing it with the highly innovative media methods of the newer and fast-growing Pentecostal churches in Ghana, and noting that the Pentecostal churches promote the linkage of prosperity, supernatural powers and religion. They attract a younger membership, often poorly educated, particularly through the radio, television, gigantic billboards, handbills distributed at petrol stations and markets, cell phone text messages, loudspeakers, and area-wide revival preaching. He stressed that there is an increasing interface between religion, the media, and politics in Ghana as those running for office are eager to obtain the votes of the Pentecostals and Islamic adherents.

The Pentecostals urge their members or prospective members "to lay their hands on their televisions and radios as they pray with their leaders"; they anoint their members with oil; and call upon the charism of the Holy Spirit to infuse their lives. He argued that the very large young and frequently uneducated population in Ghana needs to develop critical thinking skills but that with the lack of proper education, the Pentecostals use this lack of education to attract young people who are seeking fast and easy religious answers as the youth want "dynamic, exuberant, and expressive mass continuous prayers," saying that "it is alright to be wealthy, prosperous, and Christian." The Pentecostals continue to build churches for young congregations of 4,000, 6,000, and even 14,000 members while the mainstream churches are maintaining the more traditional worship for older members. He sees these mainstream churches barely attract their younger congregants, but he believes that in fifteen years, Ghana will see a major loss of the influence of the traditional churches.

In the discussion with our group, Professor Asamoah-Gyadu included the role of the mainstream religious groups in Ghana as well as the Pentecostals and traditional religions in linking the widespread environmental destruction which is occurring, with the competing religious themes among these religious groups, saying that western development continues "to desacralize the natural environments and results from the devastation of poverty among a large portion of the population." Even if prime forests are cut, he noted, the Pentecostals preach that "God will provide." Additionally, based on student questions about the role of the churches in mental health and depression, he said that generally Ghanaians distrust mental health practices, and that those with such problems are typically hidden away in the family homes, as these are taboo topics for many poor people who prefer the supernaturalism of the Pentecostal churches, and consider discussions of mental health issues as "affronts against God." Women who suffer depression still are frequently treated as "witches" and are marginalized, beaten, raped or killed.

Finally, in a discussion about the role of women in Ghanaian society, he pointed out that many men and parents in the society believe that women's role is to become wives, and therefore they do not need a high level of education. Although more women are becoming political leaders in Ghana, they still are far behind the men. However, education of girls and women remains an important role for the traditional mainstream religious churches and an area in which they continue to make major contributions to the society, thus slowing their gradual decline in memberships.

Although the information for this program emphasized "Christianity and Islam in West Africa," Professor Asamoah-Gyadu paid rather little emphasis on the impact of Islam in Ghana, perhaps since its spread remains presently limited to Northern Ghana rather than in the south. No Muslim scholars were invited to participate in the lectures and discussions, and we had the impression that it would be considered inappropriate to invite them to Trinity Theological Seminary since its role was to train Christian ministers and leaders. So these potential expectations on our part for a potential Christian-Islamic dialogue did not entirely materialize. Nonetheless the impact of the Pentecostal linkage with the media was most instructive for us as a group.

Professor Asamoah-Gyadu's books and journals were passed around among the group participants, perhaps to illustrate his credentials with our group as the only full professor at the Seminary:

o   Anaba, E. (2004). The workability of faith. Bolgstanga, Ghana: Desert Leaf Publications.

o   Asamoah-Gyadu, J. K. (2005). Current developments within independent indigeous Pentecostalism in Ghana. Luden, The Netherlands: Brill.

o   Asamoah-Gyadu, J. K. (2010: December 16). Taking territories and raising champions: Contemporary Pentecostalism and the changing face of Christianity; Inaugural lecture in commemoration of promotion to the position of full professor. Legon, Ghana: Trinity Theological Seminary.

o   Asamoah-Gyadu, J. K. (Ed.) (2011). Christianity, missions, ecumenism in Ghana: Essays in honor of Robert Kwasi Aboagye Mensah. Accra: Assembpu Publishers. Christian Council of Ghana.

"WE BRING THE WORLD TO YOU; YOU BRING THE WORLD TO THEM!"

Torogorme Village Cultural Immersion, September 17, 2011

Three Semester at Sea groups, possibly totaling more than 100 in all, visited the isolated Torogome Village, about an hour and a half from the harbor for a cultural immersion experience with members of a local Ghana traditional village, two groups for one day, and our group of thirty for an overnight experience. The total community represents about 8,000 individuals. Crossing a dam and arriving on September 15, our group was met by the chief, all of the village elders, the local citizens of the village, and all of the primary school children, totaling several hundred in a ritual ceremony of greeting. As we entered the village, we shook hands (right hand only) with all of the village elders and the chief and other local persons. Children in their green school uniforms played drums for us, and danced in a traditional and ritualistic manner, forward and backward. Each of us was called up to the front, where we were given a clay pot made by the women in the village, with our name on it, and a local name was given to us. (Mine was Sesoafia.) We met our hosts. After the ceremony, we were taken to a luncheon at a community center outside the village.

When the lunch ended, we returned to the gathering spot, where we were shown the village's pottery making kilns, their weaving of kinta cloth, and their fishing area, several children leading us by the hands. The pots are sold in local nearby markets, but the village leaders hoped that a broader market for the kinta cloth weavings and the pottery might be found. Again we met our hosts, and were taken to their simple one or two room clay homes. The compound where I was staying had two bedrooms, one for my host "mother" and one for her 70 year old mother, a separate outdoor kitchen, and an open area.

In 1991, while teaching in Swaziland, I visited similar traditional villages. There the village adults were polygamous, but in Torogorme village, adult individuals appeared to be monogamous. At least, we were not being introduced to several wives for the adult men and elders. Some compounds had TV antennas, most likely brought back by some young men who had gone outside the village to work. The bedrooms had a limited amount of electricity. We learned that while a number of the men had gone out of the village to work or sell in Ghana's capitol Accra, very few of the women and most of the school children had never been out of the village. Nonetheless, we saw many cell phones in use during our visit which was curious in such a simple highly traditional village structure. The men had built a community library with funds donated by a generous foreign individual, and they were building a large community center. Otherwise, there appeared to be very little work opportunities in the village itself.

My Torogorme host "mother," a single woman about forty, her brother in his late thirties, and her children and nephews and nieces provided a seat for me, and various adults and young children came to meet me throughout the afternoon. Most of the villagers belong actively to the Assembly of God Church. They all had fair English, and the children were singing many Pentecostal songs for me in English. My host's brother repeatedly asked us to help him come to the United States to work. Unfortunately, with limited education and skills, such an opportunity is very unlikely for almost all men of the village.

A catered evening dinner was brought in from outside the village, as was our breakfast on September 16. The elders answered questions through the aid of an interpreter. Many of our mostly middle class students were very touched by the poverty that they saw in the village, and wished that they had the capacity to do something constructive for the village. A young woman twenty-year old seatmate of mine said that "when I grow up" I hope to be able to do some of the things that you have done. We talked about first simple steps that individuals might take, perhaps to help her own host and his or her family, rather than expecting to assist an entire community at once.

CAPE TOWN

Culture of Poverty; Culture of Oppression; Culture of Reconciliation and Hope

The Semester at Sea community had a six day port visit in Cape Town. In my case, at a township school, I attended a play by shipboard participants of three combined African stories, in a style called "body theater" with the props being only the actors' bodies and sticks, written and directed by shipboard faculty member South African playwright Michael Williams and with actors from his Semester at Sea acting class, for a highly excited township primary school of 900 children. Williams' opera "Mandela," demonstrating three phases of Mandela's life with three different actors portraying him, which we saw clips from in our shipboard seminars, has been performed in Africa and in the spring of 2012 will be performed in London. A small group of us attended a dance review "Hello Cape Town" by an amateur group of nine young South Africans, at a small former church and now a theater in District Six, a previously mixed race community which the Apartheid South African government abolished, except for the churches. This review celebrated Cape Town' progress since 1995 toward a more racially tolerant society but criticized it for its continuing exclusion of disadvantaged groups.

A number of us attended an enthusiastic multiracial charismatic Pentecostal Sunday worship service in one of the townships with about 150 participants, including many children and teenagers. On another day, I joined a group participating in a hunger alleviation project in an extremely poor township, supported in part by USAID, and we visited many of the shack homes of the residents. On our last day in Cape Town, many of us visited Robben Island, where Mandela was imprisoned for 18 years in maximum security.

Archbishop Desmond Tutu (80), twice a full Semester at Sea voyager with his wife, spoke on September 28, 2011, to the entire shipboard community, just before its departure from Cape Town. Recalling the Genesis account of God realizing that Adam was lonely, and therefore creating Eve, he reminded us all that none of us are intended to be alone but part of a community, with a conscience for those who are poor and oppressed.

I am reminded of the 17th century quote by John Donne, "No man is an island, whole and entire of himself. Everyone is a part of the whole." Tutu called upon the student voyagers to remember that God (whether He or She) created them all in His/Her own image, and therefore they all were neither white nor black, Indian nor colored, but one human race, and responsible for others in that context. Humorously, however, the Archbishop stated that there is historical evidence that humans began in Africa, and so all of us might be black or white by skin, but under the first layer of the skin we are all the same.

This suggests in the study of intercultural communication the principle of similarities among cultures, or what joins us together, rather than the principle of differences, or what separates us. Although he didn't repeat the statement that he has often made that "God is not a Christian" nor by implication – a Jew, a Muslim, a Hindu, a Buddhist, etc, but the God of all peoples and all religions, his implied principle of similarities among all peoples and cultures was about members of a conscientious community responsible for other humans, white, black, Asian, or colored. He recalled three great leaders Mahatma Ghandi, Martin Luther King, and Nelson Mandela who had all had a profound impact on overcoming societal oppression.

Tutu received the Nobel Peace Prize in 1984, the Albert Schweitzer Prize for Humanitarianism in 1986, the Pacem in Terris Award in 1987, the Sydney Peace Prize (1999) the Gandhi Peace Prize in 2005, and the Presidential Medal of Freedom [from President Obama] in 2009. Among his books that have inspired me have been: The Rainbow People of God: The Making of a Peaceful Resolution (1996); God Has a Dream: A Vision of Hope for Our Time (2005); and God Is Not a Christian and Other Provocations (2011). His earlier books, Nelson Mandela's The Long Road to Freedom (1994), as well as the 1984 movie "Cry Freedom," and Mark Mathabane's Kaffir Boy (1986) have all been central to my teaching university courses such as "Communication and Social Change."

Oscar Lewis (1914-1970), an American anthropologist, is best known for his vivid depictions of the lives of slum dwellers and for postulating that there was a cross-generational culture of poverty among poor people that transcended national boundaries. Lewis contended that the cultural similarities occurred because they were "common adaptations to common problems," and that "the culture of poverty is both an adaptation and a reaction of the poor to their marginal position in a class-stratified, highly individualistic, capitalistic society". Among his books on "the culture of poverty" were his Five Families: Case Studies in the Culture of Poverty (1959) and his La Vida: A Puerto Rican Family in the Culture of Poverty: San Juan and New York (1966).

This culture of poverty is widely evident in many cities in the United States and Europe, and such Latin American countries as Bolivia and Haiti, and often centered among marginalized individuals and families. In the United States alone, there are nearly 40 million people living in such long-term cross-generational situations. More broadly, almost half of the world's seven billion persons suffer an even worse fate, living on less than $1.25 a day, without adequate clean water, sanitation, electricity, housing, health care, education, and nourishing food. Many countries have large populations nearly starving regularly, or trapped as child soldiers or sex slaves, or prostitutes to care for their families, such as Lewis described in La Vida. Those of us who have passed by deplorable shanty towns viewed from the windows of luxurious tour busses in Mumbai, Mexico City, Sao Paulo, Cape Town, Lagos, or Accra may have a slight tinge of sadness that so many people are living in such abject poverty.

While many of us on the Semester at Sea visited Torogome Village, a Hunger project, shanty towns in South Africa and Mandela's Robben Island prison, the next day as we crossed the Equator we had a "King Neptune Day" on ship, celebrating our moving from "Poliwags" to "Shellbacks" with great fun and hilarity. It was all a rather shocking transition from witnessing the grinding poverty, where nonetheless, our hosts were most kind, loving, and generous with their hospitality to the King Neptune Day. Happiness or perceived happiness comes of course in different ways, and the many children and adults that we met in Ghana and South Africa appeared to have a high degree of happiness, despite their poverty.

It is certainly true that "happiness" is not solely defined by our middle class or wealthy lives, and that happiness surveys indicate that some of the poorest people in the world are happy. It is all relative to our own experiences and lives. Aristotle, writing to his son Nicomachus, identified a number of characteristics that had the potential to lead people, even 500 years before the common era, toward happy lives or "the good life:" good parents, a good family, a good community, good friends, a good educa-tion, good health, sufficient wealth for one's station in life, and loyalty to one's country, among other factors. Thus, many of the people whom we saw in Ghanaian poor villages and the shanty settlements around Cape Town have a relative degree of happiness that money alone cannot buy.

For many years in South Africa, Indians, "coloreds," and native Africans "Bantu" not only suffered the desperate "culture of poverty" but also the excesses of the Apartheid system in what we might also call "the culture of oppression." It reminds us of the quote by Daniel Rops: "The despair of being a man." The March 21, 1960 Sharpeville massacre, the June 16; 1976, Soweto uprising and massacre of youth; Mark Mathabane's 1986 book, Kaffir Boy, about growing up as a black person in Apartheid South Africa; and the movie "Cry Freedom," indicate that many other atroci-ties committed by the South African Apartheid government from 1948 until the early 1990s all had a negative impact on world public opinion. It started in Canada, India and the Netherlands, as did the international sanctions against South Africa's multinational industries, sports partici-pation in the Olympics, and the efforts of the banned but active African National Congress (ANC). During the 1980s, Margaret Thatcher and Ronald Reagan preferred the concept of "constructive engagement" with South Africa rather than active confrontation at the United Nations or economic sanctions and boycotts. The South African white population, representing about 15% of the total, claimed 85% of the benefits of what is now one of Africa's most prosperous countries, while those native Africans whose country it was originally were squeezed into untenable settlements or imaginary countries, where the pass laws required them to remain in the cities as laborers only from 6 a.m. to 6 p.m., unless they had special governmental permission. Mathabane's Kaffir Boy describes well the situation of growing up in tin and scrap board shacks, always afraid that the military or police would invade their home, or take away his father for not having his pass book or being out of his designated area during the curfew periods.

As I was teaching at the University of Swaziland in 1990-91, and saw that this poor country with an overloaded royal family of thousands of people constantly drained the national wealth while more than half of the one million population were living a hard scrabble existence. More than half of the country's people were almost always on the edge of starvation, while some nevertheless benefited greatly economically from the international sanctions against South Africa's Apartheid oppression. Many multinational companies, bowing to the international sanctions against South Africa, had moved to Swaziland, but when the Apartheid era ended and sanctions were halted, they moved back quickly to South Africa.

I saw an illustrative example of the oppression of the students at the University of Swaziland on November 14, 1990, when the young King, Maswati III, the same age as the students, sent his young drunken soldiers into the campus of 1600 students, probably killing 2-4 students and injuring perhaps 300-400 by their brutality. The uneducated soldiers boasted that they would beat the English out of the students, and were harshest in their fury against the women students, beating them severely and simulating rape with their truncheons. The University closed for two months; a national enquiry was held for two months; students were verbally humiliated by those in the enquiry commission; and eventually no report was issued. The problem lingered for years. The inequality continues there even today as the extensive royal family benefits while the poor barely can exist in what was earlier called "the paradise of southern Africa."

Unfortunately, throughout much of Africa, the poor continue to get poorer and more desperate, while kleptomaniac leaders enrich themselves, their families, and friends. When I visited Zimbabwe for two weeks in December 1990, I was struck by what appeared to be a very healthy racial climate and the generally progressive society. Now, however, the aging Robert Mugabwe's decision to throw the white farmers off their large and productive farms, many of whom had been born in Zimbabwe, and to give them to unskilled native blacks, and his continuing oppression of his own people led to a country which is far less successful than it was in 1990 when I visited there. Many African countries are wracked by the HIV/AIDS endemic, leaving many sub Saharan African countries with a loss of 40% of their population, mostly in the fifteen to forty-five year old range, as orphans being cared for by aging grandparents. Every thirty seconds in South Africa, a woman is raped, thus spreading the pandemic widely among the heterosexual population. More than a million persons die annually from malaria; parasitical diseases are rampant because of impure water and inadequate sanitation systems. Hunger stalks the townships and settlements.

Nelson Mandela explained in his autobiography, The Long Road to Freedom, for a new South Africa for which he and F.W. DeKlerk jointly received the Nobel Peace Prize, Mandela, even in prison, began the process of negotiating with DeKlerk the first South African election in 1994 with universal sufferage, and with Mandela's election as South Africa's first black president, new hope emerged for what Archbishop Desmond Tutu called "the rainbow nation." Tutu led the Truth and Reconciliation Commission which had a potentially very healing effect on the nation. It has served as a model for overcoming major conflicts and continuing oppression in other countries. Neither Mandela's nor Thabo Mebeki's presidencies were entirely successful, failing, for example to fulfill all of the campaign promises, and giving a very low level of support for curing or alleviating the HIV/AIDS crisis, but in general South Africa has moved forward somewhat and is now considered one of the three major countries in Africa, with Nigeria and Eygpt.

After the elections of the ANC as the national leaders in 1994 and more recently, they promised extensive new adequate housing, electricity, pure water, sanitation, and the means to move out of their abject poverty. Cape Town, "the fairest cape" as it was called by Sir Philip Drake, has become from one perspective one of the most prosperous cities in Africa, where 15% of the population in the Cape area pay all of the taxes and thus support the entire population. On the other hand, it is still coping with rampant crime. Unemployment is as high as 50% among the poorest population still living typically in shantytown settlements and townships, facing the provincial and city's inability to provide them modest housing, electricity, clean water, and reasonable sanitation.

While the national government, headed by Jacob Zuma, is frequently charged with high levels of corruption, and failures to meet ANC campaign promises for the people of South Africa, the Executive Mayor of Cape Town, Patricia de Lille, is given generally high marks for her government's efforts to improve the lives of the area's poorest people and to provide the needed resources for a world-class city. Several of us in our visit to Robben Island, now one of Cape Town's seventh most visited tourist site, joined thousands of other daily visitors, to witness the former "culture of oppression" that existed there. Many of us were moved both by our former prisioner guides who told us personal narratives of their own past experiences with Apartheid, It was a drastic situation where the criminal gangs as wardens repeatedly abused the political prisoners through a systematic process of humiliation.

Also a number of us visited the Operation Hunger Western Cape project, partially supported by a USAID grant, whose goals in as many townships as possible included local development, nutrition and relief. As an NGO, the project today works with the following goals: HIV/AIDS prevention; AIDS home-based care projects; TB projects; targeted family-feeding; soup kitchens; community kitchens; food gardens; self-help food projects; water projects; maternal care; infant creche projects; nutritional well-being of children; income-generating projects such as bakeries, poultry raising, weaving, and brick-making projects; and sanitation and health and hygiene projects.

The Operation Hunger project began in the 1980s and continues to be an influence in the lives of thousands of very poor South Africans in the Cape Town area. The project's emphasis is not simply to make the poor more dependent on external aid and relief, but to partner directly with the vulnerable communities to assist them in improving their own lives in reducing chronic poverty, malnutrition, and health, recognizing "that vulnerable people are not passive recipients of exogenous developments but active agents of change...long-term processes that clarify when, how, and if Operation Hunger can assist local initiatives" (Operation Hunger manifest). In the settlement where we visited and several participants actively assisted Operation Hunger, all of the local residents were extremely kind to us, perhaps giving us much more than we were able to give to them by our very modest and brief help.

As we have now left South Africa, many of us have seen at close hand, the triple cultures: "culture of poverty," "culture of oppression," and even the "culture of reconciliation and hope," leaving us and our prospective student global citizens with an introduction to various aspects of positive and negative modern life in Africa (Morocco, Ghana, and South Africa).

Plato provided the notion of four cardinal virtues: justice, wisdom, courage and moderation. In the New Testament, and in the writings of St. Paul, three more were added: faith, hope, and love (charity), and he argued that among these three, love was the most important. In her 2010 book, Gender, Humiliation, and Global Security: Dignifying Relationships from Love, Sex, and Parenthood to World Affairs, whose foreword is by Archbishop Tutu, Evelin Lindner writes: "Global brotherhood and sisterhood, global connectedness, global cooperation, cohesion, mutuality, solidarity and loving care for our human family and its habitat are desperately needed... solidarity among all of humankind for the common good" (xvii). She comments: "I am an intercultural voyager.... Unlike a vindicator, a voyager uses the challenges of cultural diversity and intercultural conflicts as a stage for forging new relationships and ideas. Consequently, I cherish meeting strangers and encountering strangeness with the entire range of my vulnerabilities." For a short time, we as participants on the Semester at Sea also had the potential be be intercultural voyagers.

CAPE TOWN JAZZ

Johnny Snelgrove
Willamette University, Salem, Oregon

Some terrific jazz musicians live in Cape Town. My first night in South Africa I met a bassist named Wesley Valentine who, like myself, studies jazz at university and has just started making a name for himself. He saw my guitar and called the tune Joy Spring as I entered the front door of his house with my SAS [Semester at Sea] tour. Joy Spring is a pretty complex bop tune featuring a hefty number of key changes. I used to play it all the time in high school, but couldn't remember it without a chart. Nevertheless, I stumbled through Joy Spring, all the while hoping there existed some past residual muscle memory in my fingers. Nope. We had a good time jamming on other tunes, though.

I asked Wesley about good jazz spots in town and without hesitation he exclaimed: Swingers! Swingers? As in a sexual-partner swapping couple? This place sounded questionable. Maybe the club's name referenced the swing of a good groove. That seemed more likely. Wesley told me about a

Monday night open mike I should attend. This was perfect. Monday night I caught a cab and taxied out to the Swingers Jazz Club.

I've made it a goal thus far to jam with locals in every port–especially in Africa, seeing as the continent spawned the music I so love to play. Jazz came from Africa. You can hear it in the swinging rhythm, the cyclic form, the improvisation–everything! The origins of jazz are actually a bit more complicated than that, though. The origins of any music, for that matter, are fairly complicated. Almost all the musics of the world are born from cultural mishmash, trade, adoption, and innovation. The choral music of Africa that usually accompanies stereotypical scenes of elephants and giraffes galloping about the savannah is actually a relatively new style that developed when (probably Dutch?) missionaries first arrived and started teaching hymns to the native people. These hymns soon transformed into a uniquely African style as the natives adopted western music theory and mixed the concepts of harmony with their own culture's musical aesthetics.

The interconnectedness of the world is pretty interesting in itself–even outside the sphere of music. I might even go as far as to say that there is almost nothing that developed in one part of the world that was not exported or influenced by another part of the world. Moroccan mint tea, for example, didn't exist until Morocco started importing green tea from China. Morocco was one of, if not the first, importers of green tea from China. The green tea mixed with Moroccan aesthetics and gained several sprigs of mint and a whole lot of sugar. Many of the things we think of as being distinct and unique to one culture actually came about through centuries of trade and cultural diffusion.

Such is the case with jazz in Africa. Jazz grew out of African musical traditions crossing the ocean to America. These stylings merged with western harmony and form, then became more and more complex as musicians got bored with II-V-I patterns (hehe, musician joke). Jazz began making it's way back to Africa and affecting its initial parent styles after the abolishment of slavery. This process is like kneading dough by stretching out a glob and folding it back onto itself. Musical bread.

Even this is a rudimentary description of the mobility and plasticity of music (especially jazz). Cape Town jazz, specifically, is not as clear a picture. Here's why: if you follow the history of jazz, you eventually get to the point where jazz becomes a highbrow musical style. This is pretty much the case now (excluding those numerous but relatively obscure souls who continue to push the music in new and creative ways, and who I am eternally grateful towards). When you go out to a fancy restaurant or some sophisticated event, there's usually a band or solo pianist playing a bunch of corny standards. Gotta love Autumn Leaves. In Cape Town, there is a stark division between the rich and the poor, the slums and the upscale, and even race to some degree, whether we like it or not. For the most part, the majority of wealth in South Africa is distributed among the white community. As a result, the styling and lifestyle of this community have had the most profound impression on the city. In other words, there are lots of fancy restaurants. And what's a fancy restaurant without a bit of Sinatra nonchalantly cooing in the background? This influx of upscale restaurants demanded that there be an adequate supply of jazz musicians to complete the scene. Good wine, high prices, and background jazz are all you need to open a fancy restaurant. Stellenbosch to the north provided fine wine, an affluent westernized community paid the high prices, the only thing left was fancy jazz, which is now remarkably prevalent in Cape Town.

The mechanism behind jazz's arrival in Cape Town seems a bit less triumphant and liberating than at first glance. Whether or not the need for restaurant jazz really drove the jazz community in Cape Town is still open for interpretation. This is just my take on what seems likely. However it happened, jazz is alive and well in Cape Town today.

When I arrived Monday night at Swingers, I thought the place had gone under. The taxi drove up a dark alley and stopped outside a dilapidated building in the middle of some urban sprawl part of town. The windows were either barred up, broken, or boarded up, and the lean-to entrance looked ready to tip and splinter if provoked. Even my cabbie seemed doubtful and gave me the impression he didn't want to stick around too much longer to find out about this place. Oh well. Into the club I plunged, guitar in hand, ready for whatever was to come. The inside reassured me only slightly more. A few slot machines stood propped against a wall, the air smelt like cigarettes, and the bar did justice to the word vacant. The stage looked promising, though. A rack-mount unit and PA in a dark corner of the stage made me feel better about my situation. I had a few beers and waited for musicians to show up. The bartender told me they didn't usually start playing until eleven and it was only nine.

After about an hour, musicians started pouring into the club carrying keyboards and saxophones and electric basses and guitars. The whole shebang. A bassist named Alistair Andrews sat down next to me and we struck up a conversation. He taught at the University of Cape Town and had toured the world playing all sorts of styles from Afro-Jazz to world fusion projects. Alistair became my best friend there, and gave me a ride back that night with his trusty cab driver. Not all South African cabbies are to be trusted, so Alistair gave me the number of his cabbie friend. I told all the musicians that Wesley Valentine had directed me here. I felt more initially integrated at Swingers than anywhere else I'd played so far.

The band hit the stage hot once all the instruments and electronics warmed up. Only a few people had gathered in the club, but everyone knew who they were. No strangers save for myself had found their way to Swingers that night. These musicians knew how to swing. The first tune took up a quick tempo, the sound guy set the levels right, and the night took off. After the head, a young man with thick-rimmed glasses and a shock of hair got on stage and lit up a saxophone. The band still swung behind him. This place was for musicians; the atmosphere stayed informal and everybody who showed up knew this place had the hottest jams in town. The sax-man jumped outside the changes and began singing in multiphonic squawks. This wasn't fancy dinner music.

After a few tunes, the house invited me up to play. The horns stepped down but Alistair, the keyboardist, and the drummer stayed up to hold down the floor. We got going with an extended jam version of Miles Davis's So What. The band caught onto grooves and ideas incredibly fast. This made for a very explorative jam session. Everybody had a good time playing music without worrying about offending any posh diners. After So What we played a Wayne Shorter tune called Footprints. It's one of my favorites to play. I'm not a real big fan of playing over changes, but Footprints has just enough to keep the tune interesting–this is why Wayne Shorter rocks. I'm glad I brought my handheld recorder along because I got some great jams on tape (which you can listen to at http://snd.sc/qm6qKg). I don't have much more I could say about the music. That night at the sketchy jazz club probably took the award for best time on this voyage so far. Everyone invited me back for another jam session on Thursday, but the ship left Wednesday. I contemplated staying in Cape Town. That would have caused quite a messy logistical situation with SAS, though. I'll have to return to Cape Town someday so I can take all the musicians up on their Thursday jam offer.

I'm still not certain how the jazz scene in Cape Town started up. If it did grow out of dinner music, it has come a long way and defined itself as a uniquely South African brand of jazz encompassing local influences. Alistair and Wesley didn't just play jazz. They also played Goema, a specifically Cape Town style of jazz. The existence of Goema suggests the "dough kneading" style of jazz reintroduction with local styles in South Africa did occur at some time in history. In the end, there was probably a combination of sources through which jazz in South Africa sprung up. The musical landscape is so intricate it's hard to say how any one style evolved. That's the case for most musics though. It's a big tangled up world out here.

Supporting the 'Do Ubuntu' Orphan Bracelet Campaign

Mary Finocchario
Kansas City, Kansas

I was amazed to have sold 220 Do Ubuntu orphan bracelets on the Semester at Sea 2011 Fall Voyage. That is nearly $3,300 raised for the Orphan Bracelet Campaign that directly benefits women living with aids and the aids orphans whose parents have died from the epidemic. Students even knocked at my cabin door the final day of the voyage and asked to buy the last three bracelets in my possession (which I had daily worn on my wrist during the 110 day voyage). They wanted to give them as Christmas gifts and to have a memory of their visit to South Africa, as well as to be in solidarity with those living with aids on the planet.

How did I get involved with this issue, you might wonder? It happened 3 ½ years ago when I met Louise Hogarth, who founded her own non-profit, independent film company (Dream Out Loud Productions). She specializes in true stories about people and events that focus on social issues and human rights. I was in Mexico City with my daughter Sarah, who presented at the 2008 International Aids Conference. I came along to nanny her 3 month old daughter (my granddaughter), still being nursed by her mother.

While I wandered through the Global Village outside the conference hall, I met Louise. She was showing her documentary film, "Angels in the Dust" and selling Do Ubuntu aids bracelets. The Orphan Bracelet Campaign was a direct outcome from her film, as others wanted to know how they could help after viewing the Angels documentary. The film depicts the struggles of Marian Cloete and her husband Con from Johannesburg .They took all their retirement money and created the Botshabelo community that is "home" to nearly 450 aids orphans. The Cloetes shelter, feed, educate and provide anti-retroviral drugs to some of the children there who are HIV positive. I made a commitment that day to help this woman with her cause each year, either through fund raising or personal donation. I asked Louise to send me some bracelets to take on the SAS voyage. While on the ship, I presented Explorer Seminars to the Lifelong Learners and to the students. Two professors asked me to tell their students about the bracelets, and the rest of the sales came from the line of students who found their way to my cabin door. On World Aids Day, eight students involved with the program, came to buy bracelets so they could wear them on stage that night. Donors should know that 100% of the proceeds go directly to benefit the aids orphans.

Louise suggested that if others want to help they can order bracelets for their own fund raisers at their church, work or sorority. They can also order and show the documentary film, "Angels in the Dust" to better inform others about the aids epidemic in South Africa. To order the film or the bracelets, interested parties can go to the website: www.orphanbracelet.org

It is estimated that 25 million children will be orphaned due to HIV/AIDS by 2012. The Do Ubuntu Orphan Bracelet Campaign was inspired by the plight of the orphaned children from around the world. The attractive bracelets are made from recycled rubber from the United States and metal from India . Your donation provides a living wage to a woman in Africa, and an orphaned child with food, education and shelter.

D)   PUBLIC CONVERSATIONS

1.   ELEVEN QUESTIONS FOR TYRONE L. ADAMS, THE KAZAKHSTAN INSTITUTE OF MANAGEMENT, ECONOMICS, AND STRATEGIC RESEARCH (KIMEP)

Michael H. Prosser
The University of Virginia, Charlottesville, Virginia,
Shanghai International Studies University, Shanghai, China

Biography: Tyrone L. Adams

Tyrone L. Adams (Ph.D. in Communication from The Florida State University) has been the Acting Vice President of Academic Affairs at the Kazakhstan Institute of Management, Economics, and Strategic Research (KIMEP). He is also a Professor of Communication at the University of Louisiana, Lafayette and an independent consultant specializing in persuasion and global Internet communication strategies. Dr. Adams was a CIES Fulbright Senior Specialist focusing upon communication and journalism curriculum design since 2010.

He has also been a Visiting Scholar of Common Law at Oxford University (1997), a Visiting Professor of Computer-mediated Communication at the University of Iowa (1998), and a Visiting Professor of Corporate Communication and Public Affairs at the Southern Methodist University (2000). He has authored four textbooks on leveraging the Internet for communication campaigns and has edited three academic volumes on "achieving excellence" in everyday business and professional communication practices. As an internationally-recognized scholar, speaker, and former-President of the American Communication Association (2002-2003) he has rendered strategic communication analysis reports and action plans for multiple private clients.

Michael Prosser: 1. In your doctoral dissertation at Florida State University: "Terror-rhetoric: An Historical-critical Account of Peruvian President Alberto Fujimori's Coercive and Rhetorical Responses to Shining Path's International Terrorism Campaign following the Suspension of Parliament, April 1992 to December 1993," can you briefly summarize your main findings? How did you choose this particular subject?

Tyrone L. Adams: Would be happy to do that, Michael. However, I haven't touched this area of research for about ten (10) years, to be perfectly honest. I began the discipline as a global rhetorician, and quickly moved into Internet and global media when the computer revolution of the 1990s swept through the academy (and world). So, I actually had to read some of what I wrote (just now) to be able to correctly answer this question. Amazing exercise, really, because you get to see, intimately, just how poor your writing really was back then, Know what I mean?

This dissertation was a highly detailed account (hour by hour) of Peruvian President Alberto Fujimori's (Fujimori is now incarcerated for government corruption) use of both coercion and rhetoric/persuasive communication against Shining Path's international terrorism campaign. The dissertation considers the full spectrum of physical and persuasive ploys–from his 5 April 1992 autogolpé (disbanding of Congress, and thereby establishing a dictatorship) to the 13 December 1993 reestablishment of significant direct international investment as measured by Barron's DFI index–used by Fujimori to create the perception that Peru was "safe" for international investment.

Chapter One describes the social, political, and economic conditions that Fujimori faced, while pointing to the absolute dearth of communication research concerning Shining Path and Fujimori. Chapter Two reviews the varied generic literature concerning nonviolent and violent rhetoric, leading to an explanation of the terror-rhetoric genre–where the use of physical force can be regarded as meta-communication. Chapter Three presents the historical-critical methods and procedures used in the research. Chapter Four narrates the exchange between Shining Path's international offensives and Fujimori's use of force to contain the group's dissuasive power as a grand nation-state master narrative. And, Chapter Five then concludes the study by examining how Fujimori's use of terror-rhetoric affected its various audiences.

I chose this subject because I have always had a love for Latin America. Plus, my wife (now divorced) was of Peruvian descent, and her family was very high up the food-chain in governmental affairs. So, I had access to original documentation (and insurgent leader Abimael Guzman's personal library that was captured in a Peruvian National Police raid in Cuzco) that made the dissertation both possible and topical. A lot of my early work on the dissertation was done in Lima, where I could get a good cultural "feel" of the climate. So, to be very honest: I was connected.

Michael Prosser: 2. Besides having two half-Peruvian children, you have had several years of cooperative experience with the University San Martin De Porres in Lima, Peru and have helped organize the 2007 Congress of the Americas there, where you and my daughter Michelle and I may have first met. Also, you have indicated that twenty years from now when you are approaching retirement from the University of Louisiana you would like to retire in Lima. It appears that your professional, cultural, and personal life is closely connected to Peru. Can you explain these interconnecting aspects of your life?

Tyrone L. Adams: I have a very serious Latina fetish, to be perfectly blunt. But, even more honestly, I am absolutely in love with the entire Peruvian lifestyle. Living costs are cheap for an American, and the people are exceedingly friendly. Plus, the University of San Martin de Porres and I have produced three (3) books together, and plan to do more. Luckily for me, they translate all of my English into perfect Spanish. Or, I would be a very poor author. Again, having been married to a Peruvian family for 16 years will do something to your cultural perspective, too. After a while, you start thinking in Spanish. And then, all of the oddities of the culture seem to be "no major issue." A very warm and loving people, all in all. My children are a cultural reflection of those predominantly Catholic values, as well.

Michael Prosser: 3. You have been president of the American Communication Association, which was a joint sponsor and developer of important North and South American communication conferences, for example in Peru and Mexico. As a much smaller communication association than either the [US] National Communication Association or the International Communication Association, did it get formed out of a special interest in creating more productive links between communication professionals in

North and South America? If so, how did the Association help to develop these links, and what specific role did you play in creating these links?

Tyrone L. Adams: I had a very good mentor that you know personally, Michael: Steve Smith out of the University of Arkansas. One weekend while I was visiting him in Fayetteville at his home for an SEC football game, he asked me to serve on ACA's newly formed Board of Directors. At that time, I had no idea of the largesse that we would be tackling. ACA was constructed by some very good minds–Rita Kirk from SMU, Bud Goodall from Arizona State, Dale Herbeck from Boston College, and Bob Schrag from NC State–to be the shadow association for NCA. Many of us believed then, and still do today, that NCA's membership fees are outrageous, and their non-online approach to producing scholarship (paper journals for a fee) was antiquated. So, the truth is, ACA was an effort to supplant NCA, and uproot the hyper-capitalist tendencies of an academic association gone mad. However, as we began to draft our mission statement in 1996, one thing became patently clear: we were the "American" Communication Association, which, by default, included the "Americas" by definition. So, several of us started exercising our Latin American contacts, which was a brilliant move for the discipline. Soon, we were in contact with some very big players in Communication in both Central America and Latin America, and were planning conferences. Upon visiting with some of the executives at the International Communication Association in Washington, DC one weekend (Sam Luna and Michael Haley) we got financial backing from ICA's Board, and the Congress of the America's series was birthed. I think that Argentina is the next target, but have fallen out of those planning conversations with ACA, ICA, Monterrey Tech, and USMP (who are the juggernauts behind the conference series) since I'm based in Central Asia, right now. But, I would like to know, if anyone else knows.

Michael Prosser: 4. Among your authored or edited books, your coedited book with S. A. Smith, Electronic Tribes: The Human and Social Implications of Internet Communication, (Austin: University of Texas Press, 2006), and your Communication Shock: The Acceleration and Integration of Everything, (Lima: University of Saint Martin de Porres Press, 2009). (Translated into Spanish) both sound especially interesting in this intensifying age of the internet. What do you see as the major contributions to the field of communication that you develop in these books? Are the two books complementary, and if so how?

Tyrone L. Adams: No. The two books are not complementary. They are starkly different, in fact. Electronic Tribes is a collection of academic essays which tries to make the argument that online "communities" are really more like online "tribes." The collection of essays in that Texas Press run are very anthropological in their communication take. We closely examine the roots of tribal-based societies, and extend many of the fundamental social processes and norms that occur within those societies into the online arena. (My campus here in Kazakhstan blocks YouTube! for bandwidth reasons, or I would show you a link to a news segment that was done on the book by our local affiliate – go to YouTube! and search: "electronic tribes adams" and it will come up).

When we initially imagined what this collection of essays might become, we had to admit that we were awestruck by the term "tribe." Before engaging in a discussion of electronic tribes, we had to note our intrigue with the term tribe, and how it relates or does not relate to other terms similarly used to describe groups. "Tribe" is a core construct in sociological, anthropological, and political thought with hotly-contested significations. Its use evokes different imagery, even regional passions, in different scholarly traditions. The essays in that book did the same.

On the other hand, Communication Shock is a deep analysis of nanotechnology engineering, and how it relates specifically to communication technologies. Building upon a thick, engineering-based description of nano-engineering processes – and outputs – I make the argument that within the next decade we are going to experience an avalanche of highly small, ultra-sophisticated, disposable electronics. Then, I make the argument that HUMAN communication is, once again, going to be radically "shocked" and "rocked" by these cheap, nascent technologies (just as we have witnessed because of the Internet and handhelds over the past decade). This is the work of which I am the most proud, to date, not including the dissertation which took me two (2) years to write – non-stop.

Michael Prosser: 5. As the internet continues to expand, with new platforms and search engines since the creation of MySpace (declining in importance just as Alta Vista did), You Tube (You Kou as a Chinese clone), Facebook (with QQ and Jhous as Chinese clones), Twitter, Google (with

BAIDU as a Chinese clone), Bing, LinkedIn and others, we know that we are only really at the beginning of this internet revolution worldwide. If you have a sense of new internet developments in the next few years, what would be your predictions?

Tyrone L. Adams: In 2008, I was invited to an exclusive think-tank session at the US Army War College in Carlisle, PA (which is where colonels go to become generals) to listen and give my thoughts on this very subject. After sharing my thoughts, I was invited by the think-tank director to be a Visiting Professor of Strategic Communication for a year, but personal reasons involving my divorce kept me from taking the appointment – which really could have altered my scholarship in some very significant, "classified" ways.

Basically, I'll tell you what I told them: the Internet is not going away, and it is going to be the de facto backbone for World War IV (assuming that the Cold War was WW III), where information will be the currency of the insurgents and the civilized. You have to really understand the Internet from a programmer's level first, like I do, to be able to see how the code functions in an open-source, open-society, transparent way. The Wikileaks of late are just scant evidence of what's actually going on in the "undergrounds" of the Web; I cite the proliferation of peer-to-peer technologies to counteract the information firewalls that governments establish, to wit.

After all, the Internet was built to circumvent a global thermonuclear holocaust, so certainly it can be effectively used to circumvent even the best defense we try to establish for our information. But, that's the "private" story. There are people who are up very late at night, fending off hackers from all spots on the globe, trying to keep our information "safe."

The other side of the coin is what the Internet brings to us, as a society, in the public fora. I have been online for about 12 hours a day since I downloaded my first web-browser from NCSA (then "Mosaic") in 1993. That's a sum total of about 20 years of surfing (and web-design), so I've seen fads come and go. I think that Google and Apple are very well positioned, financially, to make "cloud computing" a cheap reality for – well, everyone. That's the really big next revolution.

When you can share your documents in a cloud, instead of on a password-protected hard-drive, it is really going to make the Internet a powerful driver in the Information Age. Also, Microsoft plans to unveil "lazy shopping" in the next 4-5 years, where you can select a jacket that an actor is wearing in a movie by touch-screen at home, and it will take you immediately to the web-site (opening a browser on your Internet-connected TV monitor) where it can be purchased with a Visa Card and shipped to your home, overnight. So, each company that I know of (from watching stock reports) is currently investing heavily in R&D.

As a result, I predict that we are going to have some very sexy applications in the next decade, that will (once again) define how we do business and personal communication.

Michael Prosser: 6. Kazakhstan is one of six post-Soviet states which has implemented an Individual Partnership Action Plan with NATO. Can you comment on this foreign policy balance, between its relationship with Russia and NATO as you see it? What special interests does the United States have in its relationships with Kazakhstan?

Tyrone L. Adams: Well, 20 years ago there were 1400 SS-20 ICBM's distributed throughout Kazakhstan; all of them pointing back at the USA. However, today, I have found the Kazakhs and Russians here to be very welcoming to Americans. On a personal level, you couldn't find a more hospitable people. On a governmental level, I'm not really sure that I have the full policy knowledge to properly respond to this question. But, I will say that these people do not see themselves as Asian, even though most of them look Mongolian or Chinese. They like to regard themselves as "Europeans" and watch football (soccer), play table tennis, throw darts, and drink Guinness by choice.

I do know that several nation-states are trying to position themselves nicely for the oil and gas reserves in the west, by the Caspian Sea near Aktau. Kazakhstan has an estimated 30,000,000,000 barrels of light sweet crude that remains untapped, which places it ranked at position 12 in the world (just above Qatar at 13th). That's a lot of hydrocarbons, my friend. What Kazakhstan does not have, however, are the coke-cracking plants that are along the border with Russia (in Russian territory) to process the crude into different fuels. So, there is still a heavy reliance on the North (Russia) to process the raw materials into useable resources.

Diplomatically speaking, the Soros Foundation is very active in this part of the world. Not as much as Budapest, Hungary, of course, where Central

European University was given $770 million recently as an endowment for an institution of 1,500 select students. But, Soros is very interested in the country. Likewise, there are other various rogue NGO's operating out here, trying to do democratic "good" without being cited by Glenn Beck or Rush Limbaugh for "spreading socialism." This, frankly, is really funny, since Soros and others are trying to keep these countries from falling back into their old Soviet mentalities, with organizations like Transparency International.

The institution that I am at (KIMEP) by the way, was charged by President Nazarbayev in 1992 to be the elite school of "capitalism" and "diplomacy" there. Subsequently, Nazarbayev University in Astana (where it gets down to -40C in the winters) is opening in a couple of years, and has "government money" to execute its mission. So, educational changes are afoot here, even as schools try and emulate the Western World, and become more and more democratic. As an aside, it is really interesting to hear the Scorpion's song "Winds of Change" played in a bar, when you are an American behind the old Iron Curtain. Very intriguing.

Michael Prosser: 7. Both of us have had Fulbright experiences. I began the communication major at the University of Swaziland in 1990-1991 and you have been involved directly in academic administration under the Fulbright program for Kazakhstan since 2010. How do you assess the significant contributions that the Fulbright program is making for the development of academic excellence and growth in Kazakhstan? What do you see as your own important contributions to this program?

Tyrone L. Adams: I think the Fulbright program in Kazakhstan is underrepresented by academics from the West, because it is not as glamorous of a destination as, say, Athens. Everyone I know of in Fulbright tries to get placed near the rails in Europe. It's the rare breed who goes to an exotic destination like Swaziland or Kazakhstan. More academics should apply to these locales, because these people are in need of academic direction.

Within one year, for instance, I have been promoted from Visiting Professor of Journalism and Mass Communication to Acting Vice President of Academic Affairs! So, I know of that which I speak. More important than the flow of academics into Kazakhstan, is the flow of academics out to the West, however.

Kazakhstan has a special program which is rather wide-spread, called Bolashak. If you qualify for a Bolashak Scholar's Award, you get to go to your choice of admitted school in the USA or Europe for some "free-ride" higher education (I told you there was a lot of oil out here, didn't I?). These students are getting the full American and European experience, and returning with the intentions of opening businesses, changing government, and streamlining international affairs. It is very exciting stuff, really.

Still, the government plans to revolutionize the education by opening Nazarbayev University soon, and importing Westerners to teach and train on-site in Kazakhstan. The salaries offered for communication scholars at Nazarbayev begin at around $120,000 USD, and go up depending upon academic record.

Michael Prosser: 8. Kazakhstan shares a long border with China's Xingjiang Autonomous Region, one of the reasons that it is part of the Shanghai Cooperation Organization. Also China has built extensive roads and rail lines to the border of Kazakhstan to improve cross-border commerce between China and Kazakhstan. Residents of the Xingjiang Autommomous Region are often thought to have more in common with the residents of Kazakhstan than with the main Han nationality in much of the rest of China. In the last several years, there has been considerable violence and riots in Xingjiang, which the Chinese government has often brutally repressed. What insights can you offer about the developing Chinese-Kazakhstan relationships, potential cooperation, and the problems of violence and protests in both regions?

Tyrone L. Adams: To be very honest, I am not "up" on these relations, so I would be completely lying if I tried to answer you. I will say that I know that the railroads running from Kazakhstan into China operate on a different gauge rail system. So, when rail cars head to China, they have to be stopped, then lifted by crane onto a new rail system, in order to flow. This makes trade slower and more time-consuming than it ordinarily should be, of course. The Tian Shen mountain range, which I am looking at right now out my window, is the geographical divider between China and Kazakhstan. However, I have not had either the time nor money to venture into China, yet; let alone, read up on the politics, which is not discussed much (or, so I've noticed) out here.

Michael Prosser: 9. Kazakhstan's widely spread-out population is 70% Muslim, and a reasonable part of the other 30% of the population are Christians. China's Xingjiang Autonomous Region is also predominantly Muslim in background. What do you see as the essential characteristics of Islam in this region, as compared to other Muslim countries with which you are familiar? Are the relationships between the Muslims and Christians positive or tense? Why?

Tyrone L. Adams: I am located in the city center of Almaty, which is very cosmopolitan by any standard. Here, you don't hear prayer calls over loudspeakers. But, if you go about 10-15km outside the city, they can be heard very clearly. It is as if there are two Kazakhstans: the city-dwellers in Almaty, and the rural-dwellers outside of the city. Most of the Muslims I know of also drink vodka by the bottle, so it really isn't an issue that is front-and-center, out here. But, then again, my experience may be different here in the city center.

As a low-intensity protestant, myself, I have found no problems with people that think I am out to convert them, or, them to convert me. Everyone mostly leaves well-enough alone. Then again, you have to remember that religious freedom didn't exist here until the Republic was formed. Under Soviet rule, the churches were converted into Opera Houses, and religion was regarded as a "threat" to Communist ideology. Plus, Kazakhstan is special, because all of the Russian dissidents were purged here by Stalin to reside alongside the Kazakhs. So, there is a tendency to acknowledge religion as a personal choice, by and large. Once again, I haven't spent much time outside Almaty, so my report may be ultimately biased.

Michael Prosser: 10. You give the impression that through the Rosetta Stone program, you have been able to learn a reasonable amount of Russian. Since you no doubt speak Spanish fluently, it appears that you have an easy adaptability toward learning and using efficiently other languages besides English. With the Germanic structure of English, the romance structure of Spanish, and the acrylic nature of Russian, how has your native English as well as your acquisition of both Spanish and Russian been complementary or difficult to learn and communicate effectively?

Tyrone L. Adams: First, I am not fluent in Spanish. Yo intiendo mas que yo hablar. (I understand more than I speak.) However, I am street functional in Spanish, and can get around with no problems or worries.

As to Russian, that is another animal altogether. It is a completely different alphabet (Cyrillic), and there are no Latin roots to interpret, in order to even guess what people are saying. However, Rosetta Stone is very sophisticated language acquisition software, and I have picked up about 40-50 words that I use regularly to "survive." Luckily, many people here also speak some broken English, so it is not so bad. I highly encourage you, or your students, to invest in Rosetta Stone, accordingly. If you are dedicated with the software, it will do wonders for your language skills. And, it is tax-deductible as a learning tool!!!

Michael Prosser: And last, can you briefly identify your own professional, cultural, and personal goals in the next few years?

Tyrone L. Adams: Well. Professionally, I think I'm looking for my next academic home. I've been at the University of Louisiana now for about 15 years. And, when you do that at a place like Louisiana, they start to treat you like a local. Which is nice in some respects, don't get me wrong. But, I've got kids and a Chapter 13 bankruptcy to wrestle with. And, given that I am 29% below average on salary (as reported by the Chronicle), I believe I'm up for sale – internationally.

I've enjoyed this year abroad, and think that tenure is a big lie. Who wants a lifetime contract at hourly wages? So, I'm being very deliberate with my job searches: Dubai, Abu Dhabi, Hong Kong, Budapest, and even here in Almaty. I'm not really sure where I might wind up, but I want to be working on doctoral dissertations. And grants. I've met some interesting people here who have become friends. Good pedigrees, too: Oxford, Cambridge, Boston College, Southern Cal, etc.

It's very nice to be in the company of critics, again. These people take their academics very seriously, and rarely, if ever, are impressed. All in all, the experience is upping my game.

Culturally, I want to get back to Peru, soon. Those people know how to live life. I don't drink alcohol much, so it's not the party scene I'm talking about. There's a special feel in the air that just says, "Be at peace." That is precisely how I want to feel when I am 65, thinking about retirement. I don't want to worry about whether I am going to eat cat food or dog food that day. I just want a nice hot plate of steaming green corn tamales, an Inca cola, and a night at the beach without a cell phone in my pocket.

Plus, when my son (15) and daughter (10) get in their 20s, I want them to be able to come see me in the summer in Lima.

2. Observations on Roles of Women in America

Public Conversation between

Mansoureh Sharifzadeh
Ministry of Education, Tehran, Iran

and

Rebeccah Kinnamon Neff, Ph.D.

Rebeccah Kinnamon Neff: In any society, gender roles are largely determined by traditional mores and values, which in turn come from economic, political, and religious forces. History is replete with stories of women who defied traditional female roles to support the causes of revolution and of freedom from suppression and to advance democracy.

From its founding, America was a patriarchal society in which women assumed roles to men. Their scope of activity and influence was bound by home and family. Within this sphere they sometimes found themselves alone in managing family property while their husbands were off fighting in wars or serving in political bodies, from which women were excluded. By the middle of the 19th century, women were beginning to assert themselves as workers and to organize for economic and political rights. But both of my grandmothers and their daughters, including my mother, were born before women could vote. It wasn't until 1920 that American women were granted voting rights. In addition to helping on the farm, my six maternal aunts worked in mills, factories, and shops over the course of their lives to support themselves and their families. I was not only the first grandchild of this family, but also the first to attend college. Even then, in 1958, occupational choices for women were limited. In the mostly agrarian South, women were expected to be homemakers and those who did aspire to a career usually looked no farther than teaching or nursing. We didn't aspire to be doctors or lawyers or engineers because we had no role models in these fields.

By the time I was in graduate school in the 1960s and 1970s, this was no longer the case. Our horizons had broadened. With the growth of educational opportunities for women, came increased awareness of career possibilities. The Feminist Movement in America encouraged women to lobby for equal employment opportunities, equal pay for equal work, and increased political influence. Although the Equal Rights Amendment that was approved by the U. S. Senate in 1972 was not ratified by a sufficient number of states to make it a part of the Constitution, there was no turning back. Women were becoming more active and more visible in every arena of American life: in medicine, manufacturing and the military, in business and politics; from space exploration to the Supreme Court, women were making a contribution and being acknowledged for their leadership.

Six Questions on American Women by Mansoureh Sharifzadeh

Mansoureh Sharifzadeh: 1. What limitations do the American women have in their careers?

Rebeccah Kinnamon Neff: Women in the United States have greater access than ever before to education and employment; however, female workers still do not earn as much as their male counterparts in the same jobs. And recent legislation to remedy this situation failed to pass in Congress. Social, economic and political conservatives, in particular, view women primarily as caregivers, whose first responsibility is to their husbands and children. Therefore, even though a woman might have entered the workforce before marriage, once she becomes a mother, she may feel pressure to give up any career-related ambition to focus on the needs of her family. Even if she re-enters the labor force after her children are grown, she will face the challenge of making up for her lack of experience when compared with men in similar positions, which also affects her ability to earn a comparable wage.

In addition, women in the military are still prohibited from combat positions. This limitation probably stems from the patriarchal tendency to protect women from risk and danger. Even though women have proved themselves in other military roles, and have risen to the top ranks in all branches of service, they are still not allowed to take a place alongside men in combat situations.

Mansoureh Sharifzadeh: 2. Do they consider this limitations or customs?

Rebeccah Kinnamon Neff: Women who feel themselves limited in their ability to earn a fair wage or participate fully in their chosen career would probably say there were limitations based on traditional patriarchal values.

Mansoureh Sharifzadeh: 3. What steps do you think the modern women may take to change some of those limitations?

Rebeccah Kinnamon Neff: Women will continue to lobby legislators, encouraging them to submit and support congressional bills to remove these limitations.

Mansoureh Sharifzadeh: 4. How do the traditional values cope with the new ideas?

Rebeccah Kinnamon Neff: Americans are known for their flexibility and adaptability. Whereas some citizens would prefer to hold on to traditional customs and values, most acknowledge that women have a fundamental right to be treated equally under the law. And while women who "want it all," will continue struggling to balance home and family duties with career demands, there is also widespread acceptance of a woman's right to choose the kind of life she wants.

Mansoureh Sharifzadeh: 5. What do you personally think about changing the traditional values, is it a necessity or not?

Rebeccah Kinnamon Neff: I would say the changes that allow women to make their own choices are inevitable.

Mansoureh Sharifzadeh: 6. Do the limitations have religious bases or just cultural bases?

Rebeccah Kinnamon Neff: American cultural values have a strong basis in not just one, but several religions, most of which are traditionally patriarchal. Religious practices in America vary widely in the extent to which they support women's right to make personal choices, and in their acceptance of women as religious, social, economic, and political leaders. Diverse views make for lively debate, as well as sometimes frustrating delays in achieving changes in the status of women and extension of our role in the life of our country.

E) Cultural Stories

1. The American Millennials

Michael H. Prosser
University of Virginia,
Shanghai International Studies University

Always a multicultural country, like a "salad bowl" rather than the old description of a "melting pot," in the not too distant future for the United States, several states such as California, and major cities will have the white population in the minority, while those from Latin America will represent 40% and African Americans 14-15% of the population. More minority babies are now being born in the United States than white babies. Frank Rich, writing in The New York Times, said that in 2010 births to Asian, African American, and Hispanic women in the United States consisted of 40% of the children being born (2010: March 27). African Americans represent about 14% of the American population. Martin Jacques writes that there are 3,376,000 Chinese in the US Chinese disaspora, following Indonesia (7,566,000), Thailand (7,153,000), Malaysia (7,070,000), and Singapore where the Chinese represent more than half of the population. Even Canada has 1,612,000 Chinese residents (2010: 437).

Neil Howe and William Strauss' article, "The New Generation Gap," in The Atlantic Monthly (1992: December) , provided a very insightful look at various American generations: the "Silent Generation" (born from about 1925 to about 1942) the : "Boomers" (born after the end of World War II: 1943-1969), the "Thirteeners," or sometimes labeled "Generation Xers," born around 1961, representing the thirteenth generation since the founding of the United States and about 80 million in the population, and those born after the early 1980's whom the authors called "The Millennials," because of the then coming Third Millennium (since the birth of Christ). In China they are called the "Post 1980's Generation". Henry

Luce, the creator of Time, in 1941 stressed that "American jazz, Hollywood movies, American slang, American machines and patented products are in fact the only things that every community in the world, from Zanzibar to Hamburg, recognizes in common" (Martinez, 2010: March 22, 41). Howe and Strauss identify two contrasting generations: in the 1960s the young generation claimed the high moral and cultural ground, attacking their elders, but the baby-boomers representing 69 million Americans, at the time of Howe and Strauss' writing and ranging in age from 32 to 49, now were attacking their juniors (67).

The 1960s and first half of the 1970s in the United States were the periods of flower children, hippies, the Civil Rights movement, the Gay Rights movement, the Feminist movement, the anti-Vietnam war movement, and the assassinations of President John F. Kennedy, Martin Luther King, Jr., Malcolm X, and Senator Robert Kennedy. In the late 1960s, young Americans, and many others around the world denounced the Vietnam War, chanting "Hey, Hey, LBJ [President Lyndon B. Johnson] how many kids have you killed today?" and "Hell, no, we won't go" (CNN Cold War Series: The Sixties, 1998). Peter M. Hall and John P. Hewitt (1973: 530) wrote that during the Nixon White house period in 1970, with the war in South East Asia heating up, many young people were protesting in the streets, having "speak ins" about the Vietnam war and the American bombing of Cambodia. Some, however, were becoming violent. President Nixon called for "communication, not violence." On May 1, 1970, the relatively quiet anti-war movement was filled, as Hall and Hewitt explained it, with renewed "rallies, demonstrations, bitter rhetoric, anger, frustration, and outrage.... Strikes, confrontations, building burnings, tear gas battles, and arrests, and law enforcement agencies were mobilized on numerous campuses" (Hall & Hewitt, 530).

On that same day at the Pentagon, the President contrasted the heroic action of the American military in Vietnam with the violent dissenters whom he characterized as "bums." However, on May 4, young national guardsmen opened fire on peacefully demonstrating students at Kent State University, killing five and wounding others. It was widely reported in the American and world press, and also for several days on the front page in People's Daily. President Nixon held a press conference in which he adopted what appeared to be a conciliatory attitude toward the protesters, and during the dawn hours of May 9, he came to the Lincoln memorial in Washington, D.C. to talk to young demonstrators assembled there. On May 9, 75,000 to 100,000 protesters came to Washington, many of whom were students, for an anti-war rally. Hall and Hewitt stress that some members of Nixon's own cabinet had criticized the US administration for its insensitivity toward the young Americans, and that "the main response of the administration was to cool its own rhetoric, establish lines of communication...and lend verbal support to the right of [peaceful] dissent" (531). Hall and Hewitt note that "Underlying the emphasis upon communication as a tool for conflict resolution is an American myth of common values"(531).

Howe and Strauss suggest that the "Boomers" started as the most indulged and self-indulged young people in the United States, and for middle class youth, poverty, disease, and crime seemed invisible. In 1965, Time claimed them to be on the edge of a "golden era," but all that they found was a cultural "generation gap" and many of them began to sing the Beatles' song, "Let it be." The term "yuppie" was coined to describe the "young upwardly mobile professionals" as they moved past their teens and twenties. Later, the New York Times called them the "grump-ies" ("grown up mature professionals"), more value-oriented, involved in various spiritual movements from evangelical Christianity to Asian or New Age humanism, and even creating an "American cultural civil war" and moving conservatively to the right politically (Howe and Strauss, 74).

However, Howe and Strauss claim that the cynical "Thirteeners" were youth in the suburbs, often children in divorced marriages, as the ethni-cally and racially more inclusive school education often found them later in low-paying jobs, while in the inner cities, there were more and more unwed teenage mothers and unconcerned and uninterested teen aged fathers (75). At the same time, these young people had to be "pragmatic, quick, sharp-eyed, able to step outside themselves and understand how the world really works" facing, however, "a rising tide of mediocrity" (75). Mark Bauerlein's book The Dumbest Generation, details this continuing tide of mediocrity among American youth (1999). Inner-city high schools were often called "the blackboard jungle."

Many high schools had signs, "The largest reason for teenage poverty is teenage pregnancy," The Charlottesville, Virginia High School during the "millennials" generation, with a mix of students who were the children of highly educated parents in a small town with the prestigious University of Virginia and many others from inner city poverty had 47 young unwed pregnant women in 1994, and some for the second time. The school needed a baby-care center so that these young unwed mothers could complete their high school education On the other hand, many "Thirteeners" and later "millennials" students competed vigorously to enter the best American private and public universities. For example, at the University of Virginia, between the mid 1980's and 2009, 20,000 high school students applied annually for approximately 2,000-2500 freshmen seats and 500 transferring students from other colleges and universities. More and more college and university educated graduates were entering such fields as computer and information science, but often entering science and engineering students from the United States were far outmatched by bright Chinese and Indian students.

Reihan Salam notes that three of every ten students in American high schools as recently as 2006 were graduating and less than a third of young people in the United States have finished college or university. He calls it the "cusp of a dropout revolution, one that will spark an era of experimentation in new ways to learn and new ways to live." Nonetheless, "the millennial generation could prove to be more resilient and creative than its predecessors, abandoning old, familiar and broken institutions in favor of new, strange and flourishing ones... many of the young embrace a new underground economy, a largely untaxed archipelago of communes, co-ops, and kibbutzim that passively resist the power of the granny state while building their own little utopias.... This new individualism on the left and the right will begin in the spirit of cynicism and distrust that we see now, the sense that we as a society are incapable of solving pressing problems. It will evolve into a new confidence that citizens working in common can change their lives and in doing so can change the world around them" (Salam, 2010: March 22, 46-47).

Martinez speaks of American cultural influence today: "...seven of the ten most watched TV shows around the world are American, "Avatar" is the top-grossing film of all time in China, and the world is more fixated on United States brands as ever, which is why US multinationals from Mc'Donalds to Nike book more than half their revenue overseas. If you bring together teenagers from Nigeria, Sweden, South Korea and Argentina – to pick a random foursome – what binds these kids together in some kind of community is American culture: the music, the Hollywood fare, the electronic games, Google, American consumer brands" (42). Tim Wu writes: "Face it: Americans love their smart phones and Internet television as much as they love their cars and air conditioners.... The bottom line is that if everyone keeps using the Internet and other services as much as they like, something will have to give. It is unlikely that the American appetite for bandwidth will diminish anytime soon, nor it is even clear that we want it to" (2010: March 22, 45-46). Salam concludes his Time essay with the words: "Somewhere in the suburbs there is an unemployed 23 year-old who is plotting a cultural insurrection, one that will resonate with existing demographic, cultural and economic trends so powerfully that it will knock American society off its axis" (47). As we have mentioned in Communicating Interculturally, when Mark Zuckerberg founded Facebook, he was 19.

In practical terms, the UCLA's "American Freshman National Norms Fall 2009" survey was administered to 219,864 entering students at 297 bachelor-awarding colleges and universities in the United States, as it has been annually since 1966, the largest annual study of American higher education. The 2007-2009 recession caused the largest financial concerns for first year college students in nine years, with more than half of the incoming students reporting "some concern" about financing their college expenses, and 53% having to take out loans. Only 63% of the incoming students reported having worked as high school seniors, compared to 69% in 2007. "Being well off financially" was a top goal in 2008 and at 78% in 2009, the highest since 1996.

A new recognition of the importance of developing "excellence, integrity and civic responsibility" was noted by 31% saying that there was "a very good chance" that they would take part in civic engagement and volunteer work, with 57% of those who had volunteered in high school, expecting to do so. However, only 33% said that they discussed politics frequently, down from 36% in 2008, and only 33% said that they would seek to promote racial and ethnic understanding, down from 38% in 2008. Among the entering classes, 65% said that they had taken at least one or more high school Advanced Placement courses, which could be used for college or university credit, and thus speeding up their college or university graduation. At the same time, 21% of the entering college classes had had special tutoring or remedial work in high school, the largest number reported since the surveys began, and 39% indicated that they probably would need such tutoring or remedial work in their college or university study (Prior, et al, 2009: Fall).

Mark Bauerlein in his book, The Dumbest Generation (2008), argues that American students make excellent "Jaywalking" targets because their ignorance is so widespread; they don't read books and don't want to read them either. He says that with the computer, they do not need to spell. Even when they have original thought and good writing, their peers ridicule them and they spend too many hours playing with computer games. He states that they do not memorize or store the information which they receive, since their teachers don't tell them to do it or test them on it. A final problem is that they are still young and immature. Bauerlein's arguments are plausible, but at the same time the serious students are very serious as noted above. Sharon Begley (2008, May 24) counters his arguments by reminding us that young people who play computer games have to be cognitively active and demanding, requiring players to create "elaborate fantasy" narratives, use deductive reasoning, identify causes and effects, test hypotheses, and become problem solvers: "Writing off any generation before it's thirty is what's dumb."

In an informal and unscientific survey of teenagers from around the United States, Shine from Yahoo: "Ten Things your [American] Teenager Won't Tell You" (2010: December 1), gives the teenagers' own advice to American parents: Teenagers may want: (1) having more privacy; (2) parents listening to their own views without nagging them; (3) dating even if the parents say that they can't date; (4) sometimes not getting good grades on every assignment (5) not talking to their parents about sex; (6) hating it when parents don't hold their brothers or sisters accountable for their own actions; (7) giving them some slack or leeway without always criticizing them; (8) sometimes lying to their parents to stay out of trouble; (9) getting frustrated when parents use their young age against them as a parental advantage in an argument; (10) wanting their parents to trust them.

2. EXCUSE ME, YOUR GOD IS WAITING: LOVE YOUR GOD, CREATE YOUR LIFE, FIND YOUR TRUE SELF.

Michelle Epiphany Prosser
Energy Focus Executive Coaching

As a corporate life coach I am writing about the biggest stumbling block my clients encounter to living the law of attraction. I provide proven healing therapy–with exercises and meditations–and connect the dots between readers' faith in God and their ability to converse with God.

Excuse Me, Your God Is Waiting expands and intensifies two of the most powerful teachings so you can live the secret of a life filled with love, joy and miracles, closer to God: Conversations with God revolutionized the thoughts of millions by explaining how God wants us to create our lives and become the magnificent, powerful spiritual beings God intended. Excuse Me, Your LIFE is Waiting inspired half a million readers to transform their lives through the "astonishing power" of positive feelings. In this book, I help readers to understand the language of God. Through exercises and meditations, readers we will discover a God they can connect and converse with. Just as I guide my clients in how to pray in their own words and invite God into their lives I teach readers how to have their own conversation with God just as I have done.

Beginning my book, Excuse me, your God is waiting, which was published in 2008, I write:

A river runs through these pages, like it runs through our lives. We don't have a choice of whether or not we are in this river. What we do have a choice about is whether we struggle against it, try to push it along, or surrender to its current and go downstream. We have a choice to approach our life with joy, with playfulness, with power, and with love. We can fight the river or turn and flow with the current.

Images of rivers have always run through my life. I had images of drowning when I was a teenager and my parents divorced. As one career success after another occurred in my twenties and thirties, I felt like I was riding a river current.

When my children arrived as miracles in my life, I knew I was in a river filled with grace.

Finally, when I went to a woman's shelter for counseling because of my marriage, I told my therapist I was having dreams and visions of myself struggling to wade upstream in a river, fighting the current. As I went through my divorce, there were times when I felt like I was barely keeping my head above water.

I am drawn to rivers. I have swum, canoed, and floated lazily in an inner tube down rivers. With my heart beating widely, I have ridden a raft in Class V rapids. The metaphor of rivers shows up in my coaching. I urge clients to see that they have a choice in their lives. They can view themselves as dog-paaddling in the river, struggling to keep their head above water, or they can choose to be the navigator of their own boat. Either way, they are on the water, experiencing both the gentle flow of the river and rough water, rocks, and storms. To be in the river, caught up in the current and in danger of drowning, is to be a victim. As a navigator in life, we take back our power and make choices regardless of what the river throws at us. And always, we can decide to play with the river or fight it.

It is my hope that what is contained in these pages will help you navigate the river of your lfe with joy and ease. And that you can live your life by going downstream, not upstream against the current.

I can only have one request as we start out on this leg of the journey: Fill your boat with joy and playfulness as you push it into the water.

3. Honor and Integrity: Two Important Little Words

Speech for St. Mary's High School Student Body Honor Week
September 11, 2001 Commemoration

Elizabeth Marie Prosser
St. Mary High School, Raleigh, North Carolina

Honor and integrity are little words, however they mean so much. Here at Saint Mary's we have an honor code. Have you ever stopped to think what it means? Honor? Integrity? It is doing the right thing even no one is watching. It is having the courage to do what is right even though it may not be popular. As many of you, I spent a lot of the weekend reflecting on the events of 9/11. I was 8 years old when the towers fell. Many of you may have been four or five years old. This was probably our first significant memory of our lives.

I was touched by the story of Rick Rescorla. Rescorla was a retired military officer responsible for the security of 22 floors of South Tower of the World Trade Center. He had learned the importance of being prepared as he led soldiers in Vietnam. He made the soldiers clean their weapons, dig fox holes every night and stay alert. His men sometimes grumbled about having to dig perfect fox holes every night. One night they were attacked and due to his preparation he was credited with saving the lives of many men during Vietnam.

Mr. Rescorla took his responsibility for his 22 floors of the World Trade Center very seriously. He made evacuation plans, team leaders and a buddy system. He made all of the workers on his floor practice evacuation at least twice per year. Many of the employees grumbled at having to walk down the stairs in practice. Every employee was assigned a buddy that would work together to leave the building. Once outside, there would be a rally point and a head count to make sure everyone got out safely.

On 9/11, Mr. Rescorla received official instructions that everyone should stay put because of the accident in the North Tower. Mr. Rescorla ignored this official word and activated his evacuation plan. Within three minutes of the first building being hit, team leaders orchestrated the plan to descend the stairs with their buddies two by two. Over two thousand five hundred people evacuated from Mr. Rescorla's floor just as they had practiced for years. He was calm and collected as he was giving instructions for people to leave. Mr. Rescorla was last seen heading up the stairs to help other people evacuate.

Mr. Rescorla had honor and integrity. He knew his job was the safety and security of the people he was responsible for. How many times had he practiced the evacuation when he would hear the mumbling of employees expressing displeasure about another drill? It would have been easier not to practice. Mr. Rescorla needed honor to step forward and demand practice and then make a decision to activate the evacuation plan. He had learned from his experience in Vietnam that practice and preparation would save lives. I was also struck by his name Mr. Rescorla.... Mr. Rescue.

The example he provided reminds me of what Christ says in John Chapter 15, verse 13, "No man has more love than to lay down his life for a friend" How many children still had their parents because Mr. Rescorla was prepared? How many parents were able to see their children because of his actions? How many husbands were able to come home to their wives and hug them and say, "Thank God I made it out alive?"

Like Mr. Rescorla, we strive to make honor a daily habit here at Saint Mary's. We trust each other here. We know that grades are fairly earned, that our possessions are safe, the administration will deal with us in a fair manner and we deal with them in a respectful way. The Honor Code is not just for the students, it is for everyone on campus, including the staff, faculty, administration and even visitors. We have an obligation to protect the reputation of this school both on and off campus. We show good sportsmanship not only to our team, but our opponents. We congratulate people when they deserve congratulations. We console someone when they experience defeat. We compete in a strong and vigorous manner, yet are humble when we achieve success. The adults at Saint Mary's are genuinely concerned about each one of us reaching our highest potential. Honor is proactive; honor is acting in the right way; honor is having the courage to do the right thing no matter what the consequences. This year, let us follow the example of Rick Rescorla. AMEN.

4. Argentinian and Latin American Youth

Daniel F. Alonso
Universidad Austral, Argentina

Approaching their respective bicentennials (among other, Haiti 1804, Argentina 1810, Venezuela 1811, Paraguay 1811, Chile 1818, Peru 1821, Guatemala, Costa Rica, El Salvador, Honduras y Nicaragua 1821, Mexico 1821, Brazil 1822), Latin American countries face the challenge of educating their twentieth first century generations to adapt to democracy and globalization. Since their independences, Latin American countries have struggled to strike an elaborate balance between the growing demands of affirming native traditions, European ancestry – which usually included the Catholic faith, Spanish language, and certain other cultural traits imported from noticeably England or France – and the growing North American influence coming from the United States.

Demographic diversity is noticeable throughout the continent. Indigenous descendants, called Amerindians, constitute majorities in Andean countries such as Bolivia and Peru, while white European descendants constitute substantive majorities in other former Spanish colonies, such as Argentina and Uruguay. African population is noticeable in some Northern South American countries, particularly in Brazil, while mestizos – the mixture of White and Amerindians – and mulattoes – the mixture of Africans and Amerindians – have spread around the continent. Twentieth century immigration has been led by Italians, with contributions of several other European nationalities (Encyclopedia Britannica Online, retrieved on April 30th, 2010).

Sharing such a cosmopolitan composite, younger generations have merged into the common tendency to keep closer ties with (North) American culture, by being influenced by American way of life, pop culture, and Hollywood cinema. Nevertheless, this has sometimes been in tension with more rebellious groups who have yielded towards active social involvement, more leftist political – or even Cuban-friendly – preferences, and non-alignment. In spite of being quite similar in these previous attitudes and traditions, educational backgrounds have been quite different. The fight against illiteracy has been a fundamental one throughout the continent, with results being diverse. Some countries have dropped illiteracy to seemingly developed countries rates, while others still stand afar from such coveted standard. On the one hand, Argentina (according to the 2001 National Census, illiteracy in people under 30 was 2.3 %), Uruguay and Chile enjoy a less than 3% illiteracy rate, while others (Guatemala, Bolivia and Brazil) suffer illiteracy rates of over 10%. However, the region as a whole has the lowest illiteracy rates among developing regional groups (UNESCO, World Adult Literacy Rates, 2000).

Some countries, particularly Argentina, Colombia, and – perhaps – Mexico, have enjoyed a profound leadership among their neighbors in formal education, editorial work, and – very particularly – in university studies. According to Argentina's 2001 National Census, over 26% of the working population (población ocupada) over 15 years of age have undergone some university studies and another 19 % have completed secondary school studies. Most recently, other countries have significantly improved their university prospects in order to catch up with their neighbors. Meanwhile, others continue to have their upper classes educated in US universities, with a lesser number of students pursuing postgraduate studies in Europe.

Though many times Latin American university studies have been reserved for the elite, a wider social base for university education has been growing. This is essentially the case for Argentina where the number of university graduates has increased. In addition, there is a tendency to enlarge the number of post-graduate studies for students leading to Masters or PhD degrees. With comparatively high unemployment levels, job opportunities and salaries for people not pursuing university studies are less attractive than for those holding a degree. For poorer classes, the risk of governmental dependency and populism arises.

Exchange programs, including semesters abroad, have been gaining popularity both at university and at secondary school levels. Once again, though many students prefer the North-South America exchange, some choose European placements. Argentina's cosmopolitan background and ethnical compound have fostered intercultural dialogue at university level with many European countries, particularly, Spain, Italy, France, Germany, and England.

As for foreign language studies, English continues being the most popular foreign language to learn throughout Latin America. American English has always been the most popular choice, though Argentines learn both British and American English on a similar basis. For South American countries, Brazilian Portuguese is lately enjoying some momentum. With Brazil's leadership blooming and GNP consistent growth, most neighbors' youth perceive some benefit from learning the Brazilian language. Viceversa, many Brazilians choose to master Spanish in order to nurture liaisons with their fellow countries. Foreign language study of French, Italian and German have some stronghold in areas where these countries' culture has excerpted influence.

Asian culture has expanded in very diverse ways in the different countries. To begin with, Chinatowns and the like are not so common in Latin America. And though most large urban conglomerates have their share of Chinese, Japanese and Korean immigrants, they usually have not become a power of their own. Chinese and Japanese immigrants are more numerous in Brazil and Peru. Exposure to Chinese culture has increased lately. First, there is the undeniable presence of Chinese products which range from the simplest to the more complex which include electronics and cars. Needless to say, the youth are particularly acquainted with this phenomenon. Second, the Beijing Olympic Games have been widely seen and opened a window of interest in China's geographical, historical as well as present traits; this factor –again– has had an influence on Argentine youth. Finally, Sino-Argentinean bilateral relationships – as well as with other Latin American countries- have thrived during the last decade, this due to tourism as well as commercial ties, and some investment interests of Chinese companies in Argentina.

While fostering intercultural dialogue, global awareness has sprung cultural change in areas such as human rights, and the environment. It has simultaneously triggered Pan American understanding and cooperation, and, in some cases, reciprocal acquaintance has developed the sense of a common nation: Latin America, with common roots and traits bringing populations closer, but yet distant from political or economic union.

5. BELGIAN YOUTH: A FREE PERSON WITH RIGHTS AND RULES

Helene Dislaire
Malmedy, Belgium

(Translated from French by Jean-Louis Dislaire)

A Belgian teenager is a person between thirteen and nineteen years old. The teenager is a free person with rights and rules, under the supervision of his or her parents. During this period, we young Belgians will seek our limits, like most Europeans. We will experience life, like me, and will get autonomy little by little. The young Belgians are not only young persons who like to watch TV eating snacks; we are also young persons who test the others. We set for ourselves our own limits and rules. Thus many young people like to cross the rules: it is like a game. When we know the limits, we will have to decide on our way. Then several choices are given to us. For me, the choice was quickly done. The situation of my family was not always marvelous. I have a sister and a father but an empty space will always remain with no mother at home. My current relation with my sister is rather good, she left the house and lives with her boyfriend. She works as a manager in a nursing home. The relation with my father is the only parental relation I have. It was not always easy but we work on it every day.

The young Belgian, in the best situation, has a mother and a father, and even sometimes brothers and sisters. This is what we call a "close family" with blood ties. But for some time, marriages here are breaking up. In this case, most of the young Belgians have a mother and a father but that they see them only at a regular interval (this week with mom, and the next week with dad) It is what is called in Belgium a family "with shared guardian." Many families are recomposed; a Belgian thus finds himself or herself sometimes with three sisters and two brothers whereas he or she had only one sister in his or her own family. It is what is called a recomposed family. Sometimes we have a family with one parent, because the other died or left. We call this a "single-parent" family. It is actually my situation. I think that in Europe and everywhere in the world, we will find this type of families. We are not the only ones in this situation. Unfortunately, the "adults" forget sometimes that they have children.

When I grew up, I have made grow with me my imagination and my eccentricity (which I entirely assume). I always wanted to draw and create in order to share my feelings with others. In compensation of my mother and our wound from her leaving us, my father sent me to a painting class which I took for seven years. We young Belgians must often carry our sufferings with us. Either we decide to accept them and to make our richness out of them, or we mope and get rid of them only with difficulty. However, every choice we will make during our adolescence will influence the rest of our lives. The relations we will have with our parents can depend on our lives and our parent's lives and experiences. It is possible that there is no communication; in this case, we young people are often left to our own devices. We test our limits without comments or restriction given by our parents. Often, some young Belgians come to a bad end as drug dealers, convicts, or racketeers. It is not a job; it is sad and lamentable to be there at the end.

My values are peace, serenity, frankness, respect and love. I am not a believer in a religious faith but I hope to give this love that I did not receive as I would like to be the one I did not have and I would like to stay free. I have received these values from my close relations, but for some of them I have built them from my experiments and research of myself. Young Belgians who want to be successful in life, will seek values from their experiments, good or bad, but in their own way. We can always find positive things in bad situations. I think that young Belgians stay in a continual conflict with themselves. We try to find our goals in life.

I want to be a drawing teacher; I want to see my children growing, to have a husband and to love him for what he is. Cannabis looks old-fashioned and like a pain-killer these days but just try it and you will understand. Drugs also are also included in our adolescence. There are a few people who did not try to smoke. But a lot of people will continue. In my country, the law says that people cannot take drugs before 16-18 years old and when we are 18 years old, we can have only three grams of cannabis. The cannabis is considered as soft drug, which is not the case for heroin, coke and other drugs which are hard drugs. Cigarettes are prohibited for teenagers who are not 16 years old. It is not allowed to smoke in restaurants, schools, buses and other public places. I do not deny smoking sometimes, but always reasonably, once in a while. Alcohol is easier to find and to buy. It is the subject of many ethylic comas and serious car accidents for our young people. But each of us wants to know our limits. I drink and I smoke.

I am disgusted and disappointed to see the way in which the young people consider love and romance. Of course, love is not presented as "dirty" but it becomes dirty romance in the ways it is practiced. We receive a lot of information from the media against the transmissible diseases and the dangers of pregnancy. It is not in our practice to be mothers at 14 years old but it happens nevertheless. All these topics can bring problems, incomprehension and questions from the young Belgians and Europeans. Faced with this problem, we can find answers thanks to our parents, our close relations, doctors and psychologists. Personally, I had to receive help from those people and for many reasons.

The media attack us everywhere, that is through television, Internet, cell phones, people magazines or others, and of course the newspaper. We know what happens in the world (for the young people who are interested) and we have the right to have our own opinions. Personally, I always like to listen to the radio and I appreciate medical information, news and the newspapers. I like to know in which world I live, the position I have in my country and what are my rights as a citizen. We do not all have the chance to travel. When I was six, I stayed for 6 weeks in Morocco. This experience opened my mind. When I was eight, I came to the United States. Also, I learned a lot of new things but also the sonority of the English language. When I was 12 years old I had another opportunity to go to Morocco; at 14 I went to Senegal and last year, I spent 3 weeks again in the States. I had the chance to travel quite a lot when I was young. Every Belgian is not that lucky.

As I have said, my values are peace, serenity, frankness, respect and love and I want to be free. How about you?

6. YOUTH IN MODERN RUSSIA

Sergei A. Samoilenko
George Mason University, Fairfax, Virginia

In the Soviet Union, young people were the symbol of progress, the guarantee for socialist future, and the indelible part of Soviet ideology and propaganda. The Soviet system tried to preplan their life scenarios and set down rules of conduct for its youth. Raised through the Young Pioneers and the Komsomol (the Young Communist League), young people entered the Party at the age of 28 and followed the career ladder according to the hierarchical rules: when their promotion depended on age and length of service with the same employer, rather than actual merits and qualifications. On one hand, such a paternalistic approach assured the attention that the Soviet system paid to young people and their problems; on the other hand, it prevented any deviation from the plan designed by the Communist Party. At the same time, this overprotecting strategy was ineffective in preparing youth for any social or political changes. In the late 1980s and early 1990s the political and economic reforms introduced in June 1987 by then Soviet leader Mikhail Gorbachev engendered the disintegration of the Communist Party and Komsomol. These political reforms and collapse of the old Soviet system caused many years of uncertainty, social transformation and search for a new social status of Russian youth.

In modern Russia, young people (age group 17-26 years) are more individualistic, self-dependent and feeling responsible for their own destiny than their former Soviet youth peers. They are experienced gamers and Internet users, less concerned about moneymaking compared to the youth from the 1990s, but more eager to get a high-quality education and follow their life goals and professional calling. According to the analytical report "Youth in new Russia. Values and Priorities," Russian youth think of life in their country more positively than their parents or earlier generations did. This fact can be explained by their growing financial stability and increasing job placement for Russian youth. According to this research, about 87% of young Russians are satisfied with their financial status and life overall.

Although young Russians consider financial well-being among the most important criteria for success, they believe that a good education, strong family and interesting/challenging work are equally important. When looking for work, young Russians are not only interested in how much it pays, but also whether this job is interesting and what kind of social status it represents.

A large family represents another important criterion of success for many young Russians. Since young people prefer to rely mostly on themselves, they start working early to assure their financial independence and stability by a certain age. These goals dictate their motivational behaviors and life decisions, including their choices for education and career.

Similar to the generation of the 1990s, young Russians nowadays prefer occupations related to law and finance. However, the popularity of professions, such as managers, scientists, computer specialists and doctors is increasing. Many young Russians consider Gazprom, the largest extractor of natural gas in the world, and the administration of the Russian president as top employers.

In today's Russia the political preferences show (Milyukova, 2002) contradictory political consciousness of the Russian youth. Liberal values coexist with a desire for authoritarianism and for a strong personified leader. Numerous political youth groups in Russia include: Pro-Kremlin movements (e.g, Nashi or "Ours", Youth Democratic Anti-Fascist Movement); Democratic Oppositional movements (e.g., Oborona), and Oppositional Youth movements (e.g., National Bolsheviks). Although the majority of young Russians mainly believe in democratic changes supported by the ruling and largest political party United Russia (or Yedinaya Rossiya), chaired by Prime Minister Vladimir Putin, studies show (Institute of Sociology RAN, 2007) a correlation between socioeconomic status and party preferences in this country. Young people supporting Pro-Kremlin organizations are usually satisfied with their financial standing, as opposed to those who support liberal national-patriotic and left-wing parties. According to sociologists (Pautova, 2009), Russian youth are less critical of the government than older generations and consider work for local or federal authorities among other top career options. The popularity of the Russian government can be explained by the relative economic growth and stability that allowed many of young Russians to find new ways for self-actualization.

Despite the apparent popularity of political youth movements, only 14 percent of young Russians are actively interested in politics. It could be explained by other aspects of life that young Russians consider important. Besides typical hobbies and traditional interests, such as sports, music, and reading, Russian youth combine the customary ways for rest and recreation with new opportunities introduced by globalization and technological innovations. For example, now more Russians spend their leisure time in chat rooms, forums and on social networking sites. The most important resources include Vkontakte (Russian version of Facebook), Moi Mir (My World), Odnoklassniki (Russian version of Classmates.com) and instant messaging services. The Internet has become a trustworthy news channel for many young Russians that is only second to television (Pautova & Lebedev, 2008) .

Traditionally, Russians highly appreciate the value of interpersonal communication and call interaction with friends and relatives among the most important ways to spend their leisure time. Besides its primary communication purpose, human interaction with friends and family members is also used as a strategy for bonding, establishing new connections and maintaining good relationships with the community to assure their help and support in times of need.

Unlike their parents, who believe in a slow but sure strategy for life planning and career building, Russian youth are more ambitious, goal-oriented, and aggressive. They aspire to integrate into the international youth scene, and to participate in global economic, political and humanitarian developments.

The new generation is not afraid to take risks, believes that success implies playing for high stakes, and has no doubts that they will become more successful than the generation of their parents.

References

Agranovich, M., Korolyova, N. , Poletaev, A., Sundiev, I., Seliv-
erstova, I., & Fateeva, A.(2007). Youth Development Report:
Condition of Russian Youth. Retrieved May 20, 2010, from
Diuke, N. (2006). Pervoe svobod-noe pokolenie. Retrieved,
May 20, 2010, from http://www.ecsocman. edu.ru/images/
pubs/2006/11/16/0000295102/07-dyuk-53-62.pdfhttp://unesdoc.
unesco.org/images/0014/001431/143147e.pdf

Diuke, N. (2006). Pervoe svobodnoe pokolenie. Retrieved,
May 20, 2010, from http://www.ecsocman. edu.ru/images/
pubs/2006/11/16/0000295102/07-dyuk-53-62.pdf
Fürst, J. (2001). Cutting edge: Anti-Stalinist youth groups. Retrieved, May
20, 2010, from http://www.timeshighereducation.co.uk/story.asp?sto
ryCode=160227&sectioncode=26, Chicago, il;: University of Chicago
Press.
Institute of Sociology RAN (2007). Molodyozh novoi Rossii: Tsennostnye
prioritety. Youth in New Russia. Values and Priorities. Retrieved May
20, 2010, from http://www.isras.ru/analytical_report_Youth.html
Milyukova, I. (2002:). The political future of Russia through the eyes of
young students. Young, 10, 3/4, 12-25.
Pautova, L. (2009, December). iX izuchaet Y i vospityvaet Z. Russki
reportyor. Retrieved 20, 2010, from www.rusrep.ru/2010/12/
sociologi_o_pokolenii
Pautova, L., & Lebedev, P. (2008). Molodyozh kak tselevaya auitoriya v
internete: Segmenty i podxody k nim. Retrieved May 20, 2010, from
http://bd.fom.ru/report/map/pokolenie21/pr_r210410np

7. A RUSSIAN GIRL, LOVING PARENTS, AND A RUSSIAN PASSPORT

Anya Klyukanova
University of Oregon, Eugene, Oregon

My name is Anya Klyukanova and I am a sophomore at the University of Oregon in the midst of obtaining a degree in Political Science and Journalism. I was born in Tver, Russia and I moved to the United States when I was just a toddler. However, I started returning to Russia every summer since I was about four. Because of the careful upbringing of my parents and my repeated returns to the motherland, I proudly consider myself to be Russian and I have many traits that are characteristic of Russians. Many of these traits are not prevalent in the American culture but they are still a major part of my life.

A big difference I've noticed between the Russian culture and the American culture is the value placed on family. I consider my parents to be the two most important people in my life and I interact with them a few times a day, whether it be by phone, e-mail or Skype. However, none of my American friends seem to place such high importance on family values; most talk to their parents once a week for five minutes and do so begrudgingly. Although I never resent talking to my parents, I argue with them often. This is another difference I have noticed between the two cultures. In America, it seems to be considered almost a taboo to argue with anyone but in Russia, arguing is simply a part of life. A quiet discussion can turn into a loud argument and back to a peaceful discussion within a matter of minutes and no one will think twice about it.

Next to my parents, I value my education as a critical part of my life. I take school very seriously and try very hard to excel in my studies. However, many of my American peers seem to view college as a place to party and socialize. Their lack of concern for their grades has always appalled me but if they put in half the amount of effort they put into beer pong and sports, they would have straight A's. Unfortunately, this lack of concern for grades is also shown through their lack of respect for authority. In Russia, students must stand up when a teacher enters the room and are only allowed to sit back down when told to do so. In America, students are playing games on their computer and texting on their cell phone with their feet on top of their desk when a teacher enters the room. In a Russian institution, this sort of behavior would cause a student to be expelled.

Although these are just a few of the cultural differences which I have encountered in America, I also have many traits which I share with my American friends. I have become accustomed to living with constant hot water, a full refrigerator, a laptop, a car as a mode of transportation, etc. Ultimately, I have a higher standard of living than many people in Russia. Also, I keep up with both western fashion and media much more than I do with Russian fashion and media; I shop at American stores and my favorite source of information is The New York Times. But even though I've become more accustomed to the American way of life, I will never forget my roots and I will continue to live as a girl with a Russian passport.

8.   CORRIDOR AND SMILE OF WESTERN AFRICA

Yves Assidou
Togo,
Shanghai University of Finance and Economics, Shanghai, China

Togo is a small country located in western Africa. With an estimated 5.2 million inhabitants among whom 43% are less than 15 years old, Togo is a multicultural and multiethnic state. The official language is French and the most spoken national languages are Ewe (in the south) and Kabye (in the north). At least 40 ethnic groups live within boundaries of this land which historically was a refuge for those who were escaping from wars and persecutions of ancient Kingdoms of Ashanti (now a part of Ghana), Abomey (Benin) or Ife (Nigeria) among others. German and French colonization brought Togo into modernity but ancestors' culture is still in practice in rural areas while Christianity is almost always practiced in cities.

Togolese youth are then influenced by all these ethnics, with many cultural and linguistic differences that observers consider as a great advantage. Meanwhile, Togolese young people are very open-minded like their parents because they desire to establish a common society in peace with multicultural characteristics. Although political factors influence the behavior of people from different regions, it is easily noticed that mixed marriage in Togo is becoming more and more a lifestyle. Togolese people generally believe that marriage between two persons from different ethnic groups is a factor that would eliminate regionalism and promote better understanding among the population. That's why for a long period, the country has never experienced ethnic conflict even if there were political troubles and instability during the last decade 1993-2005 of democratic process.

One policy that all Togolese governments undertook since 1960 was to send public servants from their origins to another region in order to promote Togo's multiculturalism and make people know more about others. I was personally involved in such an experience as my parents were public servants. I know the southern and northern part of Togo and their ethnic groups. Much more, I have a lot of friends from different regions of Togo, as well as my parents. This situation is not a unique one because other persons also experience this kind of life. But I think that much improvement in multicultural integration has to be done because there is still existing some kind of conservatism in some areas or ethnic groups. The conservatism factor is due to the lack of education and sometimes to religious fanatics. The wrong interpretation of religious prescriptions leads to such exaggerations and conflicts.

At regional levels, African youth culture differs across countries that are either French or English speaking. The colonization heritage plays a central role in these differences. A Nigerian or a Ghanaian would not be easily understood certain cultural behaviors of a Togolese or Senegalese. This captures the fact that a vertical cultural relationship originating from Europe is still influencing young people's behavior across the countries in western Africa. Even when some ethnic groups are dispatched across countries, the horizontal cultural relationship that might exist between western Africa countries is not so deep. For example, the Ewe-Mina ethnic group is present in Togo, Ghana and Benin. Even when those people can speak a common language, their belonging to different national entities makes them more influenced by either French or English taste. However, such differences were more pronounced in the early 1960s but with the current regional economic integration process, there is a hope that in the future, intercultural distortions will be eliminated.

About the Youth's Future in West Africa

Youth experience in West Africa has been impacted by some armed conflicts and political instability that restrain their hope about the future. Young people seem less optimistic about the political leaders' will, especially concerning the building of a society of peace and justice. They believe that political leaders are so linked to corruption that the dilapidation of common resources by a few people in-power is the main cause of the streaming state of poverty within the population. There is less confidence in political leaders in western Africa than in other region like southern Africa. This fact might be an explanation of high emigration rates in that region towards Europe. However, some countries undertake a huge battle against corruption and injustice among which is Ghana, the best example of democracy and governance in the region. Non-governmental organizations also are making great efforts to enhance young peoples' daily life by providing relief programs in rural and post-conflict areas. Despite the current situation, there is still a hope among young intellectual leaders about the future of West African youth, since multicultural settings play an important role in melting people in the region. The regional economic integration project must be the leading enterprise for the consolidation of hope about future among young people in West Africa.

Personal experience in China:

As an international student, my personal experience about intercultural communication in Asia and China is relating to some facts that capture differences with my country of origin. I experience a lot of differences with Chinese but less with European students. I think a lack of knowledge about Chinese traditions and Chinese peoples' behavior made me sad the first days of my arrival in this great country. I find Chinese students so silent that I could not imagine making friends. But later I discovered that people here are friendly in ways that are not ours in Africa. This finding is not especially true for Chinese but also for those originating from other Asian countries as well. There are other simple facts that can illustrate such differences in culture with Chinese people. For example, red color means positive things in China while in Togo this means negative things or a perception of a danger. Young people in West Africa are accustomed to shake hands in ordinary greetings but here it not a very common habit. Broadly speaking, it is not easy for one coming from outside to feel well in his or her first days in China but the more time passes the more one complies with Asian and China specificities.

References:

Chant, S. and G.A. Jones, G.A. (2005), Youth, gender and livelihoods in West Africa: Perspectives from Ghana and Gambia, Children's Geographies, Vol 3, No 2, 185-199. London, England: London School of Economics.

Williams, T.& Myers, M. (2004: August). Evaluation of search for common ground activities in Sierra Leone.; http://www.sfcg.org/programmes/westafrica/youth.pdf

West Africa http://www.waynyouth.org/Files/Programs.htm

West Africa http://ceas.iscte.pt/docs/ym_africa_programme.pdf

West Africa http://www.westafricareview.com/issue11/toc11.htm

9. The Pied Piper: "Condemned Isolation," and Liberation from Rape and Shame

Evelin Lindner
Founding President, Human Dignity and Humiliation Studies
Network

I assume you know the story of the pied piper? This story is profoundly connected to my work, did you know that?

Let me explain: Circa 1,000 years ago, the city of Hamelin (Hameln in German spelling) was infested with rats. A man with a flute came and offered to get rid of them, if paid. As he was promised payment, he went through the city playing his flute. All the rats followed him and he went into the river Weser, where they all drowned. When he asked to be paid, he was betrayed. He was told: "there were no rats in Hamelin!" To take revenge, he went through the streets the next Sunday, when all adults were at church. The children followed him and he went into the next mountain, where the children disappeared.

So far for the story.

Considerable historical truth is hidden in this story. Roughly 1,000 years ago, indeed, young people disappeared. They were often "shanghaied" to become settlers in the newly conquered east, which is today Poland. For about one thousand years, these territories (Silesia, Pomerania, East Prussia) were part of a German political sphere. A thousand years after the pied piper's story's historical roots, more precisely, after WWII, in 1945 and 1946, many millions of people with an ethnic Germanic background were thrown back west again, among them my parents. Posters were posted in the streets, ordering all expellees to leave the keys of their farms, their houses, and flats outside the door so that Poles could move in. They had to abandon everything they owned. Breslau, my mother's hometown, was almost completely emptied of its inhabitants and "refilled" with new ones. It was renamed Wroclaw (I visited it, for the first time, together with my parents, in 2007).

For people identifying with Poland, this expulsion was an utterly happy moment. They were finally liberated. And Hitler's unspeakable treatment of slaves as second-class beings was finally avenged.

Also I rejoice, deeply!

My parents, however, are profoundly traumatized by the loss of their beloved homeland. Everyday they say: "If we only could go home to Silesia!" My father walks the land of the farm he was to inherit every evening, in his mind, and speaks with his beloved two elder brothers who died in this war.

My father himself tried to oppose Nazi culture when he was 18 and was almost executed for that. He lost one arm, and lives with one arm since he is 19. His grandfather had been Jewish, and even though this had been successfully covered up by his family during Nazi times, his "Jewish" looks had added to his aggravation and opposition.

My parents say this, almost everyday, still 60 years after the war: "Hitler has destroyed our lives. Hitler has raped us."

For me, displacement went even further. My parents have a dream of their homeland, I do not even have that. Until I was about 45 years old, my main identity was, "Where I am born, I am not at home, but there is no home to go to for me. I do not belong to the human family, I have no place on this planet."

My parents were displaced to Hamelin (just by chance, there was no choice). Hamelin was filled with displaced people and grew from ca. 25,000 inhabitants to about double the size. It thus received back the children they lost 1,000 years ago, one could say.

I am born in Hamelin, but I do not feel much connection to it. It is not my home and it is not the place "where I am from." I am not "from Silesia" either. I am "from rape and displacement" – this would be the most appropriate description. (Today, my identity of being a global citizen has healed my pain of not-belonging.)

I grew up in a home so traumatized, until the day today, that trauma is normality. My parents have never had the courage to attach themselves to "life on Earth" since WWII; they live with God, beyond life and death, often praying for many hours a day.

This, in turn, has hurt me profoundly, since childhood, because I could not follow them into the dogma that underpins their religiosity. Beginning at the age of 9, I developed "religious doubts" as to the dogmatic foundations of this belief system (I felt that dogma profoundly contradicts the very essence of religious quest, only decades later would I find discussions of my stance, for example, in Carse, 2008). As a result, I became alienated from my own family. As a child from a displaced family, I had not made real friends outside the family; now I became completely isolated also inside the family. Until the age of 19, I do not remember speaking a single genuinely private word with anybody, not inside the family, and not outside of it. It was like solitary confinement, not just on Earth, but also beyond. The conclusion I felt compelled to draw from my family's belief system was that even suicide would not remedy my situation, since I would be condemned by God also after death. I felt thus crushed as a "legitimate" being very early in my life; I was a walking dead, condemned even after death: and all this due to war and displacement.

The only person, whose unconditional love, beyond any religious dogma, I remember feeling during this period, was the love from my father. He put a little bag with chocolate into my room from time to time, quietly. These little pieces of chocolate did not dry my tears, but I am sure they helped me survive.

Today, I deeply understand that my parents need their religiosity for survival, and to what degree they must have felt their very existence threatened by my doubts. I love them profoundly and empathize with their suffering. This loving empathy is among the principle driving forces for my work. The withholding of dignity and the humiliation my parents suffer, even today, is so deep and so cruel that it touches my heart thoroughly. They have never received the acknowledgment for their suffering that they deserve. Their predicament is taboo and covered under a thick carpet of silence.

They share this fate, at least to a certain extent, with moderate Hutu, for example, who opposed the killing of Tutsi, as I found out when I did my research for my doctoral dissertation on the genocides in Rwanda and Somalia, on the background of Nazi Germany.

"Condemned isolation" is a fitting phrase for the being-in-this-world of my parents. It was coined by psychiatrist Jean Baker Miller when she speaks about relational trauma. "The most terrifying and destructive feeling that a person can experience is isolation. This is not the same as 'being alone' in the more straightforward sense. It is feeling locked out of the possibility of human connection" (Miller, 1988, p. 1).

My family's suffering has opened my eyes for the suffering of humans on Earth. Apartheid-like conditions, the Holocaust, genocide, ethnic cleansing, mass killings, destruction of our habitat, this is the sad reality that we as humans have created for ourselves.

This is also the reason for why I will not and cannot simply close my eyes and try to "make the best of it." I cannot live a "normal" life in the wealthy West, the "palace" of this world, while millions suffer outside of the palace's walls, and the ecosphere we all depend on is being destroyed.

Your support touches and humbles me and I promise to deeply honor the responsibility that is connected with your trust!

All my loving gratitude,

Evelin

PS: See here the English translation of two posters that were posted in the streets, from which my parents were expelled (my mother got these posters many years after the war from somebody who collected them):

Poster 1:

Poster to the population of Lower Silesia and the Southern regions of Brandenburg!

The primordially Slavic territories that have been torn away from Poland by the imperialistic Germanic urge, are now won back for our homeland thanks to the victorious advance by the allied Red Army and the heroic Polish Army.

On the grounds of a decision by the Ministerial Council of the Republic of Poland, I assume the administration of the state on these re-conquered purely Slavic territories.

I request from the population loyal and total obedience to all decrees by the Polish administration and strict compliance and implementation of all orders.

All active or passive resistance are broken by the use of violence and the guilty are punished according to military law.

The Slavic population that has been Germanized with violence and insidiousness, is cared for by me and is given the opportunity to return to Polishness, for which the best daughters and sons of these primordially Slavic territories have been bleeding.

Signed: Stanislaw Piaskowski, April 1945

Poster 2:

Special Order to the German population of the city of Bad Salzbrunn including Sandberg

According to the order of the Polish Government it is ordered:

1. On 14th July 1945 from 6 to 9 a.m. a resettlement of the German population will take place.

2. The German population will be resettled in the territory west of the river Neisse.

3. Each German is permitted to take only 20 kg of travel luggage.

4. No transport (cars, oxen, horses, cows) is permitted.

5. The entire living and non-living inventory, in an undamaged condition, remains as property of the Polish government.

6. The last deadline for resettlement expires on 14th July, 10 o'clock.

7. Non-compliance with the order will be responded to with severest punishments, including the use of weapons.

8. Sabotage and looting will be responded to with the use of weapons.

9. Gathering place is at the street Bahnhof Bad Salzbrunn-Adelsbacher Weg in rows of 4 persons. Head of the row 20 meters in front of Adelsbach.

10. Those Germans and their family members, who have a certificate of non-evacuation, must stay in their houses from 5 a.m. to 2 p.m. and not leave them.

11. All houses and appartments in the city must stay open. The keys must be put into the doors from outside.

Bad Salzbrunn, 14th July 1945, 6 o'clock

Section Commander Zinkowski, Oberstleutnant

F) Book Reviews on Intercultural, International, and Global Topics

Michael H. Prosser
University of Virginia,
Shanghai International Studies University

1. Brzezinski, Z. (2012). Strategic Vision: America and the Crisis of Global Power.

New York, NY, Basic Books 208 pages; Introduction; Part 1 "The Receding West" (3 chapters); Part 2 "The Waning of the American Dream" (3 chapters); Part 3 "The World After America: By 2025, not Chinese but Chaotic" (3 chapters); Part 4 "Beyond 2025: A New Geopolitical Balance" (3 chapters); "Conclusion: America's Dual Role"; Notes 195-196; Index; Maps and Figures.

Zbigniew Brzezinski was the National Security Advisor for President Jimmy Carter. He is a counselor and trustee at the Center for Strategic and International Studies and is a Professor of American Foreign Policy at the School of Advanced International Studies at Johns Hopkins University. Among his fifteen published books, his book Second Chance: Three Presidents and the Crisis of American Superpower was a New York Times best seller.

Among the prepublished individuals endorsing this book on the back jacket, are President Jimmy Carter; Democrat Senator John Kerry and Republican Senator Richard G. Lugar; Former World Bank President Jim Wolfensohn; Lt. General Brent Scowcroft; former President of the Council on Foreign Relations, Leslie H. Gelb; and Harvard Professor Joseph S. Nye, Jr.

Brent Snowcroft, former National Security Director for both Presidents Gerald Ford and George H. W. Bush, writes: "In Strategic Vision, Zbigniew

Brzezinski, one of our nation's wisest statesmen and most farsighted strategists, has made yet another vital contribution to the public debate about America's role in the world. His latest book is a must read." Senator Luger writes: "Informed by a lifetime of comprehensive scholarship and many years of responsibility on the front lines of our diplomacy and national security, Zbigniew Brzezinski provides in Strategic Vision a comprehensive blueprint for successful planning and action."

Challenging the long-held argument for continuing American exceptionalism and the idea that the twenty-first century like the twentieth century will be an American century, Brzezinski's first part, "The Receding West," has three chapters, 1. "The Emergence of Global Power," 2. "The Rise of Asia and the Dispersal of Global Power,"and 3. "The Impact of Global Political Awakening."

Martin Jacques' 2009 book, When China Rules the World is one of the major books that proposes that the twenty-first century is at least an Asian century, and very likely a Chinese century. Jacques' thinking is that as modernity comes to Asia, and especially China, it is doing so on Asian and Chinese terms, rather than Westernization and Americanization. Brzezinski begins his Introduction by stating: "The world is now interactive and interdependent. It is also for the first time a world in which the problems of human survival have begun to overshadow more traditional international conflicts. Unfortunately, the major powers have yet to undertake globally cooperative responses to the new and increasingly grave challenges to human well-being – environmental, climatic, socioeconomic, nutritional or demographic. And without basic geopolitical stability, any efforts to achieve the necessary global cooperation will falter" (1). He states that he seeks to respond to four major questions:

1. The movement of global power from the West to the East, and how is it being affected by the new reality of a politically awakened humanity?

2. Why is America's global appeal waning, what are the symptoms of America's domestic and international decline, and how did American waste the unique global opportunity offered by the peaceful end of the Cold War? Conversely, what are America's recuperative strengths and what geopolitical reorientation is necessary to revitalize America's world role?

3. What would be the likely geopolitical consequences if America declined from its globally preeminent position, who would be the almost-

immediate geopolitical victims of such a decline, what effects would it have on the global-scale problems of the twenty-first century and could China assume American's central role in world affairs by 2025?

4. looking beyond 2025, how should a resurgent America define its long-terrm geopolitical goals, and how could America, with its traditional European allies, seek to engage Turkey and Russia in order to construct an even larger and more vigorous West? Simultaneously, how could America achieve balance in the East between the need for close cooperation with China and the fact that a constructive American role in Asia should be neither exclusively China-centric nor involve dangerous entanglements in Asian conflicts? (2)"

These are hard challenges that he presents, one which so far in the US Republican primaries and general election, in the absence of Jon Huntsman as the one wise voice in the earlier Republican primary debates, neither Mitt Romney, the all but sure Republican presidential nominee, nor Rick Santorum, nor Newt Gingrich have considered carefully, or perhaps honestly. Although Romney spent two years as a nineteen-twenty-one year old Mormon missionary in Paris, he sneers that Obama is trying to turn the United States into a European socialist country. The term is loosely used, but one paradox that seems present for some time is "that the United States is becoming a capitalist-socialist country while China is becoming a socialist-capitalist country." Since the United States began its experiment in Roosevelt's New Deal in the 1930s, there has always been a socialist welfare-state leaning in American policies. Perhaps the best example of socialism working well can be found in the Scandinavian countries. Basically, except as a derogative, the term socialism has a very different meaning than communism, and it has no special importance in American political and economic thinking. Even China's leaders insist in the words of Deng Xiaoping, that communism in China works with Chinese characteristics. Essentially, though China continues to require all of its students to study Marxism-Leninism, Mao Tsedong thought, Deng Xiaoping theory, Jiang Zemin's "Three Represents," and Hu Jintao's "Scientific Development" theories are much more dominant in Chinese political thinking.

Also, leaning backwards to the Cold War era of the 1960s, Mitt Romney calls the current Russia our greatest foe. But, as US Secretary of State

Hillary Clinton has recently said in TV interviews, one should see clearly where the United States and Russia agree and cooperate and where they disagree and fail to cooperate or confront each other. Now that Vladimir Putin has won reelection as president of Russia, with the potential of ruling the country until at least 2018 because of the change in the electoral term from four years to six years, and his pushing aside President Medvedev, whose policies appeared more US-friendly, there are likely to be continuing, but not insurmountable, tensions with Russia. In Europe, Brzezinski sees the possibility of a greater French-German-Russian alignment which on the other hand could be a French-German-Polish initiative. However, he believes that while "the West is not finished, but its global supremacy is over.... Only by demonstrating the capacity for a superior performance of its societal system can America restore its historical momentum, especially in the face of a China that is increasingly attractive to the third world (34-35)." China's state-run media's allusions of China as America's emerging rival in global preeminence, are nonetheless confronted with serious internal difficulties: "rural vs. urban inequality and the potential of popular resentment of absolute political authority" (21) before China can really claim to be an equal with the United States.

Brzezinski claims that the US political leaders (and we might emphasize particularly the Republican candidates for president and members of the elected Republican leaders in Congress) are potentially immersed in self-delusion, and must recognize six critical factors in America's waning of global influence: "First is America's mounting and eventually unsustainable national debt.... Second, America's flawed financial system is a major liability.... Third, widening income inequality coupled with stagnating social mobility is a long-term danger to social consensus and democratic stability.... America's fourth liability is its decaying national infrastructure.... America's fifth major vulnerability is a public that is highly ignorance about the world.... The sixth liability, related to the fifth, is America's increasingly gridlocked and highly partisan political system" (46-53). Still, although Brzezinski appears to be very pessimistic about the US' liabilities, he notes the following assets: overall economic strength, innovative potential, demographic dynamics, reactive mobilization, geographic base, and democratic appeal (55-63). Concluding Part 2, he proposes that "Success at home cannot compensate for a foreign policy that does not enlist and generate cooperation from others but instead engages the United States in lonely and draining compaigns against an increasing number of (at times) self-generated enemies. No success at home can be truly comprehensive if resources are wasted on debilitating foreign misadventures" (73-74)."

Part 3, "The World after 'America': by 2025, not Chinese but Chaotic," is an especially troublesome view of the future thirteen years from now: the potential of "a sudden and massive crisis of the American system would produce a fast-moving chain reaction leading to global political and economic chaos, a steady drift by America into increasingly pervasive decay and/or into endlessly widening warfare with Islam would be unlikely to produce even by 2025, the 'coronation' of an effective global successor. No single power will be ready by then to exercise the role that the world, upon the fall of the Soviet Union in 1991, expected the United States to play. More probably would be a protracted phase of rather inconclusive and somewhat chaotic realignments of both global and regional powers, with no grand winners and many more losers, into a setting of international uncertainty and even of potentially fatal risks to global well-being" (75). He discusses "The Post-America Scramble; The Geopolitically Most Endangered States (Georgia, Taiwan, South Korea, Belarus, Ukraine, Afghanistan, Pakistan, Israel and the greater Middle East); and The End of a Good Neighborhood (Mexico and Canada where China, India, Brazil, and Russia "are playing a more integral role in this global management process"). Brzezinski stresses that: "the strategic complexities of the world in the twenty-first century – resulting from the rise of a politically self-assertive global population and from the dispersal of global power – make such supremacy unattainable. But in this increasingly complicated geopolitical environment, and America in pursuit of a new, timely strategic vision is crucial to helping the world avoid a dangerous slid into international turmoil" (119-120).

In Part 4: "Beyond 2025: A New Geopolitical Balance," Brzezinski states firmly that "America's global standing in the decades ahead will depend on its successful implementation of purposeful efforts to overcome its drift toward a socioeconomic obsolescence and to shape a new and stable geopolitical equilibrium on the world's most important continent by far, Eurasia. The key to America's future is thus in the hands of the American people." He outlines such global aspects for Eurasia as 1. its "geopolitical volatility, 2. a larger and vital west (with Europe embracing Turkey and Russia positively), and 3. a stable and cooperative new east. Speaking about what he calls the geopolitical fact that "Asia currently is not or at least is not yet the center of world military power.... Contemporary Asia thrives now in a setting of worldwide commercial interdependence... the historical contrast between Europe and Asia" even centuries ago "the most important states of East Asia – from Japan, Korea, and China to Vietnam, Laos, Thailand, and Kampuchea... had all been linked to one another, directly or throuth the Chinese center, by trade and diplomatic relations and held together by a shared understandings of the principles , norms, and rules that regulated their mutual interactions." Finally," Brzezinski claims, "the motivating impulse of the threats to peace in the Asia of the twenty-first century likewise tends to be different from Europe's of the twentieth century." Again addressing China's role, as he does consistently throughout his book, Brzezinski identifies five major problems for China's emergence as the dominant global power in the next several decades: disparity between the rich and the poor, urban unrest and discontent, a culture of corruption, unemployment, and loss of social trust (170). Concluding Part 4, Brzezinski articulates that "In Asia, an America cooperatively engaged in multilateral structures, cautiously supportive of India's development, solidly tied to Japan and South Korea, and patiently expanding both bilateral as well as global cooperation with China is the best source of the balanceing leverage needed for sustaining stability in the globally rising new East" (181).

Brzezinski's "Conclusion" would certainly agree with Martin Jacques' When China Rules the World, in his argument that "the United States must recognize that stability in Asia can no longer be imposed by a non-Asian power.... Geopolitical equilibrium in twenty-first century Asia has to be based more on a regionally self-sustaining and constructive approach to interstate relations and less on regionally divisive military alliances with non-Asian powers... that save for its obligations to Japan and Korea, America should not be drawn into a way between Asian powers on the mainland... America's role as conciliator in the East will be especially critical, particularly in regard to the relationship between Japan and China.... The American-Japanese relationship, and through it the promotion of a Chinese-Japanese reconciliation, should be the springboard for a concerted effort to develop an American-Japanese-Chinese cooperative triangle" (191). He concludes: "In brief, an active role in Asia is essential not only in order to promote stability in the region, but, even more-so, to create circumstances in which the American-Chinese relationship evolves peacefully and cooperatively, and eventually grows into a wide-ranging political and economic partnership" (192). And last, Brzezinski posits: "a stable global order ultimately depends on America's ability to renew itself and to act wisely as the promoter and guarantor of a revitalized West and as the balancer and and conciliator of a rising new East" (192).

In watching the earler debates and statements of the Republican candidates for the Republican presidential primary election, and in reading their and other Republican leaders' countless and often widely misinformed foreign policy views, we might wish that they would read more thoughtful arguments, such as those of Brzezinski, which would than at least give them a basis for intelligent critiques on their parts, and moving them beyond the Party of "No" to constructive views of America's potential contributions to both European and Eastern stability and development than their own pandering to the often uninformed right-wing Republican current thinking. Personally, I do not know whether all of Brzezinski's and Jacques's arguments are basically correct, but my own understanding of American foreign policy and the US relationships with Europe and Asia, particularly China, has been greatly informed by Brzezinski's and Jacques' arguments. With more or less ten years of teaching at four Chinese universities, and giving many lectures and lecture series in China, I follow Chinese-American relations closely, and thus tend to accept Brzezinski's arguments as sound, though certainly troublesome for the strength of America as the twenty-first century progresses, and its potential confrontation or cooperation with Asian societies, and particularly with China in its present and coming G-2 relationship.

2. HAIDT, J. (2012). THE RIGHTEOUS MIND: WHY GOOD PEOPLE ARE DIVIDED BY POLITICS AND RELIGION

New York, NY: Pantheon, 422 pages; Introduction: Part I: Intuitions Come First, Strategic Reasoning Second (four chapters); Part II There's More to Morality than Harm and Fairness (four chapters); Part III: Morality Binds and Blinds (four chapters); Conclusion; Acknowledgements, Notes (323-376); References (377-406); Index.

"Haidt's research has revolutionized the field of moral psychology. This elegantly written book has far-reaching implications for anyone interested in politics, religion, or the many controversies that divide modern societies. If you want to know why you hold your moral beliefs and why many people disagree with you, read this book." Simon-Baron-Cohen, Cambridge University, author of The Science of Evil. (Back jacket cover)

"Jonathan Haidt is one of the smartest and most creative psychologists alive, and his newest book is a tour de force – a brave, brilliant, and eloquent exploration of the most important issues of our time. It will challenge the way you think about liberals and conservatives, atheism and religion, good and evil. This is the book that everyone will be talking about." Paul Bloom, Yale University, author of How Pleasure Works. (Back jacket cover)

"Los Angeles and Rodney King 20 Years Later: Both Better, Not Perfect, But Better"

By Madison Gray, Time, Apr. 27, 2012

[In an article about Rodney King (recently deceased) his beating in Los Angeles by four policemen, and their acquittal by a jury, King, the author of The Riot Within, Gray notes that twenty years after the last riots in Los Angeles, where fifty-three persons were killed and more than 7,000 buildings were torched, there is a much greater recognition that the racial situation there has greatly improved. Gray writes]

"King is one of the people who feels this way, even though he has long since left Los Angeles proper to settle in Rialto, 50 miles away from the epicenter of the [1992] riot. To his famous question, "Can we all get along?" he now feels there is a positive answer. "There was a lot of good that came out of it, in that era it didn't feel like it because you're living it," he chuckles lightly, even noting that having a black president may have been indirectly made possible by what happened. "I can't tell you what the future holds," he says. "I can tell you how I would like it: to be peaceful and everyone getting along. Hopefully I can leave something positive here and make it better for the next generation, that's what it's all about."

Jonathan Haidt (an undergraduate philosophy major, and then graduate student at the University of Pennsylvania, followed by a post doctorate at the University of Chicago, is now a social and moral psychologist at the University of Virginia. He begins his book with the quote by King, "Can we all get along?" He claims that while the statement by King is now seriously overused and has become a cliche, there were two reasons why he starts the book with this quote: "The first is because most Americans nowadays are asking King's question not about race relations but about political relations and the collapse of cooperation across party lines.... The second reason I decided to open the book with an overused phrase is because King followed it up with something lovely, something rarely quoted. As he stumbled through his television interview, fighting back tears and often repeating himself, he found these words: 'Please, we can get along here. I mean, we're all stuck here for a while. Let's try to work it out.'" Haidt repeats the expression: "This book is about why it's so hard for us to get along. We are indeed all stuck here for a while, so let's at least do what we can to understand why we are so easily divided into hostile groups each one certain of its righteousness (xii). He ends his book as well: "We're all stuck here for a while, so let's try to work it out" (318).

Haidt, a social psychologist, calls his highly autobiographical (my author preference labeling) and complex challenging book about moral psychology a reasonably new term in the field of psychology: "In 1987, moral psychology was a part of developmental [rationalist]psychology [Jean Piaget, Harold Kohlberg]. Researchers focused on questions such as how children develop in their thinking about rules, especially rules of fairness. The big question behind this research was: How do children come to know right from wrong?? Where does morality come from? There are two obvious answers to this question: nature or nurture If you pick nature, then you're a nativist [Charles Darwin].... But if you believe that moral knowledge comes from nurture, then you are an empiricist [John Locke]" (5).

The field of psychology whose American father was William James, is very broad, including moral (David Hume and Lawrence Kohlberg); cultural (Alan Fiske); developmental (Erik Erikson); evolutionary; political; and social (Solomon Asch, Leon Festinger, and Kurt Levin) psychology which he discusses in the book. Additionally, among psychological branches which he either does not discuss or does so very briefly, we have the following examples: abnormal (Sigmund Freud); analytical (Carl Jung); applied (Hugo Munsterberg); behavioral (Ivan Pavlov and B.F. Skinner); biopsychological; clinical (Freud); cognitive (Albert Bandura); counseling; cross-cultural (Michael Harris Bond and Shalom Schwartz); educational; experimental (Wilhelm Wundt); forensic; health; human factor (Carl Rogers); individual (Alfred Adler); industrial/organizational; personality (Gordon Allport, Eric Erikson, Freud, and Richard Shweder); school,; sports psychology; and values (Michael Harris Bond and Shalom Schwartz).

Haidt's linkages to the University of Pennsylvania, University of Chicago, and University of Virginia (about which he uses a number of examples, especially about the group psychology that surrounds its American football games) have apparently provided him a very strong basis for moving from his background in social psychology (where he published his dissertation research, without much success, he says), to moral psychology, in which he has made a substantial reputation for himself, particularly through this book. He writes that he chose to call his book The Righteous Mind rather than "The Moral Mind," to convey the sense that the human mind is designed to 'do' morality, just as it's designed to do language, sexuality, music, and many other things described in popular books reporting the latest scientific findings. "But I chose the title The Righteous Mind to convey the sense that human nature is not just intrinsically moral, it's also intrinsically moralistic, critical and judgmental" (xii-xiii) and that, fundamentally, as humans, we are righteous hypocrites (xvi)."

Haidt offers a basic principle for each of the three parts of his book: 1. "Intuition comes first; strategic reasoning second." Here he develops the metaphor (often actually a simile) that "the mind is divided, like a rider on an elephant [rather than a horse], and the rider's is to servant the elephant." Part II: His second principle of moral psychology is "that there's more to morality than harm and fairness." His central metaphor (simile) is that "the righteous mind is like a tongue with six taste receptors (with the analogy of adaptive challenge, original triggers, current triggers, characteristic emotions, and relevant values. In Part III, his third principle is that "morality binds and blinds" with the central metaphor that "human beings are 90% chimp and 10 percent bee.... Once you see our righteous minds as primate minds with a hivish overlay, you get a whole new perspective on morality, politics, and religion" (xiv-xv)

In Chapter One: 'Where Does Morality Come From?" Haidt asks several questions about actions that respondents might say are disgusting, but not morally wrong. He traces his interest in Piaget's and Kohlberg's earlier development of moral psychology and moral dilemmas relating to children's emergent ability to rationalize moral questions, then Kohlberg's former student Elliot Turiel's technique in telling stories to children about other children who break rules and then give them a series of similar yes and no probing questions: "young children don't treat all rules the same, as Piaget and Kohlberg had supposed... they are busy sorting social information in a sophisticated way. They seem to grasp early on that rules that prevent harm, are special, important, unalterable, and universal" (10-11). Taking a course from Alan Fiske, who had spent many years in West Africa, he and class members read ethnographies on different anthropological topics.

These topics led Haidt to develop an appreciation for intercultural approaches to moral psychology, and later as researcher in Brazil and still later as a Fulbright scholar in Orissa, India, where Fiske's former advisee Richard Shweder had done comparative field research in the area in Chicago around the University of Chicago, to develop the theme of moral psychology still further. Haidt came to believe that Shweder's explanation of sociocentric morality clearly resonated with his ethnographic readings in Fiske's class, leading him to also begin writing stories to test their relationship to moral psychology and which supported Shweder's findings in his own research. In summarizing his first chapter, he concluded that "The moral domain varies by culture.... People sometimes have gut feelings about disgust and disrespect – that can drive their reasoning.... Morality can't be entirely self-constructed by children based on their growing understanding of harm.... If morality doesn't come primarily from reasoning, then that leaves some combination of innateness and social learning as the most likely candidates" (26).

Chapter Two: "The Intuitive Dog and Its Rational Tail" begins by his assumption that "the mind is divided into parts that sometimes conflict. To be human is to feel pulled in different directions, and to marvel – sometimes in horror – at your inability to control your own actions" (27). Haidt notes that Plato, David Hume, and Thomas Jefferson sought to understand the human mind, without Charles Darwin's theory of evolution to assist them, with an emphasis on the problems that social Darwinism attacked, that 'the richest and most successful nations , races, and individuals are the fittest" leading to what he argues is a fundamental logical error. A second attack against nativism emphasized that the (Locke) theory of humans being born with a blank state, and "if evolution gave men and women different sets of desires and skills, for example, that would be an obstacle to achieving gender equality in many professions (31). Writing about the scientific attacks on sociobiologist Edward O. Wilson who claimed that "human nature constrains the range of what we can achieve when raising our children or designing new social institutions," sided with the humanist David Hume: "He charged that what moral philosophers were really doing was fabricating justifications after 'consulting the emotive centers' of their own brains. He predicted that the study of ethics would soon be taken out of the hands of philosophers and 'biologized,' or made to fit with the emerging science of human nature. Such a linkage of philosophy, biology, and evolution would be an example of the 'new synthesis' that Wilson dreamed of' (32).

Haidt began to look outside psychology for the emotional basis of morality with the rebirth of sociobiology under a new name 'evolutionary psychology... I had already arrived at a Jeffersonian view in which moral emotions and moral reasoning were separate processes' (35). Conducting several early experiments at the University of Virginia, he introduces the metaphor (simile) of the rider and the elephant, stressing the role of the emotions in moral psychology, and writing his 2005 book, "The Happiness Hypothesis" where he called two kinds of cognition, "the rider (controlled processes, including 'reasoning-why') and the elephant (automatic processes, including emotion, intuition, and all forms of 'seeing-that')" (45). Summarizing this chapter, he states: "The mind is divided into parts, like a rider (controlled processes) on an elephant (automatic processes).... You can see the rider serving the elephant when people are morally dumbfounded.... The social intuitionist model starts with Hume's model and makes it more social.... Therefore, if you want to change someone's mind about a moral or political issue, talk to the elephant first" (49-50).

Chapter Three: "Elephants Rule," begins with Haidt's discovery that he was a chronic, though not entirely purposeful, liar, at the time that he was writing about core aspects of moral psychology, relating to his principle, "intuitions come first, strategic reasoning second" "1. Brains Evaluate Instantly and Constantly," 2. "Social and Political Judgments Are Particularly Intuitive," 3. "Our Bodies Guide Our Judgments," 4. "Psychopaths Reason but Don't Feel," 5. "Babies Feel but Don't Reason," 5. "Affective Reactions Are in the Right Place at the Right Time in the Brain." He stresses that he has argued that "the Humean model (reason is a servant) fits the facts better than the Platonic model (reason could and should rule) or the Jeffersonian model (head and heart are co-emperors)" but he disagrees with Hume's belief that reason is "the slave of the passions." "The rider-and-elephant metaphor works well here. The rider evolved to serve the elephant, but it's a dignified partnership, more like a lawyer serving a client than a slave serving a master" (67). Summarizing the chapter, Haidt argues the main points that he has introduced; "Brains evaluate instantly and constantly.... Social and political judgments depend heavily on quick intuitive flashes.... Psychopaths reason but don't feel.... Babies feel but don't reason.... Affective reactions are in the right place at the right time in the brain...." (70).

Chapter Four: "Vote for Me (Here's Why)" returns to moral philosophy through Plato's dialogue, The Republic, where Socrates gets his listeners to agree to what a just, harmonious, and happy city looks like, then he argues that the same relationships must rule the happy person, and happy city, "then reason must rule the happy person. And if reason rules, then it cares about what is truly good, not just about the appearance of virtue.... As is often the case in moral philosophy, arguments about what we ought to do depend upon assumptions – often unstated – about human nature and human psychology," Haidt praises Socrates' chief foil, Glaucon, in the dialogue: "the most important principle for designing an ethical society is to make sure that everyone's reputation is on the line all the time, so that bad behavior will always bring bad consequences." Following William James' concept of functionalism's usefulness for the mind, Haidt asks:

"What, then is the function of moral reasoning? Does it seem to have been shaped, tuned, and crafted (by natural selection) to help us find the truth, so that we can know the right way to behave and condemn those who behave wrongly? If you believe that, then you are a rationalist, like Plato, Socrates, and Kohlberg. Or does moral reasoning seem to have been shaped, tuned, and crafted to help us pursue socially strategic goals, such as guarding our reputations and convincing other people to support us, or our team, in disputes? If you believe that, then you are a Glauconian" (74). Haidt argues that we are all intuitive politicians; that we are obsessed with polls; that our in-house press secretary automatically justifies every-thing, that we lie, cheat, and justify so well that we honestly believe we are honest; that reasoning (and Google) can take you wherever you want to go; delusions in western history: the rationalist delusion. It's the idea that reasoning is our most noble attribute, one that makes us like the gods (for Plato) or that brings us beyond the 'delusion' of believing in gods (for the New Atheists" (88). Summarizing the chapter, Haidt argues that; "We are obsessively concerned about what others think of us.... Conscious reasoning functions like a press secretary.... With the help of our press secretary, we are able to lie and cheat often.... Reasoning can take us to almost any conclusion we want to reach.... In moral and political matters we are often groupish, rather than selfish" (91)

In Part II: "There's More to Morality than Harm and Fairness," Haidt's central simile is: "The righteous mind is like a tongue with six taste recep-tors." Chapter Five: "Beyond WEIRD [Western ,educated, industrialized, rich, and democratic] Morality," notes that most psychological studies are conducted in a very small, and elite, American setting. He does not speak much about the concept of values, and does not list the term in his index. But, in general, he is right that most psychological experiments are based in the United States and perhaps other western countries. Haidt states that "Most people think holistically (seeing the whole context and the relation-ships among parts), but WEIRD people think more analytically (detach-ing the focal object from its context, assigning it to a category, and then assuming that what's true about the category is true about the object).... But when holistic thinkers in a non-WEIRD culture write about moral-ity, we get something more like the Analects of Confucius, a collection of aphorisms and anecdotes that can't be reduced to a simple rule" (96-97).

We have here the comparison between the west as individualistic and the east as collectivistic, as it is certainly true that most members of the human race live in the Asian (and African) east. He proposes that three ethics are more descriptive than one: the ethic of autonomy versus the eastern ethic of community, and the ethic of divinity (which would be found in the Hindu and Muslim worlds, but largely absent in China as a largely atheistic society). He found himself with two conflicting identities: as a liberal atheist on one hand, and with a great curiosity about the third ethic, on which he had spent very little space in his doctoral dissertation, thus leading him to a three month Fulbright in Orissa, India. (We are both Fulbrighters in developing countries: I in Swaziland in 1990-91.) His experiments in Orissa moved him towards becoming a pluralist in terms of his psychology career and allowed him to step outside the western matrix. Summarizing this chapter, he concludes: "The WEIRDer you are, the more you perceive a world full of separate objects, rather than relationships.... The moral domain is unusually narrow in WEIRD cultures, where it is largely limited to the ethic of autonomy (individualism).... Moral matrices bind people together and blind them to the coherence, or even existence, of other matrices" (110).

In Chapter Six: "Taste Buds of the Righteous Mind" Haidt really begins to explore this overriding metaphor (sweet, sour, salty, bitter, and savory) for Part II (leaving the sixth to a later chapter) and based on a food-morality comparison by Mencius, a disciple of Confucius, where he contends that like interculturally different foods, moral judgments are also multifaceted. Thus Haidt explores the analogy (simile) "that the righteous mind is like a tongue with six receptors." Haidt returns to the Enlightenment work of David Hume, who used sensory and taste analogies, and his concerns about the problematic limits of reasoning when human nature is not included.

As Haidt explores the concept of the founding of moral science, he discusses autism, Jeremy Bentham and "then the utilitarian grill," Immanuel Kant and "the deontological diner," "in psychology our goal is descriptive (not prescriptive) . We want to discover how the moral mind actually works, not how it ought to work, and that can't be done by reasoning, math, or logic. It can be done only by observation, and observation is usually keener when informed by empathy," noting that when western societies became more educated, industrialized, rich and democratic, the minds of intellectuals changed. They became more analytic and less holistic" (120). Haidt calls for "Broadening the palate," discussing the development of moral foundations theory which would include a universal moral "taste receptor" in order to account for "cultural learning and variation."

He and colleagues proposed five foundations using the taste sensory analogy: adaptive challenge, original triggers, current triggers, characteristic emotions, and relevant virtues. Summing up the chapter, Haidt says that: "Morality is like taste in many ways.... Hume's pluralist, sentimentalist, and naturalist approach to ethics is more promising than utilitarianism or deontology for modern moral psychology.... Modularity can help us think about innate receptors, and how they produce a variety of initial perceptions that get developed in culturally variable ways.... Five good candidates for being taste receptors of the righteous mind are care, fairness, loyalty, authority, and sanctity" (127).

Haidt begins to address the book's subtitle: "Why Good People Are Divided by Politics and Religion," more fully in Chapter Seven: "The Moral Foundations of Politics." He proposes a series of five moral foundations (versus homo economicus – who would judge all actions with a price tag in mind), and arguing that scientifically it would be risky "to assert that anything about human nature was innate" with bipolar assumptions: the care/harm foundation; the fairness/cheating foundation, the loyalty/betrayal foundation, the authority/subversion foundation, and the sanctity/degradation foundation. He summarizes his descriptors as follows: "The Care/harm foundation evolved in response to the adaptive challenge of caring for vulnerable children.... The Fairness/cheating foundation evolved in response to the adaptive challenge of reaping the rewards of cooperation without getting exploited.... The Loyalty/betrayal foundation evolved in the response to the adaptive challenge of forming and maintaining coalitions.... The Authority/subversion foundation evolved in response to the adaptive challenging of forging relationships that will benefit us within social hierarchies.... The Sanctity/degradation foundation evolved initially in response to the adaptive challenge of the omnivore's dilemma, and then to the broader challenge of living in a world of pathogens and parasites" (153-154).

Noting again that he was initially liberally oriented in terms of his political beliefs and identifying himself as a former speechwriter for the

2004 John Kerry presidential campaign which had many slogans that had no moral content at all, in his Chapter Eight: "The Conservative Advantage," Haidt begins by noting that in a talk to Charlottesville, Virginia Democrats, he articulated for them that: "Republicans understand moral psychology. Democrats don't. Republicans have long understood that the elephant is in charge of political behavior, not the rider, and they know how elephants work.... Republicans don't just aim to cause fear, as some Democrats charge. They trigger the full range of intuitions described by Moral Foundations Theory" (156). Haidt, a colleague and graduate student at the University of Virginia, created the first version of the Moral Foundations Questionnaire (MFQ) so that they could measure morals from a sample internet pool of 1,600 participants. They discovered that Care and Fairness were moderately high morals from liberals to conservatives, and that everyone said that concerns about compassion, cruelty, fairness, and injustice were relevant to their judgments about right and wrong. But when they tabulated the results for loyalty, authority, and sanctity, liberals largely rejected these considerations (a two-step foundation morality, but those who identified themselves as very conservative, all five concerns came together. Others also used the MFQ, and in 2007, several of the researchers met at the American Psychology Association conference. All of them agreed that they had begun initially as liberals, but they all had the same concerns about the way that the liberal field of psychologists approached political psychology: "The five of us also shared a deep concern about the polarization and incivility of American political life." The group decided to do future studies online, and created a website (www. YourMorals.com) where people could register when they would first visit, and then take part in dozens of studies on moral and political psychology.

By 2011, 130,000 participants had provided data which demonstrated that the graph lines for care and fairness slanted downward while those for loyalty, authority, and sanctity slanted upward: "Liberals value Care and Fairness far more than the other three foundations; conservatives endorse all five foundations more or less equally" (159-161). When Barack Obama won the 2008 Democratic presidential nomination, Haidt said that: "At long last, it seemed, the Democrats had chosen a candidate with a broader moral palate, someone able to speak about all five foundations" but during the summer of 2008, his speech to a major civil rights organization it was all about social justice and corporate greed: "It used on the Care and Fairness foundations, and fairness often meant equality of outcomes. In his famous speech in Berlin, he introduced himself as 'a fellow citizen of the world' and he spoke of 'global citizenship.... The Berlin speech reinforced the emerging conservative narrative that Obama was a liberal universalist, someone who could not be trusted to put the interests of his nation above the interests of the rest of the world" (163-164). In contrast, John McCain's slogan was "Country First." Haidt then wrote an essay: "What Makes People Vote Republican" and he used the Moral Foundations Theory to understand the moral matrices of both sides. He contrasted the views of John Stewart Mills ("a peaceful, open, and creative place where diverse individuals respect each other's rights and band together voluntarily") and the French sociologist Emile Durkheim "man cannot become attached to higher aims and submit to a rule if he sees nothing above him to which he belongs" (165-166). Among the responses were statements of surprise that conservatives might have an alternative moral vision. While conservatives with military or religious backgrounds found his portrayal of their morality accurate and useful.

In Chapter Seven, Haidt recalls that he had discussed the liberty/oppression foundation, and he notes that "For groups that made this political transition to egalitarianism, there was a quantum leap in the development of moral matrices, or "self-domestication": The Liberty foundation obviously operates in tension with the Authority foundation.... The Liberty foundation supports the moral matrix of revolutionaries and 'freedom fighters' everywhere"(174). In early 2009, the Tea Party emerged "to reshape the American political landscape and realign the American culture war."

Haidt suggests that the "Moral Foundation Theory says that there are (at least) six psychological systems that comprise the universal foundations of the world's many moral matrices. The various moralities found on the political left tend to rest most strongly on the Care/harm and Liberty/oppression foundations" and "support ideals of social justice," "solidarity," "Everyone – left, right, and center – cares about Care/harm, but liberals care more.... Everyone – left, right, and center – cares about Liberty/oppression, but each political faction cares in a different way. In the contemporary United States, liberals are most concerned about the rights of certain vulnerable groups (e.g., racial minorities, children, animals), and they look to government to defend the weak against oppression by the strong. Conservatives, in contrast, hold more traditional ideas of liberty as the right to be left alone, and they often resent liberal programs that use government to infringe on their liberties in order to protect the groups that liberals care most about" (181-182).Summarizing the chapter, Haidt notes that: "We added the Liberty/oppression foundation, which makes people notice and resent any sign of attempted domination..... We modified the Fairness foundation to make it focus more strongly on proportionality" (185).

For Part III: "Morality Binds and Blinds," Haidt's central metaphor is "We are 90 Percent Chimp and 10 Percent Bee." Chapter Nine emphasizes American tendencies toward groupishness (joining groups and organizations) rather than selfishness (pursuit of self-interest). Individualism versus collectivism are certainly major emphases in Geert Hofstede's six national dimensions based on his extensive multinational research, and the United States ranks very high in individualism in contrast to several other eastern societies which rank very high on collectivism. In our 2012 intercultural communication text book for Chinese university students, Communicating Interculturally, published by Higher Education Press in Beijing, Li Mengyu and I make the following comments concerning Hofstede's national dimension of individualism versus collectivism:

This dimension attempts to describe how people in each culture identify themselves and others. Individualism places the greater emphasis on the individual, and "I" consciousness prevails in that culture. Competition rather than cooperation is encouraged, personal goals and interests take precedence over group goals and interests. Hofstede (1991) defined individualism as "societies in which ties between individuals are loose; everyone is expected to look after himself or herself and his or her immediate family." Therefore, in an individualistic culture, an individual or "I" identity is regarded as the most important unit in society, and the value of each individual is placed in the first position, often in a very egalitarian manner. While in a collectivistic or communitarian culture, "we" consciousness prevails over individuals, group goals and interests take precedence over personal goals and interests. Consequently, Hofstede (1991) explained collectivism as "societies in which people from birth onwards are integrated into strong, cohesive in-groups, which throughout people's lifetimes continue to protect them in exchange for unquestioning loyalty." Samovar and Porter (2004) analyzed the feature of collectivism in a similar view, "Collectivism is characterized by a rigid social framework that distinguishes between in-group (relatives, clans, organizations) to look after them, and in exchange for that they believe they owe absolute loyalty to the group." Thus, in collective cultures, the concept of "group" and "we" is of great importance; each person's identity is established on the social system; and the individual has a close tie with the organizations and institutions in which he or she belongs.

According to Geert Hofstede, individualism and collectivism are central to all the cultural values. According to his research, the United States, Australia, Great Britain, Canada, the Netherlands, and New Zealand are among those most individualism-oriented countries, while Pakistan, Indonesia, Colombia, Venezuela, Panama, Ecuador, and Guatemala are highly collectivistically-oriented. That is to say, individualism can be found in most northern and western areas of Europe and North America, while collectivism can be observed in Central and South America, the Middle East, Asia, Africa and the Pacific islands (Li & Prosser, 2012, p. 107).

While I see many signs of individualism in the United States, fortified by books such as Robert Putnam's 2000 book Bowling Alone, and also indications that many Americans join organizations to develop social relationships, it is interesting to see Haidt's findings on American groupishness. He admits, for example, that he also found this groupishness a puzzle, but he offers four examples of new evidence that demonstrates "the value of thinking about groups as real entities that compete with each other. This new evidence leads us directly to the third and final principle of moral psychology. Morality binds and blinds. I will suggest that human nature is mostly selfish, but with a groupish overlay that resulted from the fact that natural selection works at multiple level simultaneously.... Groups compete with groups, and that competition favors groups composed of true team players – those who are willing to cooperate and work for the good of the group even when they could do better by slacking, cheating, or leaving the group" (191-192). Haidt cites Darwin's findings about the morality of group: "Ultimately our moral sense becomes a highly complex sentiment – originating in the social instincts, largely guided by the approbation of our fellow-men, ruled by reason, self-interest, and in later times by deep religious feelings, and confirmed by instruction and habit" (194-195). Haidt points major transitions that have occurred in evolution, shared intentionality among humans, the evolvement of genes and cultures, and the potential swiftness of evolution. He argues that group selection does not require war or violence, which no doubt many people would challenge.

Summarizing this chapter, Haidt writes that major transitions produce superorganisms; the emergence of the uniquely human ability to share intentions and other mental representations; genes and cultures coevolve; and evolution can be fast: "We humans have a dual nature – we are selfish primates who long to be a part of something larger and nobler than ourselves" (219-220).

Chapter Ten: "The Hive Switch" cites William McNeill's hypothesis that "the process of 'muscular bonding'... enabled people to forget themselves, trust each other, function as a unit, and then crush less cohesive groups" (222). Haidt identifies his own hypothesis for the chapter "is that human beings are conditional hive creatures. We have the ability (under special conditions) to transcend self-interest and lose ourselves (temporarily and ecstatically) in something larger than ourselves. That ability is what I'm calling the hive switch.... The hive switch is an adaptation for making groups more cohesive, and therefore more successful in competition with other groups" (223). He describes such hivish activities as collective emotions and many ways to flip the switch, and the biology of the hive switch, hives at work, and then the nature of political hives. He concludes this chapter by stating: "Once you understand our dual nature, including our groupish overlay, you can see what happiness comes from between. We evolved to live in groups" (244). (This leads, politically, to people joining as team members in the efforts of one group to compete with, and defeat another group – Republicans and Democrats in the United States, for example, encourage this sort of groupishness.)

Chapter Eleven: "Religion Is a Team Sport" begins with Haidt's description of autumn American football games at the University of Virginia, which has, Haidt argues, all of the trappings of organized religion: "It's a whole day of hiving and collective emotions.... From a Durkheimian perspective these behaviors serve a very different function (than to encourage their team to win), and it is the same one that Durkheim saw at work in most religious rituals: the creation of a community. A college football game is a superb analogy for religion." Durkheim sees religion as binding a community together. With the destruction of the World Trade Center twin towers on September 11, 2001, many Americans equated the nine Muslim perpretrators with Islam as fostering terrorism, and so many books were written attacking not only Islam, but other religions too (except Buddhism), that Haidt indicates a "New Atheism" like Plato's rationalism was born, arguing that the Supernatural or God was nothing more than a delusion. Haidt notes that the New Atheists developed the "hypersensitive agency detection device" – or the birth of a supernatural being, where none can be discovered, and seeing something there that does not exist, and as a solution "an agency detection module" which like the detection device, operates on a hair trigger, swiftly and without necessary reasons: "According to these theorists, the genes for constructing these various modules were all in place by the time modern humans left Africa, and the genes did not change in response to selection pressures either for or against religiosity during the 50,000 years since then. The gods changed, however, and this brings us to the second step of the New Atheist story, cultural evolution." (253). Thus, in Haidt's perspective the religious story also evolved, creating new by-products, and "the cultural group selection. On the other hand, Emile Durkheim saw by-products and then "maypoles" (rituals, belonging, and groupism). Haidt asks whether God is a force for good or evil? "The New Atheists assert that religion is the root of most evil. They say it is a primary cause of war, genocide, terrorism, and the oppression of women. Religious believers, for their part, often say that atheists are immoral and that they can't be trusted" (264-265).

Finally, Haidt offers as he says, "The Definition of Morality (At Last)" which many of his readers perhaps would have preferred much earlier in the book. He defines moral systems as "interlocking sets of values, virtues, norms, practices, identities, institutions, technologies, and evolved psychological mechanisms that work together to suppress or regulate self-interest and make cooperative societies possible." Concluding the chapter, Haidt states: "We humans have an extraordinary ability to care about things beyond ourselves, to circle around those things with other people, and in the process to bind ourselves into teams that can pursue larger projects. That's what religion is all about" (273).

In the final Chapter Twelve: "Can't We All Disagree More Constructively" (which I read first and then have returned to it again), Haidt recognizes the nastiness of politics, but asks: "Does it have to be this nasty? The country now seems polarized and embattled to the point of dysfunction. They are right. Up until a few years ago, there were some political scientists who claimed that the so-called culture war was limited to Washington.... But in the last twelve years Americans have begun to move further apart This shift to a more righteous and tribal mentality was bad enough in the 1990s, a time of peace, prosperity, and balanced budgets. But nowadays, when the fiscal and political situations are so much worse, many Americans feel that they're on a ship that's sinking, and the crew is too busy fighting with each other to bother plugging the leaks " (275-276).

When he discusses the evolutionary movement from genes to moral matrices, he suggests three steps in the process: "Step 1: Genes Make Brains; Step 2: Traits Guide Children along Different Paths; Step 3: People Construct Life Narratives" (278-283). Among the narratives that people construct are "The Grand Narratives of Liberalism and Conservatism" giving the left a blind spot: "Moral Capital." Reflecting on the Taoist concepts of yin and yang, he calls yin, in this case, "Liberal Wisdom," leading the liberals to establish two essential points for a healthy life: "Point #1: Governments Can and Should Restrain Corporate Superorganisms," Point #2: "Some Problems Really Can Be Solved by Regulation" (296-300). On the other hand "Yang #1: Libertarian Wisdom, "Counterpoint #1: "Markets Are Miraculous," "Yang #2: "Social Conservative Wisdom, ""Counterpoint #2: "You Can't Help the Bees by Destroying the Hive" (300-309). Haidt calls upon people in each opposite to move toward more civil politics: "Human beings are the frontline in the battle; we contain both good and evil, and we must pick one side and fight for it" (309). He summarizes his arguments: "People don't adapt their ideologies at random, or by soaking up whatever ideas are around them" and accept the life narratives either from the more liberal political developments or the more conservative ones: "Morality binds and blinds. It blinds us into ideological teams that fight each other as though the fate of the world depended on our side winning each battle. It blinds us to the fact that each team is composed of good people who have something important to say" (313).

In his brief conclusion to the book, he ends as he has begun: "We're all stuck here for a while, so let's try to work it out" (318).

Although complex in his theories, Jonathan Haidt makes every effort to make his book quite readable for the layperson, including those of us academics who are not embedded in the field of psychology. It is quite clear that he is very well read, as he says, not just in psychology, but in many other anthropological, historical, political science, and sociological topics that help to inform us of his own understanding of moral psychology and the moral or righteous mind.

Haidt's chapter summaries are exceedingly helpful for a fuller understanding of his metaphors (which are mostly actually grammatically similes as he expresses them) and major arguments proposed in each of his chapters. The metaphors themselves (the soul of language as Kenneth Burke has proposed) provide the readers with common-sense analogies, in an otherwise fairly complex treatment of his topics related to moral psychology and the moral or righteous mind.

3. Jackson, R. L. II & Hopson, M.C. (Eds.) (2011). Masculinity in the Black Imagination: Politics of Communicating Race and Manhood

New York, NY: Black Studies & Critical Thinking Series, Peter Lang. 244 pages; Introduction, 13 chapters, Contributors, Index.

Ronald L. Jackson, II, Head of African American Studies at the University of Illinois, is the author of several books including The Negotiation of Cultural Identity and Scripting the Black Masculine Body. He is the coeditor of African American Rhetoric(s); African American Communication and Identities; and Encyclopedia of Identity.

Mark C. Hopson, who teaches communication at George Mason University, an expert on intercultural communication, African American rhetoric, and black masculinity studies, is the author of Notes from the Talking Drum: Black Communication, Critical Memory, and Intercultural Communication Contexts. He is a co-author for an essay on a founder of the field of intercultural communication, Fred Casmir, for a special forthcoming issue of the International Journal of Intercultural Relations, honoring twelve early leaders in the intercultural fields published in 2012.

In their Introduction, Jackson and Hopson maintain that "only our imaginations may properly assist us in comprehending the possibilities of liberation from a pathologized Blackness and perhaps an even more sinister, singular racial masculinity that has come to be known as 'Black Masculinity'" (p. 1).

In Chapter One, "The View from Abroad, Race, Gender and Politics" by Robert Staples, whom Jackson and Hopson call the "father of the modern Black masculinity studies," he compares race, gender, and politics in Australia, where he now lives, and the United States. He correctly recognizes that such a comparison is like comparing apples and oranges. Staples contends that because the US nonwhite population is about 40% with Latin America being very multicultural, naturally comparisons between Australia and the United States on race are highly disproportionate.

He finds it amazing that in a 2008 local Australian newspaper, the claim was made that "There seems to be general agreement among the experts that Australia is one of the least racist countries in the world," after earlier being one of the four most racist nations. Staples argues that "racism is always associated with predominantly White nations." Although this may be generally true, personally, I have seen considerable racial bigotry in China against African students there, and against their own dark skinned, most likely, rural populations with dark skinned Chinese students often being referred to by their lighter skinned classmates as "the black ants." Staples assesses Australia's 1850 move from a constitutionally all white Australia policy, to the present multicultural society, beginning in 1984, where today there is considerable interethnic and interracial marriage, thereby making policies more directed toward class than race.

Completing his essay during the 2008 general election campaign after Hillary Rodham Clinton and Barack Obama's primary campaign but before Obama's winning the general election campaign against John McCain (unfortunate for a book published in 2011), his attitude towards Hillary Clinton is far more negative than the American perception of her today as the Secretary of State, and recent surveys indicate that Obama is the most admired man in the United States (despite the Republican loathing of him) and Clinton is the most admired woman. Besides noting that much of her campaign was subtly or even overtly anti-black, he argues: "the key to Obama's success is the fact that about 60 percent of Democratic voters regarded his White female opponent as untrustworthy, dishonest, and someone who did not care about people." From my perhaps inaccurate information, she was widely expected to win both the Democratic primary election, but had the strong possibility that she would also win the 2008 general election, based in part by strong support from women who wanted to see the first US American woman president. As the primary votes were slipping away from her, Staples suggests that she shifted her campaign from racism to sexism.

On the other hand, Staples offers evidence that one reason that Obama won the primary was his attractiveness as a half white, Columbia University/Harvard law degree, and somewhat feminized candidate. While he says that Obama was able to win the primary vote by pulling together small states and 90% of the southern Black vote, he does not discuss the extraordinary use of the social media that Obama employed so well and in which the Clinton campaign was more or less a novice. Since Staples finished his essay before the general election results were in, of course, he also did not discuss the weaknesses of the McCain campaign, which were aided or hindered by Sarah Palin's selection as McCain's vice presidential running mate.

Staples concludes his essay by returning to his racial comparisons between Australia and the United States as white settler nations: " If we want to cite racism as the only cause of these race and gender disparities, we need to explain why Black females have increased in education, employment and income over the last three decades and Black men have not. Even a majority of Afro-Americans think Blacks are responsible for their own condition. Opportunities did open up over the last forty years and many Blacks took advantage of them, many were women." He continues: "the major source of conflict is mostly religion and ethnicity.... The challenge for Australia is different as it is surrounded by billions of people of color in the Asian sub-continent.... The United States benefits from having elevated its Black citizens from servitude to some of the highest positions it has" (pp.23-25).

In Chapter Two: "Am I Not a Man and a Brother?" Analyzing the Complexities of Black 'Greek' Masculine Identity," Matthew W. Hughey and Gregory S. Parks provide a useful historical understanding of the Black Greek fraternities in American universities and colleges. What I found most interesting was their discussion in "Who's the (Black) Man?" of three different perspectives: "Black Man Emasculation," "Black Male Hyper Masculinity" and "The 'Practice' of Black Masculinity." Citing authors such as Franklin Frazier, Daniel Patrick Moynihan, Oscar Lewis, Franz Fanon, and Robert Staples, which argue that the socio-cultural situation for Black men, the "sex role" paradigm: "provides the conceptual basis for much of today's academic research and layperson conjecture that defines African American men as psychologically and interpersonally impotent.... What is most insidious about the emasculation thesis is that it acquiesces to patriarchal and white normative notions of domesticity, sexuality, and gender politics writ large" (28-29).

On the other hand, the chapter authors write that often black men are considered "anything but emasculated but are hyper-masculine to the point of being 'beast-like.... Central to the imagined iconography of black men as inherently angerous is an emphasis on physical prowess, limited mental capacity, and emotional volatility" (p. 29). Hughey and Parks say that this thesis is also connected to the "sex role" paradigm, noting that both perspectives is that it can identify potentially positive or alternative forms of black masculinity. In discussing "the 'practice' of Black masculinity," space is opened in discussing the Black Greek fraternities to "more fully interrogate the social construction of black masculinity that neither emphasizes an omnipresent structural force that unilaterally emasculates black men nor frames black men as an aggregate of agency-filled monsters roaming our cultural landscape...." (p. 31).

Chapter Three: "How to Become a 'BlackMan': Exploring African American Masculinities and the Performance of Gender" by Kimberly J. Chandler is a summary of her doctoral dissertation, in which she asks: "How does one 'become' a Black Man? What influences this becoming? How does one 'do' Black masculinity as a performance of gender?" (p. 55). She asserts: "In an effort to enrich communication scholarship with a specific focus on the performance of gender, this study explores the ways in which African American males perform masculinities" (p. 55).

She offers a theoretical framework including the concepts of performativity; performances and everyday life; race and blackness: ethnicity as performance; and blackness and gender performance. Her qualitative methodology is by using a 20 question guide in an interview format of fifteen African American males representative of a wide demographic map. She describes her communal conversation as an African American woman interviewing African American men, where she sought to create a bond of understanding and trust. She describes her rich findings and provides frequent samples of the responses given to her questions. Among these findings, she identified several different African American male views: excuses for being black males; the dominant society versus their organic selves; or the black male against the world. In her discussion, she notes that Black males see themselves performing their masculinities as a result of being between various tensions, such as the cycle of victimhood; black male privilege; and black authenticity equaling black masculinity. In her conclusion, she argues that "the concepts of blackness and Manhood take on a very different tenor when society characterizes an individual as not only Black, not only a man, but a 'BlackMan'" (p.84).

Chapters Four through Eight explore the relationship of prime time television in Chapter Four by Mika]il Abdullah Petin; comic relief or super coon in Chapter Five by Shannon B. S. Campbell and Steven S. Giannino; the black body through ghetto and bourgeois characters in American films in Chapter Six by Toniesha L. Taylor and Amber Johnson; construction of black masculinity in popular magazines in Chapter Seven by Katrina E. Bell-Jordan, and scripting the black male athlete in popular magazines in Chapter Eight by Timothy J. Brown.

"Are You in the Brotherhood?': Humor, Black Masculinity, and Queer Identity on Prime-Time Television" stresses the blandness and inequality in contemporary primetime television, argues that "Noah's Arc" a series, written by a black gay male, featuring the lives of four black, gay males living in Los Angeles challenges the one-dimensionality of black males on television. Petin, calling himself a black heterosexual male, argues that "Noah's for black gay males hungry for this type of TV dealing with black characters they're not seeing anywhere else." Petin argues that "fixity is an important realization in understanding postmodern black men... the discursive forces that have aided in constructing the black male in the postmodern public space of white mainstream media have evoked the realization that this black maleness is delineated by an imposed racial/ethnic identity, a generalized hyper-sexuality, a set of prohibitive cultural mores, and a 'debilitating 'physical corporality" (p. 92) Quoting J. Doyle's five chronological roles in society, the epic male, the spiritual male, the chivalric male, the renaissance male, and bourgeois male, Petin asks where the radicalized male, the sexualized male and radicalized and sexualized male roles fit? Petin discusses the history of black men on television, why for his essay the situation comedy genre is significant for analysis, the meaning of one-dimensionality, the black male aesthetic, and the meaning of black television masculinity. He concludes by asking "How to interpret a popular television series, "Noah's Arc," as an expression of a needed reconstitution of a fettered televisual masculine identity? While it is actually jokingly referred to as the black 'Sex in the City,' it is more of a catalyst to begin a discourse on one-dimensionality that black men, whether on television or on the Internet, cannot seem to escape until they take more control over the ways in which they are represented" (p. 101).

Shannon B.S. Campbell and Steven S. Giannino's Chapter Five: "Flaaavooor-Flaav: Comic Relief or Super-Coon," discusses the popular black "reality" show 'Flavor of Love' whose main character exhibits: the rebirth of one of the most troubling mediated caricature portrayals of African Americans – the coon.... 'Flavor of Love' has catapulted Flavor Flav and Vh1 to unprecedented popularity. Nearly 6 million viewers tuned in to the finale of the first season of 'Flavor of Love.' A record-breaking 7.5 million watched the season finale of 'Flavor of Love II,' making it the number one telecase on cable (the night it aired) and the network's highest-rated telecast ever..." (p. 103). Campbell and Giannino indicate that the precedence for the show was Public Enemy, including William Drayton, Jr. (Flavor Flav) who was the visual image for the band and "quickly became renowned for his outlandish sense of style and asinine behavior.... Flav became a significant revolutionary figure in the world of rap by becoming its first 'hype man'... used for comic relief to increase audience excitement" (pp. 104-105).

As have authors in the earlier chapters of the book, Campbell and Giannino emphasize that black males are typically seen as one-dimensional characters. They argue that the concept of the black male "Sambo" as the perpetual child unable to live as a functioning adult, its 21st century interpretation as "coon," who acts childish but is an adult, and is equally dehumanizing: "The coon was a Sambo gone bad." Flavor Flav's "quest for true love" makes him not just a coon but a super-coon: "as the modern day super-coon is typecast in the same one-dimensional way as the coon of years past, and as such, he evokes and enacts many of the same troubling stereotypes.... During most dining scenes, Flav is depicted as uncivilized and barbaric".... By depicting Flavor Flav as an uneducated, uncouth, yet curiously arrogant black man reveling in the illusion of power and wealth, 'Flavor of Love' reiterates the idea of black male success as absurd (pp. 107-111).

In concluding their essay, Campbell and Giannino call for those constantly exposed to the super coon caricature to "remain critically vigilant. When viewers critically engage and participate in a thorough re-reading of the text, a redistribution of power occurs. Re-reading 'Flavor of Love' allows viewers to recognize the insidious nature of the race/gender caste that exists in American culture.... In other words, a close re-reading of the text can provide a person of color with the tools necessary to detect the historic and contemporary connections between pop culture's use of demeaning caricatures and the socio-political implications that follow" (p. 111). The authors do not indicate how many of the viewers are black or white, and why the show is so popular to the viewers if Flavor Flav's outlandish super coon image in the show does not indeed provide comic relief for an otherwise potentially stressed group of viewers. Should such reality shows not exist as a counter to those that are oriented toward "young, white, attractive, financially and emotional stable" bachelors and audiences? Are the cast members in "Flavor of Love" and audiences powerless victims of the corporate sponsors, or do audiences need comic relief, and even possible satire of the outlandish lives of such black males (and the humiliated bachelorettes in the show)? As Campbell and Giannino conclude: "re-reading might even serve as a way to identify the future trajectory of the systemic oppression one might face. Additionally, it can serve as a pretext or rallying call for women, people of color and other subjugated groups to demand some say in the stories that depict them... and can serve as an impetus for a revolutionary movement whereby marginalized people can demand to have stories told by, for and about them!" (p. 111).

Toniesha L Taylor and Amber Johnson's Chapter Six: "'Class Meet Race': A Critical Re-Scripting of the Black Body through Ghetto and Bourgeois Characters in American Films," contend that film-makers who portray a dichotomy of existence for African American men by illustrating a ghetto character who has to become bourgeois or risk remaining ghetto forever." They quote Ronald Jackson as saying that black masculine identity "has been conditioned by Western hegemonic contexts and inscribed through discourse, resulting in a script and note that Jackson encourages scholars to "analyze and decipher new scripts and their assigned meaning of bodily text (p. 113). Again quoting Jackson, "the public narrative pertaining to black men's lives comply with several racialized projections about the black men's body as (1) exotic and strange, (2) violent, (3) incompetent and uneducated, (4) sexual, (5) exploitable, and (6) innately incapacitated" (p. 114). Taylor and Johnson argue that "by framing a film rhetorically and critically interrogating film for its inclusions, silences or disallowences of specific identity constructs, scholars are able to argue that there are clear lines of cultural narratives presented within films" (p. 115).

They offer several constructions: the black bourgeois, from ghetto to ghetto fabulous, the ghetto antagonist, the ghetto protagonist, and rescripting the liberator: the bourgeois protagonist and antagonist, and finally rescripting black masculinity with class. Taylor and Johnson stress that they have found three new characters (as noted above), and "a continuation of an old character, the ghetto antagonist." They call for new analysis of gendered performances, and ask: "What do the female versions of the ghetto and bourgeois protagonist and antagonist look like? How do they affect the upward mobility of the black male character?" They conclude that a clearer understanding and critical analysis of these archetypes can lead to productive archetypes rather than negative and degrading stereotypes... provided they highlight the complexities inherent in racial, sexual, and class-based identities as well as promote other options that extend beyond the either-or dichotomy of ghetto and bourgeois." (pp. 126-127). In reading this essay, personally, I think that "black persona" could easily have been included in the essay's title rather than "black body" in terms of the characters that they introduced. Since many black and white Americans are most familiar with Spike Lee's movies, it is surprising that there is no mention of his influence as an early director of black ghetto films.

Katrina E. Bell-Jordan's Chapter Seven: "Still Subscribing to Stereotypes: Constructions of Black Masculinity in Popular Magazines," contends that in examining three popular magazines, Vibe, Sports Illustrated, and ESPN published in 2006 and 2007, all of which extensively feature black athletes or celebrities, she found that "Emergent themes were identified in terms of the ways that black masculinity is depicted in reductive, limited and one-dimensional ways in those publications" (p.135), which is the point by which she begins her essay. Quoting Jackson and Dangerfield (2004), she notes that "contemporary culture continues to signify black masculinity as violent, sexual, criminal, and incompetent or uneducated" (p. 129). She suggests that this factor calls for "the importance and implications of theorizing about black masculinity within the discourse on hip-hop culture.

And it deconstructs this discourse by giving particular attention to the ways in which hegemonic constructions of black masculinity are articulated in the advertising and cultural content of some popular magazines.

She discusses such issues as race and representation in media; theorizing black masculinity; black masculinity in hip-hop; critiquing hegemonic representations; confronting representations of black masculinity, through a textual analysis (problematic signifiers of black masculinity and black hypermasculinity, an emphasis on excess and materialism); and limited constructions of black masculinity. Bell-Jordan identifies six bipolar hegemonic media constructions of lived experiences of black men in black masculinity in contemporary culture. She concludes by noting: "An important aspect of this chapter's critique of the construction of Black masculinity in the advertising and editorial copy of popular magazines has been the history of ideological and discursive struggle over race and representations pervasive in media culture" and she calls for understanding "the lived experiences in Black males in more complex and meaningful ways" (than for example in the three magazines whose advertising and editorial policy marginalizes black me)" (pp. 142-143). She has pointed out earlier in the essay that "there are numerous photos in each issue of Vibe examined here featuring Black artists and other celebrities posed in a hypermasculine stance" (p. 139).

No doubt, she is quite correct in her broader examination than I have made recently in the supermarket quickly cursing through the most recent copy of Vibe, but I noted that there were several advertisements showing black men as clean cut, neatly attired, and there were also several advertisements showing white men both in the same manner and also as hypermasculine. Additionally, as a recent faculty member on the University of Virginia autumn 2011 Semester at Sea with 450 students, including only 5% male and female students of color, these students were uniformly neat, modestly dressed, and soft spoken. Conversely, among the white women and men students, with about 40% being male, several of the white men frequently were demonstrating their own hypermasculinity by exhibiting their bulging muscles, and sometimes with quite vulgar language which some staff members and adult parents of children on the ship calling on them to watch their language in front of the children. One interesting experience related to me privately by a dark skinned Guatemalian male was that while he had been on the ship for half the voyage, on a four day excursion in India with twenty other students, faculty, and Lifelong Learners to the Taj Mahal, in which a round trip air flight was required, on the return trip to the ship, one white male student asked him what part of India he was from. In this way, he felt quite invisible and marginalized, especially as the group had traveled together, explored together, eaten together and stayed in the same hotels.

So my question for Katrina Bell-Jordan would be whether a comparison of black and white men in advertisements and featured stories in these three magazines which she chose to examine would not only generally confirm her research about the black men but possibly also about the white men whom we would see featured there? So is it the male masculinity seen as aggressive and hypermasculine or only the black men? I would speculate, without any precise knowledge, that these magazines might focus on male hypermasculinity itself rather than just among black men.

Timothy J. Brown's Chapter Eight: "Scripting the Black Male Athlete: Donovan McNabb and the Double Bind of Black Masculinity" led me to consider my comments relating to Chapter Seven, to see if Brown's research led him to similar conclusions. In the two January, 2012 South Carolina Republican debates, a January 22, New York Times heavily criticized both the primary winner, Newt Gingrich, for his "gutter debating" and his audiences who gave him standing ovations for his "red meat" statements, and for both him and the audiences lacking common civility. Brown indicates that Philadelphia is "known for as a tough-nosed, blue-collar town, where hard work and ethnic pride run deep" (p. 147). Brown discusses "the politics of sports: the stereotype of black dominance. citing Ronald Jackson's 2006 book Scripting the Black Masculine Body, as providing a "critical historical approach to demonstrate how since the seventeenth century, the mass media have engaged in scripting the black body to perpetuate stereotypes and negative images of African Americans – which continues today.According to Jackson (2006), scripting is not simply the construction of an image, it draws upon racialized, politicized, and commodified black bodies that over time are accepted as having a negative meaning... – a worldview that perpetuates negative assumptions, characteristics, anad behaviors of African Americans" (pp. 152-153). Brown states that there are two features to scripting: the gaze and social prescriptions: "First, the gaze is the process of being aware that there is an Other (based upon the visibility of difference.... For African Americans, difference is defined through physical features such as skin color, facial features, and hair texture, Second, social prescriptions are worldviews that devalue and perpetuate negative and stereotypical images toward the black body" (p. 153).

With his theoretical approach, Brown explores the scripting of the African American Philadelphia Eagles star Donavan McNabb, who has led the team to five time Pro Bowl Selections and has made the Eagles one of the most successful pro football teams, however, "has endured heated criticism from fans, the media and his teammates." The" criticism goes beyond abuse that starting NFL quarterbacks take. This criticism reflects long-held inscriptions society has imposed on black masculinity" with three categories: identity politics, expressiveness, and style of play" (pp. 154-155). Brown explores these three categories in relation to McNabb's often harsh treatment by the media, fans, and teammates. This leads Brown to argue that in general black athletes are scripted, and: "The double binds (as represented by McNabb) highlight contradictions that can be said about black athletes in general; black athletes are valued when they do not have any identity politics, black athletes are valued when their physicality can be controlled and black athletes are valued when they confirm to 'organized' styles of sports" (p. 161). He concludes: "As a society, we have trouble when individuals such as a Tiger Woods, a Barack Obama, or a Donavan McNabb come along and provide a different image, a different persona that constructs identity on its own terms. This is the ultimate challenge of the 21st century – to understand and accept the range of identities that comprise black masculinity" (p. 163).

In Chapter Nine: "Bearing Witness and Paying Mind: (Re) Defining the Meanings of Black Male Success": Rachel Griffin reflects on the stigmatization of black men as "a dangerous, unintelligent, at-risk, endangered and hopeless demographic in crisis" (p. 167). Although she is concerned about how a biracial woman such as herself can engage in research "in the hopes of liberating black men? Quoting bell hooks who says "Black women cannot speak for black men. We can speak with them," Griffin undertakes the task in this chapter to theorize healthy and productive black male identities. She finds that there are "urgent circumstances surrounding black males, and identifies numerous studies that interlocking systems of oppression have on black men. Griffin discusses the complexity of "the cool pose" exhibited by many black males, with both positive and negative effects. She proposes progressive black masculinities aiding black males to obtain positive results. As a part of her research methodology, she conducted a number of critical ethnographic interviews with former black professional male basketball players and encouraged them to engage in performance writing and poetic transcriptions. In her analysis and discussion, she provides several pertinent examples, which illustrate how the men spoke of attaining success as a process, and that in this aspect, they were able to see their own worth and answered the call to employ progressive black masculinities. Griffin concludes by assessing what it means for these former athletes to be "progressively cool." She calls for future research to provide spaces for black teachers, parents, and community members to join in being able to speak and be listened to as progressive masculinities: "How can black men be taught and encouraged to define success through family, spirituality, education, and community in a manner that speaks to who they are, who they can be, and who they wish to become?" (pp. 182-183).

In Rex L. Crawley's Chapter Ten: "Black Man, Black Boy: An Auto-ethnographic Exploration of the Issues Associated with Black Men Raising Black Boys," he acknowledges that "There is a plethora of work focused on absentee fathers, work on incarcerated fathers, deadbeat dads, and unemployed/underemployed fathers.... It becomes apparent to me that there is a need to respond to the dearth of communication literature on black fatherhood" (p. 188). Using auto-ethnographic research methods, at the birth of his son, he began journaling to document "some of the experiences and emotions associated with being a black father.... The extended research project will include black men who play a nurturing and permanent role in the lives of their black sons.... the majority of the co-researcher for the study will be college graduates and members of a black fraternity" (for which he served as the local president of the alumni chapter). He developed five themes: black son, black mother; gender rolls and perceptions; discipline; displays of emotion; and relationship with God. Crawley concludes: "These five themes represent the beginning of the exploration into the experience of black men raising black boys. Each day represents a new adventure for me as a new black father; however, as I encounter black men across the country, I likewise uncover new issues and areas of inquiry" (p. 195). Unlike most other essays in the volume which have reasonably rich references (for example Brown and Griffin), Crawley has only one, making it less useful than many of the other essays.

Chapter Eleven: "'Where My Citizens at?' The Criminalization of Black Manhood in Contemporary America," by Christopher Davis, begins his essay discussing his grandfather's feeling of urgency in voting, even on a very cold and snowy morning, when he was only about nine years old. Davis says that his grandfather left him an important legacy: a model of manhood "rooted firmly in his citizenship." His "role as active participant and stakeholder in his community made him the man he was. In my mind, my grandfather's manhood was linked directly to the fulfillment of his role and responsibility in American democracy... my grandfather and many black men of his generation ironically found courage and purpose in embracing American democracy and civic duty... simply living a citizen's life was masculine" (pp. 198-202).

Following his discussion of both Athenian and American citizenship, where slaves were the antithesis of citizens, but, nonetheless, "this concept of manhood on a day-by-day basis became a badge of honor, the reward of struggle," Davis questions what has happened to black men born after the Civil Rights Movement: "No longer does a democratic manhood (for middle-class values and lifestyle) hold the same value or regard for many young Black men today.... The large percentage of Black men today who are or have been incarcerated and suffered the socio-cultural effects of the crack cocaine epidemic of the 1980s, have altered the Black male image and identity" (pp. 203-204). He argues that "Black manhood now is commonly associated with anti-social behavior, criminality; and violence, not with democracy" (p. 204). He notes that the popular culture now centers on "an image of Black masculinity as one of anti-citizen, an image of thuggery and gangsterism.... A way of life limited to prisons and street corners has now come to characterize manhood" (p. 204).

Davis contends that this concept of manhood is fundamentally anti-democratic, anti-citizen, and anti-community: "Criminal manhood is an ideology of masculinity built on hubris destructive both to the individual and to society" (p. 205). Concluding by recalling when he was about fourteen that his grandfather made an anonymous call to the police, resulting in a drug raid next door, many black men might criticize him as a bitch according to the "Stop snitching" ethic that was then prevalent. Quoting Michael Kimmel's book, Manhood in America:"Personally, I believe that in the twenty-first century, we need a different sort of manhood, a 'democratic manhood.' The manhood of the future cannot be based on obsessive self-control, defensive exclusion, or frightened escape. We need a new definition of masculinity in this new century, a definition that is more about the character of men's hearts and the depths of their souls than about the size of their biceps, wallets, or penises, a definition that is capable of embracing differences among men and enabling other men to feel secure and confident rather than marginalized and excluded (1996, p 329), Davis ends his essay: "I do not think the thugs get it… and that is the problem" (pp. 207-208). It is a powerful essay.

It is not quite clear to me why this excellent and inspirationally motivational essay, Chapter Twelve: "Letter to My Sons: A Black Father's Ruminations on Black Manhood and Identity," by Baruti N. Kopano, a Ph.D. and university department chair, belongs in this academic book, unless it is with the assumption that as if the book is used as a text, it will implicitly speak directly to young black men enrolled in the class, encouraging them to become good husbands and loving and present fathers to their own sons. The book is not designed as a text, but might easily be included for that purpose, and in this case, Kopano's essay might be useful, which it certainly would be in a popular men's magazine.

The final chapter: "Exploring Intercultural Sensitivity and Black Manhood Development in The Autobiography of Malcolm X," by the book's coeditor, Mark C. Hopson begins his essay, identifying himself as a black man who hopes that his lived experience "might somehow represent, with honesty and sincerity, the lived experiences of other black men. He relates his own surprise meeting of Malcolm X's youngest sister and his mother. He provides a narrative where he received and passed on Malcolm X's own autobiographical narrative, first as a popular school leader; second as a street leader; third as a prison leader; fourth as a national spokesman for the Nation of Islam; Fifth as an International Pan-African leader. By "viewing Malcolm X through these five stages, we see the development of a transformational leader and educator" (p. 220).

Hopson utilizes and expands Milton J. Bennett's 1993 developmental "Model of Intercultural Sensitivity" as his own research focus in studying Malcom X's autobiography: "Stages of ethnocentricity include a worldview that is limited by notions of race, ethnicity, class, and general ideas about differences which assume that one's own culture is all that is central to reality. This position further asserts that cultural difference is wrong and/ or abnormal. According to Bennett, ethnocentrism encompasses acts of (a) denial, (b) defense, and (c) minimization" (p. 219). On the other hand, Bennett describes ethnorelativity includes the goal "to understand, and to work within, the concept of difference rather than seeking to eliminate it. Bennett's ideas of ethnorelativity include stages of (a) acceptance, (b) adaptation, and (c) constructive marginality" (pp. 218-219).

Hopson continues by discussing ethnocentricity in AMX (Autobiography of Malcolm X): isolation and separation; defense inferiority versus superiority, ethnorelativity (acceptance, adaptation, constructive marginalization: a call to action); and critical memory and black masculinity development (the impact of intercultural interactions, identification and acceptance). Hopson speaks autobiographically of his own growth as a black youth and man, facing discrimination, but learning that he cannot become a white man, as he sometimes wished, but must exist in white society as a black boy and man. Like Malcolm X (who later, after his pilgrimage to Mecca where he worshiped with peoples of all cultures and classes, changed his name to El Hajj Malik El Shabazz), Hopson indicates that he takes a constructive marginality approach to intercultural communication: "In conclusion, I am a black man. I am a work in progress. To understand me, you must understand the world in which I exist. It is neither a simple nor static world, but a world of continuous motion. In honor of Brother Malcolm and all the brothers of the world, I remain in continuous motion" (p. 228).

This statement ends the book well, linking both Hopson's ethnorelative position as a black man, and as a scholar on black masculinity and intercultural communication.

I note that Rex L Crawley does have a section in Chapter Ten "Relationship with God," and that Ronald L. Jackson II begins his acknowledgements by stating: "I am ever grateful for the head of my life, my savior Jesus Christ, for his unconditional love, humility and sacrifice. Without him, none of this would be possible." Although he does not explain why this is true, with this first line beginning of the book, and seeming rather curious in an academic volume such as Masculinity in the Black Imagination, it would appear logical for there to be at least one full chapter relating to the role of religion, or its absence, among black males. While there are passing references to religion, the index includes no references to religion. Additionally, in a book relating to black or males, it is surprising that there are no essays relating to African black men, nor any references on this subject in the index. Both the relationship of religion to black African American and African men's lives could provide added useful chapters.

Recently, in Ghana, I saw the extraordinary influence of Pentecostalism through many very large billboards everywhere we traveled promoting one or another Ghanaian charismatic male preacher. I would have liked to attend one of these charismatic worship services there. Also, I attended a conversation by a Ghanaian traditional religious seminary professor, who lamented that traditional Christianity in southern Africa was rapidly losing out to Pentecostalism as an attraction for young Africans. Apparently, these Pentecostal churches are filled to overflowing several times a week in the economically depressed and seriously unemployed Ghanaian population. Finally, I attended a charismatic Pentecostal interracial worship service in a South African ghetto township, which while the witnessing by both the speakers and the congregation raising their hands in praise was much more calm than in such services that I have attended in the United States, or in the exaggerated film depictions in American cinema, it is still apparent that charismatic Pentecostalism is a major religious force among black southern Africans.

To conclude my review, Masculinity in the Black Imagination is an important academic accomplishment for Jackson and Hopson as communication scholars, and is entirely relevant to contemporary studies of race, masculinity, and black men in America. Continuing their joint scholarship, I would encourage them to develop additional volumes related to black women and other marginalized groups of people of color or perhaps to encourage others to undertake such volumes.

4. Kriese, P. & Osborne, R. E. (Eds.) (2011). Social Justice, Poverty and Race: Normative and Empirical Points of View

Amsterdam, the Netherlands: Value Inquiry Book Series. It includes 226 pages, with a Preface, and Introduction to the Work. Part One emphasizes "Theoretical Approaches to Social Justice," with five chapters; Part Two: "Teaching about Social Justice, Poverty and Race" with five chapters; Part Three: Practical Applications of Knowledge about Social Justice, Poverty and Race" with five chapters; plus a "Conclusion to the Work," "Works Cited" [identified for each chapter], "About the Authors," and an index. The front and back covers have a photo of an old woman at a soup kitchen. This volume is 234 in the series, and is specifically a volume in "Studies in Jurisprudence."

In teaching at the University of Buffalo, Indiana University, the University of Virginia, University of Swaziland, and the Rochester Institute of Technology, I made various efforts to encourage my students to increase their awareness and active involvement in social justice issues. At Indiana University, I hosted a day long program with African American and white students on positive aspects of racial cooperation. For a course in communication and social change, I included as texts Mark Mathebane's book Kaffir Boy; Paulo Friere's book Pedagogy of the Oppressed; and Guatavo Gutieriez' The Power of the Poor in History, among others which emphasized the concept of social justice and poverty. I also showed various movies such as "Romero" and videos such as "The Panama Deception," and "Falun Gong."

In 1980/81, I participated in a faculty study tour of the PLO in Lebanon, the Council of Foreign Relations in Jordan, and the occupied territories of Israel, engaging in conversations with academics, diplomats, refugees, women's groups, and we had a two hour conversation with Chairman Yassir Arafat in Beirut. In 1988/89, I participated in a "Solidarity with the Poor" retreat in Puorto Prince, Hinche, and Soltidare, Haiti. All of these activities helped increase my own sense of social justice and informed my teaching of university classes on communication and social change.

After hosting international high school exchange students from Sweden, Belgium, France, and Spain, I requested students from developing countries to provide some the same opportunities that the middle class European students were receiving, and I hosted students from Brazil and South Africa, as well as a refugee boy from El Salvador. When I returned from teaching in Swaziland, I brought two Swazi teens for extra high school education. Later, I had three adults from South Sudan living in my home. As the 7800 South Sudanese "lost boys" started to come to the United States in 2001, Rochester, New York was to receive 78 of them, and I involved myself in their independent educational efforts before I began to teach that autumn in Chinese universities. In China, I encouraged my students to become global citizens and to increase their own conscience for the poor in their own society, following the saying of Socrates: "I am neither a citizen of Athens, nor Greece, but of the world."

On the University of Virginia/Institute for Shipboard Education Autumn 2011 Semester at Sea voyage, many instructors, classes, discussions, and experiential learning situations were offered to help not only to increase our awareness as elite and privileged participants, but to encourage us to become actively involved in social justice issues in our own communities. On the ship, many people participated in simulations such as "Bafa Bafa" and the Oxfam Hunger Meal, and we had many speakers whose emphasis was the creation and awareness of social justice issues, and encouragement to become actively involved later as global citizens but also as local problem solvers on such issues. Most of the twelve on-shore ports included the ability to engage as volunteers in Habitat for Humanity, the Torgome Ghanian village experience, the Cape Town Hunger Project; visits to impoverished villages; donation of school supplies to poor students; visiting orphanages and hospitals, and serving in soup kitchens. Indeed, a great effort was made to send us disembarking passengers home with an enhanced awareness of our role in our own communities in regards to social justice. Locally, many groups are organized around issues such as social justice race, and poverty and my grandson's scout troop is involved weekly as volunteers in a community food pantry "Loaves and Fishes."

In Social Justice, Poverty and Race's Chapter One, "Barriers to Truth Concerning Social Justice," Lawrence J Hanks considers, from different evaluative arguments, the concept of social justice. He offers three fundamental assumptions: absolute or virtual objectivity does not practically exist; it is almost impossible to prove the strengths and weaknesses of a particular argument; and although humans value rationality, objectivity and the greater good, arguments are often clouded by emotions, subjectivity and self-interest. He proposes six problems in understanding arguments: "Perspective: From What Angle Is Your View?" "Persistence: Have You Checked Your 'Truth' Lately?"; "Proximity: Closeness and Concerns"; "Peculiarity: The Need to Conform"; "Programming Potential"; and "Perfection: How Our Lack of It Impedes Our Search." He ends the chapter with a section on "Creating a Common Vision: A Win-Win Scenario" as a means of evaluating arguments, and concludes that scholars should be passionate in their analysis, acknowledge their own biases, and approach their work as critical thinkers. Though he does not offer Rene Decarte's famous quote, "Dubito, ergo Cogito, ergo Sum" ("I doubt, therefore I think, therefore I am"), it would seem to be a good slogan for this chapter theme. In Li Mengyu's and my intercultural communication book for Chinese students, Communicating Interculturally (2012), as we seek to encourage them to become critical thinkers, we offer this saying as a major theme, helping them to understand their own views of truth, based on their own society's development, and to overcome their biases by looking at arguments from various angles.

In Chapter Two, "The Limits of Western Democracy," Wazir Mohamed contrasts the historical impact of indentured contract immigration in Mauritius and Guyana, exploring how the complex ethnic makeup of their societies from the nineteenth and early twentieth century, vastly complicated their possibilities to achieve democracy and social justice, where Mauritius reached these goals for immigrant laborers much more easily than in Guyana. He notes that Mauritius sustained democracy by holding elections, maintaining an independent judiciary, and by protecting civil and political rights, while Guyana was unable to do so, thus creating a much greater ethnic divide than in Mauritius today.

In a very contemporary analysis, Jerome Dean Mahaffey's Chapter Three: "Imaginary Leaders," and using a social media framework, discusses some of the recent events informed and enlarged by the anonymous social media, in what has become known even more currently as "the Arab Spring" through the torture and beating to death of a young businessman,

Khalid Said, in Egypt by uncover police for his efforts to expose police corruption. First analyzing media evolution and activism, credibility and public discourse, and constructing credibility in a text Mahaffey uses this event as a case study for social justice. Through anonymous reporting on Facebook, more than 100,000 persons joined the protests within a few months, leading to the widespread slogan on a website "We are all Khalid Said." Applying Aristotle's definition of ethos with credibility and trustworthiness, he demonstrates how the websites, despite their anonymous character, can create widespread public attention to examples of social injustice provided by social activists.

Deductively, I personally would have preferred to see Chapter Four: "International Perspectives on Social Justice" by John M. Davis before the case studies in chapters Two and Three. Additionally, it would seem that the book's last five main chapters could have been developed with the case studies in Part One. In his first paragraph, Davis identifies as an important author in his argument, (Smith, 1958) without indicating his or her importance, and forcing readers to go to the end of the book for the sources relating to this chapter to know who Smith was. Davis does note that much of the scholarly work on social justice has been directed toward identifying an "ideal, universal conception of social justice," starting in the west with Plato, but without making a comparison with eastern views on this topic. His approach is not toward the pursuit of this ideal, universal justice, but for one that seeks a means of reducing concrete injustices. He offers examples of major historical injustices such as human slavery, Apartheid in South Africa, and ethnic cleansing of indigenous populations Davis provides a very helpful overview of social justice from a four volume 43 nation study of war, peace, and government aggression, with individual country profiles by the group of authors. Davis explains the nature of realism and post realism in international relations, emerging cultural influences on social justice, and what makes cultural views influential with July 2011 statistics with four different tables. He explores abstract and concrete justice, offering personal experiences of disparate cultural views, and concludes by considering the value of cultural explorations. Curiously, he offers a three page annotated bibliography of suggested readings, the only chapter in the book which does this, and therefore seeming a bit unbalanced with the other chapters. Unfortunately, both this chapter and Chapter Five have serious proofreading problems.

Chapter Five: "Murder on the Bayou: The Demand for Social Justice Following the Death of Jose Campos Torres [by police brutality in Houston, Texas]," by Dwight G. Watson is another very interesting case study, which in my perspective, should, with Chapters Two and Three, follow the current Chapter Four. Watson's analysis includes sections on how to examine Torres' fate, the impact of the case locally and nationally, moving beyond the Hispanic community wounds caused by the police officers' acquittal in Texas, and the national calls to change the perspective on issues of police brutality and repression where the Houston police department became victims of their own racism.

Part Two of the book, "Teaching about Social Justice, Poverty and Race" has five useful chapters about how to teach students and their own educators to understand these topics, but also how to implement this teaching positively in their own lives through various experiential explorations on their part. In Chapter Six, "Sociocentric Social Justice," the book editors, Osborne and Kriese, report on "three elements of teaching that appear to predict success in fostering 'a social justice pedagogy'": 1. Liberatory pedagogy; 2. Emancipatory pedagogy; and 3. Transformative thinking. They apply and explore the well-known communication scholar, Milton J. Bennett's development continuum, also known as his developmental model of intercultural sensitivity: denial, defense or reversal, minimization, acceptance, adaptation, and integration. Osborne and Kriese indicate that it is difficult to assist student development towards social justice, and link their own assignment from their ten years of teaching on the topic to stages in Bennett's model. They conclude by offering four points on teaching social justice: perceptions of social justice follow the same development as Bennett's development of intercultural sensitivity; advanced thinking in the area will not occur without focused assignments for the students and forcing the six stages of the model; the assignments must be well designed and force students to progress beyond simple recitation of facts or opinion; and the teaching can best be developed by focusing the students' thinking both on individual and collective aspects of social justice. Still, they claim that these four aspects are only half of the battle: faculty also must understand how to translate the knowledge of social

justice and goals into pedagogical practice and course assignments, causing everyone to learn together, both students and teachers.

Chapter Seven: "Navigating New Worlds of Social Justice in Teacher
Education," by Karon LeCompte and Stephanie Sefcik, about creating a
documentary on the attitudes toward the campus gay and lesbian culture
and an unexpected campus hate group's attempts to block the showing
of a short documentary is interesting, but with the analogy of Sefcik as
Dorothy in "The Wizard of Oz" and the invisible hate group as the invisible
flying monkeys in the play makes the essay seem more appropriate for
a magazine article than an essay in this academic volume. None the less,
their point if well made about the need to overcome the efforts of such
hate groups towards a campus marginalized student group.

Margaret A. Syverson's Chapter Eight, "Social Justice and Evidence-
Based Assessment with the Learning Record," demonstrates how test-based
teaching is less effective than expected, and illustrates how a national
US policy such as "Leave No Child Behind" actually marginalizes minority student populations with disabilities or limited English proficiency.
Syverson quotes researchers whose findings indicate that test measurements in high stakes populations is not only a political error, but also a
serious policy error that "discriminate against all of America's poor and
many of America's minority students." She argues that "an alternative
to this madness does exist" by using the Learning Record as an assessment model, empirically informing both parents and teachers through
interviews and observational techniques, and thus becoming a source
of restorative social justice and restores a fundamental humanity to the
educational system. The basic requirement is that "teachers must focus
their observations and interpretations of students' actual development,
rather than potentially stereotypical assumptions about students with
different backgrounds. As a collaborative, public and open assessment,
Syverson claims that use of the Learning Record uses different kinds of
evidence and analysis rather than simply depending on mandated tests
for the entire age-level population being assessed. She concludes that real
data about "student activity, experience, performance, and achievement"
help to provide "the best hope for working toward the amelioration of
social injustices inflicted and supported by the institution of school and
ultimately the social injustices perpetuated by the larger culture."

Marilyn D. Moore, in Chapter Nine: "Bearing the Burden: Will the Elite Be America's Only College Education?" argues that three recent changes have played a significant and widening gap between the rich and average Americans: the cost of living, he rising costs of consumer goods made in the United States, and the current recession and individualism. She suggests that the most troubling problem is an "ideological shift in American thinking related to the idea of justice." She asks the following questions: "Is there justice in the financial system? Is there still a middle-class in America? Is there still a place for the middle-class student? Is there myopia in the American middle-class?"

Chapter Ten: "Developing An Understanding of Best Practices for Teaching Undergraduate Students about Poverty" by Kevin D. Blair examines "current approaches to teaching [American university] students about poverty" and "presents initial findings from a study that examines the impact of participation in a poverty simulation on undergraduate students' knowledge about people living in poverty and the impact of the simulation on their ability to empathize with the challenges and difficulties faced by those who live in poverty." He reviews the current, but limited, literature in teaching poverty issues to undergraduate students and the impact of simulations on attitudes, and briefly identifies successful programs for poverty education, such as at Washington and Lee University, Baylor University, Rice University, University of California at Berkeley, plus poverty surveys, including the Niagara University poverty survey. Blair, a faculty member there, indicates that the data analysis, results and discussion of the University's program and survey are in progress at the time of the book's publication. Although the polled students tend to see a "flawed character" as the underlying cause of poverty, he finds it encouraging that 80% of the students acknowledged that the poor are not treated as well as others, and about 48% who felt that they might personally make a difference in the lives of the poor.

Part Three of the book "Practical Applications of Knowledge about Social Justice, Poverty, and Race: includes five chapters: Eleven: "Social Justice and the Integration of Aboriginal and Torres Strait islander Worldviews in Australian social Work Practice and Education" by Joanna Zubrycki; Twelve: "Can GMO [genetically modified organism] Solve World Hunger?" by Sabry Shehata; Thirteen: "Reconceptualizing the Story of US Cultural

Adaptation?" by Elvenet S. Wilson; Fourteen: "Poverty, Immigration and Latinos in US Texas Colonias" by Cecilia Giusti; and Fifteen: "Victory in the Fields: Cesar Chavez's Quest for Dignity and Social Justice for Farm Workers through Non-Violence and Spiritual Power" by John E. Valdez. These chapters reinforce the importance of understanding the major themes of the book.

Finally, in "Conclusion to the Work: Thinking about and Acting to Advance Social Justice: A Dilemma," a brief epilogue, by Paul Gomberg, he identifies several books related to the book's themes, but says that "The chapters in this volume address social justice from three pathways.... Thinking about social justice in theoretical ways – the focus of Section One – is really only as beneficial as the ability for these theories to be used to educate others to want to do something about those injustices – the focus of Section Two. Lastly, the measure of whether these theoretical and educational efforts will have dividends, comes in the form of practical applications where people can see social justice in action – the focus of Section Three of this work."

Personally, while I find some of the chapters rather uneven in their approaches, overall, I very much appreciate having this volume to aid me in furthering my own understanding of the book's themes of social justice, poverty, and race and in encouraging me to continue to involve myself actively in support for social justice, the alleviation of poverty where I am able to help, and improving racial equity where I have the opportunity to act. It is, of course, a lifelong requirement for those of us who are both critical thinkers and aspirants toward global citizenship.

5. LEFFLER, M. P. & LEGRO, J. W. (EDS.) (2011). IN UNCERTAIN TIMES: AMERICAN FOREIGN POLICY AFTER THE BERLIN WALL AND 9/11

Ithaca, NY: Cornell University Press. 243 pages; Introduction; 10 chapters; Conclusion; Notes (199-226); Notes on Contributors (227); Index.

Robert Jervis, the Adlai E. Stevenson Professor of International Politics at Columbia University, offers this recommendation: "Bringing policymakers, political scientists, and historians together, Melvin P. Leffler and Jeffrey W. Legro's collection provides a wealth of insights and arguments into where we are and how we got here. There is a lot to think about and to argue with in these essays" (back cover).

Leffler is the Edward R. Stettinius Professor of American History in the Department of History at the University of Virginia and Legro is the Randolph P. Compton Professor in the Department of Politics at the University of Virginia.

The book's promotional information offers the following: "In Uncertain Times considers how policymakers react to dramatic developments on the world stage. Melvyn P. Leffler and Jeffrey W Legro have assembled an illustrious roster of officials from the George W. H. Bush, Clinton, and George W. Bush administrations. These policymakers describe how they went about making strategy for a world fraught with possibility and peril. A group of eminent scholars probe the unstated assumptions, the cultural values, and the psychological makeup of the policymakers. Together, the two communitites impel us to rethink how our world has changed and how policy can be improved in the future" (back cover).

In 1959 when I was twenty-three, shortly before the July 24 Khruschev-Nixon "Kitchen" debate at the American exhibit in Moscow, I was among a group of about two dozen young adults moving by train from Finland into the Soviet Union heading toward Leningrad, each of us carrying a Torah for one Jewish young man to give out to Jews. We visited a former cathedral in Leningrad which then was a museum of religion (negatively presented and atheism, which was positively demonstrated). Later in Moscow, we all registered at the US Embassy, where we were each given about a couple dozen copies of the USIA magazine in Russian Amerika, to distribute during our visit. As I indicated in my recent blog review of Allen C. Lynch's 2012 book, Vladimir Putin and Russian Statecraft (Post 390), an intentionally lightly guarded collection of 15,000 books by American authors at the American exhibit in Moscow had already lost 7,500 books by the time that we were at the exhibit and many more disappeared (into Soviet society) before the exhibit ended (American soft power). Although some of us were invited to visit Russian student apartments, the young Russians did not appear at our meeting place, hindered perhaps by officials or by worried families. GUM, Moscow's largest department store, had very few consumer items on the shelves and there were very few autos on the Moscow streets. Some of the Americans sold western blue jeans or cigarettes on the "black market" in Red Square, and fortunately none of them were arrested. Later in 1977, I visited East Berlin and Dresden; Budapest, Warsaw and Krakow, and Prague.

After meeting members of a small Soviet delegation in Charlottesville, Virginia in the summer of 1989, I was invited to participate as a member of a small American delegation in an international conference in Moscow in late October on "Communication and Peace in the Satellite and Internet Age," sponsored by the Soviet Peace Institute (funded no doubt by the government) and taking place about two to three weeks before the fall of the Berlin wall on November 9. I presented a paper in the social science division of the conference and gave a very well attended speech to enthusiastic students at Moscow State University. In that period of perestroika and glasnost, many television debates on Moscow stations were taking place about their importance and future and the "revolutions of Eastern and central Europe" (Poland, Hungary, Czechoslovakia, Bulgaria, and Romania) which had been occurring, plus the attendance of Mikhail Gorbachev and leaders of the Warsaw Pact at the October 7th fortieth anniversary of the founding of the German Democratic Republic, at which time protesters outside the hall were calling "Gorby, help us! Gorby, save us!"

We had many intense discussions and contacts about the events with the Russian conference participants and students, and I was a dinner guest in four different Russian apartments, including a Jewish home, the first time that a foreigner had entered those buildings. There were many autos on the Moscow streets and the shelves in GUM had many consumer items for sale. Communist-approved Patriarch Pimem of the Russian Orthodox Church had worked carefully with the government to open many of the formerly closed churches and monasteries which we were able to visit and the churches were filled with worshipers. When I returned to the University of Virginia, I gave class presentations on my presence in Moscow before the fall of the Berlin wall, and on what was happening in Eastern and central Europe. The later 1996 CNN "Cold War" series had many vivid illustrations of what had been taking place in Eastern Europe from August 1989 to the dissolution of the Soviet Union in 1991.

In late August of 2001, I flew to Shanghai to teach at Yangzhou University (four hours west by train) and when 9/11 occurred, I learned about it at 1AM China time from a telephone call from my son (1PM Eastern US time). At that time China Central TV only had two or three daily twenty minute news programs in English on the Chinese Channel 4, at a time when the Chinese government only allowed its channels to present delayed breaking news, though Phoenix TV could broadcast such an event live. . One of the early Chinese language television images that I saw after the photos of the destruction of the twin towers of the World Trade Center and at the Pentagon were displayed was Chinese President Jiang Zemin announcing his government's support of the US government and citizens. (About thirty-five Chinese citizens were among the casualties in the World Trade Center.)

It was only at the beginning of the March 20, 2003 US/UK-Iraq War that CCTV was permitted to broadcast that occurrence live. At the Beijing Language and Culture University, I had been already been scheduled to give a public presentation on "The Culture of War; The Culture of Peace" very close to the date of the beginning of the invasion, which, with the imminent American "shock and awe" attack, caused considerable nervousness by university officials, requiring all audience members to show their identification cards, and having university guards posted outside the lecture hall where I was speaking (perhaps in case a spontaneous student protest might develop).

Teaching, more or less, from 2001 to 2011 in four Chinese universities, I subsequently gave a lecture series at Kursk State University in 2003 (Kursk, the site of the last great Russian-Nazi tank battle in World War II); I was a speaker at the Fourth Russian Communication Association Conference in St. Petersburg in 2006; and I gave a 2008 lecture series at the Volgograd State Pedagogical University (Volgograd, earlier named Stalingrad, the site of the half year Nazi siege along the Volga River); and I made academic presentations at the fifth Russian Communication Association Conference in 2008 near Moscow.

Based on my professional, cultural, and personal experiences in Russia around the period of the fall of the Berlin wall and more recently and in China around the time of the 9/11 event and since, my recent blog reviews of Allen C. Lynch's 2012 Vladimir Putin and Russian Statecraft [Post 390] and Zbigniew Brezezinski's 2012 Strategic Vision: America and the Crisis of Global Power (Post 436) and their extensive examples related to China and Russia have made me very interested in learning more about these periods by reviewing Melvyn P. Leffler and Jeffrey W. Legro's 2011 book, In Uncertain Times: American Foreign Policy after the Berlin Wall and 9/11.

In William R. Slomanson's 2000 Fundamental Perspectives on International Law (updated in 2010), he notes that in the spring of 1989 virtually no scholars nor policymakers anticipated the following events: the global rise of uncertainty, unpredictability, and rapid social transformation; the economic and political rise of China; the demise of the Soviet Union and rise of the United States as the only superpower (hyperpower); the dramatic changes a few months later in Eastern and central Europe; the fall of the Berlin wall on November 9th and reunification of Germany in December 1990 (leading many to think that in the near future South and North Korea might also be reunited); the full end of the Cold War and beginning of a "post-Cold War" period; the economic and political transformation of Western Europe toward the establishment of the European Union and the currency formation of the Euro; the ending of the war in Afghanistan, but then the Gulf and Iraq wars; extreme Islamic and Al Quaeda terrorist attacks against the United States, Russia, Spain, and even Islamic countries; the beginning of the end of Apartheid in South Africa; or the genocides in Rwanda, Bosnia, Kosevo, and the Sudan.

Coauthoring In Uncertain Times' "Introduction: Navigating the Unknown" and "Conclusion: Strategy in a Murky World," Leffler (history) and Legro (political science) identify some of the same major concerns, as does also Mary Elise Sarotte in Chapter 1: "The Wall Comes Down: A Punctuational Moment." Leffler and Legro ask these fundamental questions:

How did US officials and bureaucracies interpret the events surrounding 11/9 and 9/11?

How did their understanding of these events shape their subsequent thinking and planning for foreign policy or international order? Did they accurately grasp the international landscape they were about to encounter?

Were they successful in conceptualizing and implementing their policies?

What factors accounted for their success or failure? What lessons can be derived for meeting future challenges in making foreign policy in uncertain and shifting strategic circumstances? (3).

They identify several thoughtful authors' comments on this period, noting that "In many of these sympathetic yet critical portrayals, post-Cold War officials are pictured as struggling to find a unifying strategic theme to define their foreign policy (of deterrence and containment).... (George W.) Bush and his advisers dismissed (these policies). (In his 2005 inaugural address) Bush declared that it was American's mission to end tyranny and create a democratic peace. Most writers conclude that the strategy was deeply flawed for simplifying the world and overextending American power. Many of these critics claim that it was the product of a relentless neoconservative campaign to embed their views on official policy" (4-5). Recently, I note that Clark Rountree's 2012 book, The Chameleon President: The Curious Case of George W. Bush, which I reviewed (Post 333) offers many of the similar concerns, particularly Bush's hubris, in several of his chapters. Leffler and Legro offer reassessments both of "The Policymakers' Perspectives" and "The Views of Scholars" and call for "Reexamining Strategy in Uncertain Times" "As we reexamine the history of the post-Cold War era, we have a unique opportunity also to rethink some of the most fundamental challenges that inhere in the making of strategy" (12).

In their concluding chapter, they argue that "We aim both to clarify and analyze what the United States did and how it fared during the momentous years that followed the end of the Cold War. First, we sketch the evolution of strategy from the fall of the Berlin Wall to the onset of the Obama presidency. We then attempt to identify the accomplishments and failures of US planning under uncertainty. Finally, we explore some of the key impediments to effective strategy-making in times of uncertainty and outline what we might learn from the record so that we can do better in the future" (179). Personally, since their book was published in 2011, instead of considering only the foreign policy of the presidencies of the two Bushes and Clinton, I would have liked to see them also extend this evolution at least through the first year of the Obama presidency on several strategic topics of his foreign policy (for example, his outreach to the Middle East, Iran, China, and Russia). No doubt, they would argue that only one year of the Obama presidency was not enough to establish his own coherent foreign policy strategy. Still, much of it began to develop tentatively in his 2007-08 campaign for the presidency, and that period could be reasonably compared with his strategies as they developed in his first year as president.

Mary Elise Sarotte in Chapter 1: "The Wall Comes Down," provides a very thorough analysis of that period, suggesting also "what this particular case study can contribute to our broader understanding of decision making in times of rapid change" (14). She explains what had been happening in the context of the fall of the wall, and German Democratic Republic spokesman Gunter Schabowsky's fumbling press conference, an unusual event for the GDR even to hold a press conference, late in his remarks, when he looked at a paper that had been handled to him earlier, responded to a reporter's question "When does that (a new travel procedure) go into force?" by saying "immediately, right away." This became the impetus for East Germans to surge to several border crossings with West Berlin, and for the guards who were armed with lethal ammunition, to become overwhelmed, and without instructions, to allow the opening of the gates. Lynch, in his book Vladimir Putin and Russian Statecraft, points out that this was, with Putin's realization that he had no backup Soviet troops at the KGB headquarters that he was defending in Dresden almost singly handedly from angry protesters, another major disillusionment for him when he realized that "Moscow was silent," and therefore in grave danger for Soviet disintegration. Sarotte argues that both in Washington and Bonn, "unsurprisingly, leaders in both countries viewed the Wall's opening with a mixture of shock, happiness, and deep concern." The event forced Chancellor Kohl to rush back to West Germany from Poland, for a visit marking the fiftieth anniversary of the Nazi invasion of Poland. Reaching the stage in West Berlin just before a press conference called by the opposition, Kohl told the crowd: "I would like to call out to everyone in the German Democratic Republic: You are not alone! We stand at your side! We are and will remain one nation, and we belong together!" (19). In the meantime, Sarotte believes that President Bush and Secretary of State Baker were trying to figure out precisely to handle this development, with Bush saying to CBS Lesley Stahl "I'm not an emotional guy, but I'm very pleased" but that "developments had caught him by surprise and had said that he was determined not to incite a Soviet backlash by acting in a triumphalist manner" (19).

Calling the fall of the wall a "punctuational moment" that would demand a strategic US response: "Bush indicated to Kohl that he agreed with the latter's plans to push for unification as rapidly as possible, as long as a united Germany remained in NATO.... Washington's aim was to capitalize on the unexpected opportunity at the expense of the dying USSR." (21). Sarotte continued her discussion with her section of her paper: "The Legacy of the Punctuational Moment of 1989-1990 for 2001" by identifying that the US foreign policy strategy was still locked in a Cold War mentality, even when the 9/11 event happened: "The US foreign policy response the punctuation of Cold War institutions, specifically NATO, in the post-Cold War world." She concludes her essay by stressing: "When thinking about strategic planning it is worth remembering that US decision makers will not control the punctuational moments.... The events of 1989-90 demonstrate that crises are terrible things to waste; they constitute rare chances for dramatic change" (24-25).

In Chapter 5: "A Crisis of Opportunity: The Clinton Administration and Russia," Walter B. Slocombe states that "the new administration expected to have a reasonable chance to operate in a genuinely new world order – however unwilling its spokesmen would have been to accept this particular phrase, so ridiculed when used by Clinton's predecessor" and in his section "Russia: An Opportunity Recognized" acknowledges President Clinton's efforts to shore up the Russian economy and also to support the very weak President Boris Yeltsin: "Clinton and his advisers, however did have a strategic vision for US foreign policy: to reinforce the positive trends that seemed so pervasive, based on the judgment that 'for all its dangers, this new world presents an immense opportunity.... Nowhere was this more the case than in regard to Russia" (79-80). "Implementing the strategy," however was filled with challenges, and as Slocombe argues, the priorities were in conflict: "Clinton's priority of working with Russia because of its long-term strategic importance promptly collided wiih other, more immediate, if arguably less crucial, priorities that he could not ignore or afford to sacrifice.

The Russia question was not the only unexpected and unprecedented challenge, and opportunity for American interests in Europe that followed from the collapse of the Soviet system." Among other challenges facing Clinton was open warfare in the Balkans and the future role of the NATO alliance, and still later the Kosovo crisis Slocombe argues that there were four explanations that Clinton's strategy did not work: "First, the US government, like Yeltsin and the Russian reformers, simply underestimated the inherent difficulties of the task.... Second, there was a serious overestimation of the degree to which any external efforts could shape Russian politics, economics, and society.... Third, the vision of a full-scale US-Russian partnership, even in international affairs, was too optimistic and neglected real conflicting interests.... Fourth, the Yeltsin-centric tactic was inherently a risky way to pursue the overall strategy of promoting internal reform" (92-95).

University of Chicago Professor Bruce Cummings in Chapter 8: "The Assumptions Did It," provides specific case studies which skewed academic reactions to these events and biasing future policy decisions: the shattered world of 1945, the fall of the Berlin wall, the collapse of the Soviet Union, 9/11, and North Korea. He posits that all of the theories, models, and predictive measures so often used by academics and policy analysts often fail in terms of practical unpredicted or modestly predicted regional or world events, noting McGeorge Bundy's startling admission twenty-five years after the Vietnam war ended that he had not taken his Vietnamese enemy seriously. Just as do Chapters 9: "Faulty Learning and Flawed Policies in Afghanistan and Iraq" by Odd Arne Westad, and Chapter 10: "How Did the Experts Do?" by William C. Wohlforth, Cummings recognizes that the experts often get their expectations for future occurrences wrong. Cummings stresses that historians, policy experts, and social science experts, simply do not have the correct background to make such assessments adequately, and that often common sense rule of thumb often produces just as strong results: (Gorbachev's) "idea is a good one: we make predictions in the present, and life tells us whether we are right or wrong. The bipartisan Washington consensus through three Bush and two Clinton administrations was that post-1989 North Korea was on the verge of collapse.... Any honest person of the Left has to admit that the past two decades have been full of utterly unanticipated events, beginning with the fall of the Berlin Wall and culminating in the unimaginable collapse of the Soviet Union.... A third method of finding out we are wrong is to have history prove it to us, and then sail ahead undaunted" (134-135).

Unlike neocon philosophical Defense Department architect of the US invasion of Iraq and scandal-marred head of the World Bank, and author of Chapter 3, "Shaping the Future: Planning at the Pentagon, 1989-1993" Paul Wolfowitz (who fails to mention his role in formulating the Iraq invasion policy), other authors in In Uncertain Times offer explicit or implicit critiques of his thinking process and other policy planners of the period. Odd Arne Westad gives readers several arguments for why the US interventions in Afghanistan and Iraq: "In the wake of the military victory of US supported forces in Afghanistan, the Bush administration made two major mistakes that undermined the positive effects of that victory for the United States and for the Afghans. First, it let the remnants of the political leadership of the Taliban and their al Qaeda escape into Pakistani territory without forcing the military dictatorship in Islamabad to accept a US-led offensive against them.... Second, instead of concentrating almost exclusively on aiding Hamid Karzai's regime and the northern warlords, the United States and the Western allies should have offered far more civilian assistance to the Afghan regime, especially in the Pashtun-dominated south and east, in the crucial two years after the victory over the Taliban" (151-152). Among the problems that Westad articulates were the US belief in the superiority of American technology over local fighters; the failure of the United States to seriously understand the problems of regime change; the role of moral absolutes and national values in a region of the world where these absolutes had vastly different meanings than the American leadership supported; the unintended negative consequences of past US covert operations; and the American effort to speed up change after the end of the Cold War. He contends that: "there is reason to believe that unsuccessful attempts to learn from the Cold War played an important role in the renewed US interventionism in the 2000s.... What will remain, I believe, of the present critique of the Bush administration's failures after a generation or so has passed is not so much the immediate response to 9/11, the mishandling of alliances, the scant attention to civil liberties, or the invasion of Iraq. It will be that the administration chose the worst possible places to attempt the spread of democracy, and thereby set pluralism and political participation worldwide back by many years" (161-162).

In Chapter 10, "How Did the Experts Do?" William C. Wohlforth argues that "A large and influential scholarly literature holds that an expert consensus against a policy is a powerful signal that the policy is ill advised" (162). He stresses the two major case studies in the book "imply a more qualified role for outside experts in strategic planning. The conventional view fails to distinguish between normal levels of uncertainty and the extreme levels that decision makers had to confront in the kind of paradigm-shifting events considered in the book.... Officials' information advantage might assume unusual importance in an especially fast-moving situation.... Second, and most important, it is the very style of reasoning that lends experts such apparent analytical power both in normal times and in hindsight may hamper their ability to update quickly when the underpinnings of a long established strategic equilibrium come unhinged" (164-165). Wohlforth offers four phrases of the Bush administration's responses: 1. "a strategic reassessment that entailed a pause in the rapidly ripening entente with Moscow initiated by President Reagan and General Secretary Gorbachev; 2. A diplomatically competitive phrased premise on the continuance of the bipolar Cold War framework in which Washington sought to regain the initiative under the slogan "a Europe whole and free"; 3. A brief effort to bolster the two-bloc status quo as the GDR's position unraveled in the summer and fall and fears of instability mounted, and 4. The late fall decision to back Helmut Kohl's unification drive with united Germany's membership in NATO as the conditio sine qua non" (166). From 1994-1999, Wohlforth proposes that the assumed necessity of NATO's enlargement was a key assumption of American foreign policy and strategic planning. He writes that four propositions informed regional experts, terrorism scholars and international security scholars: a policy of deterrence and containment would work, the substantial costs and spreading instability in the region, even if victory could be assured, there was no exit strategy, and war with Iraq would jeopardize the campaign against al Qaeda. He notes that many of the forecasts costs did not materialize: many of the critiques that scholars made retrospectively were absent from their prewar assessments; and prospects for a strong Sunni insurgency were not stressed in prewar assessments as they did in retrospective evaluations rather than in the prewar assessments. Nonetheless, Wohlforth believes that despite the problems of hindsight versus foresight, the outside expert perspectives remain valuable in such strategic thinking after major events like the reunification of Germany and the expansion of NATO, and later events.

Concluding the book, Leffler and Legro offer the hope that a better understanding of how the United States has reacted in the past "will help illuminate the say forward – that has been the goal of bringing together the views of former policymakers and scholars" (197).

Overall, the book is very helpful for those of us who have an academic or lay interest in such major world events as the aftermath of the fall of the Berlin Wall and 9/11. The insights of historians and political science academicians, as well as the views of the policymakers, are very valuable and deserve our thanks. The chapters included are illustrative of the book as a whole.

Part II

Cross-Cultural Common Ground in Contemporary Asia and China

A) Essays

1. Asian Modernity and Intercultural Communication

Michael H. Prosser
University of Virginia,
Shanghai International Studies University

Globalism and Globalization

We can define globalism as "the belief that political policies should take world-wide issues into account before focusing on national or state concerns, or the advocacy of this belief," while globalization is "the process by which social institutions become adopted on a global scale" or "the process by which a business or company becomes international or starts operating at the international scale" (Encyclopedia Encarta, 1999). Globalization always includes the geographical movement across nations and cultures of goods, currency, people, and ideas. Migration is one of the most important aspects of globalization, from one country to another, and internally within a country or region. Chinese internal migration has been one of the largest movements in the world suggesting the term the "Mingyong" Chinese Migration because rural Chinese migrate to the cities to work and then home again briefly for the Lunar New Year celebration, encompassing 560 million or 43% of the population (2005). The labor surplus was 150-170 million in 2009. There were also 98 million residents in the top ten developing cities in 2009 (Global Times, 2009: November 30). The Chinese overseas diaspora has gone to Indonesia, Thailand, Malaysia, Singapore, United States, Myanmar, Canada, Vietnam, Philippines, and

Russia in that order, 38 million residents in 15 more countries with large Chinese populations (Jacques, 2009).

Evelin Lindner in her book, Gender, Humiliation, and Global Security (2010) writes that "A global culture and global institutions of social and societal cooperation can create meaningful life on planet Earth. We need too seek optimization of balance within each individual's life, and one integrated life, embedded in one united global community. Today, it takes a decent global society to give humankind a future." In Europe, she proposes, we have the term "social cohesion" for the move toward "global connectedness" among the human family and its habitats. In Asia, "the harmonious society" is more common. Whatever the phrasing, the meaning behind the words is solidarity among all of humankind for the common good." (Lindner, 2010)

Samuel Huntington's 1996 The Clash of Civilizations leads toward the proposal of a "Dialogue of Civilizations." Huntington asks: Are the Judao/Christian West and the Muslim Middle East and North African nations and cultures and the Asian/Confucian/Buddhist/Hindu cultures fundamentally different and unable to cooperate together on a global scale? Or, can we have a "dialogue of civilizations" in which it is imperative that we work together globally, internationally, and regionally?

Randy Kluver and John H. Powers in their 1999 book Civic Discourse: Civil Society, and Chinese Communities stress that China's earlier periods before 1949 were a period of "fragmentation, civil war, and Japanese occupation". It was a very long civilization, but with a short period of "civil society with Chinese characteristics," only since 1976 after the death of Chairman Mao Tsedong. From a communication framework, civil society may develop either as top down or bottom up depending on the internal communication, world-wide disapora, and between central government and global actors. Civil Society allows citizens a voice to influence social and political life outside the power of state. "Civic Discourse", Kluver and Powers argue is the ability to define the nature of society and people, including economics, cultural and social issues, popular culture (arts, architecture music, books, internet) by which their national identity can be expressed. Civic discourse helps create society; society helps promote civic discourse, like Edward T. Hall's axiom: "Communication is Culture; Culture is Communication" or Clifford Geertz' statement, "Humans create culture and culture creates humans." The future is likely to bring an even more diverse set of ideas into a culture and society that is rapidly constructing a new identity, and a new Chinese world."

Arthur Kroeber (2010: April) cites what he considers five American myths about China: 1. China will quickly overtake United States in economy, 2. China's holdings of US treasury bonds means holding Washington hostage on the economy, 3. Letting Chinese currency grow in value is the most important step to reduce its trade surplus. 4. China's hunger for resources is sucking the world dry and seriously increases global warming. 5. China's economic growth has occurred mostly with its cheap labor force.

However, in his 2009 book When China Rules the World, Martin Jacques states that: "Previously, the United States was regarded as the overwhelming agent and beneficiary of globalization. Now the main beneficiary is perceived to be East Asia and especially China," as its civilizational (versus nation state) dimension, "gives China its special and unique character. "Should we then consider globalization, not as moving Asians towards westernization, but increasingly the West moving more toward East Asia and China?

Jacques offers five measurements of Asian identity and values: language, the body, dress and cosmetics, food, power, and politics.

For Asian language fluency in English, Jacques points out that in China 350 million are learning English annually, and it is the elite language which is required for entrance into university and graduation, but in India it is only one of the 15 official languages, while in Japan the English language level is rather low despite 15 years of learning for each student. In Pakistan it is a frequent teaching language, in Singapore, Hong Kong the English language level is high, and it is a typical school language. In the Philippines English is the language for middle school and above.

In Asia for the body, dress and cosmetics, Jacques notes that many Asians seek to be lighter in skin color with women carrying umbrellas in the sun and the models have a lighter skin, seeking a Western appearance with an increasing amount of Western cosmetics. Western dress is typical in China except for the prewedding celebration photos and at the wedding celebrations the brides tend to wear both white and traditional dresses. Western dress is popular also in Japan, but the kimono for women remains still popular on weekends and for celebrations. In India, Hindu dress patterns still dominate, and there is widespread Muslim dress in India, Indonesia, Malaysia, Pakistan, Bangladesh, with traditional dress in South East Asia.

Discussing Asian food, Jacques notes that most Asians eat Asian foods most of the time, even though it is noted that Yum is the largest restaurant chain in the world owning franchises including 36,000 for KFC, Taco Bell, Pizza Hug, Long John Silvers, A & W. KFC has 15,580 restaurants in 109 countries and in China 2,200; McDonalds has 950 restaurants in China: 3,500 in Japan, and in Malaysia, 300 as well as a growing number in india. "Yum is the most successful fast food firm in China" (Economist, 2009: October 29). However, personally traveling widely in China, I do not personally see the English signs for Yum.

In considering Western and Eastern Views of Power, Jacques finds profound differences, where in the West – individual autonomy, identity, utilitarian government, democracy, freedom are the norm, but in East Asia, North Asia, and South-East Asia – group identity with the family as the basis of society, there is a consistent desire for stability and harmony. He argues that: "First, the impact of Westernization is limited; thus modernization depends on Asians' ability to transform themselves and adapt." "Second, if modernization is simply a transplant, it will not succeed in Asia. People must believe that modernization is their own."

Politics is a vibrantly alive democracy and often chaotic in India; in Japan, governments have changed hands frequently in the last several years; but in China, the leaders stress that politics should be left up to them, while as Deng Xiaoping's axiom "To get rich is glorious" is the common mantra for young people. Chinese foreign policy is based on the 1954 agreement between India and China and remains a continuing policy for Chinese foreign relations. 1. mutual respect for each other's territorial integrity and sovereignty, 2. mutual non-aggression, 3. mutual non-interference in each other's internal affairs, 4. equality and mutual benefit, and 5. peaceful co-existence. Deng Xiaoping's policy: "adopt a low profile and never take the lead" was China's major strategy until early in the twenty-first century, but now China is an increasingly active international political stakeholder.

While globalism as the concept and globalization as the process continue rapidly, at the same time, Martin Jacques argues that Asia will only modernize at its own pace, and within the context of Asian society. What works well from the West is adopted, but if it does not work well in the Asian context, it will not be adopted. In the meantime, Asian values and society are having an increasing influence in Western societies.

Jacques does not significantly discuss the role of religion in Asia, but we can see the following dimensions, China is basically nonreligious/atheistic/Confucianist/Buddhist and with a very large number of Muslims, especially in Western China; India is both predominantly Hindu/Muslim; Japan has many Buddhists and Shintoists; Pakistan, Bangladesh, and Afghanistan are mainly Muslim; in the Philippines, Roman Catholics are the dominant population; in South East Asia the Buddhist/Confucianist traditions prevail; and in South Korea there is a mix of Buddhist/Christian beliefs. Naturally, the religious tendendicies in the various countries and cultures play a major role in their societies, and often prevent greater Westernization for them.

CNN likes to call itself the creator of McLuhan's Electronic "Global Village" "Marshall McLuhan got it wrong" according to Auletta who states that maybe technology has leaped beyond McLuhan's conception and is no longer (CNN) Ted Turner's ally. Maybe, instead of one wired global village, there will be hundreds of villages, each broadcasting in its own language, with its own anchor and news team, its own weather and sports and local slant. The idea of a global village was initially appealing because of its simplicity, "But it's a misleading simplicity" (Auletta, K. (1993, August 2). The Electronic "Global Village" with CNN's earlier global dominance "faces challenges from new multinational network linkups and changes in what the world wants to watch." Auletta proposes that there are "At least two competing future models for world news."

One is Ted Turner's. "Nationalism is not growing," he says. "Internationalism is growing." Two: "Localization is growing." Turner also admits, but "We're the only distribution system that goes out to the whole world." And this will remain a low-cost network" (1993, August 2). Still, despite the fact that CNN is in 200 countries, there are now many global TV media competitors such as ABC. Al Alia, Al Jazeera, BBC. BBC/ABC, CBS, CCTV, Eurovision, Reuters TV, Ruport Murdoch's Sky TV News, and Telemundo, to name a few.

Media Globalization

We can ask, "What are the implications of Western media globalization for indigenous cultures in developing Asian countries? What kind of influence, if any, is Western media globalization having on indigenous media industries? In this age of media globalization, are there any indications that cultural influences may be taking place both ways – between the East and the West – rather than only from films: Holliwoodization vs. Bolliwoodization. There is a growing Hollywoodization of Asian films. Hollywood is getting Asianized to some degree, with influences of the Indian, Hong Kong and Korean movie industries. The two-way cultural symbiosis is likely to grow to serve the entertainment and cultural needs of a cosmopolitan audience who is open to consuming and appreciating foreign cultural influences without entirely rejecting their own. The internet grows exponentially; is censored; and grows again. China now has more people using the internet today than the entire populations of the United States, Canada, Australia, New Zealand, and Belgium. There are currently 30 million websites, a large proportion of them in China alone. New social media keeps springing up, as older ones fail or are censored.

Chinese Media Billionaires

Russell Flannery, writing for Forbes Magazine online (2010, November 12) notes that among the 400 richest people in China, with many billionaires, 20 % of the total or 80 live in Guandong Province. Zhejiang Province has 46; Jiangsu Province has 44 of the richest, accounting together for 170 of China's richest individuals. The largest number in one city is in Beijing where Robin Li, Chairman of Baidu lives, followed by Charles Zhang, Chairman of the Nasdaq-listed Sohu, and property developers Pan Shiyi and Zhang Xin who head Soho China. The second among cities is Shenzhen, one of the first to open up in 1978 under the direction of Paramount Leader Deng Xiaoping. Shanghai has 37 of the 400 richest, including Shi Yuzhi, the billionaire chairman of the New York-listed online game company, Giant Interactive. The fourth is Hangzhou, home to the 39% Yahoo-owned ecommerce giant Alibaba chaired by Jack Ma. Guangzhou and Hong Kong are tied for fifth with nine members each.

Forbes China identifies the best cities in China to do international business with as Guangzhou, Shanghai, Shenzhen, Hangzhou and Souzhou. In an intercultural communication text book, it is interesting for us to note that most of these billionaires are involved heavily in the media which are themselves both intercultural, international and global in scope. This suggests for our intercultural communication students that your future may well be linked to the media field in China. Some of you will be entrepreneurs, opening up your own businesses, or working outside of the State Owned Enterprises (SOEs) and in already very successful businesses and international trade, many of which will be intercultural or international and media related.

Baidu, incorporated January 18, 2000, with $902 million dollars in total assets in 2009, was founded by Robin Li and Eric Xu, both of whom studied and worked in the United States. Li graduated from Peking University, studied computer science at the State University of New York at Buffalo, and worked at Infoseek developing one of the California Silicon Valley's earliest search engine companies. Baidu was the first Chinese company to be listed on Nasdaq 100. This service engine provides 740 million web pages, 80 million images, and 10 million multimedia files (See for example, Kulich & Prosser, 2007 in the Baidu listing). The name was taken from a quote in Xin Oiji's classical poem, "Green Jade Table in the Lantern Festival:" "Having searched for him hundreds and thousands of times in the crowd, suddenly turning back by chance, I find him there in the dimmest candlelight."

Founder and current Baidu chairman Robin Li writes: "Many people have asked about the meaning of our name. 'Baidu' was inspired by a poem written more than 800 years ago during the Song Dynasty. The poem compares the search for a retreating beauty amid chaotic glamour with the search for one's dream while confronted by life's many obstacles. '... hundreds and thousands of times, for her I searched in chaos, suddenly, I turned by chance, to where the lights were waning, and there she stood.' Baidu, whose literal meaning is hundreds of times, represents persistent search for the ideal."

In terms of market share of Internet providers, Baidu held 60% in 2010 and Google China held about 31%, with Yahoo.cn sold to Alibaba, having only 9-10%. In 2008, the Internet advertising market (3.3 million rmb) was dominated by Baidu, Sina, and Google China. David Barboza, writing in The New York Times, (2010: January 13) noted that Baidu had 300 million visitors, a market share of more than $15 billion, or 63% of the Internet search engine in China, but that should Google leave China, while Baidu could expect much short-term gain, by becoming a monopoly, it would tend to become less competitive and innovative. However, after significant difficulties between Google and the Chinese government in 2010, Google did have its license renewed on June 30, 2010.

Conclusion

Two-fifths of the world's 7+ billion people live in Asia. As the nineteenth century is often called the industrial age, or the British century, and the twentieth century is labeled the American century, Martin Jacques thinks that the twenty-first century might indeed be the Asian century, or even the Chinese century, as the title of his book When China Rules the World suggests. It would appear that Arthur Krueger would disagree, but there are many books being written as bestsellers about the China threat. Whether Asians more broadly, and especially China and India, represent the coming global tendencies, or not, as Jacques suggests, serious attention needs to be paid as the century progresses to whether Huntington's "clash of civilizations" will be the dominant factor, or whether both East and West can move toward a more serious "dialogue of civilizations."

References

Auletta, K. (1993, August 2). Raiding the global village. New Yorker.
Huntington, S. P. (1996). The clash of civilizations. New York, NY: Touchstone.

Jacques, M. (2009). When China rules the world. New York, NY: The Penguin Press.

Kuldip, R. R. (2005, Spring). Cultural imperialism or economic necessity? The Hollywood factor in the reshaping of the Asian film industry. Global Media Journal 4, 6.

Li, M. & Prosser, M.H. (2012) Communicating interculturally. Beijing, China: Higher Education Press.

Lindner, E. (2010). Gender,humiliation and global security. Santa Barbara, CA: Praeger.

Powers, J.H. & Kluver,R. (Eds.) (1999). Civic discourse: Civil societies and Chinese communities. Stamford, CT: Ablex.

2. BETWEEN CHINESE AND JAPANESE: BRIDGING THE GAP

Ray T. Donahue
Nagoya Gakuin University, Nagoya, Japan

Heartwarming was a scene of Chinese college students in China collecting donations for the Great East Japan Earthquake, known also as 3/11. A Chinese pointed out that Japan had helped China after a natural catastrophe in the past. The CNN broadcast noted the significance given political tensions between the two countries, particularly unresolved issues related to World War II history. I recall myself how after giving a lecture on Japanese culture to students of Japanese at Tianjin Foreign Studies University, a student came to me at the end and asked, "Why do you like Japan so much" (despite that I made no direct statements as such). Or more recently in Japan, a Chinese exchange student in my sociolinguistics class asked "How come you live in Japan?" Such irony that the first was a Japanese major and the second chose to study in Japan! Their questions belie volumes that could be written, I am sure, about past deep historical feelings. In both cases any reply short of a treatise would likely be insufficient.

In a small way, I would like to contribute to Chinese-Japanese understanding with an anecdote about the Nanking Massacre. This anecdote comes from a very close friend, a Japanese, who is a college professor but also whose father it is about. His father was a retired violinist who was a soldier in Nanking during the massacre. The story is this: My friend once visited his dad only to find him crying. His dad was crying because of so much remorse about the wartime atrocities committed. He told my friend some of the shameful acts committed, such as lining up Chinese in single file to see the power of a Japanese bullet by the number of people it could go through. Nothing can condone such acts of course. But we can well imagine that this man felt a heavy burden throughout his life. Although there are those Japanese ultraists who try to deny such a massacre or that there has been relative silence by the soldiers themselves, it is stories like this man's and others that clearly show not only the profoundly tragic event occurred but it also evinces humanity. However these men may have tried to forget their actions, they could not. They likely lived a tortured life, their souls in so much unrest. Surely they wish(ed) that the tragedy never had happened.

In the absence of such stories, it is easy to imagine that such Japanese, if not the whole nation, are cold hearted, numb of feeling. But, my friends, that is completely untrue. As so often the case, we need to separate a government and its people. Governments are usually unfeeling; but not people. Stripped of politics, we find that people across the world share much in common – that which makes us human.

A principle of intercultural communication is the assumption that others are well intentioned (unless proved otherwise). Without this assumption, we are likely to make the cultural gap much larger than it is. Removed of their humanity, Japanese easily can be imagined as the worse (falsely); therefore not deserving a second look. I hope that stories of remorseful Japanese soldiers will help viewing Japanese in their full humanity and thus possibly narrowing the cultural gap that divides the two peoples.

3. THE PERCEPTION OF THE USCC TOWARD CHINA AND ITS INFLUENCE ON SINO-US RELATIONS

Zhang Shengyong
Dezhou University, Dezhou, China

The US-China Economic and Security Review Commission (USCC) was formed on October 30, 2000 to provide reports concerning relationships between the United States and China with respects to national security, trade and economy. According to the purpose on its website http://www.uscc.gov/about/facts.php, Public Law 109-108 directs the USCC to focus its work and study on the following eight areas: proliferation practices, economic transfers, energy, US capital markets, regional economic and security impacts, US-China bilateral programs, WTO compliance, and the implications of restrictions on speech and access to information in the People's Republic of China. Its first annual report was in 2002. However, as the Commission did not publish an annual report in 2003, so it has submitted seven annual reports to Congress (2002, 2004-2009).

In a letter to congressional leaders in the 2002 annual report, the former chairman of the USCC, C. Richard D'Amato, pointed out that the immediate reason for its formation was the approval of the Permanent Most Favored Nation Trade Relations (PNTR) by the US Congress. During congressional consideration of that legislation, the Clinton Administration asserted that passage of the PNTR and China's entry into the WTO were in the "vital national security of the U.S" (USCC, 2002). Congress charged it to evaluate that assertion over time. Analysis of USCC reports shows that it believes that some of the current trends in US-China relations have negative implications, and as a result, US policies are in need of urgent attention and corrections (USCC, 2002, 2004-2009). Based on the USCC reports themselves and related writings by scholars, such as Sun (2003, 2004), Yu (2003), Xin (2003), Zhang (2003), Jiang (2005), Sun & Liu (2006), Xie (2006), Li (2007), Sun (2007), and Zhang (2009), the perception of China in these annual reports will be discussed from various aspects.

Basic Reasons for Believing That the Commission Reports Are Necessary

In this report, the author tried to explain why the Commission believes that current trends in US-China relations have negative implications for long term economic and national security interests from historical and current perspectives. US misperceptions about China's significance in world affairs (See Cohen, 1990; Schaller, 2000) have a long history. As Sutter (2004) argues, "many Americans think that US leaders made a mistake following President Richard Nixon's historic trip to China in 1972 when they widely believed that as a great power China could force the Soviet Union to abandon its expansionist policies and accommodate the West" (p. 75). Sutter continued to explain that "China was actually a weak state with a stagnating economy and an obsolete military enmeshed in a wrenching leadership struggle, and on the other hand, the United States grossly underestimated Chinese resolve when a million of China's Soviet-backed 'volunteers' first entered the Korean War in 1950 and then misjudged the fighting endurance of those volunteers, who would engage US soldiers for three years of hard combat" (p. 75).

However, the May 4-June 5 Tiananmen Square incident in 1989 quickly replaced the 1980's US perception of China, and "aggressive Chinese military behavior toward Taiwan and the dispute over Taiwan's independence along with other Chinese territorial disputes prompted US concerns about China as a long-term strategic threat capable of contesting US power in the not-so-distant future" (Sutter, 2004, p. 76).

According to many scholars, the "China threat" concept includes both China and the Chinese language as a risk to the United States and other dominant European countries as well as English as a global language (Timberlake & Triplett, 1989; Bernstein & Munroe, 1997; Gertz, 2002; Yee & Storey, 2004, Gold, 2004; Wang, Huters & Karl, 2006; Li, 2008; Jacques, 2009; Karabell, 2009; Wang, 2010; Naisbitt & Naisbitt, 2010, etc.). Zhang (2009) discusses the role of the United States Congressional Commission's annual report on Chinese security, identifying a genuine congressional concern about China's potential threat to the United States Other Chinese scholars (Wu & Liu, 2007; Yao, 2007; and Zhu, 2009) also worry consistently about the United States as a long term threat to China.

Several commissions about China have been established over the years, such as the House US-China Inter-Parliamentary Exchange (1999), the Congressional Executive Commission on China (2000), the US-China Economic and Security Review Commission (2000), the Senate US-China Inter-Parliamentary Exchange (2004), the Congressional China Caucus (2005), the US-China House Working Group (2005) and the US-China Senate Working Group (2006). The Commission holds that the "report will provide a baseline for assessing changes in US-China relations – the positive and the negative – in the years ahead" (USCC, 2002). However, this author concludes that the USCC considers China as an ongoing threat to the US

The USCC General Perception of China

The Commission's evaluation of China holds that China is and will be a major competitor of the United States Its first annual 209-page report in 2002 evaluated China in 10 different fields including China's perceptions of the United States and strategic thinking, trade and investment, China and the World Trade Organization, its political and civil freedom, growth as a regional economic power, presence in US capital markets, China's proliferation and relations with terrorist-sponsoring states, cross-strait security issues, China's defense budget, military economy, technology transfers and military acquisition policies. As a result, twenty recommendations on guiding the relations between America and China were given to the US Congress based on the above evaluations.

In 2004, those central issues included the questions of China's progress in four broad areas: (1) market reforms and trade commitments, (2) cooperation with the United States on national security matters, (3) policies toward openness, human rights, democracy-building, and the rule of law, and (4) the quality of the overall bilateral relationship. In most of these areas, the USCC believed that China's progress had been far from satisfactory, and that it is in the US interest to continue to press China to take more international responsibility (USCC, 2004). Concerning questions such as openness, human rights, democracy-building and the rule of law, USCC regularly stated that China simply failed to meet a minimal standard of progress (USCC, 2004-2009).

The 2006 annual report borrowed the notion of a "responsible stakeholder" in the international community – that is, a state that not only observes international norms but works to strengthen those norms – as a measure of Chinese activities (USCC, 2006). However, it was USCC's judgment that, while China's influence was growing as its national strength increased, and there remained many reasons to think that China might in the future stand as a pillar of the world, its behavior as yet was far from that standard. Furthermore, it suggested that many of the trends (trades in China's foreign policy, China's military modernization and China's regional activity) of 2005 had raised serious doubts whether China was willing or prepared to play the role. For example, although China is integrated increasingly into the international economy, the USCC believed that profound differences remained between "the open-market US approach and the managed trade principles and predatory practices observed by the Chinese government" (USCC, 2006). In particular, the USCC reported that "China's record of adhering to the obligations it incurred upon its entry into the WTO had been inconsistent, and it remains an open question whether China would change its domestic practices to observe international trade norms or will continue to bend current norms to suit its domestic practices" (USCC, 2006).

The USCC also concluded that China to become a responsible stakeholder was urgent because of threats to international security, terrorism and weapons of mass destruction, the challenges of the economic globalization, the weaknesses of failed and failing states, environmental degradation, etc. According to the 2006 report, world security and prosperity, public health, and liberty all needed China to devote to the world interest rather than to focus on its own national interests (2006).

On the contrary, other international media watched China and the Chinese role in the world very differently. China Daily, the official language newspaper of the Chinese government, covers the cooperation between China and the United States frequently, such as the report on March 4, 2007 that China and the United States should work together to maintain world stability and peace. US Deputy Secretary of State John Negroponte disclosed that the United States was seeking to work cooperatively with China on many issues, which would benefit the two countries and the rest of the world. (China Daily, March 4, 2007).

Also, as reported in the New York Times, the US undersecretary of state for economic, energy and agricultural affairs commented at Davos 2010 (The Davos meeting is designed to offer a platform for stakeholders to discuss world pressing issues) that if the United States and China "work together we can deal with almost all the major global crises, and stressed that success in clean technologies was not a 'zero-sum game'" (Bennhold, 2010).

There seem to be differences between the Commission and the media's perception towards China. An open and objective truth should always make communication smooth and healthy. However, the Commission's view on China has been mostly negative as analyzed by the author.

At Presidents Hu Jintao and Barack Obama's meeting in Beijing on November 17, 2009, China and the United States agreed that "the US-China Strategic and Economic Dialogue (August, 2010) ... offers a unique forum to promote understanding, expand common ground, reduce differences, and develop solutions to common problems." Presidents Hu and Obama further agreed that: China and the United States have an increasingly broad base of cooperation and share increasingly important common responsibilities on many major issues concerning global stability and prosperity; the two countries should further strengthen coordination and cooperation, work together to tackle challenges, and promote world peace, security and prosperity and the two sides are determined to work together to achieve more sustainable and balanced global economic growth (US-China Joint Statement, November 17, 2009).

I believe that it is normal for the United States to concern itself regarding the development of a rising superpower such as China or, in contrast, for China to worry about perceived threats coming from such world powers as the United States or Russia. Facing China's development and its difference in political structure and ideology, the United States Commission has argued that the United States had the right to show its concern over the emerging China and to be anxious about some trends that would influence its own interest (Zhang, 2009). However, from the perspective of China, its leaders and spokespersons have consistently affirmed that such a concern is meddling unfairly in its internal affairs and the Ministry of Foreign Affairs of the People's Republic of China has consistently and firmly opposed all the Commission's annual reports.

Evaluation of the China-US Trade and Economic Relationship

According to the USCC's 2006 annual report, China was America's third largest trading partner behind Canada and Mexico, but the report argued that China's trade relationship with the United States was extremely unbalanced as China was then exporting to the United States six times the value that it imported from the United States which led to an increasing trade deficit for the United States. This deficit witnessed twenty-three percent of the total US deficits in 2006. Therefore, the USCC argued that the increasing US deficit and the pouring of the private capital into China as well as China's investment in US capital markets had caused China's increasing national power.

The Commission repeated regularly in its annual reports that the major drivers of China's comparative advantage were considered to be unfair trading practices. These included China's undervalued currency, counterfeiting and piracy, export industry subsidies and the lack of protection of US intellectual property rights. The Commission held that those violations and unfair practices also contributed to a growing US trade deficit with China (USCC, 2004-2009).

Concerning the reform of the Chinese currency, China has been denying the criticism from the United States, Europe and others on the RMB's exchange rate to the dollar. The USCC reports agreed that "currency reform alone was not the solution to rebalancing the US-China relationship because the deficit and disadvantages were compounded by China's other unfair trading practices" (USCC, 2006). In Davos 2010, the People's Bank of China Deputy Governor Zhu Min told the World Economic Forum at its annual meeting on January 30th that China will maintain an accommodative monetary policy, aiming for annual economic growth of 8% to 9% (Watts, 2010). Meanwhile, Zhu Min pointed out that China will stick to the current monetary and fiscal policy to keep the RMB at reasonable level.

The Commission recommended that the United States should cooperate with the EU, Japan, and other interested nations to address mutual – and security – related concerns with China, such as to move China to increase the value of the Chinese RMB, to issue an annual joint assessment of China's compliance with the rules of WTO, and to develop embargos on China. Meanwhile, the USCC has continued to ignore the progress that China has made in market reform, such as property rights reform, market (pricing) reform, enterprise reform, and reform of the political system, which allowed China to become the world's third-largest economy, surpassing Germany in 2009, and expected to surpass Japan in 2010. This author believes that these recent Chinese achievements could not have been completed without progress in market reform.

In contrast to the Commission's conclusion, the cooperation between the United States and China has become more important than any period, and the US-China Strategic and Economic Dialogue (S&ED) provided a platform to reduce differences (Liu Hong, July 30, 2009). David Loevinger, senior coordinator for China Affairs and the US-China Strategic and Economic Dialogue, has told Xinhua that the United States and China act very quickly and aggressively on global economic crisis (July 30, 2009). Even though the world was facing a serious global economic crisis in 2008, the USCC's 2008 Annual Report mentioned nothing about the issue. Continually, the reports recommend that the Congress adopt more sanctions on China (USCC, 2008).

Following US President Barack Obama's visit to China in November 2009, the two governments issued a joint declaration saying "they are committed to building a positive, cooperative and comprehensive China-US relationship for the 21st century, and will take concrete actions to steadily build a partnership to address common challenges" (US-China Joint Statement, November 17, 2009). In the new era of China-US relationship, trade and economics both have strategic significance. Today, China and the United States are each other's second largest trade partners and their trade volume has increased by 130 times in the past 30 years (2009: A Year of Cooperation and Conflicts for China-US Trade Relations, December 23, 2009).

Regarding compliance with the rules of the WTO, the USCC stated that China's adherence to its many WTO obligations remained spotty and halting in important areas five years after China attained WTO membership. As a result, US exporters and investors had been facing a variety of non-tariff barriers and major impediments in conducting business in

China. China's failure to enforce intellectual property rights provides such an egregious case of its noncompliance with WTO rules in the view of the Commission (USCC, 2006, 2007). However, in the Commission's 2007 report to Congress on China's WTO Compliance, it pointed out that China "did make some progress" in complying with the rules of the WTO (2007 Report to Congress on China's WTO Compliance, 2007). In the report, it said that China has taken many impressive steps to reform its economy, making progress in implementing a set of sweeping commitments that required it to reduce tariff rates, dispel non-tariff barriers, provide the same favorable policy to foreign countries as what the Chinese enterprises enjoy in the domestic trades, and protect intellectual property rights. Although not complete in every respect, "China's implementation of its WTO commitments has led to significant increases in US-China trade, including US exports to China" (2007 Report to Congress on China's WTO Compliance, 2007). In this case, the Commission did have some rare positive statements about China's progress, but it is clearly possible to notice in general the Commission's negative attitude towards China. This author believes that the Commission reports tend to focus on its perceived negative perspectives of China's current condition and has quoted a one-sided outlook to promote its own China threat speculations and recommendations.

Evaluation of China's Military Power

China's growing military power has been another great concern in the USCC's annual reports, including China's nuclear proliferation, China's military modernization and its effects against American interests and regional security. Generally the USCC has consistently held that the development of China's military power and weapon exportation was threatening America's security. In its annual report of 2002, it pointed out the reasons for such a concern in this field. On one hand, China's power growth and the increasing world politics improved China's confidence to compete with America. On the other hand, China had particularly developed relationships with oil-rich terrorist-sponsoring countries to provide China with long-term economic and strategic interests and extend China's global reach. In the Commission's opinion, the Chinese government had made numerous multilateral and bilateral promises to stop weapons and nuclear proliferation originating in China, but despite repeated promises had not kept its word. This situation was a major item at the summit meeting between Presidents George W. Bush and Jiang Zemin in February 2002. However, less progress has been made during the meeting.

Meanwhile, the Commission denied that China was exerting its full efforts to work with America in joint anti-terrorist efforts. The USCC stated that since September 11th, 2001, Beijing had expressed support for and had implemented a working relationship with the United States on some elements of anti-terrorist efforts, but that the Chinese nuclear proliferation and cooperation with terrorist-sponsoring countries had continued (USCC, 2002). These relationships, the Commission warned, enhanced Beijing's political and military influence and helped ensure a diversified source of energy to meet its own growing energy needs. Therefore, the USCC concluded that the US military sanctions policies to deter China's proliferation practices need immediate review. Then, the Commission recommended that Congress should create new authorization to broaden proliferation sanctions (USCC, 2002). However, US Secretary of State Hillary Rodham Clinton has more recently stated that China is "very much engaged" in working with the United States to punish Iran for its nuclear program (Rozen & Negrin, January 29, 2010).

In its 2006 annual report, the Commission said that "China was pursuing measures to try to control the Western Pacific seas and was developing space warfare weapons that would impede US command and control" (USCC, 2006). In 2007, the USCC stressed that Chinese espionage behavior in the United States was so extensive that it comprised the single greatest risk to the security of American technologies. In addition, the 2007 annual report emphasized that Chinese military strategists had embraced disruptive warfare techniques, including the use of cyber attacks, and had incorporated them in China's military defense practices. In all, such attacks could have extremely harmful consequence on America's critical infrastructure. Regarding cyber attacks, the Commission argued that China was actively engaging in cyber reconnaissance by probing the computer networks of US government agencies as well as private companies (USCC, 2007).

Hillary Clinton also attacked China's internet policy, saying that China is one of the countries to see "a spike in threats to the free flow of information" (Clinton, January 21, 2010). China "resolutely opposes such remarks and practices that contravene facts and undermine China-US relations" according to Foreign Ministry Spokesperson Ma Zhaoxu in his remarks on her China-related speech "Internet Freedom" (January 22, 2010). Ma replied that China's internet is open, so hacking and attacking others' privacy is forbidden by law in China. As a major victim concerning the problem, China believes that "the international community should intensify the cooperation in jointly combating internet hacking so as to safeguard internet security and protect the privacy of citizens in accordance with law" (January 22, 2010).

On China's nuclear proliferation, the Commission pointed out that it was vital for US national security for China to ensure that it was not the source of proliferation contrary to its commitments, and recommended that it was "equally vital for other nations committed to nonproliferation to monitor China's adherence to its commitments and insist that China honor them" (USCC, 2007). As a result, one of the conclusions of the Commission was that if China wanted to be perceived as a responsible stakeholder, China must stop providing trade and diplomatic support to North Korea and Iran, which were under international pressure to end their WMD programs (USCC, 2006-2008).

Evaluation of China's High-Technology and Science Development

Briefly speaking, China's technological development caused America's anxiety and suspicion about the potential threat that China posed to US interests (USCC, 2004-2009). Throughout the reports, this author finds that the USCC has shown greater and greater concern over the development of China's science and technology. In 2002, its annual report mentioned only a little information in this respect. But in 2004, the USCC provided four pages to illustrate China's developing science strategy. In 2005, twenty-seven pages' evaluated China's technological development and implications for the US defense industrial base. It was noted (USCC, 2005) that

China's plan for science and technology incorporated elements of previous similar plans, but also collected important social factors such as needed institutional and cultural reforms. The Commission also emphasized on the importance of domestic innovation rather than reliance on imported high-tech products. It can easily be seen that China's great achievements in science and technology these years from the Commission's evaluation were a source of considerable concern to the United States The Commission stressed that Chinese policies promote "leapfrogging" by adapting already existing technology from the United States (USCC, 2006). "This speeds product development and saves China the time and cost of accomplishing the intermediate steps" (Excutive Summary of USCC 2006 Annual Report, p.8). However, according to the USCC's (2007) view, industrial espionage by China had contributed to this process. A major objective of the Chinese Science and Technology policy is to acquire technology that will strengthen the PLA (People's Liberation Army) while it also realizes commercial benefits (USCC, 2007).

Most of the Commission's reports to Congress recommend that the US government develop a comprehensive national strategy to meet China's challenge to the leadership of the United States in science and technology, as America's economic competitiveness, standard of living, and national security depend on such leadership. Therefore, the Commission recommended the following:

(I)   that Congress urge the US administration to publish a national strategy on security that strengthens American's interest all over the world.

(II)   that Congress direct the Department of Commerce and the Office of the US Trade Representative (USTR) to study and report on China's improvement of domestic technology standards and "whether non-performance-based standards are creating an unjustified market barrier to US goods" (USCC, 2007).This echoes its previous recommendation that: if the study finds that China's standard setting process is acting as a market access restriction, Congress should direct USTR to identify standards under development and to intervene with Chinese officials early in the standard development process, and to consider filing a WTO case to address restrictive standards that are already in effect (USCC, 2005).

(III)   that Congress increase intelligence community resources for collection and analysis focused on China's technology development, as it is vital that "US policy makers have access to current, accurate, and complete information on China's technological development" (USCC, 2005).

(IV)   that Congress direct the US administration to prepare and submit quadrennial reviews of any strategies by foreign countries or companies to get critical defense technologies (USCC, 2008).

However, China has been emphasizing cooperation in science and technology with the United States since 2007, and the US Commerce Department and China signed "Guidelines for US-China High-Technology and Strategic Trade Development," which outline the importance of working cooperatively to achieve the mutual benefits of promoting secure, bilateral civilian high-technology trade. Under the principle, the US-China Joint Commission on Commerce and Trade (JCCT) High-Technology Working Group agreed to share more information on market opportunities and identify and eliminate unnecessary barriers to bilateral, civilian high-technology trade (The United States-China Government Signing Ceremony fact sheet, December 11, 2007). When Chinese Premier Wen Jiabao met with US Delegates to the US-China Strategic Forum on Clean Energy Cooperation on October 21, 2009, he "called on the governments, enterprises and scientific research and academic institutions of both countries to join efforts in enhancing energy and environment cooperation. Such cooperation is important work and in the interests of both countries and the world." He said that the two countries should advance cooperation in this area to bring benefit to mankind and future generations (Wen Jiabao Meets with US Delegates to the US-China Strategic Forum on Clean Energy Cooperation, October 21, 2009).

All in all, the Commission's evaluation of China includes nearly every aspect of the Sino-US relations. Although the emphasis of each annual report differs, several reach the same conclusion: that is, based on their analyses to date, the Commission believes that "a number of the current trends in US-China relations have negative implications for the long term economic and national security interests, and therefore that the US policies in these areas are in need of urgent attention and course corrections" (USCC, 2002, p.1; 2004, p.1). As a result, it clearly reflects the US concern for China's emergence in the world and anxiety about its rising. This author, from reading and analyzing those recommendations, has argued that nearly all the recommendations consider containment as the main policy in Sino-US relations (See also Zhang, 2003; Sun, 2007).

Conclusion

Although China consistently argues that the US Commission is meddling in its internal affairs, it is normal for a superpower such as the United States to concern itself with a rising superpower such as China. Facing China's development and its difference in political structure and ideology, America has the right to show its concern about the emerging China as a superpower and to be anxious about some trends that influence its own interests. But considering the USCC's evaluation of China by comparing it with various media's views on China, its attitude is almost consistently negative. The statement by China's Foreign Ministry spokesperson Qin Gang in response to the 2008 annual report argues that the Commission always sees China through tinted lenses, and creates obstacles for China-US cooperation in extensive fields by tarnishing and attacking China deliberately and misleading the general public: The report was flatly unfounded and the Commission will never succeed in its attempts.... (We) advise the Commission to reverse its course, stop issuing reports of this kind, and stop interfering in China's internal affairs, so as not to further undermine its own image. (Qin, 2008).

As China's power grows, Chinese leaders presumably will become more confident in exerting China's influence in world affairs. In April 2009, President Barack Obama and President Hu Jintao announced a new dialogue as a part of the administration's efforts to build a positive, cooperative and comprehensive relationship with Beijing (Clinton & Geithner, 2009). The Chinese government in 2009 reported that China seeks a 20-year period to focus primarily on internal development as stressed by Chinese President Hu Jintao when he addressed the Study Session of Communist Party of China on Global New Military Changes on May 24, 2009. He stated that Chinese leaders intend to continue trying to stabilize China's international environment to preserve good conditions for Chinese economic development. With the growing communication with China, more specialists outside of China think that recent behavior and trends in China suggest a continued comparatively cooperative and accommodating Chinese approach to most world issues for the foreseeable future.

Hu Jintao and Wen Jibao represent the first peaceful transmission of power by Chinese leaders. Following the fourth generation of Chinese leaders since the founding of the PRC, the succession by a fifth generation of leaders is currently ongoing in an orderly fashion. There likely will come a point well before 2020 when Chinese leaders will develop sufficient power to choose a different and more assertive approach to international affairs. Unfortunately, the evidence is insufficient to determine if that approach will support or oppose US interests in the prevailing world order. However, according to Clinton and Geithner (2009), few global problems can be solved by the United States or China alone and few can be solved without the United States and China together. The strength of the global economy, the health of the global environment, the stability of fragile states and the solution to nonproliferation challenges turn in large measure on cooperation between the United States and China. Therefore, this author agrees with Sutter (2004) who said that "prudence seems to argue for a middle course in US policy that works for cooperation but is prepared for difficulty and challenge" (p. 88).

This analysis has longitudinally assessed the Commission's own statements from 2002 to 2009 about what it sees as the trends of the Sino-American cooperation, and cross-cultural analysis has considered the Chinese and American perspectives and statements on the major issues confronting this bilateral relationship over time. Even though some difficulties in the relationship have developed recently, this author believes that overall the Chinese-American relationship will continue to move towards cooperation in many of the areas which have been discussed in this paper.

References

2009: A year of cooperation and conflicts for China-US trade relations. Retrieved December 23, 2009 from http://www.china.org.cn/world/2009-12/23/ content_19117866.htm.

Bennhold, K. (2010: January 10). Race is on to develop green, clean technology. Retrieved January 30, 2010 from http://www.nytimes.com/2010/01/30/business/global/30davos.html?emc=eta1.

Bernstein, R. & Munro, R. H. (1997). The coming conflict with China. New York, NY: Knopf.

China and the US Lead Global Smart Meter Trend. Retrieved January 31, 2010 from http://www.smartmeters.com/the-news/794-china-and-the-us-lead-global-smart-meter-trend.html.

Claburn, T. (2007: November 21). China espionage top threat to US tech, USCC report. Information Week.

Clinton, H. R. (2010; January 21). Remarks on Secretary of State Hillary Clinton on "internet freedom." http://beijing.usembassy-china.org.cn/012110ir.html.

Clinton, H. R. & Geithner, T. (2009, July 29). A new strategic and economic dialogue with China. Wall Street Journal.

Cohen,W. I. (1990). America's response to China. New York, NY: Columbia University Press.

Foreign Ministry Spokesperson Ma Zhaoxu's Remarks on China-related Speech by US Secretary of State on "Internet Freedom" Retrieved January 22, 2010 from http://www.fmprc.gov.cn/eng/xwfw/s2510/t653351.htm.

Gertz, B. (2002). The China threat: How the People's Republic targets America. Washington, DC: Regnery Publishing Company.

Ho, K. L. & Ku, S. C. Y.(2005). China and Southeast Asia: Global changes and regional challenges. Taibei, Taiwan: National Sun Yat-sen University Press.

Hu Jintao Addresses CPC's Study Session on Global New Military Changes. Retrieved May 24, 2003 from http://xinhua.net.

Jacques, M. (2009). When China rules the world: The end of the western world and the birth of a new global world order. London, England: Allen Lane.

Jiang, X. Y. (2005). US congress and the making of US security policy towards China. Beijing, China: Shishi Press.

Karabell, Z. (2009). Superfusion: How China and America become one economy and why the world's prosperity depends on it. New York, NY: Simon and Schuster.

Knowlton, B. (2010: January 26). China Leads Better-Than-Expected Global Recovery. New York Times. Retrieved January 26, 2010 from http://www.nytimes.com/2010/01/27/business/global/27imf. html?emc=eta1.

Li, M. (2008). The rise of China and the demise of China and the demise of the capitalist world economy. London, England: Pluto Press.

Li, Q.S. (2002). US Congress and American policy towards China. Beiijng, China: World Press

Liu, H. (2009: July 30). Senior US official says cooperation with China never so important. Retrieved July 30, 2009 from http://english.dbw. cn/system/2009/07/30/ 000148765.shtml.

Ma, Z. (2010); January 22). Remarks on the China-related speech by the US Secretary of State on 'Internet Freedom.' Beijing, China: China Foreign Ministry.

Naisbitt, J. & Naisbitt, D. (2010). China's megatrends: The 8 pillars of a new society. New York, NY: Harper Collins.

Qin, G. (2008: November 24). Foreign Ministry spokesperson Qin Gang's remarks on the US-China Economic and Security Review Commission, 2008. http://www.chinaembassy.org.nz.

Rozen, L. & Negrin, M. (2010; January 29). Hillary Clinton: China helping US on Iran. http://www.politico.com/news/stories/0110/32199. html.

Schaller, M.(2002).The United States and China. Oxford: Oxford University Press.

Seldin, R. (2006: June 23). The commissions in US Congress. Asian Times.

Sun, L. (2007). Analyzing US-China Economic and Security Review Commission. Tribune of Social Sciences, No.3.pp. 36-46.

Sun, Z. (2003). Study of US Congress. Shanghai, China: Fudan University Press.

Sun, Z. (2004). Studies of US congress and sino-US relations----case and analysis. Beijing, China: Shishi Press.

Sutter, R. (2003-2004; Winter). Why does China matter? The Washington Quarterly, 27:1. pp. 75–89.

The big issues between China and America from 1972 to 2008, Retrieved December 31, 2009 from http://world.people.com.cn/GB/8212/142261/142271/8610214.html.

The United States-China government signing ceremony fact sheet, Retrieved December 11, 2007 from http://beijing.usembassy-china.org.cn/121107jcct3.html.

Timberlake, E. & Triplett II, W.C. (1989). Red dragon rising: Communist China's military threat to America. Washington, DC: Regnery.

Tkacik Jr., J. J. (2008: August 8). Trojan dragon: China's cyber threat. Backgrounder, No. 2106.

United States Trade Representative (2007). 2007 Report to Congress on China's WTO Compliance. http://www.ustr.gov/sites/default/files/asset_upload_file625_13692.pdf.

USCC. (2002: July).The US-China Economic and Security Commission Annual Report. http://www.USCC.gov/index.

USCC. (2004: June). The US-China Economic and Security Commission Annual Report. http://www.USCC.gov/index.

USCC. (2005: November). The US-China Economic and Security Commission Annual Report. http://www.USCC.gov/index.

USCC. (2006: November). The US-China Economic and Security Commission Annual Report. http://www.USCC.gov/index.

USCC. (2007: June). The US-China Economic and Security Commission Annual Report. http://www.USCC.gov/index.

USCC. (2008: October). The US-China Economic and Security Commission Annual Report. http://www.USCC.gov/index.

USCC. (2009: November). The US-China Economic and Security Commission Annual Report. http://www.USCC.gov/index.

US-China Joint Statement, Retrieved November 17, 2009 from http://beijing.usembassy-china.org.cn/111709.html.

US seeks closer cooperation with China in securing world peace, Retrieved March 4, 2007 from http://www.chinadaily.com.cn/china/2007-03/04/content_819174.htm.

Wang, H. (2010). The end of the revolution: China and the limits of modernity. London, England: Verso.

Wang, H., Huters, T., & Karl, R.E. (2006). China's new order: Society, politics, and economy in transition. Cambridge, MA: Harvard University Press.

Watts, W.L. (January 30, 2010). No change for China's monetary, currency policies, Market Watch. See also: http://www.marketwatch.com/story/china-sticking-to- monetary-currency-policies-2010-01-30.

Wen Jiabao meets with US delegates to the US-China Strategic Forum on clean energy cooperation, Retrieved October 21, 2009 from http://www.chinaconsulatesf.org/ eng/xw/t622137.htm.

Wu, L. & Liu, X. (September, 2007). The 'China Energy Threat' thesis and Sino-US relations: A critical review. Journal of Middle Eastern and Islamic Studies (in Asia).1. 1.

Xin, Q. (2003). US congress and Taiwan issue. Shanghai, China: Fudan University Press.

Yao, K. (September, 2007). Development of Sino-Arab relations and the evolution of China's Middle East policy in the new era. Journal of Middle Eastern and Islamic Studies (in Asia). 1.1.

Yee, H. & Storey, I. (2004). China threat: Perceptions, myths, and reality. New York, NY: RoutledgeCurzon.

Zhang, S. Y. (2009). USCC's cognition on China and its influence on Sino-US relations. Unpublished MA thesis. Shanghai, China: Shanghai International Studies University.

Zhu, W. (March, 2009). Understanding and respect: On establishing a Chinese discourse for Middle East studies. Journal of Middle Eastern and Islamic Studies (in Asia). 3.1.

4. Chinese and Japanese Relationships: Observations of Three Generations of Chinese Citizens

Zhang Shengyong
Dezhou University, Dezhou, China

Introduction

The relations between China and Japan always make people alert and sensitive. In China, we know the general description about Japan from the geography book in primary school. That is, China and Japan are neighbors that are separated only by a strip of water. However, we just couldn't get through the water. As a result, although Japan is close to China in geography, it is also a country that remains a huge distance from China for us as Chinese emotionally. As a learner in intercultural communication, I feel strongly that what China and Japan need badly is to communicate with one another. However, to communicate easily with Japan is just as difficult as to cross the water between the two countries.

This essay presents the relations between China and Japan from three generations of Chinese citizens and also some background on these relationships. Therefore, the content related to my three family generations reflects the perceived truth in China about how the relations change from one generation to another.

The story covers mainly my own family. But the family can be considered as a mirror of many families in China. On one hand, it is subjective to some extent in describing the relations because many more families in different parts of China should be interviewed to add evidence of the Chinese attitudes toward Japan and the Japanese. On the other hand, it is objective because it tells a true story in my family about how the relations influenced their life in each generation. Besides, as an individual family in China, it is inevitable to communicate with others, to share the current thinking and to accept some information that is closer to the perceived truth. Then the content could be more convincing.

I as a member of the family was born in 1980, a period for China opening its gate to the outside world. My father was born in 1955 and my mother was born in 1952, a period for China depending mainly on its own power to develop its economy. My grandparents were born in the 1920s, about 10 years before Japan invaded China. So they survived the war and witnessed the foundation of the new China. My grandmother died in 1998 and my grandfather in 2008 respectively. So this essay is also for remembering my grandparents who told me the suffering in their growing up and the hard life in the anti-Japanese war. Then it is necessary to introduce the profession of each generation. My grandparents were both peasants. The peasants made up as high as 90% of the whole population at that time in China. So their life and attitude towards Japan could reflect the basic condition in their time.

My parents were the early group to find a job in a town instead of continuing farming as their parents did in rural areas. My father worked for the government and my mother worked in several state-owned enterprises (all which went bankrupt in the process of economic reform). Meanwhile, they experienced the Cultural Revolution from 1966–1976. My mother became a laid-off worker in 1998, influenced by the economic reform. I joked with my mother that she was the victim of reform. Then my mother smiled sadly without saying anything. She expected to find another job. However, after several short-life works, she decided to sell plastic bags to shops. Thus the life of their generation is so complicated that the rise and decline of their destiny represent the transition of China both in politics and its economy. I teach at the university of Dezhou, a relatively small city in Shandong Province.

Since I was born in a very common family, education seemed to be an ideal way to change my life. I am happy that I got well educated. So I represent the generation who benefited from the reform. Meanwhile, this generation faces challenges in every aspect of our life, dreams and reality, individuality and collectivity, rebellion and compromise.

*The relations between China and Japan in my grandparents'
generation.*

When I was a child, my grandparents always told me about their life
when growing up. Life was tough and poor already under the Nanjing
KMT government in the 1920s. Japan's invasion made it worse.

On the 18th of September 1931, the Japanese army attacked Shenyang,
a city of the Northeast provinces of China. Meanwhile, Japan started to
invade all the three provinces in the Northeast. However, the leader of the
Kuomingtang, Chiang Kai-shek, telegrammed to General Zhang Xueliang
"... try to avoid the clash with Japanese troops no matter how they make
belligerent acts in Northeast provinces, and your army cannot resist ..."
(Composing team for anti-Japanese war, 2011, p.137)

Although Japan threatened to invade the inner land of China, Chiang
ignored this potential threat and concentrated all his forces against the
Communists. As a result, with a crushing force, Japanese troops conquered
dozens of coastal cities despite brave resistance by the Chinese army
and civilians. After the September 18th incident in 1931, Japan's troops
continued the policy of invading China. Consequently, the Northeast
provinces (Heilongjiang Province, Jilin Province and Liaoning Province)
were occupied by Japan very quickly.

As soon as the news spread that we lost the territory in the Northeast
of China, the young people in China, including my grandfather, expected
the KMT government to fight against the invaders. However, the news
that they received became worse and worse.

On 7th July 1937, Japanese troops launched a "practice with live
ammunition" at the Lugouqiao (Lugou Bridge) in Beijing. As a result, the
Lugouqiao incident broke out. It was the prelude of the struggle of all
the Chinese people against the Japanese aggression. Soon in September
1937, Japanese forces arrived at the gate outside of Dezhou, the district
which my grandparents' hometown belonged to. Although the national
army was outnumbered by the enemy, they defended the city bravely
and fearlessly. Consequently, Dezhou City was occupied because of the
huge disparity between the Chinese army and Japanese force. After the
Japanese army conquered Dezhou, they committed monstrous crimes by

killing people, burning houses, raping the women and plundering the property of ordinary citizens.

My grandfather was about 18 years old. He had joined several protests against the Japanese's heinous behavior in Dezhou, including a general strike along the Majiahe River. In order to control the protests in this area, Japanese troops were stationed in Renjia Village, only 2 kilometers away from my grandfather's. At that time my grandfather made a living by being a stonemason when farming was not busy. However, the Japanese had forbidden all the local trades. Much metal equipment was taken away by the Japanese soldiers in case they could be used as weapons against them. Facing losing his home and outraged by Japan's cruel control, my grandfather secretly joined the local militia to fight against the Japanese control. My grandfather was appointed as the company commander of the local militia because of his courage and meritorious service.

I had asked my grandfather once before why he joined the militia and whether he knew that his action could bring disaster to the whole family. He answered me very briefly, "I want my home." After a short while, he continued the question. "I know my family could be killed by Japanese soldiers at anytime. But I had nothing because the soldiers took away all my belongings. How can I protect my family? You know, your grandmother and other members could starve to death." After these words, my grandfather paused for a long time. At last, he said, "The war made me homeless. I hope the peace could be always with you." My grandfather died in 2008. At that time, I was in Shanghai. So I didn't see him at the last moment. But I could remember clearly the words he told me when I visited him, which is "May the peace be with you." He died as a Christian. He became a Christian in his 70s. From his words we can know the anti-Japanese war influenced him deeply and the humble feeling from a common Chinese how important peace is for people.

My grandfather loved me most in my opinion. Maybe it is because I was the only one among his 11 grandchildren who entered the university. So every time when I was with him, he liked to tell me his early life. However, I was young, and sometime I became very impatient to stop him or find an excuse to get outside of his room. But I know about him as he left me forever. "I do miss you, grandfather!"

According to my broken memory, grandfather told me what he did in the war. "We did everything we could to cause trouble for the Japanese troops," my grandfather told me one day. I found the similar description in The Anti-Japanese War in Dezhou written by Guo Xinzhong (2010) of Dezhou University, a part of Columns of Dezhou Local Culture Research. It says:

"In order to break the roads built for the advance weapons of Japanese troops, the villagers united together to dig a hole with 5 meters width and one meter deep every 10 meters in the road. Or they cut the power lines to destroy the enemy's communication system. In the autumn of 1940, more than thousand of villagers organized by 4 team leaders gathered in the two roads, one from Qingyun to Banying, the other from Qingyun to Renjia Village (2 kilometers away from my grandfather's village). They spent one night in breaking the roads as long as 50 kilometers. And a local song was very popular at that time. It records how the villagers broke the road. ... Japs (Japanese) built the road in the day, and we broke it in the night. Then the earth on the road became sand alike. So it delayed the Japs' horse and car, which made them desperated." During the 8 years of the war, the villagers in Qingyun broke the road as long as 500 kilometers and cut the power lines as heavy as 5,000 kilograms (pp.146-147)."

He also told me a story that happened in a village near his. And I also found it in the book. It reads:

"The local militias united together to fight against the enemy. On 8th December 1944, Brigade 6th of the puppet troops (mainly Chinese soldiers organized by Japanese officers to control the local people) surrounded Liugui Village. The village militia and villagers had a fierce battle with the enemy in the galleys. A militia named Wang Xianfa, after using up all the bullets, took the hay cutter to fight till his last moment (149-150)."

The stories like this lasted all through the war. When I asked my grandfather whether he worried about the possibility of losing the war, he said firmly, "Impossible!" "Why are you so sure?" I continued. "Because we are the right side, it is Japan who invaded us. So they have to return all belongings to us." The answer is very simple but deserves reflecting on Japan about the historical problem. My grandfather was just an ordinary peasant. But he used the simplest words to express the most significant meaning. What Mencius (n. d.) said, that a just cause enjoys abundant support while an unjust cause finds little, conveys the exact meaning of what my grandfather said.

So here we can find very different attitudes towards history in China and Japan. The people of my grandfather's generation experienced the war themselves. They have enough qualification to tell the truth because the war brought disaster not only for them but also for Japanese. Therefore, to face the war truly was their basic attitude to show the respect for all the people who died in the war. Besides, the top-level visits by Japanese leaders, including recent prime ministers to the Yashukuni Jinja shrine that honors convicted war criminals have deeply hurt the feelings of Chinese and Asian people, and have also formed political obstacles in Sino-Japanese relations.

At present, every country should try to be a responsible stakeholder in the world. However, if Japan always denies its history, how can it deserve the trust from other countries, especially from the countries which suffered a lot, such as China, South Korea, the Democratic People's Republic of Korea, Singapore and other Asian countries? Besides, one of the government's functions is to let its citizen know their roots and original identity, that is, the truth in its historical development. However, the Japanese government approved several history textbook changes used in the secondary education (junior and high schools) of Japan. The changes "primarily concern what some international observers perceive to be Japanese nationalist efforts to whitewash the actions of the Empire of Japan during World War II" (Wikipedia, July 2012). So when we think about it, if the youth of a country couldn't face its history, how do we expect them to take an honest attitude towards its county's future? If a government couldn't take a responsible attitude towards its neighbor countries, how do we expect it to be responsible for the rest of the world?

History is written by human beings. So history should record the truth, although different cultures and countries may identify their version of truth differently. Only by doing this can we know about our ancestors and continue to walk forward. The war caused extraordinary suffering and disaster to China and other Asian countries. The war is like a scar in the heart. It is impossible for any country to change it or whitewash it. It reminds me of my trip in New Zealand in early 2009. When we visited the Auckland Museum, there was an exhibition named "Scars on the Heart to honor World War II Asia Wars." Lots of photos and video programs reflected what had happened in the war. So we remember history not to revenge but to remind ourselves to cherish the peace.

History shouldn't be a burden to improve the relations between China and Japan. On the contrary, history should be an accelerator to strengthen the positive relations between China and Japan. Both governments have to take a responsible attitude to educate their youth to remember the history and lead the patriotic spirit correctly.

The relations between China and Japan in my parents' generation

After 8 years' anti-Japanese war from 1937-1945 and another 3 years' civil war, the People's Republic of China was founded on October 1, 1949. However, the conditions were unfavorable. New China was isolated by the capitalist countries with the United States as the head, despite the fact that the United States had fought along side the Chinese in World War II against the Japanese. They cut all the economic trade and political dialogue with China. Consequently, after several years' hot war, China was dragged into the Cold War.

However, the Americans' assistance combined with Japanese government's interventionism contributed directly to Japan's economic miracle after WWII. On one hand, as we know, the Korean War broke out in 1950. And it strengthened Japan's role as one of America's arsenals in Asia. So the American government played a crucial role in Japan's initial economic recovery. This also partly explains why Japan's foreign policy very often follows the American order. On the other hand, the Japanese government's measures fostered rapid postwar growth. According to Mikiso Hane(1996), the period from the Korean War leading up to the late 1960s saw the greatest years of prosperity in economy. Besides, the Japanese government paid more attention to post-war education, which contributed strongly to its modernizing process. As a result, Japan had become the second largest economy of the world, after the United States, since 1968. Of course, China formally overtook Japan as the world's second largest economy in 2010.

But the new China was dogged by misfortunes. Facing the severe situation of the world, Chairman Mao Zedong advanced the principle of "Starting anew," "putting the house in order before inviting guests" and "leaning to one side." This is a major decision made in the light of China's historical and real situation and in accordance with the existing international environment at that time. However, only one year after the foundation of new China, the Korean War broke out. And the new-born China was involved into another hot war lasting for 3 years, with more than 390,000 Chinese soldiers dying in the war. Furthermore, the Chinese famine of 1959-1961 caused the death of millions of Chinese people. According to Yuan Longping, a Chinese agricultural scientist and educator known for developing the first hybrid rice in 1970s, he disclosed that in an interview made by Guangzhou Daily 40 million people died in the three years' disaster (Anonymous, August 2009; Anonymous, May 2010). Professor Cong Jin (2009) wrote in his book China in 1949-1976: Development in Zigzags that "the number of non-normal death...reached 40 million from 1959-1961" (p. 272).

My parents experienced both the famine and Cultural Revolution. I had asked my parents how they survived the days of famine. They said, "To survive the days is a miracle for them." All the villagers tried to find anything that could to fill their stomach, such as leaves, the roots of the tree, Bentonite and other things. At that moment, my grandparents led five children to beg for food from one family to another. However, they still felt starved everyday. In order to feed the whole family, all the members had to do all kinds of tough jobs to earn a little money.

During the ten years of the Cultural Revolution from 1966-1976, my parents were students. But they nearly spent most time on farming or learning the "Quotations from Chairman Mao" to answer the calls of "Down to the Countryside Movement." As a result, they couldn't receive the formal and scientific education. At that moment, China's youth answered to Mao's appeal by forming Red Guard groups all over the country. And they spread into the military, urban workers, peasants, students and other fields of life. Millions of people were persecuted in the violent factional struggles that ensued across the country, and suffered a wide range of abuses including public humiliation, arbitrary imprisonment, torture, sustained harassment, and seizure of property. In a word, the movement significantly affected the country economically and socially.

Liu Changyuan and Wang Song write: "In 1958, Mao publicly set forth his notion on the revolutionary advantage of being 'poor' and 'blank' and asserted that the more backward the economy was, the easier it would be for the socialist and communist ideas to spread and help rebuild into a completely new and modernized one.... He criticized individualism and valued collectivism as a cardinal tenet underlying communism and pointed out that individualism, egoism, and liberalism were extremely harmful to the revolutionary collectivism. A human life was trivial and meaningless unless it was immersed with 'communist consciousness,' and devoted to the revolutionary movement" (Liu and Wang, 2007, pp. 180-181). About the Great Proletariat Cultural Revolution, Liu and Wang write: "It was a radical movement that closed schools, slowed production, and virtually severed China's relations with the outside world. It was proletarian because it was a revolution of the workers against high ranking party and government officials. It was cultural because it meant to alter the values of society in the Communist sense. It was great because it was on a mammoth scale" (Liu, C. & Wang, pp. 181-182).

According to the talk by the Vice-Chairman Li Xiannian on the 20th of December 1979, "The 10 years of Cultural Revolution caused 500 billion Yuan losses in national income" (Li, X. N. personal speech, 1979: December 20). However, the rest of the world made use of the peaceful period after WWII to develop its economy rapidly. China was far less developed than other countries by losing the ten years of that golden period. Especially, our neighbor countries made great achievements in development, such as Japan, Korea, Singapore and other countries, among which Japan developed fastest.

Facing the great gap with other countries in development, Deng Xiaoping, as the core of the second generation leaders after the Cultural Revolution, set up a new strategy in developing national economy. And the strategy was to focus on the central task of economic construction and open China to foreign investment and global market. In foreign relations with other countries, Deng made two decisions. One was to sign the Treaty of Peace and Friendship between the People's Republic of China and Japan; the other was to establish diplomatic relations with the United States.

Henry Kissinger's secret trip to Beijing in 1971 produced an agreement that President Nixon would visit China. So Nixon's visit in 1972 marked that China and America began to work to establish their diplomatic relations. The two national leaders, Premier Zhou Enlai of China and President Nixon of the United States signed the Shanghai Communique in February 1972. The Shanghai Communique emphasized that the normalization of relations between the two countries was not only in the interest of the Chinese and American people but also contributed to the relaxation of tension in Asia and the world. Nixon's visit and the Communique totally changed China-US relations, leading to official establishment of full diplomatic relations between the countries on January 1, 1979.

Nixon's visit to China in 1972 shocked the whole world, which also caused Japan to take a passive position in dealing with the relations with China. Since Japan was a follower of American foreign policy, it expected the United States to inform the news to Japan in advance. However, Japan failed in the expectation. As a result, how to improve the relations with China became one of the most important political issues at that time for Japan.

The two countries normalized their diplomatic relations in September 1972 when Prime Minister Kakuei Tanaka visited China, and concluded a treaty of peace and friendship in August that year. The present relationship between Japan and China is based on two documents: the 1972 Joint Communique, which formed the basis of diplomatic relations between the countries, and the 1978 Treaty of Peace and Friendship. However, it took 6 years to reach the Treaty of Peace and Friendship. Mainly the difficulty was whether the treaty should include the item of "anti-hegemony"

Actually, the content of "anti-hegemony" was included in the 7th item of the 1972 Joint Communique, "The normalization of relations between Japan and China is not directed against any third country. Neither of the two countries should seek hegemony in the Asia-Pacific region and each is opposed to efforts by any other country or group of countries to establish such hegemony" (Joint Communique, 1972, September 29). So since the two countries had reached consensus on this item, China thought it would be reasonable to include it in the Treaty of Peace and Friendship. However, according to the Japanese government, the treaty would be interpreted into one against Russia with China if the term "anti-hegemony" was included.

Besides, it would not be in accord with the Japanese constitution. Apparently, Japan's pressure was from the Soviet Union. In the 1960s and 1970s, the relations between China and the Soviet Union were influenced badly because of the sharp debate on ideology.

The two countries held fundamentally different opinions on socialism, which had caused the rupture of strong Sino-Soviet relations in 1960. Consequently, Japan didn't want to be involved in the conflict between China and the Soviet Union. However, if the term of "anti-hegemony" was included in the treaty with China, it would be read by the Soviet leadership as the combination of China and Japan. Furthermore, "Japanese Premier Miyazaki Kiichi met the Foreign Minister of the Soviet Union Gromyko to discuss the peaceful treaty with each other on the same day of the meeting with the Chinese delegation" (Japan Diplomacy Association, 1978, p. 12). The problem lasted 3 years to discuss which words would appear in the treaty. At last, China and Japan reached the agreement in 1978. The term of "anti-hegemony" was included. But it reads "The Contracting Parties declare that neither of them should seek hegemony in the Asia-Pacific region or in any other region and that each is opposed to efforts by any other country or group of countries to establish such hegemony" (Treaty of Peace and Friendship 1978: August 12). It explained that "the present Treaty shall not affect the position of either Contracting Party regarding its relations with third countries" (Treaty of Peace and Friendship 1978: August 12).

Then on August 12, 1978, China and Japan signed the Treaty of Peace and Friendship. On October 22, Chinese vice Premier Deng Xiaoping visited Japan. On October 23, China and Japan exchanged documents of ratification of the Treaty. Then the relations of China and Japan entered a new stage. According to the Japan Federation of Economic Organizations:

In the economic arena, the amount of bilateral trade rose to an all-time high of over 85 billion dollars in 2000. From China's perspective, Japan has been its largest trade partner for eight years in a row, and from Japan's viewpoint, China became its second largest trade partner after the United States. Japan's direct investment in China soared after 1990, with the amount of investment already implemented totaling 24.88 billion dollars at the end of 1999. Not counting the combined investment of Hong Kong and Macao, Japan became China's second largest source of investment after the United States. At present, as many as 20,000 Japanese businesses are said to be operating in China, providing job opportunities to more than 1 million people. Apart from expanding bilateral trade, Japanese investments have also played a role in transferring high-tech industries to China (Keidanren, 2001: February).

"Statistics show that their bilateral trade volume hit a record high of nearly $300 billion in 2011. Japan has benefited greatly from China's booming economy" (Xinhua, 2012: July). Therefore, both countries should take various advantages to explore new fields for cooperation in order to achieve a win-win situation.The relationship also contributes directly to other fields between China and Japan:

The number of visitors between the two countries has increased year by year. According to figures released by the Ministry of Justice, the number of Japanese visitors to China topped the 1 million mark in 1996, and the level was sustained through 1999. The number of Chinese visitors to Japan (including those from Taiwan and Hong Kong but excluding those who traveled to Japan on reentry permits) reached 150,000 in 1998. From September 2000, Japan started issuing tourist visas to Chinese group tours from Beijing, Shanghai and Guangdong Province. Although there are still certain restrictions, it is now possible for the Chinese people to visit Japan as tourists, and their number is expected to increase in the years ahead. Also, there are approximately 32,000 Chinese studying in Japan, accounting for 54% of the total number of foreign students. More than 250 Japanese cities have established formal friendship ties with their counterparts in China, while academic exchanges between the two countries have expanded every year (Keidanren, 2001: February).

So again, cooperation brings benefits to both sides, while separation is harmful to both. And it is time for the new Japanese Prime Minister Shinzo Abe (since December 26, 2012) to show his vision, sincerity and leadership in steering China-Japan relations to a more stable and healthy track.

The relations between China and Japan in my generation

Generally speaking, Deng's 1978 policy of opening up and reform and the developing foreign policy changed the picture of China. He is considered "the architect," having developed socialism with Chinese characteristics. In 30 years of opening up and reform, China has created its own miracle.

When I took the cruise from Australia to New Zealand in 2009, I met an old man from America. He happened to visit China in 1980 and thus enjoyed first-hand knowledge of what the country has undergone in the past three decades. "China was grey, and everybody wore grey," he said when I talked with him about his trip to China then. However, "things have changed greatly since 1980." said the old man. He went to China again in 2008. And in just 30 years' time, "China has emerged as a colorful and self-confident society with a significant influence on world affairs." he said.

According to Martin Jacques (2010), "China is in the midst of what Marx described – writing about the British Industrial Revolution – as primitive accumulation, or what we know as economic take-off: the process in which the majority of the working population moves from the land to industry, from the countryside to the cities"(p. 159). Between 1952 and 2003, agriculture's share of GDP fell from 60 per cent to 16 per cent and its share of employment from 83 per cent to 51 per cent (Ferguson, 2006, October). Meanwhile, it took China only 10 years to double its per capita output (1977-1987) – a measure of the speed of economic take-off – compared with 58 years for the UK, 47 for the United States and 11 for South Korea, after three decades of economic growth averaging 9.5 per cent (Maddison, 2006, p.128).

As a Chinese being born in 1980, I had the opportunity to witness the great reform and opening up practice which brought about the tremendous changes. You can find my story in Cultural Stories of Part II: Cross-cultural Common Ground in Asia; China.

Rapid and sustainable economic development is the most remarkable achievement in the new period of reform and opening up. In 1978, China's total GDP was only 364.52 billion yuan, and the GDP per capita was 381 yuan; in 2007, China's total GDP amounted to 24.66 trillion yuan, 67.7

times that of 1978, with an average annual growth of nearly 10%, much higher than the same period of the world's average of around 3% growth rate (Anonymous, November 14, 2008).

However, in the second half of the 1980s, rising stock and real estate prices caused the Japanese economy to overheat in what was later to be known as the Japanese asset price bubble. The economic bubble came to an abrupt end as the Tokyo Stock Exchange crashed in 1990–92 and real estate prices peaked in 1991. "Growth in Japan throughout the 1990s at 1.5% was slower than growth in other major developed economies, giving rise to the term Lost Decade" (Wikipedia, 2012, July). And it never fully recovered from the stagnation of the 1990s and has yet to address deflation, an ageing population and ballooning public debt. Therefore, China surpassed Japan to be the second-largest economy after America in 2010.

In the past three decades, China's comprehensive national strength has continuously increased. Hongkong and Macao returned to China on July 1, 1997 and October 22, 1999 respectively. On August 8, 2008, Beijing hosted its first Olympic Games, attracting thousands of athletes around the world, which turns out to be the greatest event ever in the Olympic history. China has more say in the world affairs today. In the face of the global financial tsunami, China calls on the joint efforts of the global community and tries to make its contribution by maintaining its own economic growth.

China is emerging as one of the strongest global economies since the last two decades and increasing even more dramatically more recently. Joe McDonald (2010) writes that China has now edged past Germany in 2009 to become the top exporter.

Nick Edwards writes "In China - the biggest marginal generator of growth - politics are shifting policy into pro-growth high gear. "In the second half as we get closer to the Communist Party (leadership transition) and GDP growth falls closer to their 7.5 percent target for the year, the government will become much less tolerant of a further slowdown," Zhang Zhiwei, Hong Kong-based chief China economist at Nomura, told Reuters.

The once-a-decade handover of power in China is a showpiece event which the government is determined to ensure takes place against a backdrop of social stability and economic prosperity (Edwards, 2012: July 9).

However, the successful cooperation in the economy between China and Japan couldn't lead to the mutual understanding in politics. In the recent years, the conflict of historical perception has become the primary factor plunging the Sino-Japanese political relationship to the lowest point since the normalization of bilateral relations. According to a poll conducted by the Institute of Japanese Studies of the Chinese Academy of Social Sciences in September and October 2004: 54% of those interviewed consider Japan "far from amicable" or "not amicable", 10% higher than that in 2002. 26% gave the reason that "Japan invaded China in the modern history", while 62% thought that "Japan has till this day failed to criticize itself for its past aggression." This shows that the impact from the textbook dispute and Yasukuni Shrine visits on the thinking of the Chinese people is greater than that of memories of Japanese aggression against China. According to a public opinion poll conducted by China Daily, Japan Genron NPO and Peking University in July 2005, most Chinese and Japanese interviewees regarded understanding of historical issues as the main obstacle in the way of the sound development of Sino-Japanese relations. Among all the interviewees, 93% of Chinese university students, 80% of Chinese urban residents, and 77% of Japanese held this view (Liu, November 3, 2005).

These figures indicate that the understanding of historical issues remains the major contradiction in Sino-Japanese relations.

An opinion poll sponsored by China Daily and the Japanese nonprofit think tank Genron NPO released results in Tokyo on June 20, 2012, serving as a barometer for people to gauge the dynamics of China-Japan relations. It says:

The number of Chinese who have positive attitudes toward Japan has increased after a dip in 2011. About 32% of those polled in China say they now have good feelings toward Japan. But it is noteworthy that of all the issues that are preventing bilateral ties from growing more healthily, it is the Diaoyu Islands that are cited as the top concern by Chinese respondents to the survey. In contrast to the growing positive attitude toward Japan among Chinese people, the survey suggests that the number of Japanese people who harbor a negative attitude toward its neighbor has continued to rise. In 2011, 78 percent of Japanese respondents said they had "negative" or "relatively negative" impressions of China. This year, the figure increased to 84 percent (China Daily, June 21, 2012, p.8).

Just as in the result of the poll, I have good feelings toward Japan. I went to Japan in September 2009 to attend the 15th International Association for Intercultural Communication Studies annual conference held by Kumamoto Gakuen University. After the conference Michael Prosser and I made a nice trip in Japan. We visited 7 or 8 cities, including Osaka, Kyoto, Nagasaki, Fukuoka, Kumamoto, and Kokura, etc. It leaves me a very good impression. It is clean and in order everywhere. And the people there have a strong sense of environmental protection. So mini-cars or eco-friendly autos are commonly seen on the Japanese roads. People are polite to each other and friendly to our travelers. We stayed in Japan for about two weeks. Maybe it is not long enough to know about the country. But at least it gives me a chance to witness the current Japan and its people. The young Japanese I met there were interested in China and Chinese youth. And nearly all of them hoped they could visit China one day. So it implies that the people of China and Japan do want to understand each other, which could serve as a useful reference for decision-makers to recalibrate their interaction and cooperation.

Facing the so-called "cold politics and hot economics" of Sino-Japan relations, experts and scholars put forward different solutions or read the problems from different perspectives. Ma Licheng's (2002) article "New Thinking on the Relation with Japan" caused hot debate in China on patriotism and nationalism. The "New Thinking" also caused attention outside of China. Peter Hays Gries (2005) gave his opinion on Sino-Japan relations from a perspective of an European scholar in his article "China's "New Thinking" on Japan" Jin Xide(2001;2002;2006;2007;2008) wrote books and articles to analyze the problems existing in Sino-Japan relation. Particularly, he focuses on the future development of the relation in his China-Japan Relation in 21st Century, Reflection on the 30th Anniversary of Sino-Japan Relation after Normalization, Politics and Foreign Relations of Japan in Early 21st Century," and "Choices for Japan in Foreign Relations," etc.

Other famous scholars on Sino-Japan relations, such as Feng Zhaokui (2001; 2004; 2007), Jiang Lifeng (2002) and Liu Jiangyong (2006) also contribute greatly to the study. Several experts from China, Japan and other countries hope the economic cooperation and success could improve the political relation between two countries. Min Gyo Koo and Vinod

K. Aggarwal (2005) pointed at different solutions in their joint paper "Beyond Network Power? The Dynamics of Formal Economic Integration in Northeast Asia." Min Gyo Koo (2009) made a series of research on "hot economy and cold politics" in "The Senkaku/Diaoyu dispute and Sino-Japanese political-economic relations: cold politics and hot economics." Sara Newland and Kristi Gavella (2010) also think a sound cooperation in economy could produce a good relationship in politics. Other scholars study China-Japan relations from the multiple relations among China, America and Japan, such as Xia Liping's (2007) China-US-Japan Strategic Relations: Seeking Common Benefits and Avoiding a Security Dilemma, and Andrew K. Hannami's (2010) The United States, Japan and Asia in International Politics. Furthermore, several articles discuss China-Japan relations in the period of China's rise. Kentaro Sakuwa (2009) and Barry Buzan (2007) are the two main representatives in this aspect.

When I co-edited an earlier book, I have been thinking about the result of the opinion poll sponsored by China Daily and the Japanese nonprofit think tank Genron NPO asking why more Chinese take a positive attitude towards Japan in 2012. To some extent, this favorable change is inseparably linked with the continuous efforts the Chinese government and society have made to nourish its good neighborly ties with Japan, and the opposite. However, how to look at and handle the Japanese aggression against China and its other neighbor countries in Asia, the issues of textbooks and Yasukuni Shrine as well as Diaoyu Island, have been serving as a hurdle to the improvement of Sino-Japan relations. Just as the Chinese proverb says, "harmony benefits both and confrontation hurts both." It needs patience and wisdom to solve the problems existing in Sino-Japan relation.

Reflection

Three generations' observation toward Sino-Japan relation shapes a long history, a history that was carved into our soul because our ancestors contributed a peaceful environmental to the current generation with their sacrifice and devotion. The history will be always in our minds because it has been encouraging us to cherish peace today. Bai Yansong (2010), a prominent Chinese news anchor and journalist affiliated with China Central Television, China's national television network, had a conversation with Tsuneo Watanabe who has a great influence on Japanese politics. "'What should Japan do to make China satisfied?', asked Tsuneo Watanabe. I answered, 'We all know Germany's attitude towards history. Germany made apologies to the victimized countries. The Sino-Japan relation could be improved if Japan could apologize for its crimes in WWII'" (p. 176).

For the answer from Japan, China actually does not ask for much except that Japan stops doing things to hurt the feelings of the Chinese people. President Hu Jintao of China has made it clear that, "The war of aggression launched by the Japanese militarists brought grave disaster to the Chinese people, as well as the Japanese people. To understand and treat the history correctly means that Japan should translate its remorse into action and stop doing things which will hurt the feelings of the Chinese people and the people in other Asian countries concerned" (Hu, personal speech, 2005: September 3). Past experience, if not forgotten, is a guide for the future. As an individual citizen of China, I hope that Japan could take a responsible attitude toward history and then improve the relations of the two countries. For my part, as a young Chinese, I am encouraged by my 2010 travel to Japan that young Japanese also want to continue to improve these positive relationships.

References

Aggarwal, V. K. & Koo, V. K. (2005). Beyond network power? The dynamics of formal economic integration in Northeast Asia. The Pacific Review, 18(2), 189-216.

Bai, Y. S. (2010). Are we happy? Beijing, China: Changjiang Literature and Art Press.

Buzan, B. (2007). Sino-Japanese and Sino-US relations in China's peaceful rise. World Economics and Politics, 2006-07, 21-29.

Composing team for anti-Japanese war. (2011). The anti-Japanese war. Beijing, China: Renmin Press.

Cong, J. (2009). China in 1949-1976: Development in zigzags. Beijing, China: Renmin Press.

Consequence of the natural disaster from 1959-1961.(n.d.). Retrieved May 17, 2010, from http://club.china.com/data/thread/1011/2712/88/00/3.1.html .

Different attitudes. (2012, June 21). China Daily, p.8.

Economy of Japan. (n.d.) Retrieved July 6th, 2012 from http://en.wikipedia.org/wiki/Economy_of_Japan .

Edwards, N. (2012: July 9). Global economy weekahead: Downside risks dominate as China G.D.P. looms. Reuters.

Feng, Z. K. (2001). Poverty in Japan's strategy. World Affairs, 7, 8-11.

Feng, Z. K. & Lin, C. (2007). Report of China-Japan relation. Beijing, China: Shishi Press.

Ferguson, N. (October 2006). Empire falls. Retrieved 5th July, 2012, from www.vanityfair.com .

Gries, P. H. (2005). China's "new thinking" on Japan. The China Quarterly, 184, 831-850.

Guo, X. Z. (2010). The anti-Japanese war in Dezhou. Beijing, China: Xianzhuang Press.

Hane, M. (1996). Eastern phoenix: Japan since 1945. Boulder, CO: Westview Press.

Hannami, A. K. (2010). The US, Japan and Asia in international politics. San Diego, CA: Cognella.

Japan Diplomacy Association. (1978). China-Japan Treaty: Negotiation and ratification. Tokyo, Japan: JDA Press.

Japanese history textbook controversies. (n.d.). Retrieved July 4, 2012, from http://en.wikipedia.org/wiki/Japanese_history_textbook_controversies .

Joint Communique of the Government of Japan and the Government of the People's Republic of China. (n.d.). Retrieved July 3, 2012, from http://www.mofa.go.jp/region/asia-paci/china/joint72.html .

Jiang, L. F. (2002). The fact of Chinese distant attitude towards Japan. Japanese Studies, 6, 38-43.

Jin, X. D. (2001). Rebirth or declining: Decision of Japan in 21st century. Beijing, China: Social Sciences Academic Press (China).

Jin, X. D. (2002). Thinking on the 30th anniversary of Sino-Japan relation after normalization. Beijing, China: World Affairs Press.

Jin, X. D. (2006). Politics and foreign relations of Japan in early 21st century. Beijing, China: World Affairs Press.

Jin, X. D. (2007). China-Japan relatiosn in 21st Century. Chongqing, China: Chongqing Press.

Jin, X. D. (2008). Choices for Japan in foreign relations in 21st century. International Politics Quarterly, 1, 1-16.

Keidanren. (2001, February 20). Japan –China Relations in the 21st Century: Recommendations for building a relationship of trust and expanding economic exchanges between Japan and China. Retrieved July 4, 2012, from http://www.keidanren.or.jp/english/policy/2001/006/index.html .

Koo, M. G. (2009). The Senkaku/Diaoyu dispute and Sino-Japanese political-economic relations: cold politics and hot economics? The Pacific Review, 22(2), 175-182.

Liu, C. & Wang, S. (2007). Who are we and where are we going? – cultural transformation in the past twenty-five years in China in the global context. In S. J. Kulich & M.H. Prosser (Eds.), Intercultural perspectives on Chinese communication. Shanghai, China: Shanghai Foreign Language Education Press.

Liu J. Y. (2005, November 3). On correct understanding of the historical issues between China and Japan, Retrieved July 4th, 2012, from http://www.china-un.org/eng/zt/af60/t219660.htm .

Liu, J. Y. (2006). Influence of Japan's adaption in economic cooperation with China. Contemporary International Relations, 11, 35-42.

Ma, L. C.(2002). New thinking on the relation of China and Japan. Strategy and Management, 6, 84-96.

Maddison, A.(2006). The world economy.A millennial perspective. Paris, France: OECD.

McDonald, J. (2010, January 10). China becomes biggest exporter, edging out Germany. Retrieved July 6th, 2012, from http://www.newsvine.com/_news/2010/01/10/3735910-china-becomes-biggest-exporter-edging-out-germany .

Newland, S., & Govella, K. (2010, September). Hot economics, cold politics? Reexamining economic linkages and political tensions in Sino-

Japanese relations. Paper presented at the APSA 2010 annual meeting, Washington, DC.

Reasons for the natural disaster from 1959-1961. (n.d.). Retrieved August 18 2009, from http://forum.home.news.cn/detail/69635389/3.html .

Sakuwa, K. (2009). A not so dangerous dyad: China's rise and Sino-Japanese rivalry. International Relations of the Asia-Pacific, 9(3), 497-528.

Thirty years of reform and opening up in my eye. (2008, November 14). Retrieved July 5th, 2012, from http://blog.sina.com.cn/lqs6738 .

Treaty of Peace and Friendship between Japan and The People's Republic of China. (n.d.). Retrieved August 12, 1978, from http://www.mofa.go.jp/region/asia-paci/china/treaty78.html .

Xia, L. P. (2007). China-US-Japan strategic relations: Seeking common benefits and avoiding a security dilemma. World Economics and Politics, 9, 31-36.

Xin, H. (2011, August 31). Time to elevate China-Japan relations. China Daily, Retrieved July 4th, 2012, from http://www.chinadaily.com.cn/china/2011-08-31/content_13396720.htm

5. Harmony as a Major Value: On the Traditional Chinese Value of "Harmony"

Li Mengyu
Ocean University of China, Qingdao, China

Intercultural communication is a field which focuses on the exploration of the relationship between communication and culture. The ultimate aim of the discipline is to help people from diverse cultural backgrounds communicate more effectively with one another and to establish a harmonious relationship. To some extent, to create a harmonious communicative relationship among people from different cultures is of vital importance to the successful intercultural communication. The traditional Chinese value of "harmony" can provide the field with new and illuminating resources either on a theoretical basis and/or practical usage.

In the traditional Chinese culture, the notion of "harmony" is often interpreted as a dialectical and dynamic term. The conception of "Supreme Harmony" or "Great Harmony" (tai he) was first mentioned in The Book of Changes (Zhou yi). Fung Yu-Lan in his book, A Short History of Chinese Philosophy, stated: "Harmony of this sort, which includes not only human society, but permeates the entire universe, is called the Supreme Harmony. In 'Appendix I' of the Yi, it is said: 'How vast is the originating power of (the hexagram), Ch'ien.... Unitedly to protect the Supreme Harmony: this is indeed profitable and auspicious" (2007: 286). The term "Ch'ien" (also translated as "Qian") denoting the ultimate way the universe operates, is regarded as the perfect reconciliation of opposing forces of nature. As Yu Dunkang illustrated: "It explains that all beings find the ultimate and proper purpose of their existence by transformations of the Qian path: hard and soft are reconciled and united, producing the perfect harmony by which all beings are created and on which they thrive, and bringing a state of ultimate peace to the world" (1991: 53).

The notion of harmony is also elucidated in Tao Te Ching: "Tao gave birth to the One: The One gave birth successively to two things, three things, up to ten thousand. These ten thousand creatures cannot turn their backs to the shade without having the sun on their bellies and it is on this blending of the breaths that their harmony depends" (90). Hence, the conceptions of "Ch'ien" in The Book of Changes (Zhou Yi) and "Tao" in Tao Te Ching can be respectively interpreted as the originating power or intrinsic principle of the universe which involve the harmonious interaction of opposing forces such as ying and yang, light and dark, hard and soft, water and fire. "The Supreme Harmony" is thus regarded as the dynamic balance of the forces. The notion of harmony is also illustrated in Chung yung, (or the doctrine of the Mean), within which Chung and Ho serve as the two crucial terms. It explains: "To have no emotions of pleasure or anger, sorrow or joy, welling up: this is to be described as the state of Chung. To have these emotions welling up but in due proportion: this is to be described as the state of ho (harmony). Chung is the chief foundation of the world. Ho is the great highway for the world. Once chung and ho are established, Heaven and Earth maintain their proper position, and all creatures are nourished" (284). Therefore, harmony (or ho) in Chung yung, can be perceived as the perfect state of appropriateness, which lays great emphasis on the proper position and due proportion of the various elements being involved.

In another famous Chinese ancient book called Tso Chuan, Yen Tzu further expounded the notion of harmony by employing the famous analogy "Seeking harmony is like making a soup. One uses water, fire, vinegar, soy source and prunes all together to stew with fish and meat. The chef mélanges harmoniously all the ingredients for a tasteful soup"(47). Harmony is a also a key word of understanding Confucius's thought, the term has appeared in The Analects eight times. Confucius' entire life was engaged in the perfection of one's virtue and personality as a gentleman (or a perfect person). "Jen" (humanism) and "li" (ritual) were two main concepts in The Analects. Confucius particularly interpreted the two concepts in terms of harmony. Jen, according to Confucius, is "the ideal relationship which should pertain between individuals" (Smith, 1994: 110). And he stressed "In practicing the rules of propriety, it is harmony that is prized" (Pan, et al. 2004: 6).

Confucius had further broadened the thought of harmony by stating "The gentleman harmonizes his relationship with others but never follows them blindly (he er bu tong).The petty man just follows others blindly disregarding any principle (tong er bu he)"(45). Thus, in Confucius's eyes, a gentleman (or a perfect person) is a person who has accomplished the maximum development of one's virtue and personality by being kind and considerate to others on the one hand and maintaining his or her independent mind on the other hand, and this reflects Confucius's unique interpretation of the harmonious relationship among individuals. Above all, harmony is a very important conception in traditional Chinese culture, and it embodies the supreme ideal of Chinese culture that regards "All things are nurtured together without injuring one another; All courses are pursued together without collision" (Fung, 2007: 286).

Although the above typical views of harmony quoted are illustrated in different ways, they express the common dialectical and dynamic interpretation of harmony, which underscores the value of difference, reconciliation and creation. First, they do not regard harmony as a category denoting sameness, uniformity and conformity; instead they underscore in particular the value of difference, diversity, multiplicity and plurality within the concept. Next, they lay great emphasis on the reconciliation of the heterogeneous things rather than contestation, conflict and strive among them. Finally, they conceive harmony as a source of constructive creativity which can bring mutual benefit for all in the process of transformational synthesis of various components. The interpretations of harmony in traditional culture mentioned above have offered rich revelations to the intercultural communication study.

6 . Chinese Civilization's Crisis and Hopes

Sheldon Xu
Ocean University of China, Qingdao, China

As a Chinese citizen, I am very proud of myself, due to the enormous culture legacy. Undoubtedly, the five thousand year's brilliant culture, including various forms of rites, festivals, traditional arts, even life styles, and philosophies, is definitely our precious gift that ancestors endowed to us. However, along with China's opening up to the outside world, our fascinating and unique culture risked being eroded gradually, which is surely the biggest challenge that China has to bravely confront in order to survive and develop in the 21st century.

Chapter 3 and chapter 7 of Communicating Interculturally give us detailed examples about the lives of youth or previous youth from different cultural backgrounds, which are very interesting. And I feel like listening to them telling their own stories by face to face, which is helpful to be familiar with contemporary youth's behavior, habit, customs, etc. It also pushes us to reflect on ourselves seriously in turn. Here I want to demonstrate my thought of contemporary youth in China against youths from western countries, such as the USA under the context of global culture communication and culture erosion.

"We are more westernized" said a student in Ocean University of China in chapter 7 of Communicating Interculturally. But what is the definition of westernized? Simply by the mere fact that we watch a lot American movies and listen to British Broadcasting Corporation and Voice of America, we should not judge that we are more westernized. It is entirely possible that watching American movies is just for fun and the time we spend on it may be equal to or less than we spend on watching Chinese movies. In addition, I cannot agree with the students who say that we listen to BBC and VOA a lot. The "we" actually includes only a small amount of people, such as those English majors or those students who want to further their studies in America, like me. It is hard to imagine that a youth without a bachelor's degree enjoys listening to BBC. Even a student like me who has taken exams in Test of English as a Foreign Language (TOEFL) and

Graduate Record Examination (GRE), sometimes could not understand the news very well. In a word, some college students' personal behavior cannot stand for a large number of contemporary Chinese youths.

When it comes to KFC or McDonalds, I have to say that most young people around me do not reject these fast food restaurants. But that's not to say that we show much interest in these western-style food. As reasonable people, we may easily figure out that it is beyond our ability to cover for the expenses for eating many times in these restaurants. What's more, these fast foods are not healthy and it turns out that they are the main cause for the over-weight and suffering from chronic diseases, such as diabetes in western countries. Most importantly, as a "post-1980s" who grew up in a rural area, I have no access to these fast foods, thus I am not inclined to eat these fast foods. And I believe a lot of young people in China agree with me.

As with the western festivals, I admit that many young people would like to celebrate them, such as Christmas, Valentines Day or Thanksgivings Day. This is partly due to the influence of globalization and many people just follow the current. However, another reason is that young Chinese do not have their own festivals in traditional Chinese culture. The spring festival is mainly for those elderly people because young men have to visit their elders respectfully. The tomb sweeping festival is also the time for people to memorialize their ancestors. In a word, there are no particular festivals for the young. So it is no strange situation that western festivals are popular among the young. They are popular not for offering a kind of culture identity, rather, they serve as a platform for young people to communicate with each other, to concentrate on their own things.

However, with western festivals sweeping China, it follows the raising of people's awareness of protecting and developing our own festival cultures. As a result, the traditional Chinese festivals were made official festivals for the whole nation.

Until now, I had always been defending contemporary Chinese youth of not being westernized. It does not mean that I try to ignore various aspects of changes of Chinese youth under the influence of globalization. Some of my friends like to watch the Japanese cartoons and South Korean's TV series. Some girls like to follow the dressing trend of the Japanese and South Korean women. With easy access to the internet, friends are more connected with each other through instant online services. But these kind of changes are just an indispensable component of modernity, which is equally shaped by history and culture, not limited by markets or technology.

Here I'd like to illustrate some similarities among the youths from China and America. In the survey of "Ten Things your (American) Teenager Won't Tell You", teenagers want more privacy, respect, freedom, equality and encouragement. This is the same case with contemporary Chinese youths. And I think these things go beyond culture differences and belong to uniform humanity that everyone values.

Now it comes to the core of my argument, namely the values of contemporary Chinese youth. It is apparent that our values have changed a lot against our parents' generation. Moreover, my sister, who is post-1990s, shares little common value with me. So what invisible forces drive the changes of our values? To answer that question, we have to make it clear what has happened in China for the past thirty years.

Everyone says that China has made a huge progress in industrialization in 30 years against western countries with more than one hundred years. But the fruits of opening up to the world were not allocated to people equally. Rather, there is an overwhelming trend that the gap widens between the poor and the wealthy. And the original blueprint that people are governing our country was substituted by privileged bureaucracy's domination, whose roots hide deeply in China's society and have flourished after the opening up since 1978. To some extent, the contemporary Chinese youth can be categorized into four segments, which is Rich 2G, Official 2G, Poverty 2G and the large group of ordinary youth. Actually, I believe I belong to the fourth one.

To begin with, I want to tell a story that happened recently and inspired a hot debate over the internet. Yao Jiaxin, a Rich 2G, who bumped down a young mother, Zhang Miao when driving to his college, instead of sending Zhang to a hospital immediately, he was concerned that Zhang would remember his car number and get him into trouble if he just ran. An evil idea occurred to him instantaneously. He stabbed Zhang eight times and killed her. When Yao was caught, his family used various channels to rescue him, like debating for him on famous media and employing famous criminal experts to rationalize his inhumane behavior. Apparently, people can easily tell that justice is not equal to everyone and justice stands closely to the rich.

So the rich value money a lot. Money can get power and even has a great impact on a person's life. But it is not only confined to the rich that put much emphasis on money. Actually, the whole society worships money crazily, according to a survey. It is astonishing when you contrast people with those born fifty years ago. Dating back to Chairman Mao's times, people were cultured with such pure minds that they valued kindness and truth more than money. Although materials were limited, at that time they were much happier than we are now.

However, the fast growing economy has completely changed this situation. With the breakdown of collectivism in the economy, people were much concentrating on their own business. When it comes to running business, profit is the most important element that all activities are moving around it. Many traditional merits are outmatched by money. Actually, money is so dominant that it can gradually change a generous and kind person into a mean and greedy one. When this kind of people increases, it becomes a phenomenon that people are not feeling strange about evil or false things. Under this atmosphere, it is not strange that people's values have changed a lot. And because China has such huge amounts of people, the competition between people has intensified and so does people's curved soul.

The exception is the fourth category of youth in China, namely the ordinary youth. These people, include me, can make ends meet and do not desperately want money. We value friendship, benevolence, and love a lot. We are not jealous of those with money and power and we are compassionate with poor people. And I think we are the guardian of truth, kindness and beauty. We emerged when the earthquake hit Wenchuan. We emerged when Zhang was killed by Yao Jiaxin. I think we are the consciousness of China, we are the hope of China.

Chapter 7 of Communicating Interculturally mentions that many contemporary American youth read less books and the ratio of college students is low. This phenomenon is explainable taking into consideration the fact that United States has such advanced technologies that they can easily earn a bigger piece of the cake in the fierce competitive global market. Americans can easily get large amounts of resources by means of the strong dollar. So they do not need to read too many books. Ironically, people from all over the world further their study in America and serve for this country.

I have talked a lot about the present. What about our future? Will our culture fade away by the great impact of western culture? Will we become westernized? Or will Chinese culture be resilient enough to survive and make Chinese less materially-driven and more mentally healthy? At least I am optimistic about my culture. I equally believe that Chinese culture will rejuvenate and shine brightly in the 21st century. People will be released from being slaves of money and find real meaning of their existence.

References

Li Mengyu's and Michael H. Prosser. Communicating Interculturally, Beijing 2012: Higher Education Press (262 pages in English).

7. Wu Hsian Mei - The story of a child bride

Cui Wu
Beijing, China

Translated from Chinese and edited by Kelly Ni

My grandmother Wu Hsian Mei (also known as Wu Hsiao Mei) was born in Yiwu, a county in Zhejiang Province, China, into a poor farming family. For generations, her family worked for the local land gentry as laboring tenants. Her mother gave birth to ten sons and daughters; but due to poverty, and not being able to provide for themselves, her siblings were given to other people, and some of the girls were drowned in the toilet upon birth. Yet due to the (farming) villagers prejudice against women in general, Wu Hsian Mei became the only girl to survive infancy. But because of food scarcity, in her sixth year, she was sold to the Song family as a child bride by her father.

The Songs were a big family, and kept several acres of land, one cow, and over a dozen chickens, as well as five pigs. The Songs, in keeping with the traditions of local farming communities, had ten brothers all living under one roof. Wu Hsian Mei entered the Song household, she had to wake up at 4 a.m., then carry the water from the nearby well to put underfoot. And thus, she was able to carry out the work of twenty some odd number of people, helping with the cooking and washing jobs. After meals she would carry a carrying pole; carry a vat of water to feed the pigs, cows, as well as chickens. It was perhaps hardest on her three inch feet also deemed "three-inch lotus blossom." Her feet were bound when she was two or three years old, as in keeping with Chinese rural village traditions. Her feet would be covered with blisters.

Nana Wu Hsian Mei refused to eat beef; she even told us that the aged cow in her household had spent its entire life plowing the fields, and finally reached an age where it was old and quite weakened in its body. The household decided to kill it over spring festival. But on the day of the killing, the old cow kneeled within the cowshed, tears streaming down its face, and brayed nonstop. Wu Hsian Mei held onto the neck of the old cow. After that time had passed, Wu Hsian Mei refrained from eating beef, and turned to Buddhism.

And thus till she was in her teens, Nana started to raise children. She continuously gave birth to ten children, but only three boys and one girl survived past infancy. The females all went through the same fate of drowning, other than a few children who died from sickness or illness. Several of the girl infants suffered the same fate of drowning, other than that, a few children died by illness. None of the parents wanted to drown their own daughter, due to poverty, and lack of sufficient food and could not provide for their nutritional needs. Nana was adept at sewing. She hand-made all the shoes worn by her family. The shoe bottoms were hand crafted as well. Whether it's young, middle aged, or the elderly, in the family they all wore the cloth made with broadcloth, which were spun and woven by the loom. Each piece of cloth had the same history of three years new, three years old and three years of patchwork. Yet all this needlework was composed with Nana's handiwork. When I was little, Nana would make several shoe pads, layers of old cloth stuck together by glue, sewn by hand with beautiful pattern of flowers, birds and animals, I held onto the shoe pads, and I was so excited; it was really soft and comfortable. Nana also made two pairs of shoe with red corduroy, and the shoes were very comfortable, and well worn.

I remember the first time I saw Nana, she was in her sixties. She came from her old home far away in Zhejiang Province, Yiwu County to Beijing, and we have lived at Beijing Dong Si 10th, Renmin Daxue apartments. In our backyard, she was sharecropping a small piece of land, in which she planted sunflowers, vegetables, as well as other flowers.

In one corner of our yard, we built a chicken coop, kept ten chickens, nine hens, one rooster. Watching the furry critters growing up day by day, I felt grateful. Every morning, I was wakened from my dreams by the rooster's crow, I would be following Nana, reach into the nest and get a couple of eggs, and I was very happy and jumping around with joy. Nana would follow behind, with a smile plastered over her face, only a few remaining teeth exposed when she was smiling. And her gray hair was shaking when she laughed. These ten chickens were growing up fast, especially the rooster getting big and strong with red crown, bright feathers, looking proud and dignified. I used to like this little rooster, but with its growing up, I began to resent it, eventually growing to hate it, because it was mean to the hens which were weaker than it. One day I saw it riding atop the hens, all mean looking. I thought, this dirty bastard, I vowed that I would punish it. Thus, I found a big wicker basket, about half my height, put some food in as a bait, and when I saw the rooster jump into the basket, I took a blanket and covered the basket immediately, I took the basket and shook it with all my might.

"Save me!" the rooster was screaming loudly inside the basket. Nana came running towards me, and prevented me from continually abusing the rooster. She asked me why I am doing such silly and stupid things; after letting me tell her the reason to punish this rooster, she laughed heartily. She said "Kiddo, it's the rooster and the hen mating." I asked Nana "what means mating? Why the rooster is using its size to bully others?" Nana said "mating means getting married. You are too young to understand, you will understand when you grow up. Would you please release this rooster?"

Nana could make peanut sesame candy by hand. She was using raw peanuts and sesame, added some brown sugar and flour, and then baked them; it turned to be very sweet and crispy. She gave two paper boxes to me and my sister, one for each of us. We saved these candy bars in the boxes, served as snacks every afternoon. Nana had a big smile when she watched us eating and enjoying the candy like hungry kids.

One day, my Uncle Wu Han's secretary came to see us, and brought us a basket of green apples and a cardboard box. We rugrats couldn't wait to take a bite of the apples, but our taste buds were piqued by the sourness, till we screamed with delight. The apple was too hard for Nana to chew, because she had only several teeth left. She stood aside and watched us while we chewed on the apple. She said, "Oh my, I am starting to drool." That night, when my mom came home and opened the little box, she said, "oh my", what appeared in front of us, is a piece of root, looks like an old man with white hair and long moustache. Mother said, "This big wild ginseng and green apple are a gift to Chairman Mao from Korea Leader Kim Il Jong, and Chairman Mao sent them to Uncle Wu Han. Uncle Wu Han then gave to his younger sister (my mom)". Since Mom had high blood pressure, ginseng was unhealthy for Mom; thus mom gave it to Nana. Every day Nana would chop off a few slices of this ginseng, boil it with water and rock candy, then drink the soup.

One day, I returned home after playing jump rope, sweating from head to toe, and I was very thirsty. Nana provided me a half cup of the soup and added a few slices of white roots into the cup. Nana coaxed me by saying "the rock candied roots are very delicious!" I thought what I ate was some root-like turnips. After a while, I felt my body getting hot and starting to burn. My nose was bleeding nonstop the next day. Mom came back home that evening, and asked me, "Why does your face look all funny?" I stammered, and could not utter a single word.

Nana was hard working all her life. She was never given a chance to go to school. She could not read or write. Every day when I came back from school, she would touch my backpack and said, "Now all women know how to read, you are very lucky!" One day, she took a pencil and a piece of paper, asked me to teach her how to write her name. I asked Nana about her name. She told me her name was Xiao Mei. I said that is a nick name, it doesn't count. Nana said she was sold to the Song family when she was six years old, and had never had a regular name. The Song family always called her Xiao Mei (which means little sister). She said she had just been given the family name "Wu Xiao Mei". I took out my own blackboard and chalk, and started teaching her how to write. Nana practiced one stroke after another stroke; her attitude towards learning was as serious as she stitched the shoe bottoms. Every character she practiced about twenty times at least, but the writing tablet was so small that she had to write and erase and erase and write. She could write her own name finally after two weeks. She was so happy and smiled all day long and we could even see her few remaining teeth. She made a box of sesame candy to reward my sister and me. I could not help but laugh through the teeth when I looked at her messy handwriting for her name "Wu Xiao Mei". Since then, she would practice one or two phrases per week, and later increase to four or five phrases per week. Believe it or not, two years later, Nana could read my elementary school text book. After several years, Nana could read the headlines of People's Daily Newspaper – Renmin Ribao. When I watched Nana practice writing so seriously under the dimming electric light, one stroke after another, it is hard to believe that Nana was a child bride, sold to another family as a child slave, but she got up to the reading level of an elementary school student only when she reached sixty-eight years old.

When I was a teenage girl, I was very playful and naughty. After school I would play jump rope with my teenage friends almost daily, then go climbing up some hills and trees; afterwards we would pick the fresh dates and fruits in our back yard. My family had been living in the dormitory of People's University (Renmin Daxue). The dormitory of People's University located in East Fourth No. 10 of Beijing, used to be a Regional Governor's mansion during the Qing Dynasty. There were forestry glen, pond, and man-made artificial hills. My friends and I would play hide and seek on the imitation hills around the pond. We had a lot of fun. When I returned home, Nana saw me as a mud caked monkey, drenched with sweat; she would drag me to a water hose to wash my face, feet and hand. I would come home very tired; after I came home I would fall to my easy chair and sleep. One day when I slept on my easy chair in my semi -conscious state, I found someone using a nail trimmer to cut my nails. and it was Nana! She took a small pair of scissors, wore a pair of spectacles cutting my toe nails.

But one thing made me wonder for a long time that I had never seen Nana washing her feet or cutting toe nails while Nana used to help me wash my feet. I started to pay attention and discovered her secret that she would wash her feet behind our backs. One day, I found out that Nana might be washing her feet in her room, but she happened to forget to lock the door, left a crack open, from that I sneaked a peek; indeed, she was washing her feet. I pushed the door open; Nana immediately covered her feet with a towel. I gently lifted up the towel; the scene shocked me! I had been never seeing such horrible feet. There was a big hump on the back of the feet due to the broken back bone on the fore of the feet. Except for the big toe which was straight, the bones of all other four digits had been either bent or broken, and buried under the fore of the feet. A thick layer of callus and carbuncle developed under her feet bottoms. She had to cut the callus with a sharpened switchblade layer by layer. Oh, dear Nana, you had walked since the time when you were three years old, with this pair of three-inch long bloodied feet. I could feel how much torture and suffering you had been through, I could not hold back my tears anymore. Nana wiped off my tears gently, and said "Don't cry kiddo, let me make some candy for you."

Soon, the peace in our household vanished. In its place were either end-less arguments or silence. The house became deadly silent after a series of violent arguments. Children's laughter also went away. Although Nana would come up with a recipe for tasty desserts, yet the house was devoid of our usual joy and laughter. Nana would shake her head upon looking at my parents' faces. The white hair on her head would shake and shiver, and in turn our hearts would be gripped in fear. The teachers at my school were labeled as rightists one after another. Even my favorite English teacher was labeled as a rightist. Watching her cleaning the hallways, my heart trembled with coldness; I was often perplexed as to why this is happen-ing. Looking upon the school hallways plastered with big letter posters, I could not understand why the teachers I had usually respected would have an "X" over their names. Upon returning home, I saw Nana sighing to herself, her face full of pain. I wanted to ask my parents, but the cool expression on their faces, made me swallow back what I was going to say.

Many years later, after I'd grown up and begun to understand things, I learned that during the anti-rightist movement, my father had responded to our great leader Chairmen Mao's call to criticize the Chinese Commu-nist Party. My father wrote and published several papers in the People's Daily and the Central Journal "Call" of Democratic Party Affiliates. At the time he suggested that the Chinese Communist Party give up its political policy of following in Soviet Union's footsteps, and furthermore, learn from Europe and America their advanced science and technology as well as management. He even went as far as to suggest having a professorial committee on the college campus, and having an expert committee within the factories and companies for management to change the condition of philistine leading experts. My father was later labeled as a rightist. The definition of a rightist was that he represented capitalism seizing power from communism. He was openly criticized in large meetings and small group meetings. The department head forced my mother and father to betray each other. Then my family lost its original peace and harmony. Since the great leader Chairman Mao set up the strategy by using the bait to catch the snake, so many intellectuals were labeled as rightists like the snake to be caught in the trap. As a young teenager I was stunned and could not understand what was happening, and why my father became a rightist of anti-Chinese Communist Party and had fallen from the pedestal of being a professor. It's hard to estimate how many families were suffering and torn apart during this political movement storm. My family was only one of many.

My parents were sent into exile from China People's University in Beijing to a remote area in the west of China next to Tibet, a small university named "Tsing Hai University". It was during the time of the Tibetan rebellion. The agriculture, animal husbandry and economy were nearly destroyed completely over there; there were not enough food supplies. From the letters of my mother I had learned that they were starving. Nana often took my two younger sisters; dug out grassroots in the mountainside to eat. Nana and my two younger sisters had edema due to lack of nutrition. From the letter I also learned that Mom and Dad would carry a gun to go on patrol; they were trained as local militia to suppress bandits.

I was left alone in Beijing and in the girl's boarding school. My mother required me to visit and live in the home of my uncle Wu Han in Beijing during the weekends and summer vacations. I remembered that at the time when I was a student of Beijing Teacher's Middle School for girls. I was in the second year of junior high, and I was missing Nana, my two younger sisters, and my parents so much that I was itching to fly to Tsing Hai to visit and reunite with them. But what I could not understand was why my mother would not let me go and visit them. She even wrote a letter to Uncle Wu and my homeroom teacher to stop me from going. I started saving money in secret. I used to go to Uncle Wu's home to get monthly allowance from Aunt. I saved all my money except for each month's food allowance. I put all my saved money into a wallet and counted daily.

One day I played the Chinese jump rope with my classmate, and I lost my wallet, and it had slipped out from my pocket. I was so sad and I cried loudly; my hopes of visiting Tsing Hai fell short. However that wallet was picked up by a classmate and handed back to the homeroom teacher. My homeroom teacher gave it back to me, and told me with concern "I understand that you miss home, but it might not be wise for you to go there alone." When I visited my Uncle that weekend, my Aunt talked to me in a serious tone, she said, "The railroad to Xi'ning (Nana's hometown) has not been fixed, some of the railroads had been destroyed by rebels, the public transportation had been disrupted. It's not safe for you to go alone". After some days, I received a mail package. I opened it; it was from my mother. There was a smaller package inside, which contained watermelon seeds from my younger sister; they were homegrown. There was another package, which contained fish jerky strips, cooked by Nana. It was bitter and made my mouth tingle. The fish was caught by students of Tsing Hai University. Since those fish lived in the salt water lake, their taste was so bad, it became inedible. Nana made them into fish jerky strips. It served as delicacy food for them. Later I learned that the salt water in Tsing Hai Lake contained a high concentration of salt and heavy metals; that was the reason it taste so bitter and inedible. The fish in Tsing Hai Lake were respected and worshiped as gods, it was not allowed for anybody to catch and eat them. Thus the fish in that lake grew to a large size, and there were lots of them. But during the three year's famine period, people lived in those provinces next to Tibet, including Anhui Province, Sichuan and Tsing Hai Provinces, and tens of thousands of people were starving and dying. People rushed to Tsing Hai Lake to catch fish and ward off famine.

Several years later, one day my Aunt told me, "Your mother is coming to Beijing to visit you." I was shocked and felt pleasantly surprised. Every day henceforth I would look forward for that day to arrive. But I was stunned when my mother and two younger sisters appeared in front of me. My mother's frame was a bag of bones. My two younger sisters were skinny as hell. I almost could not recognize them. My mother's eye welled up with tears when she saw me. Mother touched my head and said, "You have grown so tall, I thought I might never see you again." When I heard this sentence, my brain went blank. Then I learned that mother had fainted in front of three hundred students when she gave a lecture due to malnutrition and depletion. The Doctor said, even though her life was spared, her blood pressure was so high that it would be life threatening to her to stay on the high plateau four thousand meter above sea level. Mother returned to Beijing with medication for about one year, and her blood pressure stabilized gradually. She was re-assigned to a job at Beijing Economics Institute. She resumed her teaching career. My seventy year old grandma remained in Tsing Hai with my father; they were codependent upon each other. Nana grew some vegetables, raised some chickens and rabbits. She tried all different ways to improve the quality of life. Thus my parents lived apart for eighteen years. My father went to Tianjing

Economics Institute, until after the Cultural Revolution; finally he moved to Beijing Economics Institute by mother's side after eighteen years apart.

During the Cultural Revolution, my uncle Wu Han became the scapegoat of Mao's political struggle. He was labeled as an Antirevolutionary Revisionist by the Gang of Four and Chairman Mao. Jiang Qing, Chairman Mao's wife, labeled my uncle as a reactionary academic authority. Then he was criticized nationwide. He was to be condemned both in speech and in writing by the Red Guards and the organization of the Worker's Rebellion. But of course, my family couldn't avoid the fate of patriarchal clan [1]. Both my parents were picked out for punishment; they were forced to confess, then locked up. Later they were sent to a remote Labor Camp. My father was in Tianjin with Nana at that time. He was ordered to go to a Farm Labor Camp at Tang-Gu, separated from Nana. He had to do labor work such as planting, weeding, feeding pigs, horse, and sweeping the barn and horse stable under the overseer. Although, he was a professor, but he came from a farming family, he had been working in the field since childhood and used to do the hard labor work, so he could stand the heavy duty and hard work. Father was lucky to be with Nana that they could stand together in times of needs and to share weal and woe, although, Nana was getting old.

When I received father's letter from Tianjin telling me that Nana had palpitation, heart murmurs and stomach pain, and could not got off bed and when I heard the bad news, I disregarded everything and took a break from "Broadcasting Workforce". I bought a train ticket from Beijing running to Tianjing immediately. At that time I was a student of Qinghua University at Beijing and I was forced to confess because of my uncle Wu Han. I was naturally guilty by association with my uncle and was labeled as an "Anti Revolution Student", "Harbored Revisionist". I was sent to a "Labor Camp" for two years. Later I was back to Tsinghua University under escort and worked in another "Labor Camp" for two and a half years. During that time, when the freshmen student body took the political science class, I was their example of what not to be, I had to accept their criticism and humiliation. They said I did not hold the proper attitude and was not sincere because I refused to confess that I was against Mao's wife and the Cultural Revolution.

When I decided to go straight to Tianjin, despite any accusations directed towards me, I prepared for the worst consequence. When I walked in the door, I saw Nana lying on the bed, prostrate, full of white hair. I went toward the bedside, hugged Nana's forearm and cried loudly. Nana barely opened her eye, stroked my head, and said, "Don't cry, kiddo, Nana is still alive. I am overjoyed to see you. I am very happy, you are big child now." I went to the supermarket, and bought some lean pork meat and vegetables, I made some soup, and fed Nana one spoonful at a time. But she was unable to swallow at that time. Although father was professor of economics at a university, he was labeled as a member of the anti-communist party, "The three man village."[3]. Father was either denounced, or went through forced labor daily and all their money and belongings were seized and took away. Father's life was on the line, and he was unable to take care of Nana. When father returned home from the labor camp, and finally brought Nana to visit the medical doctor, she was diagnosed as late stage liver cancer. Furthermore she had heart angina.

Seeing me full of tears, father told me a story. "At that time, the red guards came daily to strip search our home, for the evidence of father's anticommunist party evidence, they looked through the entire house, every corner and every place, The wood floor and ceiling were pried wide open. The Red Guard wanted to steal and take away all clothing; they forced Nana to get up off the bed. Father went forth, stopped them and said, "My mother has late stage liver cancer, the hepatitis is contagious." When the Red Guard heard that they got scared and put down all the clothes, and materials and fled in helter-skelter. Since then, they never showed up again" I burst into tears and started laughing, but my tears were still overflowing.

The next day, Nana called me to her bedside. She took out a wallet from underneath her pillow, slowly opened the little wallet by her shaking hands, she took out the RMB equivalent of ten dollars stuffed it into my hand. I knew that the money was from her life savings; Nana used to collect old newspapers and used journals from the garbage, sold them and saved money little by little from the clippings. I gave the money back to Nana, and said in reply, "Nana will recover, why don't you use the money for yourself. You need to buy some food and medicines." Nana stuffed the money into my hand and said, "Your household money was all taken by the Red Guards. Father and mother only have 30 RMBs of living allowance each month. You have no job, and plus you have two sisters. Why don't you take this money, and buy some food." I accepted the money, and carefully hid it into my inside jacket pocket.

The day I was leaving, I went towards Nana's bedside, and couldn't bear telling her that I was going to return to Tsinghua University in Beijing to continue receiving labor reform. I held back my tears, and held onto Nana's hands which were dry and brittle as sticks, pretended to be happy and said, "Nana, you have to get better. I promise to return soon to see you." When I stepped out of the doorway, my tears couldn't help but roll down my cheeks. I knew that this is my final goodbye to dear nana. "Time flew by, after the Cultural Revolution, father finally moved back to Beijing to be reunited with mother.

President Nixon's China trip opened the door for culture exchange. I had the chance of coming to the United States for my Ph.D. program. When I heard that father was very ill, I quickly took a direct flight from America to Beijing and visited father in the hospital. My father got colon cancer and passed away. When I was cleaning out father's valuables, I found a small cloth bag which was locked in a desk drawer. I was wondering what it was. I surmised that it was some valuables of father's. I peeled away the layers of cloth, and inside was a strand of white hair, it was Nana's! I exclaimed and contained it with my two hands and it had held the memory of my father. Images of him and Nana passed through my brain.

My father in his youth, his family was poor. His siblings, and all cousins and nephews, none of them had finished high school. They had dropped out to tend the old farm, and support their families. Only father had finished high school, as well as college. Father had left the county of Yiwu to go to the city of Jinhua, to attend junior high school. I had heard him saying that he had been walking miles and with a bamboo carrying pole, which was prepared by Nana. One side of the pole was a bamboo basket. Inside were some books, notes, papers, several changes of clothes, and two pairs of shoes made by Nana. The other side of the bamboo pole was a clay jar. Inside the jar was dried yasai made by Nana. This dried yasai was the stuff that father ate during his whole semester in middle school, three meals a day,the same thing every day.

One summer, the weather was hot and humid; father was ill due to lack of nutrition, there was a lump of pus on his body, and he ran up a high fever. It was pyemia. Nana sold some eggs, some hand-knit woven cloth and a pig that she raised. She used the money, sought out the local doctor, and hence saved father's life.

In order to raise the tuition fee for father, Nana worked very hard, she raised more chickens, got more eggs, and raised more pigs which bred more piglets. Every day she would stay in the loom until midnight to make hand-knit woven cloth. Nana maintained good personal relationships. When she was raising money for father to go to Zhejiang University, her ten brother-in-laws and sister in-laws all pitched in and donated to father some money. When father's tuition and street change were collected, Nana made a nice supper as usual to treat one another, and to send father on his way. Father knew of Nana's diligence, and studied much harder than usual. Because he was the family's only college graduate. His hard work paid off. After many years of persistence, he had finally become a university professor.

Nana was not only diligent, but often willing to help other people out of a jam. She would often give her food and vegetables to poorer neighbors living in surrounding areas. Nana helped out Hsieh Gui's family. Hsieh Gui's father was father's nephew. Hsieh Gui used to come to visit Nana at our home in Beijing. I heard that Hsieh Gui had already attained the position of an air force naval captain in Beijing. He would often bring some good food including chocolate when he came. Nana was toothless, and couldn't chew hard stuff. All those cookies and candies were given to us rugrats. Nana told us that Hsieh Gui used to wear split bottom pants in the grassy fields to herd the cow as a little poor boy, he couldn't get a decent meal, and often went to bed hungry. Nana used to save the scraps from her own meal for him to eat. Hsieh Gui's parents passed away when he was a little boy, and he had been living with his aunt.

Hsieh Gui's aunt was widowed when she was young. When Hsieh Gui told Nana that auntie passed away, and met with a cruel fate, Nana cried her eyes out. I stood aside, and asked out of curiosity how did auntie pass away? Nana said, "She ate too much and had a bloated stomach." "How come she died with a bloated stomach?" I asked. Nana said, "Every year, the Song family at an ancestral shrine of a patriarchal clan would hold its annual remembrance of the ancestor ceremony. It was going to be a free meal for all, whether for the old or young, rich or poor, and would honor their common ancestry, having descended from the same ancestor. For those poor relatives and their children, that day meant they could enjoy the once a year food fest. It included wine, meat, porridge, and vegetables in the meal. Only on that day of the year, aunty and her offspring could have a bowl of meat. In order to enjoy more meat, aunty would fast three days prior, without realizing that such a tragedy awaited her. During the dinner reception, aunt ate too fast and too furiously, and her throat got caught by a piece of chicken bone. Aunty was suffocating.

When Nana heard of this, she sighed, "Aunty was such a kind and warm woman, what a pity that she was so poor!" After aunty passed away, Nana used to serve free meals to auntie's children. Only now do I understand why Nana would not allow me to waste my rice, and now I fully understand why father kept a strand of Nana's white hair as his treasure, and saved it into the cloth bag wrapped by many layers, and why it was locked into father's private drawer. I held a strand of Nana's white hair with my two hands, I seemed to have seen Nana, who was walking towards me with a big smile, hot tears streamed down my face.

Several years later, I heard the news from father of Hsieh Gui's passing. During the Cultural Revolution, Hsieh Gui who used to be an air force captain, was tried and interrogated. He was labeled as a member of Wu Han's Anti-Revolutionary Faction, just because he was a distant relative of Wu Han. He was reprimanded again and again. He was stripped of the right to fly, so he was banned from flying in the blue sky, that had always been his hobby and dream. He felt sick to his heart; he suffered a heart attack, and finally said good bye to the cruel world.

Hsieh Gui was only fifty seven when he passed away. He was at the top of his game in his life and work, and he probably had some dreams and aspirations that had not yet materialized. Yet history and reality had made a fool of him. Only because he was the distant relative of my father, and my father was Wu Han's brother-in-law. Since Wu Han was labeled as an Anti-Communist Party Leader by Chairman Mao. Thus Hsieh Gui was condemned to death also.

I was glad that Nana did not know of Hsieh Gui's passing until later; otherwise she would have been in the depth of despair, she would have been asking, "Hsieh Gui was at the top of his game in his life and work, it was in his golden year, and he had come from a poor farming family, yet why should he meet such sudden death?" I did not know how to explain to Nana. If I had a chance to tell Nana the truth, I was afraid that Nana would not understand the reality, to know terms such as the "Patriarchal clan" [1], "The three man village of Anti-Communist Party"[3], "Totalitarianism of un-propertied class"[4], and "political movement of the masses." At that time, I myself was actually confused with what was going on during the Cultural Revolution; I was confused about what was right and what was wrong, and basically questioned my existence and values.

Oh, may God bless that my Nana had such pure heart, a Buddhist's merciful heart. Had my Nana's heart had not been contaminated by that political conspiracy; I sincerely hope that Nana could go to heaven with a clean slate and a peace of mind. I would remember forever my dear Nana, who had the three inch feet as "three-inch lotus blossom, who had the white hair. My dear Nana, you had such a rough-hewn hand and face, yet a most beautiful heart.

8. A Glimpse of the Life of Contemporary Chinese Women – by Studying a Certain Group of Them

Joanna Liu (pseudonym)
Beijing Language and Culture University, Beijing, China

Chinese women are quite unique in the world. On one hand, they are much more free in some aspects than their sisters in other ancient developing countries. Sometimes even some developed countries. On the other hand, they are facing a lot of pressures. Pressures come from both the ancient Chinese tradition and the rapid changing of modern Chinese society. To give a general description and analysis of Chinese women's lives is too big a subject to me and to this report. Because just like a lot of other things in China, women's rights and pressures are extremely unbalanced. They differ from area to area, generation to generation, and are influenced by financial conditions, education, tradition, etc. So I'll have to limit my topic to the life of women living in the suburban district of southeast China, which is quite familiar to me and which to my opinion, is quite representative. I'll divide women and their lives into three general groups, the grandmothers, the mothers and the daughters. Then I'll focus on two things which have played and are playing important roles in their lives, family planning and the Women's Federation.

The Grandmothers

They are generally housewives more than 55 years old, with more than 3 children and are now living with one of their children. Having never taken up any formal job all of their lives, they are now mostly financially depending on their children, especially sons. So if their children treat them badly, their lives are sure to be miserable. Most of the time, the money they get from their children is quite limited. Because of this and their habits formed in the hard old days, they now live a quite thrifty life and are strongly against any form of so called wastefulness and extravagance.

If they are healthy enough, they take as much of the housework as possible and take care of their grandchildren and even great grandchildren. Sometimes, it is quite heavy work for an elderly woman. But both they and their children take it for granted. Once they are not able to help their children anymore, they tend to consider themselves as useless and a burden on their children.With little education, they have no interest in books, radios, newspapers and television. They travel little and know few people except for family members. The only way they get and exchange information is the gossip among themselves. Many of them find mental comfort in superstition. Therefore, their minds are quite narrow and out of date. They are the most faithful guards of the old tradition from which they have suffered the most.

The Mothers

They are women aged from 35 to 55, with less than 3 children and are mostly the women of families now. Very few of them are full time housewives. They work with their husbands in the local family business. Their salary is not very high but it is an important part of the family income. This earns them a comparatively important position in the family. These days, the town and township enterprises are not as prosperous as before, and the older and poorer educated are facing the danger of losing their jobs. Those who really lost their jobs are forced to take up temporary jobs with lower salaries or become housewives.

Though they work, they have to do much more housework than their husbands. Things are not so bad for those who have their mothers or mothers-in-law to help them. Quite a lot of them have to work, to take care of the whole household and take care of their grandchildren and the old people of the family at the same time. So they are usually quite busy and tired.

Most of the mothers have finished their primary school but went no further. Because they work and take care of the education of the children and deal with all kinds of social affairs of the family, they have the basic knowledge of the society, but have no interest for more things. They spend their leisure time playing mah-jong, watching TV series, swearing and gossiping. But you cannot say that they are intellectually inferior to their husbands. At least, they have equal common sense with them. I know a lot of mothers who are the mainstays of the family. They make almost all the important decisions. They are energetic, hardworking and smart, and some of them in my opinion, are the most respectable women I've ever seen.

The Daughters

They are the daughters and young mothers, living with or near their parents' family. Usually, they don't care much about money; they have their parents and husbands to support them. They take up easy jobs and, as it is more and more difficult to find a proper job, they feel quite happy to stay at home and enjoy themselves, if possible.

Most of them have finished their middle schools. Those who haven't got the opportunity to go on studying will take up a life more or less similar to their mothers, but with few burdens. Some of them are required to work hard on their books since they were little girls. They pass their examinations and get the opportunity to receive further education in technical schools or colleges. After graduation, they'll choose to stay in cities and start their own lives. They will live independently and become new women who are completely different from their grandmothers, mothers, and sisters.

Now, we can see some of the basic features of contemporary Chinese women. Compared to their husbands, they are more bound to the family. The young generation women have gotten the opportunity to work and are able to support themselves, but when jobs are in a shortage, they are the first to lose them and the last to get them. They have basic education, but many of them have little interest in developing themselves because they think it's unnecessary, or they themselves are too old, too busy, too stupid or something else. Most of the daughters, as the only child of the family, are supported as well as the boys. They are more well-educated, more independent, and believe themselves not to be inferior to boys. They are the new women of this country. The mothers and the daughters benefit a lot from the policy of the new China, especially in family planning and the Women's Federation, which enable them to live more freely and to get more opportunities than their mothers and grandmothers.

Family Planning

Many westerners criticize the family planning in China for depriving women of their rights of giving birth to more children. They have their reasons. But it's beyond all doubt that the family planning policy greatly frees women, at least in two ways.

First, it frees the mother. Giving birth to a child is quite a time-consuming and energy-taking work. If a woman gives birth to 7 to 8 children, which was quite common in old China, and takes care of them until they can take care of themselves, it will cost her the best 20 years of her life, from 20 to 40. Now, because of the family planning policy, she is allowed to have one child, and with the help of her mother and mother-in-law and kindergartens set up by the government, she can bring up her child and as well as keep her job. If she wishes, she can also develop herself by further study.

Second, it frees the daughters in a family with sons and daughters. If the money and energy are limited, parents will do their best to support the boys, and sacrifice the rights of the daughters, because they are considered to be sure to leave the family one day. And the girls are the most likely to stay at home to look after their younger sisters and brothers and help their mothers with housework, when they ought to be in school. But if a family has an only daughter, the parents will concentrate their strength on her. These girls are not only provided with equal opportunities, but also have a sense of equality to anybody.

The Women's Federation

Another thing which is quite unique and important in Chinese women's lives is the Women's Federation. Any woman, no matter where she lives and where she works is taken care of by a certain Women's Federation. The Women's Federation enjoys vast rights from the carrying out of the family planning, issuing marriage licenses, to judging the complaints of a mother-in-law to her daughter-in-law. The Women's Federation is an important part of the local government and has its own voice, usually the voice of women, in all of the local affairs. Many able women start their careers as government officials with positions in the Women's Federation. The most important function of the Women's Federation is to provide women with a place to go when they are treated badly by their families or colleagues.

Conclusion

Most of the material of this report is from my own experience and from my aunt, who has worked for our local Women's Federation for 15 years. It is too too limited to be a scientific report of the contemporary Chinese women, but I've done my best to convey the lives of the women whom I am most familiar with and whom I love the most, hoping to provide a way to understand their lives and understand our own lives as young women.

9. Translating Marshall McLuhan in China

He Daokuan
Shenzhen University, Shenzhen, China

My first encounter with Marshall McLuhan

I worked at Goshen College in northern Indiana as a visiting scholar in the 1980-81 academic year. With 17 years'experience as an EFL (English as a Foreign Language) teacher, I was supposed to learn the state of art in the teaching of English language and literature.

Yet with a burning desire to be more than a good teacher, I ventured outside the boundaries of my mission. Besides courses in British Literature American Literature, modern linguistics and TOESL [Teaching of English as a Second Language], I took European Philosophy and Intercultural Communication courses. My teacher of philosophy Professor Marlin Jesche was profound and conversant; his speaking matched that of the marvelous Marshall McLuhan. My teacher of communication Professor Daniel Hess was prolific. The textbook we used for his ICC (Intercultural communication) class was his own work From the Other's Point of View, which is teeming with wisdom and experience in cross-cultural living and teaching.

There, I was fortunate enough to strike a friendship with Professor Robert Kohls, whose gift books such as Survival Kit for Overseas Living encouraged my bolder venture into this new field of learning. The assigned reading for Dan's ICC course included Edward T. Hall's Silent Language and Beyond Culture, and McLuhan's Understanding Media. They opened up a new horizon and enriched my research interest in humanities and social sciences.

Translation of Marshall McLuhan and Edward T. Hall

In the past dozen years and more, I had a strong urge to introduce ICC and communication into China in general and McLuhan and Hall in particular. As one of the pioneers of ICC, I helped found the China Association for Intercultural Communication as one of its vice-presidents. CAFIC was founded in 1995. This association has a strong humanities background with mostly language teachers as its backbone force. At the same time I participated in the work of Chinese Association of Communication (CAC) and was elected a vice-president. This Society leans heavily on social sciences, evolving mostly media and journalism professionals. CAC was founded in 2005.

Before that I had a wonderful chance to interpret McLuhan's ideas. It was in November 1986. I volunteered as an interpreter for the "Culture and Future" seminar jointly sponsored by the Academy of Chinese Culture and China Association for Future Studies. Among the numerous speakers from abroad was Frank Feather, Secretary General of the Canadian Association for Future Studies. His speech "Hi-tech Electronic Culture" focused on Marshall McLuhan. The venue for the seminar was the big auditorium of Beijing University. The warm response from the elite audience from all over China spurred me to attempt a translation of McLuhan's Understanding Media . The three translations of mine of its three editions (McGraw Hill, 1964 ; MIT Press, 1994 ; Gingko Press, 2003) came out in China respectively in 1992, 2000 and 2011. Understanding Media made its way into the 300 most influential books of China between 1980 and 2010.

Other works by McLuhan brought out by me in China are Essential McLuhan (2001); The Mechanical Bride (2004), Understanding Me: Lectures and Interviews (2004) and Letters of Marshall McLuhan (2005). It is a pity that no publisher in China has ever got the copyrights to print Chinese editions of McLuhan's other major work The Gutenberg Galaxy up to now. Meanwhile, I published translations of works on or related with McLuhan. These include Digital McLuhan (2001) by Paul Levinson, and Marshall McLuhan: The Medium and the Messenger by Phillip Mar¬chand.

Authors similar to Marshall McLuhan in a way have been my interest focus all along. So Harold Innis, Neil Postman, Paul Levinson, Robert

Logan entered into my translation projects. I have managed to put some of their works on the Chinese Market: Bias of Communication, Empire and Communications by Harold Innis, Technopoly by Neil Postman, Cellphone, Realspace, New New Media and Soft Edge by Paul Levinson.

2012 will see my translations of two of Robert Logan's works: Understanding New Media: Extending Marshall McLuhan and The Alphabet Effect. I will bring out another two of Harold Innis's works next year too. They are Changing Concept of Time and Strategy of Cutlture. I claim two dozen academic papers on Marshall McLuhan in standard academic journals, all in Chinese though. So allow me not ennumerate them here.

My translations and research papers have gone beyond Marshall McLuhan to cover Media Ecology as a theory group. The most salient product is my tanslation of Perspectives on Culture, Technology And Communication: The Media Ecology （ed. Casay Man Kong Lum） .

I have always enjoyed the wonderful meetings and conversations with Prof. Michael Prosser at various conferences in China. I marvel at his brain power, speech, rhetoric and charism and will be only too happy to contribute to his website and to translate his 1978 book, The Cultural Dialogue. (Professor He has translated Michael H. Prosser's 1978 The Cultural Dialogue, published in June 2013 with the University of Beijing Press.)

10. MY EXPERIENCE TEACHING THE BUDDHIST MONKS AND NUNS

Zhang Shengyong
Dezhou University, Dezhou, China

Teaching the Buddhist monks and nuns was a very special experience for me. Before the teaching, I hadn't thought I would be so close to a religion. And even afterwards, I didn't think that I would be as close as that experience to a religion.

Every time when I visit a temple, such as Putuo Mountain, one of the four famous mountains for Buddhism in China, I am interested in not only the Buddha statues, architecture and the ceremony but also the monks behind the statues, beating the wooden fish (a Buddhist percussion instrument), or striking the bell, or singing Buddhist songs which can take you to a spiritually ethereal place. In my eyes, the monks are mysterious, conservative and free from mere conventionality.

When I got the news that I was recommended to be one of the faculty members for the English training program for Buddhism in November 2008, I couldn't believe my ears. "Wow..." This was my first reaction with a long and deep sound. "That should be super cool!" After several seconds, I gave my confirmation to the Overseas Training Center of Shanghai International Studies University.

In order to spread Chinese Buddhism and strengthen the exchange with other countries in religion, the English Training Program for Buddhism was sponsored by the Buddhist Association of China and China Religious Culture Communication Association. Twenty-three Buddhist monks and nuns from different temples of China gathered in Shanghai to attend the program lasting for 8 months.

I had been preparing for my teaching before the lesson. But I just couldn't focus on the books. Could I treat the Buddhist monks and nuns as common students? What if I mention something offensive to Buddhism? Could I share some stories to entertain the class? Lots of questions filled my mind. I felt nervous and excited to meet them the next day.

When I opened the door, all the Buddhist monks and nuns looked at me, which made me more nervous. They all wore the yellow or grey Buddhism robes. Some were expressionless. Others smiled at me. I pretended to keep calm to start the lesson. After my self-introduction, it was their turn. Before the introduction, they all crossed their fingers to show respect. And they said to me, "Mr. Zhang, don't be nervous. We are nothing different from your regular students." Then we all laughed making the atmosphere relaxed and light.

Soon we got along well with each other. I found them knowledgeable and peaceful. Most of them had the experience of study in foreign countries, so they could tell the difference among several countries in Buddhism. And then you could listen to them carefully and interestingly how Chinese Buddhism formed and developed. They talk slowly but powerfully. They even could quote from the Buddhist scriptures to point the significance of religion in a culture. I loved to talk with them. So the class to some extent became a forum to exchange intercultural knowledge. I tried to answer them in English about how to form sentences to narrate the story of Buddhism. And they tried to explain my questions in English. By exchanging information, they improved greatly in English. And in return, I gained the knowledge of Buddhism. It seemed that they could transfer everything into Buddhist understanding.

They believe in destiny. So they know more than our ordinary people to cherish destiny. According to Buddhism, destiny is the bridge between reason and results and everything is connected to one another. So the relation of teacher and students or classmates is prearranged in destiny. As a result, we should cherish and respect the chance to meet. Just as Buddha says, it is the 500 times of looking back in the preexistence that we get the chance of passing by each other in this life. So maybe this explained mostly why they always keep peace and quiet.

Sometime we teachers complained about our hard task or our troubles in life. The Buddhist monks and nuns first listened to us quietly. After our complaints, they always explained to us from Buddhist points of knowledge. They told us just as Patriarch Bodhidharma said that it is inevitable for a person to rise and fall in life. Since we couldn't find what we lost in life, doesn't it make it worse if we lose our temper because of it? And then the loss would be doubled. So we should collect enough good karma in life to produce a better end.

I also found them the same as our ordinary people. Before knowing them, I always thought that they lived a very humble and simple life. On one hand, they indeed live a very simple life in the temple, focusing on a pure and spiritual stage. On the other hand, they lived a modern life which surprised me. Among all the Buddhist monks and nuns, each owns a laptop and mobile phone. When I asked them how they studied in the temple, they told me they could make use of the internet and TV programs to improve their practice. Besides, during the 8 months study, I was invited to the vegetarian restaurants to have dinner with them. And nearly most of the restaurants were quite expensive for me. In the restaurants, they were just like our ordinary people to order, talk and exchange table manners. In their spare time, several monks would go to the swimming pool to exercise. And they also would go shopping in Shanghai. This kind of their life surprised me a lot because in my opinion they should stay inside to chant sutras most of the time and keep a distance from the modern society. However, they could keep pace with time. And finally I understood why they liked me to treat them as ordinary students. For some of them, to be a Buddhist monk or nun was a way of making a living. They could get a salary regularly. And if one got bored about the life in the temple, he or she could resign. In a word, they were the same as us. We all have experienced a lot in life. And in the process of pursuing life, we have difference choices. For them, they chose to be Buddhist monks and nuns.

Now I still think of the days with them. Especially, I miss the simple life in the class or in their hotel with the Buddhist monks and nuns. I will always remember the afternoons with them, staying in the room, appreciating the fragrant tea and sharing opinions about Buddhism and culture, and through the sunshine from the window we could see the whole world.

11. The Power of Weibo in Public Communications (China)

Tony Xu
Shanghai International Studies University, Shanghai, China

When July 23, 2011 witnessed the horrendous rear-end collision of two bullet trains, near Hangzhou, resulting in hitherto the most horrendous derailment accident in contemporary China, Weibo, a.k.a Microblog, the Chinese Twitter, following traditional social media network like Kaixin and Xiaonei once again came to the fore as a platform which emanated heated public debates among people from all walks of life.

It was at about 8 p.m. peak hour for Chinese netizens when scores of ordinary people rather than rescue teams or medical teams arrived and rallied around the scene of the accident after a boom suddenly pulled their heartstring. It was the same group of people with portable digital media apparatus that reported the news to a wider public through Weibo – a case which has civic journalism writ large.

There is little doubt that this tragic event will go down in the Chinese communications history, yet whoever the history-recorder, Weibo definitely will be the word that to some extent characterizes the event. And it is true. Even the first tranche of the information regarding the tragic accident delivered by the national news agency had its origin from the pictures and videos taken by the netizens who were among the eyewitnesses right that night.

Journalists vs Onlookers; professional or amateurish?

Thanks to Weibo, it of course contributed further to the technology of networks. By integrating mobile phones with mini-cameras that work together with them in a network ambit, the way of history-recording is being revolutionized to a new height, one that stirs up checkered emotions. Conduit via which messages are communicated widened by Weibo, the monopoly of information releasing is shattered, turning a pyramid-like top-down mode into a network where sporadic dots are everywhere to be found, having the potential of being both the sender and receiver.

Micro as the blog is in the real sense of the two Chinese characters, the power of it is anything but micro. In effect, we have every reason to believe that micro-blogs represent mega-force. The adoption of user-generated pictures and their weibo messages by news agencies accelerates the speed of and widens the scope of communications and in return, this makes itself more competitive and authoritative. Conversely, disregard of those simultaneous pictures and messages deports themselves from the masses who are no longer on the receiving end of communications. In an epoch like nowadays, any attempts to cover up information against the popular will tend to backfire in the sense that their opponents will use this against them to shore up their own reputation and creditability by putting on an air of candidness.

That, therefore raises a question as regards the importance of the rapidity of information communication. My answer is yes, the importance is paramount. Right after they obtained online the news of the tragedy, the masses spontaneously came down to the scene and did everything within their capacity to help the trapped individuals. What's more, people living not far from the place where the two trains derailed and fell off the rail bridge lined up all night, waiting to have their blood donated to the needy. Taxi drivers, regardless of their night business, willingly traveled back and forth, carrying the wounded to the hospital, all gratis. Switch to other on-site people. They constantly released simultaneous information onto weibo with a view to helping people in the train liaison with their families as well as reporting the truth in a timely fashion. Information was none other than life per se.

On the other hand, feedback from the authorities paled in comparison to that of the public, be it in the richness of content or in veracity. Not only was little information released by the authorities; their attitude toward the reckless rescue incurred ferocious condemnations from the public. Mocking the rhetoric of the spokesman of The Ministry of Railways who irresponsibly responded to the media "Regardless of whether you believe what happened or not, I will buy it", the e-public invented ironical responses to ridicule similar unfair treatments.

From the perspective of PR communications, nothing is more abhorrent than deliberatively hushing up news the public has every right to know, not least when they are already in the know only that their wish is to be informed responsibly and timely

12. THE BEGGAR

Sun Zhen
Ocean University of China, Qingdao, China

A usual dusk in the Qingdao spring, with cool breeze and comfortable sunshine. It was about 5:40 p.m. The sun was pale orange and the sky was pink. Though it was Sunday, the intersection was just as busy and noisy, lines of vehicles and crowds of pedestrians waiting anxiously before the traffic lights and meantime swarms of others hurrying across the street, engines roaring. This crossing was right in the center of the city, Qingdao in Shangdong Province, China – a prosperous commercial zone, Carrefour, Sunshine, ICBC (Industrial and Commercial Bank Corporation), and Inzone Center each in one of its four corners. Surrounded by several skyscrapers, the basin seemed darker than it should have been at this time of the day and even buses and trucks were like mites with those giants, let alone pedestrians. A poster as high as five stories hung on top of the Inzone Center exhibiting pictures of the latest Volkswagen and propagating how promising it should be to join the business zone here. On top of the ICBC building, commercials showing its new credit cards, smiling staff and a tidy broad business hall were alternating on an enormous screen as wide as its roof. A mixed smell of dumplings, hot pancakes, hamburgers and baked sausages pervaded the atmosphere.

Zebra crossings connected four safety islands, from which pedestrians could go on to the corners of the intersection across narrow turning roads. Every time the traffic lights turned green, crowds of twenty or more people – most with shopping bags in their hands – went across the street from one island and then onto another, some with a deadpan expression while others were laughing or chatting excitedly. Just at one of the safety islands, right near the lawn on its corner, there seemed to be a crude black stone just brought from a quarry. Most people who stepped onto the safety island, however, just walked ahead towards the zebra crossing, waited and then crossed the street as if nothing special was there.

It was an old lady. The sloppy black cotton coat and dirty brown pants made her conspicuous in contrast to the red floor bricks and verdant lawn.

She groveled on her forearms and outer side of her left leg, her elbows on a cloth pad as shabby and black as her cotton coat. She kept staring at the ground with no movement at all. Overwhelmed by the breeze like a swath of withered grass, her grey hair was completely in a mess. In front of her there stood a red instant noodle bowl. Every time traffic lights turned green, she merged into the tides of pedestrians.

It was 6:05 p.m. The sky transited smoothly from orange to blue and it was comfortably cool.

A little boy staggered towards the safety island, one hand in his mother's. On going onto the safety island, the mother bent down to whisper something to his ear and the boy, when passing by the old lady, dropped some money into the bowl in such a clumsy manner that he almost made the money fall out. For the first time, the old lady raised her head and looked at them, one of her arms waving, or actually trembling, the other one keeping bent under her body to support her trunk. As the mother led her son away, she lowered her head, withdrew her arm and transformed back to a stone.

It was 6:21 p.m. and it was getting even cooler and wind heavier. The sun dangled on the horizon.

Traffic lights were red and pedestrians were waiting on the opposite island. The old lady reached one hand towards her bowl to put notes out into a black cloth bag under her body with a slow trembling motion. Then she put out a plastic beverage bottle, lifted her head against her stiff neck, raised it to her mouth, sipped and slowly put it back into her coat. Her hair was even messier in the heavier wind. Some time later, a young lady with long golden brown hair, fitted jacket, jupe jeans, purple tights and white high-heeled shoes laid some money into the bowl when passed by. The old lady seemed to try raising her head.

It was 6:35 p.m. and it was getting cold. The sky was now dark blue.

A man in a black suit strode over her bowl in a hurry but the old lady just kept staring at the ground as though nothing had happened. Later, she tried hard to bend her legs to the other side and her right leg took over the job to support her body. When traffic lights turned green, a migrant worker in dirty camouflage passed by, with a plastic bag in his hand containing two plastic disposable meal boxes. Shortly afterwards, a man with long messy hair and a big brown spot in his face stopped his bicycle beside a trash can on the pavement near the curb, reached his hand into it, pulled out an empty tin, pushed it into a wooden box on his bike and then hurried away. Staring at the ground, the old lady obviously paid no attention to that.

A middle-aged man in a black suit turned his head to the old lady and stared at her briefly when passing by and then just went along the zebra crossing away. Another man maybe in his thirties with a maroon leather jacket and blue jeans stopped not far from the lady, reaching his hands into his pockets one after one to find some money. Though it took him a bit of time, he finally found some and bent down to put it into the bowl.

It was 6:50 p.m. The road lights were all on although it was still not completely dark.

The old lady struggled to stand with her stiff legs and staggered to the other side of the safety island, the bowl in one hand and the pad in the other hand. There she kneeled down and then groveled as before, staring at the ground and keeping still. A young lady with a black suit went by but suddenly stopped, turned back and laid some money into the bowl.

It was 7:07 p.m. and the sky was completely dark. However, the basin was somewhat brighter and more energetic. Refreshed pedestrians chatted across the street, swamping into shopping centers, coffee bars, restaurants, gyms and KTVs. Colorful neon lights hanging on the skyscrapers, street-lights on both sides of the street and headlights of cars and buses rendered the street a warm orange color. Various delicate goods and beautiful garments in shop windows were so fascinating under the colorful light that pedestrians couldn't help stopping and appreciating them. The big screen had become so prominent with the dark sky that nobody would miss the rolling commercials that it showed, except the old lady.

Still, she was groveling there, like a stone. A man with a bicycle rode by just beside her within half a meter, nevertheless attracting none of her attention. Towards her a young couple came, their baby held by the husband. When passing her, the young mother, wearing sports clothes, took a wallet out of her handbag and put out some money. She handed it down into the bowl and then went by, joking with her husband, laughing happily. Later, a young man with long hair dyed golden and a cigarette in his mouth went by with his girlfriend, dropping some coins into the old lady's bowl. After they had gone away, the old lady reached into the bowl, got the notes and put them into her shabby black bag very carefully.

It was 7:31 p.m. The basin saw another round of prosperity. Crowds of pedestrians still waiting or hurrying across the road. Cars and buses formed a long line along the street from the intersection. Streetlights and neon lights were still bright.

The old lady tried hard to bend her stiff legs to the other side and kept on staring at the ground. Every time somebody put some money into her bowl, they could hear her murmur, "thanks...thanks..." "xiexie...xiexie." I was thinking, "the poor old beggar woman!"

B) Semester at Sea Around the World Study Voyage: Asia

1. "Incredible India:" Chennai, Nagercoil, Mamallapuram

Michael H. Prosser
University of Virginia, Charlottesville, Virginia,
Shanghai International Studies University, Shanghai, China

I have returned my third time briefly to India, our first port in Asia: Chennai-earlier known as Madras. My earlier visits to India included Delhi, Lucknow (where I gave a lecture series), Veranasi, Agra, Jaipur, and Mumbai. We arrived in the Arabian Sea at the South Western port of Chennai on October 10 and leave this evening at 8:00 p.m. going to Penang, Malaysia. Seven of us (plus our Indian guide Veil) took a long night train from Chennai to Nagercoil near the southern cape of India to visit for two days the plantation and farm of our friends, who have a son studying engineering in a southern California university.

Our visit in Nagercoil included traditional South Indian meals at our hosts' home; visits to a traditional herbal pharmacy and hospital; vegetable and spice gardens; a pottery-making unit staffed by exceptionally poor Indians; a spinning factory; a rubber plantation; and a coconut plantation. At the one palace in the region, the king was noted for his generosity in feeding up to 2,000 poor neighborhood residents. There, I had conversations with twenty-five young Indian men, university engineering students from Chennai, who discussed their own academic programs and some of whom wish to study later in the United Kingdom or United States.

In the evening of our first day, we went to Kanyakamari, at the southern-most tip of India, where we saw the monument holding some of the ashes of Gandhi. This was our second view of a coastal cape, the first being Cape Hope in Cape Town. On our second day in Nagercoil, one of the special features was our visit to the Pioneer School for 500 students, founded by our hosts who continue to be the school's patrons. We were met by the principal, teachers, and a group of boys and girls. All of the students, girls and boys each separated on one side of the assembly room, sang an opening Hindu prayer for us. Two small girls performed very lovely and precise classical Indian dances for us. The students were invited to ask us questions, but they were all too shy to do so.

The Pioneer School Magazine, in its "Annual Report 2008-2010" notes that "The School has acquired the status of being a byword for excellence in academic performance." In the matriculation examinations, in 2008 and 2009, the school achieved 100% results. Many individual students were complimented on winning prestigious academic awards in mathematics, physics, computer science, biology, social science, Tamil, elocution, essay, short story, and poetry writing, fancy dress, drawing competition, and music, plus physical education and sports: javelin throw, discus throw, 400 meter race and long jump, basketball, lawn tennis, karate, chess, shuttle cock doubles, badminton, and tennis.

Teachers attended monthly workshops on communication skills, structured thinking skills, first aid training, personality development, and subject training. In the principal's remarks, he notes "to rest is to rust," "the students had a great opportunity to attend many programmes where they have metamorphosed from dull, lazy, and scared into bright, confident and courageous butterflies," and " 'not just coexistence, but an active part in the society around us'" is a value which is a hallmark of our institution." The magazine had many short essays in Tamil and English, inspirational pieces, poems, proverbs, art, and jokes by both teachers and students, plus photos of award winning students, and ads by parents of some students, including their children's photos.

Before we left her home, our host gave each of us a copy of one of her favorite books written by her personal long-time guru: Paramahansa Yogananda's 2001 Autobiography of a Yogi, Dakshineswar, Kolkata: Yogoda Satsanga Society of India. In Chennai, we visited the NGO Working Women's Forum, founded in 1978, "a pioneer in social mobilization-strategy, committed to transform over a million women in extreme poverty into powerful and confident leaders of many households, equal partners in community-neighbourhoods." The forum provides "access to credit, education, health care, training/orientation towards promoting social and financial independence to fight poverty, matching the objectives of millennium development goals of the United Nations (2000). Taking responsibilities to organize these poor women around their own households, markets, communities and neighbourhoods, the forum... now a social movement of 11,030,726 women in three southern states of India in 14 branches spread over 3,676 villages and 2,270 slums.... The credit programme of ICNW reaches over 5 million poor entrepreneurs effecting nearly 1,745,45 million rupees, accomplishing 99 % recovery rate in the urban slums/urban areas." In India, 41 % live below the poverty line of $1.00 a day." WWF is a future oriented-multi-pronged initiative and a pro-poor strategy that helps the Indian poor women to face the onslaught of globalization" (Working Womens' Forum Brochure).

In July 2011, US Secretary of State Hillary Clinton, an international advocate for women, visited the Forum, and identified cooperative ventures between the United States and Indian governments' grants to train women regionally at the Asia University of Women. Clinton noted that the US government was very interested in continuing to help the Forum to overcome violence against women in South India as well as to create smoke-free cooking stoves for the poor women in their households to protect their respiratory health. Clinton indicated that the US government has worked with many partners around the world to create the Global Alliance for Clean Cookstoves, while the Indian government created in 2009 its own National Biomass Cookstove Alliance. Paraphrasing her address at the Fourth UN Conference on Women in Beijing in 1995, Clinton concluded her remarks: ..."so that you not only help yourselves and your families but you spread the word about microfinance, about bank accounts, about starting businesses, about getting health services, about empowering the women of this state (Tamil Nadu), and giving everyone a chance to live up to your God-given potential" (Groots, Grassroots Organizations Operating Together in Sisterhood, South Asia, 2011, January-July, Vol 15, Issue 31.

We met several of the women leaders of the Forum, some speaking in English, and others in Tamil (and interpreted into English) Our participants had many questions for the women leaders and also were shown the WWF bank loaning and retrieval offices processes. The Forum has made a major proposal for grant funds from the William J. Clinton Foundation, which the Forum leaders were optimistic to receive because of the earlier visit of Hillary Clinton.

All of our ports include service projects, working with Habitat for Humanity, and making service visits to orphanages, hospitals, special needs facilities, and social development projects, all of which have been popular with a reasonable number of the shipboard community members. It is a consistent goal of the Semester at Sea to help its students and other participants to develop a social conscience toward those who are poor or oppressed in each of our various ports.

Today, October 14, our last day in India, two bus loads of faculty and dependents, students, and Life Long Learners traveled to the Shiva Temple, the Sri Parthasrathy Temple decidated to Krishna, and other Dravidian temples, monuments and sculpture constructed, as well as the bas-relief 90 feet high rock face, and representing the Gangha River cascading down the face of the bas-relief, in and near Mamallapuram, in the seventh to tenth centuries, 75 and 100 kilometers from Chennai.

2. Carnatic (Hindu) Music in India

Johnny Snelgrove
Willamette University, Salem, Oregon

I spent most my time in India studying under a Veena maestro in Chennai. I'm not exactly sure how I started with lessons. An odd series of fortunate events involving a well-connected rickshaw driver brought me and my guitar to the maestro's front door. After waiting for forty-five minutes in the office, the master soon came in and introduced himself. "My name is Subramanian, but if you have trouble with pronunciation you can just call me Superman," he told me, and then he asked me what I wanted to learn. I didn't have much of an answer so I just replied, "Carnatic music".

Subramanian chuckled then said, "Let's start with a cup of tea." We spent the first two hours of my lesson in conversation. Subramanian described the ways of Hindu thought, how these philosophical ideas related to music, how they related to life, to everybody and everything that surrounds us, and how these ideas formed the basis of individuality. Every abstract thing, he explained to me, is relative. The most important concepts exist in the connections between everything and everyone. An individual is made an individual by virtue of their relationship with the external world. A name and a body are not distinct and cannot act as the defining features of an individual. An individual is defined by the social connections he has with the people and objects around him.

For two hours, Subramanian blasted my mind with these and similarly intense philosophical concepts. I started noticing a pattern in Indian ways of thought: they love to classify everything. The Carnatic scale system, for instance, consists of seventy-two melas (scales) derived by extrapolating every possible seven-note scale from a twelve-tone system. The rhythmic structure is a collection of rhythmic cycles called tala. There are seven tala, but any number of counts larger than two within any given tala can be substituted with either a count of three, four, five, seven, or nine, thus leading to a immense number of possible tala (interestingly enough, the most common tala called Adi Tala is an eight beat count that goes 4+2+2.

Why do most cultures love 4/4 time so much? Anyway, I wouldn't recommend straining your grey matter over this unless you really want to start learning how to play the tabla drums. I'm just supporting my claim that Indian culture loves classification. The Hindu set of deities, the Vedas, the cuisine, lovemaking (kama sutra), music, the governmental system, and the ancient societal caste system are all attempts to categorize and apply a structure to the chaos of life. India's intricate classifications amplify the mysticalness of Indian culture. Classification is not unique to Indian culture, however. The magnitude of classification sets India apart from other cultures' attempts to make sense of the world. Being a big fan of symbolic logic, I loved all the classifications. There's just so much to memorize, though.

After our tea, Master Subramanian had me reflect and write about all the concepts he'd just bombarded me with. I wrote feverishly, trying to transfer all the ideas to paper before they slipped from my consciousness. Some got away, but not all. We then went over the Indian solfège system (the same concept as do, re, me, fa, sol, la, ti, do from the Sound of Music) for the next three hours of my lesson. The Indian solfège still has seven syllables but they are named: sa, ri, ga, me, pa, dah, ni, sa. We sang these and Subramanian used this as the basis for teaching me the seventy-two scales. The next of the time I spent memorizing all seventy-two scales. I now know the scales conceptually, so it's just a matter of getting each one into my ears and knowing them in a musical way.

For the next four days, I returned to study with Master Subramanian for about six or seven hours per day with a short lunch break halfway through the lesson. When I finally became mentally exhausted, we'd have dinner. Not until the second to last day did we even play anything. It took a lot of theory and conceptualizing to even get to playing music. The amount we covered in only four days was pretty impressive, though. The way I imagine music, especially melody, has drastically evolved. Indian classical music focuses more on the way you get from note to note. Even these are categorized into ten (although the number is debated) techniques called the gamakas. Transferring these gamakas to guitar has proved the most challenging part of learning Carnatic music. The notes just don't bend far enough.... But I'll try, and eventually I'll be able to at least approximate the gamakas. There is still so much to learn. Master Subramanian's daughter attends school in Portland, Oregon, so I have the feeling we will meet up again in the future. I'm shrinking the world, one country at a time, shrinking the world

3. "Good Morning, Vietnam!"

Michael H. Prosser
University of Virginia, Charlottesville, Virginia,
Shanghai International Studies University, Shanghai China

Many of us remember Robin Williams' reasonably lighthearted, but deeply satirical movie "Good Morning, Vietnam!" and perhaps also the much darker Viet Nam remembrance movie, "Apocalypse Now," or "Avatar," or the late Robert McNamara's book, In Retrospect: The Tragedy and Lessons of Vietnam. Many of the Semester at Sea participants have visited the War Remnants Museums in Hanoi and The Ho Chi Minh Museum in Ho Chi Minh City. Some of our students, born long after the war ended, felt that these museums were too anti-American.. They might be reminded that young National Guard troops actually killed students their own age at Kent State University and Jackson State University in 1970. Recently in the Semester at Sea Global Studies classes, two Viet Nam US veterans gave very impassioned presentations about their experience at war time and their imprisonment there, leading one to choke-up as he stated that he could not forgive his American government for lying to him about the purposes of the war. He also reminded us that while 58,000 American military men and women had died in the war, 60,000 Viet Nam veterans have committed suicide since the war was over.

During the late 1960s, as a faculty member first at the University of Buffalo and then Indiana University I listened to their protests, sit ins, and "speak ins,"never having been a veteran myself, I counseled students who were seeking conscientious objector status, or who were talking about going to Canada so that they could not be drafted. In my visit to Viet Nam in 2004, I often heard the saying: "The North won the war, but the South won the economy." Then the Mekong Delta area was flooded with young European tourists.

Today, Viet Nam is considered one of the economic miracles of southeast Asia, and this seemed quite obvious in my recent visit in and around the area of Saigon or Ho Chi Minh City. One would scarcely recall the southern Vietnamese Cu Chi Tunnels, except as a quirky tourist attraction.. Some of our students took a trip to to see Ankor Wat and Phnem Penh's "killing fields" museums. While we saw extraordinary poor villages in Ghana, and many of the remaining scars of South Africa's Apartheid era, hopefully this visit to Viet Nam also gave our students a serious and sobering view of America's involvement in such wars as Viet Nam, Cambodia, Iraq, and Afghanistan. As one of our staff participants articulated: "War doesn't say who is right, but only who is left."

Presidents Bill Clinton and George W. Bush both visited Viet Nam during their presidencies, and now the United States and Viet Nam have very strong trade relations. In China there is the American business concept of "China plus one" which means that many companies have major business enterprises both in China and one other Asian country (or more).

4. Saigon Jazz

Johnny Snelgrove
Willamette University, Salem, Oregon

I mostly bummed around Saigon while in Vietnam; hopping around the city, just me and my guitar on the backs of rusty old motorcycles. There are thousands upon thousands of motorbikes pouring down the busy streets of the city. The liquid traffic: a river of buzzing puttering exhaust. On foot, crossing the street is akin to fording a river – only the river can potentially run you over. One afternoon, I wandered into a ritzier part of Saigon. French influenced architecture, tall modern glass buildings filled with shopping malls, and chandelier laden hotels (complete with a pianist playing pop songs in an over-the-top, sappy, arpeggiated manner) all led me to believe that this part of Saigon belonged to the tourists. On the edge of all the glamor, though, I encountered a club with the words "Jazz" scrawled across the entrance in neon lights. A board outside the front door listed the acts for the night: Live Jazz! Special Guests Tonight: 9:00 p.m to 12:00 p.m Mr. Gnan Manh Guan, Ms. Guyet Joan, Ms. Jennifer Ghuy, and, Mr. Johnny Guitar. I shook my head, blinked, then reread the sign. "Special guest, Johnny Guitar."

Could there be another newly arriving jazz musician named Johnny Guitar in Saigon? Or maybe someone had caught wind of my wandering and minstreling and signed me up to play. At 9:00 p.m., I'd return to the club to resolve all this. I spent the rest of day in a park with a group of Vietnamese college students. I played them some songs, then a crowd started to gather, and everyone in the park seemed to want a picture with me. I'm guessing they didn't get a lot of folks wandering through playing American cowboy tunes. The Vietnamese expressed an openness and curiosity I'd not yet encountered anywhere else in the world. I think my character seemed so foreign to them, they couldn't help but ask questions and take pictures. I had a good day in the park and I made some good friends.

Later that night, I made my way back to the Jazz club (called the Sax n' Art Jazz Club). I didn't know what to expect: a welcome or another

Johnny Guitar. I pushed through the glass doors, past the doorman, and into the dark cocktail lounge. More neons light the stage. Purple, red, green. A band had already started playing and each performer glowed their own hue of neon. Front and center, a tall man, somewhat bulky, with a long dark slicked-back ponytail, coaxed blues licks from a heavy sunburst Les Paul. No doubt about it, this was Johnny Guitar. I took a seat and propped up my guitar beside me. The drinks priced steep, yikes. Ritzy. After their set ended, I wandered over to the bar to meet Johnny Guitar. The exchange went a little like this: "You wouldn't happen to be Johnny Guitar?" I ask. "Yup, that's me, born a Greek Turk, started playing piano as a kid, but couldn't stand the stuff, picked up a guitar, ya know? So I took off to Australia, what about you, man, where you from?" "Name's also Johnny Guitar." I tell him. "Your last name's Guitar?" He asks. "Nah, Snelgrove. You're Greek? I play some Greek music; rebetiko, man." "Yeah, Greek Turk, got stuck playing Greek junk making a living, got sick of it, had to get out, went to Australia, still got stuck playing that stuff, so I took my guitar, renamed myself, came to Asia, met a woman in Hong Kong – women, they're crazy, man – she went to prison, I came here, became a rockstar, I'm Johnny Guitar, man, everyone knows me around here – there's a lot of pretty ones, eh – they're crazy, man, I'm tellin' you, so what, you wanna play?"

I told him about my global music quest, he called over some band members, introduced me, then we decided on some jams. We played at the end of the night, but I had trouble getting into a good groove. I played Johnny's guitar, but couldn't get a feel for it. The thing was too touchy. I'd pluck a note and it'd yelp, so I'd lighten up the pick and it'd get too quiet. The strap also didn't fit, which forced me into tucking the brick of a guitar under my armpit to keep it steady while playing. I eventually got a stool. Nevertheless, the band dug it and invited me out to another spot called Thi Cafe the next night. I found Thi Cafe on accident. During my wandering, I came upon the Saigon Backpacker's District: a part of town filled with dance clubs, tour agencies, junk stores, drug dealers, and Australian backpackers. I caught melodic strains of a psychedelic synthesizer while passing by a little hole-in-the-wall pub. Only later did I check my pocket book and realize that this was the spot I'd been invited. The synth player was an intellectually gruff looking bearded Australian fellow who growled the name "Tim Tiger" upon his introduction. We chatted about music, jazz, then he asked if I wanted to play tonight. Of course. So I set up as the rest of the band leisurely wandered in. A drum set, keyboard, tangles of cables, amps, and microphones crowded the stage of the little club. Nobody seemed worried about whether or not I'd ruin their act. All pretty chill cats, hip, down to earth, Australian. At six, we started playing standards. The place began filling up quickly, and everyone dug the tunes. To my surprise, they didn't kick me off the bandstand. I played the entire first set with them (then they played some of their own tunes after that). Nobody from the previous jazz club showed up at Thi. I told the band Johnny Guitar had invited me out here. The bassist asked, "did he freak you out?" Then added, "that dude kind of freaks me out." I agreed, Johnny Guitar was a bit of a loony eccentric. An intense dude.

This was definitely a more happening spot. Less ritzy, more authentic – the bar even provided me a couple beers on the house (a first on this trip). The Thi band really made Saigon for me, and I'm glad I got some recordings of our show (which you can listen to and download at http://thesaltiestminstrel.blogspot.com/p/recordings. html).

They invited me back to play the next night, but I had to leave town. All the local musicians seemed pretty unsatisfied with the jazz scene in Saigon, but compared with many places, it wasn't too dismal. Saigon offered at least a few good spots to play, and a good pool of musicians to draw from. Saigon surprised me. It's interesting how jazz has permeated pretty much every society I've visited so far. I've never heard of any sort of resistance to jazz, either. Other musics have had a resistance when they enter another culture, but this all depends on social context.

The brother of a drummer I met, for example, was beaten and imprisoned for six months because he played American rock music. For (not so) obvious reasons, I'm going to leave out the name of the country where this occurred.

Jazz has almost always been favorably looked upon. Even though Jazz originated in seedy bars and dark alleyways, it has evolved to become a respectable and complex music. For this reason, any country looking to modernize and prove their progressiveness to the world is going to welcome jazz musicians. The owner of the Sax n' Art club attended Berklee College of Music in Boston. After graduating, he eventually returned to

Vietnam and started the Sax n' Art jazz club in the ritzy part of Saigon. I wonder if the Vietnamese Government sponsored his schooling. Now Vietnam has a world class saxophonist running one of the hottest clubs in Southeast Asia – something like that looks pretty impressive to the rest of the world. This makes me think of Darwin's survival of the fittest concept. If a country has the means to spend time, energy, and money on something as – this hurts to say – pointless as music, then they must be healthier and more advanced than countries that don't have jazz musicians. The nightly light-shows in Hong Kong, China's intense eagerness to host the Olympics, the excessiveness of Dubai – these are all power plays. Every little bit counts. The more a country can present itself as a modernized global power, the better chance it has of surviving in this aggressive, capitalist world we've created. Hooray for jazz musicians; we make nations look tough.

5. Japan 1974, 1980, 2009, and 2011

Michael H. Prosser
University of Virginia, Charlottesville, Virginia,
Shanghai International Studies University, Shanghai, China

Nihonmatsu, 1974

In July, 1974, besides time in Tokyo, I participated in a bicultural research conference and project in the northern resort city of Nihonmatsu, Japan, for 9 days, intended to demonstrate cultural similarities and differences between the Japanese and Americans. There were 64 of us, 32 Japanese of various ages and professional backgrounds and 32 Americans also varied in ages and professional backgrounds, plus a technical team of 8 persons. Three days included both the beginnings and endings of the project, involving an opening reception, plus pre and post semantic differential polls, each of us keeping a daily journal for the nine days, and for six days, there were 8 cross-generational groups of 4 Japanese and 4 Americans whose nonspecific goal was simply to communicate together. The six days in the small groups were all videotaped for further observations by the combined Japanese and American research team; on one half day, for some reason, all of the sound was lost on all eight video cameras, causing the research team to add research assumptions on the nonverbal dimensions illustrated on the eight cameras. One group spoke entirely in Japanese; another in Japanese and English; and six others all in English.

A number of different hypotheses were developed about the eight groups and about the participants in terms of the different research procedures being utilized. For example, it was assumed that the all Japanese group would remain more formal, while the six all English language groups would become more informal over time, and this turned out to be true. It was assumed in the absence of specifically assigned topics, that the Japanese would tend to be task-oriented and the Americans would tend to be process-oriented. However, the findings demonstrated that the younger members (both Japanese and Americans) tended toward process-orientation and the older members (both Japanese and Americans) tended to be more task-oriented. Unfortunately, in this first bicultural research project, there were both serious intercultural and intracultural tensions and difficulties, which led to the cancellation of the projected book with the research findings and results, specifically because the Japanese leaders found the process and results to be too culturally sensitive and their concern that their members would "lose face."

From my own consistent journal notes, in my 1978 text book, The Cultural Dialogue (1978, pp. 216-286), I featured one quarter of the book for the intercultural dialogue which had taken place. In 1982, the book was partially published in Japanese by Toku University Press in Tokyo. Part IV of the book "The Cultural Communicator in Dialogue: Observations on Japanese and American Cultures." To provide a Japanese perspective, I invited a Japanese participant living in Hawaii, Muneo Yoshikawa, still an important contributor to the study of intercultural communication, to write an essay for the book: "Some Japanese and American Cultural Characteristics." Following this Chapter 11, I offered additional chapters based on my own observations: Chapter 12: "A Journal of an American's Cultural Dialogue in Japan: Preparing for the Dialogue"; Chapter 13: "Beginning the Dialogue"; Chapter 14: "Communication Breakdown"; Chapter 15: "Concluding the Dialogue"; and Chapter 16: "Evaluating the Dialogue." One recent scholar writing about the bicultural research conference has noted that my observations provided a much more positive perspective on the event than that remembered by many of the participants, both Japanese and American.

More recently, continuing to propose the notion of cultural dialogue as a basis for effective intercultural communication, Professor Li Mengyu of Ocean University of China in Qingdao and I decided to write our intercultural communication text book for Chinese university students, Communicating Interculturally published by Higher Education Press in Beijing, in June, 2012. We included for each chapter and the Epilogue an imaginary dialogue between a class of imaginary Chinese students, an imaginary Professor Zhang (an extraordinarily common "Old One Hundred" name in China), and myself as really myself

Japan, 1980

I had been invited by the United States Information Agency's cultural division to give sponsored lectures in South Korea and Singapore. Enroute to South Korea, I spent a week in Japan, visiting several of my former Indiana University and University of Virginia Japanese MA students at their homes, and thus traveling extensively in that short time from home to home, near Tokyo all the way to Kyoto and then to the north of Japan. Although my former students didn't know each other, as I proceeded from one home to another, each one would call the next one who would then meet me at the train station in his locality. One of these former students wrote a large number of practical books to teach English to Japanese; another later got his Ph.D. degree in communication; and still another was the head of a Buddhist/Shinto temple complex which he had inherited at his father's death. Being reunited with these former students in their own homes was indeed a great pleasure.

Japan, 2009

My young Chinese friend and I met together in Fukiama to go to Kumamoto, Japan in September, 2010 for the International Association for Intercultural Communication Conference, where we saw many people whom we had met earlier, and we were hosted by the very gracious conference chair, an American professor married to a Japanese husband. Besides my conference presentation, I gave two speeches at the University. We visited the very sobering Peace Museum in Nakasaki and Osaka. Several groups of Japanese school students were present during our visit, but they had a hard time focusing on the terrible images of the devastation there in 1945.

Japan 2011

Following a six day visit to Hong Kong and Shanghai, as a part of the Semester at Sea voyage this autumn, the M/V Explorer docked in Kobe for two days; about 200 of us stayed on the ship for the voyage north to Yokohama (a half hour by train from Tokyo) where we were docked for another two days before departing on our eight day North Pacific Ocean crossing to Hilo, Hawaii for Thanksgiving. Japan was the most expensive set of ports on our entire voyage, and our guides appeared to have much less command of English than we expected. Some of us older participants were less active in Japan on this visit than in the past port visits. Perhaps, we were beginning to tire of the then almost three months as a part of the study tour.

C. Public Conversation: Ten Questions for Cui Litang

Cui Litang, Xiamen University
Tan Kha Kee College, Xiamen, China

Michael H. Prosser
University of Virginia,
Shanghai International Studies University

Biography: Cui Litang

Cui Litang, MA, professional instructor of EFL/ESL, teaching Chinese as a foreign language and mass communication, multilingual translator, web author and developer, podcaster, with over 25 years of teaching/consultant experiences at colleges, universities and organizations in China, USA, Australia and Germany Yangzhou University, Beijing Language and Culture University, Australian Broadcasting Corporation, Deutsche Welle, Shandong Normal University, Green River Community College, USA, Shanghai Industry & Commerce Foreign Language College, Global LT, Jiang Nan Polytechnic College of Film and TV Art, Shanghai Normal University/Tianhua College).

As a visiting scholar at Green River Community College, he has been honored as a cultural ambassador and rewarded with an honorary membership of Green River Community College Humanities Division for his excellent services. And for his continuing tenure as an EFL/ESL instructor he has received an honor for his contribution in instructions at Shanghai Industry and Commerce Foreign Language College. His translations and writings as a contributing author reflect his research interest in linguistics and media.

Michael H. Prosser: About two weeks after I arrived to teach at Yang-zhou University in 2001, the World Trade Center twin towers and the Pentagon were struck by airplanes, and one airplane was crashed in Pennsylvania as it headed toward Washington, D.C. My son called me from the Washington area about 4 hours after it happened, but at 1 a.m. in China, and I hadn't heard yet about it.

As one who was interested then in matters related to the media and since, can you speculate as to why CCTV could not have live coverage over 9/11, but only delayed coverage, and could not have live coverage of such an important event until the Iraq War broke out in March 2003?

Cui Litang: Thanks for refreshing up on the very first moment we met and got to know each other during my tenure at YZU. You're right. As a media guy since a long time ago, I have always had extensive media exposure, the print as well as the electronic media, and plus the internet. But in 2001 I was still more of a radio guy than a TV person, spending many hours daily tuned to VOA, BBC and several other international broadcasters on the shortwave, sometimes feverishly during crises. I happened to be at my favorite radio when VOA interrupted its normal broadcast giving way to the breaking news of 9/11 attacks. For a brief moment I thought it might be just an accident and then in no time when more details unfolding and flowing in, an unexpected fear began to loom large and true. Since I didn't own a satellite nor have the habit of watching TV online then due to the limited bandwidth, I watched CCTV occasionally and alternatively thereafter, in order to catch up on some live images, when I was not aware if or why preliminary CCTV coverage of 9/11 was delayed. As a state media, CCTV has strict guidelines in terms of international coverage, and on top of that all coverage is selected and edited. As for introduction of the extensive CNN live coverage of Iraq War on CCTV since March 19th, 2003, I think partially it was accounted for by China's Iraq policy and stance over sanction of Iraq, prior to the invasion. In addition, Chinese audiences were interested in watching some modern warfares and at the same time with a moral reason to keep a watch on that.

Michael H. Prosser: In the autumn of 2001, I joined the Yangzhou University College of Foreign Languages in the English Department. We met during that period, and you and your daughter, who was then about twelve, came one Friday evening for one of my English Corner open houses. Also, it was my pleasure to invite you to give some lectures in my two junior level mass communication classes. You and the class members were too kind to correct my Americanized mispronunciation of your family name which I said was "Cu ee." If I remember correctly, one of your major sources for your lectures in my classes was an Australian book on the mass media. Now you have had almost eleven more years of experience studying, teaching, and practicing in the media.

What are some of the special insights that you have gained in this period about the mass media in China in general?

Cui Litang: "Media is the message" is what Marshall McLuhan says about the human-media relationship. And this has turned out very true in my survival efforts over the past decades. I have been using the media to navigate the world, from the magic soundsphere of the radio world, to the deluge of subscribed newspapers and magazines and to the imagery world of film and TV. So it's only natural for me to have developed a profound interest and insight in man and media which has paved the way for some intellectual and academic research later, drawing on resources, not only like that of my personal media exposure, but also serious study and thinking. The Media is the Message, Cyberpunk Handbook, Neuromancer, Lines of Communication of Australian Broadcasting Corp., Intercultural Cooperation and its Importance For Survival, the Dynamics of Mass Communication, the Cultural Dialogue, Communication Theories: Perspectives, Processes and Contexts, the Diamond Age, Essential McLuhan, Radio Production, the NPR Guide to Audio Journalism and Production and Origins of Human Communication are among the publications that I have delved into in order to gain an explicit understanding of media and mass communication.

I appreciated your invitation to me that year for a guest speech in your media class, which I felt, has piloted my first media class in my life, and triggered my total plunge into media study. Since then, with this turn of interest, I have witnessed some interesting changes in my intellectual thinking involving pragmatic linguistics and about man and media relations. My published papers like " the Communication Convention and Functions of English Discourse Markers in Speech Communication" and

" A Map Without Boundary: William Gibson's Cyberpunk Novel Neuro-mancer Reexamined " have manifested this significant change.

About when I was going about launching my first course of " Let's Get to Know Mass Communication " at Shanghai Industry and Commerce Foreign Language College, I participated in a massive renovation pro-gram as an interior designer of Shanghai Municipal Situational Foreign Language and Experiencing Center which I have illustrated by presenting a brief communication history of English on the walls, all the way from Canterbury to the country in the New World.

In the meantime, as part of media practice, I have started to podcast irregularly on:

- o   facebook at http://www.facebook.com/people/Cui-Litang
- o   youtube at http://www.youtube.com/user/cuilitang
- o   flickr at http://www.flickr.com/photos/cuilitang myvoa, with media and communication related videos and photos. A better example of these is Bappa's Chinese New Year's Message at Shanghai Reman Factory of Caterpillar, when the General Man-ager, Bappa, a student of Global LT Chinese program delivered a message in Chinese to the factory.

On top of that, my website "Let's Learn Chinese the E-way!" also serves the purpose of communication. The general situation of the mass media in the last decade since 2001 has seen changes within the status of the state media, as analyzed in my contributing writing " Wrangling the Media Market Place " to Prof. Li Mengyu and Prof Michael Prosser's Communicating Culturally. Any further insights or speculations are not expected to go beyond that frame.

Michael H. Prosser: When I came to China, there were about eighty-four million users of the internet there. Today, the number is close to 500 million users. Few of my Chinese students had cell phones, there was almost no texting, and it was very unusual to see any students with a lap top computer. Now, there has been a genuine communication revolution in China.

How do you account for the rapid growth of all forms of communication and information technology in China over the last nearly dozen years? What are some of the things in this regard that the Chinese government has done well? What are of the things in this regard that the Chinese government has done poorly.

Cui Litang: Yes. Media technology has enormously proliferated over the past decades as embodied and manifested by the internet, when we have not only seen a surge of netizens but also convergence of media toward mobile and personal, to that of the media prophecy of EPIC 2014 by Robin Sloan and Matt Thompson. China has benefited from recent decades of economic growth which has fed the media consumption on the internet, and the growth of the internet in the size of e-commerce, in the number of educational, organizational, governmental and personal portals have, in turn, fed the growth of the internet and media in general. If this is to be accounted for by the favorable government policy, the sheer number of netizens shouts the story.

Chinese Premier Wen Jiabao has been reportedly in recent time to call for urgent economic and political reforms, indicating the existence of a number of unpopular issues in which the government is apparently held accountable for. The yawning gap between the rich and the poor, injustice, lawlessness and lack of freedom are believed to be among the urgent issues.

Take media censorship for instance, while there are no logical reasons why the Chinese Government should have blocked social media sites like facebook, twitter and YouTube as it has been alleged to, it is simply miraculous and remains a puzzle why more politically sensitive news sites like that of VOA and BBC are left open but not the website of similar status, of Deutsche Welle.

Michael H. Prosser: During the general period that I was at Yangzhou University (or shortly after), you had an opportunity to spend time at a college in the United States, but for some reason you were unable to undertake the experience. When it happened, you left Yangzhou University and later taught at Shanghai Industry & Commerce Foreign Language College. After the 9/11 event, the United States severely tightened visa requirements and cut the number of Chinese entering the United States significantly.

Did the problems arise because of the US Consular office, the Chinese government, or the inviting institution? Having given up your teaching post at Yangzhou University for this opportunity, what were the effects for you professionally and personally?

Cui Litang: I participated at the Beijing New Oriental School and US sponsored H-1B program in 2004, in order to fill a mutual job need in the United States. I had a hard time making a decision when realizing lots of a total 35 participants would end up teaching pre-schools.

But my urge to return to the United States was so strong that I eventually persuaded myself and spent quite some time, doing study in language development and cognitive studies which I decided were the least things that I was still interested in and might be useful in a long run in my intellectual life. Then I started to talk to some of my close friends in the United States about this move. A friend who later ran for the Congress in Silicon Valley discouraged the H1-B program by painting a gloomy picture of sweatshops as seen in the Silicon Valley, in California. Another friend who is now a VP at a community college simply pointed out the criminal nature of any fee to be charged for the H-1B program. Amid these concerns like this, the paperwork was already in process and eventually my H-1B visa petition was issued by US Immigrations on petition of my employer in the United States

By the end of 2004 I was only an entrance visa away from a real world teaching job in the United States. The president of the hiring company flew to Beijing and invited me over for a meeting, obviously for reasons that I have had many years of differentiating working experiences at colleges of higher education both in China and the United States. I was recommended for some US public charter schools rather than preschools for teaching, which I recognized as a fair and considerate gesture. Unfortunately for the exact same reason of many years of working at the university, I had trouble getting a passport when the travel document was already for easy grabs by mere presenting an ID card, according to a new policy. According to the local police, I would either have to give up the idea of going to the States or giving up my 20 year long job. With the visa petition already in place, the decision wasn't a difficult one for me, albeit after several heart to heart talk with the head of the HR department at YZU. At last I got my passport by giving up my teaching job at the university.

Unfortunately however before any entrance visa on petition was issued, all applications were put on a waiting list, for internal investigations on the side of the immigration. And this was when the whole program withdrew and I started to find my job beyond the university, while waiting for a reply of go-ahead for my return to the university as I later requested.

Shanghai Industry and Commerce Foreign Language College, as a newly developed polytechnic college, provided some unprecedented opportunities and challenges in the areas of instructions where more autonomy and creativity were practiced, in resources where efforts of creation were usually encouraged and facilitated, and with students whose level range in English was tremendously random and various, put on a curriculum that typically emphasized " doing " over "studying." At some point, I felt intellectually displaced. Fortunately all in all I have had some great classes there and good working experiences with some of my colleagues.

Michael H. Prosser: The Shanghai Industry and Commerce Foreign Language College, where I gave my first presentation outside of Shanghai International Studies University after I arrived there in 2005 had a very pleasant environmental feeling about it. Some of the students that I met seemed quite interested in my power point presentation on global media, while others seemed quite detached. While there, I attended an English corner by the Greek columns and these students seemed relatively proficient in English. Perhaps the general English level was lower than that of students whom I had taught at Yangzhou University or from 2002-2005 at Beijing Language and Culture University.

If you were to compare the English proficiency of students at Yangzhou University and the Shanghai Industry & Commerce Foreign Language College, how would you rate each general group in their English proficiency? What were the main goals of teaching English at the College and what was the success rate?

Cui Litang: Good observation. Shanghai Industry and Commerce Foreign Language College is a polytechnic college, specialized in job training and in fast process of staffing. English is taught either as a major, with students whose study slants towards a specific line of business or trade, for instance, tourism, conference and exhibition, so on and so forth, or a non-major for students whose majors are anything but English. By the nature of recruitment their level range of English is tremendously various, with some real good, many are lower than average state colleges or universities. The success rate in English should be indicated by national CET-4/6, or in this instance, PETS or equivalents when they choose to take.

Michael H. Prosser: More recently, you have had the opportunity to teach at Green River Community College and received an honor from the College for your contributions.

Can you identify what kinds of courses you provided there? Were they focused on the mass media, internet, or other information technologies? Were your students preparing for careers in the media or information technology or were they preparing to enter a four year college or university after receiving their associate's degree?

Cui Litang: I visited the United States on a J-1 visa, as a visiting scholar, for an exchange program in 1995 when I was to teach Mandarin Chinese at Green River Community College, in the State of Washington. Home to Boeing and Microsoft Company, 1995 in the State already saw the primary school year of the internet when the internet was only a notion in China, meager access was only available in several major universities in Beijing. And this was a time when my very first personal computer was yet to be donated by Prof. Bruce Haulman at Green River Community College. Since I had prepared all my teaching materials both for classes and lectures in advance, and everything was supposed to be manual, primitive and nothing in digital. During the credit course, I used my charter of strokes in the classroom, demonstrating and tracing the strokes of Chinese writing system on the blackboard and acting the reading in real voice, though I was able to project students' academic records from an Apple, retrieving e-mail messages from PINE on a Windows-based computer and voice messages on the office phone, thanks to generosity of Prof. Bruce Haulman in sharing his office.

Our Chinese class had a cross section of American and international students. Except one or two elder students, most were to transfer to a four year college or university. As a credit course, the Chinese class provided them with the credits they would need and a rewarding multicultural experience they would fondly remember.

Michael H. Prosser: No doubt you met a variety of hospitable townspeople, faculty, staff, and students during your time at Green River Community College.

What were your impressions about these people with whom you had contact there? If you were to compare your students at Shanghai Industry & Commerce Foreign Language College and Green River Community

College, how would you compare their values and world views? Did you have other opportunities for travel to other areas? If so, what insights could you draw from these experiences?

Cui Litang: My working and living experiences at Green River Community College have shaped a fundamental American outlook in me. Three of my American host-families on regular basis plus several other accidental hosts or hostesses provided not only the conveniences and comfort of a genuine home but also plenty of opportunities of learning, through no holds barred communication and occasional traveling.

All my American and international students at Green River Community College were extraordinary in pursuit of learning as well as in treating their teacher. We drove to Vancouver, Canada, to and from, buying music CDs and books, watching movies. We pigged out in the Sushi Bar devouring the Japanese delicacy, and we had our jiaozi party churning out the Chinese dim sun on our fingers and then got lost in the long lane potpourri of international food.

Oops and ouch! I missed two important organized opportunities of travel when I was at Green River. One was a fun trip to Disneyland in California, and the other one was a study trip to Ecuador. But I think I made up later by seeing more things in the Northwest of the United States: watched the baseball game at the dome in Seattle, trip to Vashon Island, yachting at the bay, a cruise to San Juan Island, a night at the Indian Beach, a picnic at the Mountain Rainier National Park, a long drive to and the Indian country in Idaho, let alone a magnificent flight over the snow-covered mountains in a sports plane.

Americans are hardworking people whose good work ethics is illustrated not only by their work, but also the way they seek fun and enjoy themselves. Yachting, kayaking and flying are their regular menu of fun. Potluck is the way they identify themselves when clubbing and a way they present their best home cooking. Yes they are busy, and they have to check their schedules for you, as they might be busy working on a project, or away in the dome watching a baseball game. And this also provides a footnote to their robust individualism.

In comparison, my Chinese students at Shanghai Industry and Commerce Foreign Language College were less ready to talk in English, though I remember trying to talk with some of them in Shanghainese, for fun. The

Shanghai students were laid back and less likely to worry their heads off over a no-pass if anyone would ever get. They might like to put on some makeup but they didn't pretend! On some rare occasion, several of us, me and several students of mine, ate out at the nearby restaurant, over some chats in Chinese, like the one before their graduation when one of them was leaving for the army. I remember fondly one student of mine volunteered to erase the blackboard, one class after another, and I quoted her as an example of shining hope.

Michael H. Prosser: In Li Mengyu's and my book on intercultural communication for Chinese university students, Communicating Interculturally, which is in press at Higher Education Press in Beijing, you provided an excellent essay, "Wrangling the Media Market," with an emphasis on the problems that Google was then having with the Chinese government over censorship.

What were your major conclusions when you wrote the second draft, as events were happening rapidly in that matter, and more recently when you consider the status of Google and its relationship with the Chinese government and its censors? It appears that Baidu benefited greatly from the problems that Google encountered. Can you discuss this matter more fully and the effects for Baidu versus Google, or other western media entering China?

Cui Litang: The Chinese media state since the Google China row has not undergone any significant changes as the state status of media remains unchanged. The alleged blocking of facebook, twitter and youtube by the Chinese government can hardly be verified by any individuals though a study released early this month by David Bamman, Brendan O'Connor and Noah Smith from the Language Technologies Institute at Carnegie Mellon University unmistakably indicates political content is subject to censorship on the Chinese social media site Weibo, based on their analysis of 57 million messages at between June 27 and September 30, 2011.

Over time, before it is commonly aware of, Baidu has edged over Google as the No. 1 search engine in China, with 83.6% query share over 11.1% since fourth quarter of 2010. And Baidu seems to have reemerged as the search engine of China.

Among a few things that favor Baidu: fast search speed at local servers and free music downloads. But since Baidu search results are filtered on government requirements, chance of penetrating by western media is significantly curtailed.

Michael H. Prosser: When the bullet train collided with another oncoming train on July 23, 2011 near Wenzhou after a lightening strike on the power system, a two year old baby was found alive in the wreckage, and the Chinese government identified considerable railway leadership corruption before the accident. Bloomberg News reported on December 29, 2011 that "Mismanagement and design flaws were the main causes for the crash that killed 40 people near the eastern Chinese city of Wenzhou, according to the report issued yesterday by the State Council, China's cabinet. The government punished 54 officials and ordered the railway ministry to improve management of the high-speed rail network, the report said."

On September 27, 2011, The New York Times reported: "Hundreds of people were injured here on Tuesday when a [Red Line] subway train slammed into the rear of another train in a sprawling transit line that opened just last year. The accident cast new scrutiny on the safety record of China's rapidly modernizing mass transit rail systems.

The state-run news media reported that 271 people were injured during the afternoon accident in the Shanghai Metro system. Xinhua, the official news agency, said that equipment failure was believed to be responsible and that the accident was under investigation."

I have heard from a student at Shanghai International Studies University that Weibo was very active in the first incident in alerting people about the accident and calling on them to go quickly to the scene to give whatever assistance that they could provide, but that the government censors shut down the website, and that it kept opening up under different website addresses. It appears in the second case that the Government was more forthcoming with transparency in the media coverage or blockage of events in such situations.

Can you provide any assessment of the Chinese electronic, print, and internet media transparency in situations like these two accidents, and whether there is continued resistance or a newer openness on the part of the Government toward reporting accurately on accidents of this sort?

Cui Litang: A very important function of the state media is to reign the public opinion, good times or bad. To get the drain along this thinking of propaganda or publicity, curbing the news or curtailing some coverage is possible and at the disposal of the individuals and supervisors, at time of crises.

Meantime panic responses of the public as a result of uncertainty pending a major accident like that could have led to massive chaos and confusion which could be disastrous and the worse thing the government would like to see happen.

I did try to follow both incidents but didn't follow through, as the state media turned out to be more transparent in coverage, and fairly explicit, down to the compensations details.

Michael H. Prosser: From your viewpoint with your understanding of the media in China today, whether from the print, electronic media, ipods, ipads, cell phones, etc. or all of them how would you assess the transparency and openness of the Chinese media both in terms of domestic and international events? What are your projections in these regards when Xi Jinping becomes the President in the near future?

Cui Litang: I appreciate all efforts being made toward making China a more transparent and open society in terms of democracy, and I believe China is on its way there.

With thanks, Michael Prosser

D) Cultural Stories

1. Japanese Youth Today: The Glocal Generation

Judy Yeonoka
Kumamoto Gakuen University, Kumamoto, Japan

Japan conjures up an image of young salary men all dressed alike, jostling for space in a crowded commuter train or on a busy Tokyo street. However, young people have been facing new challenges – and can be found more often at home with their parents, still in school, living in net cafes, or even on the streets. From ages 3 to 33 and beyond, "what these groups have in common, for all their diversity, is that they have not yet become full-fledged members of 'the adult social order'" (Matthews & White 2004: 6).

The young people of Japan today may be best described as "lost" – or perhaps more appropriately, they have (been) derailed. The 'adult social order' was supposed to be the end station of a track of "best schools", laid for them by education mamas and papas and teachers and jukus (cram schools). All the children had to do was sit tight and hold on for the ride, and they would be rewarded with a fine adult life at the end. However, nowadays their end station is no longer clearly in sight, and their train is generally seen to be going nowhere.

The causes for this derailment can be summed up in three words: demographics, economics and technology. First, a top-heavy generational displacement means that for the first time in Japan's history there are more older people than younger ones. The dangai no sedai, Japanese equivalent of baby-boomers born after World War II, are nearing the end of their careers and running out of steam. Moreover, they have fewer children and grandchildren than previous generations: the Japanese birth rate has been under 1.5 since the 1990s and currently stands at 1.21. This presents the young generation with a double whammy. First, their fathers are in a bottleneck at the top of most major companies, allowing fewer of their children to be hired; and second, these same children must look forward to being financially and physically responsible for aging parents (and their friends) down the road.

This demographic dilemma is coupled with an economic one; since the burst of the bubble in 1991, the lucrative jobs that were supposed to be at the end of their education have been absent. This produced the first generation of freeters – full time part-timers who are now in their 30s. They should be married by now, with children of their own; instead, they are living at home as 'parasite singles', and working at jobs meant to supplement college students' incomes. Finally, advances in technology have followed the younger generation throughout their lives, bringing them video games, cell phones, and Mixi (the Japanese version of Facebook). Like their counterparts around the world, many young Japanese find it easier to relate to a LCD screen than to a human face.

The results of these changes have manifested in many ways. Some young people withdraw, becoming hikikomori (hide-at-home) and futoko (playing truant). Others rebel, creating gakkyu houkai (class destruction) even in traditional schools that have prided themselves on having "perfect" students. In March 2010, when 7-year-old Princess Aiko, granddaughter of the present Emperor, could not attend her elementary school because of bullies, it made national news, and the country was shocked that even the ultra-elite Gakushuin could have such mundane problems.

On the other hand, the current generation is more globally-oriented than any generation before them. Many have been abroad, even on school trips, and all have studied several years of English. They have grown up with the internet, and are aware of what the net revolution means to the world today. They are more connected with more people in more different ways than ever before, and they relate to their peers less as fellow Japanese and more as global teenagers. In this sense they are very much like students their same age around the world.

However, they face the dilemma of harmonizing a past in which they were simply expected to "stay on track" with a future for which they must be the trailblazers. The world has changed around them, and they will have to find new ways of coping to get where they want to go. In other words, they will have to develop independence,

2. Chinese Contemporary Youth: The Post 1980s Generation

Li Mengyu
Ocean University of China, Qingdao, China

China has the largest youth population in the world. The generation has been shaped by a strong traditional culture as well as the global world culture. Nowadays in China, when we mention Chinese youth, we mainly refer to the post-80s and post-90s young people whose ways of living , values and even communication styles are quite different from those of their parents' and grandparents' generations. Since China keeps opening up to the outside world, the Chinese youth are under the influence of various foreign cultures. First, they are greatly influenced by the western cultures and they hold a more positive view towards the western developed countries and their cultures, such as the United States as well as the European countries. As one student in the Ocean University of China says: "We are more westernized. For example, we watch more American movies, TV series, we listen to BBC and VOA, and celebrate western holidays. " They also show much interest in western style fast food such as KFC, McDonalds and Pizza Hut, and like wearing Nike or Adidas clothes. Many of them choose to go abroad to pursue further study and experience a new life. Next, they are also under the influence of their neighboring countries, such as Japan and South Korea; they like to watch the Japanese cartoons and South Korean's TV series, and some girls like to follow the dressing trend of the Japanese and South Korean women. In short, nowadays, under the influence of various cultures, the Chinese youth now have diversified ways of living; their eye views have been broadened and most of them want to live a more interesting and colorful life. They spend more time on traveling, sports, music as well as watching movies, TV series and go shopping in their spare time.

In terms of the values aspect, the Chinese youth display some complex and mixed value dimensions; on the one hand, the traditional Chinese culture still exerts a far-reaching influence on them; they still adhere to collectivism and group unity as well as the Confucian values of benevolence, good conduct, practical wisdom, and proper social relationships. On the other hand, they appear to be more individualistic.They cherish the value of self-confidence, self-independence and self-esteem, and try to be different from others by seeking their unique personalities. Besides, there is more emphasis on personal choice, freedom, and more equality of the sexes among the present Chinese young generation. Even some Chinese university girls speak quite frankly that they believe that they are the center of the world. But as a coin has two sides, the tendency of individualism also has its negative effects as many of them turn out to be self-interested and self-centered which has given rise to many communication problems.

The communication style of Chinese youth has also changed dramatically. Particularly, for the urban young people, they prefer to communicate with their friends by the means of QQ, MSN in the internet, or sending short messages instead of face-to-face communication. It seems to them that the internet has become a more real world. It has become a fashion or life style for the Chinese youth to have their cyberspace on Ren Ren Network or QQ network, on which they can upload their photos, blogs and other material they would like to share with others. As Zhaojing from the College of Liberal Arts and Journalism and Communication in the Ocean University of China says: "Nowadays, writing micro blogs is popular with netizens, and as the college students are in a large proportion, we can express our personal views on hot issues. If these netizens can draw much attention and have some fans, they will become the 'opinion leaders,' and their view will be transmitted from person to person. But different students have different purposes; some are willing to be the opinion leaders while others just want to get more information from their concerned celebrities." In short, the Chinese youth, particularly the young Chinese urban people spend more and more time on the internet and cyberspace has become a public place for their personal communication.

However, there are many problems which the Chinese youth are facing, among them, one common problem is the pressure. For students, they are under enormous pressure to get excellent grades, to get into university and then compete for good jobs. For those educated urban professionals, they also work under great pressure and intense competition for high social positions, good salaries and house issues. For those in the rural population, they have to go to cities and towns to work even harder for the purpose of earning money to support their families back in the rural areas.

Anyway, the Chinese youth are generations who have dreams. As Ms. Ge, who studied Chinese literature at Beijing Normal University remarked: "It's inspired by the American dream, but different. Americans say you can build anything out of nothing. We believe that you can love your family and your country and return to your cultural roots, such as Confucius. So much was lost in the last 60 years. We want to rejuvenate our values and find our soft power as a nation." The Chinese youth are now still on their way of pursuing the "Chinese dream," that they want to enjoy life and have a life with meaning and value.

3. Confucianism, Buddhism, The Information Age, and Globalization

William Zhu
Shanghai International Studies University, Shanghai, China

Believe it or not, I have never seriously, as well as thoroughly, considered who I am and what constitutes my cultural background for the past twenty-two years. To begin with, Confucian thought carves a deep notch in the cultural heritage of all Chinese people. Its profound impact is witnessed in every aspect of our life: humanity, benevolence, courtesy, respect for the old and love for the young, family hierarchy, filial piety, diligence, harmony, thrift, and obedience, to name a few. Though those attributes were proposed by Confucius thousands of years ago, they stand the test of time and are passed down from generation to generation with few alterations. When I was a small kid, I was taught by my parents and teachers to respect the old and pay due deference to people senior of my age. I should not call my parents, elder brothers and sisters, uncles and aunts their names; instead, I should greet them by their appellations respectively. However, when addressing my younger brothers and sisters, I enjoyed the privilege to call their names directly.

In terms of respecting the old, particularly my grandparents, I have to carefully observe many rules. For instance, when eating together at the same table, the arrangement of seats is fixed and I should sit accordingly. Usually, my grandpa or grandma's seats are considered the dominant ones and signify authority. If they happen not to be present, their seats are taken by my uncles or senior male family members. It seems to me that the rules at the table are observed not only at home but also in society. When having dinner with friends, colleagues or people who are not our relatives, the senior, powerful one always sits above the salt. The same seating arrangement pattern is also demonstrated in meetings. I remembered that whenever our family had something to discuss or decide, we would customarily have an informal meeting with my grandparents sitting in the middle of the crowd and supervising the process. Small kids like me did not have a say as all we had to do was to listen attentively and carry out the decisions to the letter. We were not supposed to raise any doubts or challenge the decision, if we did, we would end up receiving either verbal or physical punishment. Besides, to sustain a harmonious state is of vital importance as I learned from my own experience. It is common that some discord or friction exists among family members. Despite dislikes or even resentment, we try to achieve, at least, a superficial harmony by avoiding obvious conflict. By doing so, we are giving each other face and being gentle.

Also, I grew up in an environment of diligence and thrift which also typifies the characteristics of the majority of the Chinese. Thriftlessness, waste, laziness and idleness are considered evils and people who are extravagant or slothful are labeled with derogatory epithets, condemned and even chastised. I once received a good beating because I bought something from a neighborhood grocery on credit. My mother considered the incident to be extremely serious and thought I might end up as a spend-thrift idler if no intervention was carried out. Another example is that as a kid, I had to eat all the food in my bowl and if there were any leftovers, my parents or relatives would repeat the invariable story how precious rice is and how hard farmers work to harvest it under the scorching sun. One salient traditional breakfast in south China is "paofan," rice soaked with water. Actually, they are the leftovers of the previous night's supper. In addition, diligence is a great virtue that my parents tried their best to cultivate in me. With the proverb that the early bird gets the worm, diligence is the means by which one makes up for one's dullness.

Those adages are carved into my head as a stimulus to urge me get up early and study with might and main. My parents were excessively proud of me as I was a top student through primary school to university. They often tell me that as my genetic makeup might not be very favorable because neither of them has obtained a bachelor's degree, I have to be much more industrious than others and spend ten times as much efforts on study than my smart peers.

As Confucian thought may exert a positive influence on my cultural context, the Cultural Revolution, a devastating political as well as social catastrophe, has taken its tolls. Both my grandfathers on my mother's and father's side were put into prisons and forced to reform through labor, and were displaced and tortured. My mother's father at that time was a graduate from one of the leading universities working in a bank; he was persecuted because as a liberal and young person with high aspirations, he voiced many discontentments and disagreements with the authorities. As a consequence, he was sent to a remote backwoods province laboring in the field, enduring unspeakable ordeals which affected him physically and psychologically all through his life. It is by no means exaggerated to say that his life had been totally transformed. My father's father, who at that time worked as a cadre in the local government, had a very promising future for he was eloquent, charismatic and knowledgeable. Unfortunately, due to his dishonorable family background (my grandfather's father served as a military official for the Kuomintang party before new China was founded), he was dismissed, jailed and forced to cut his connections with all the family members. The tragedy did not end up here as my mother and father, and their brothers and sisters, as the offspring of the rightist, underwent tremendous humiliation, unfair treatment and hardships. They were deprived of the right to receive a higher education; they were also forced to labor after school to be educated. All these experiences left a great impact on their life. They are apolitical, distrustful of the government and place enormous expectation on us.

My parents, since I could remember things, instructed me not to be too aggressive, not to voice discontent in public, not to offend others, not to get involved in politics, to study hard and be in a low key. Actually, the golden rule seems to be "reticence is better than eloquence" and "a ready tongue is an evil." Evidently, they drew the lesson from their parents. They did all they could to ensure that I got the best education which they were deprived of. They know how horrible and painful a political upheaval could be and their last wish is that I should repeat what they went through during those turbulent years when nobody trusted each other and human evil was revealed to the most as even spouses set up against each other. There is no doubt that the psychological aftershock of the Cultural Revolution will exert its power not only in my generation but also my offspring.

Another point that I want to elaborate on is religious belief as it is very closely connected with culture and it has a powerful impact on my cultural background. My mother is a Buddhist, so is my mother's mother. The first thing my mother and grandmother do after they get up every morning is to offer incense to Buddha. And each first as well as fifteenth day in the lunar calendar, they will put some fruits, pastry, and a bowl of rice in front of the Buddha statue, which is placed in the living room to serve as a tribute. Whenever a family member has to travel to a far away place, or I have to sit in for an exam, or some family member has some trouble, be it illness, misfortune or whatever, my mother or my grandmother will pray before the statue, kneeing and kowtowing. Bad times are interpreted as a test that Buddha has for us and achievement or luck is interpreted as a blessing of Buddha by my mother and grandmother. Our lives are considered to be predestined and all we have to do is to accept our destiny and act accordingly (this perspective is quite paradoxical in Buddhism for we both accept our destiny and pray for good things to happen), As Buddhists, we have a pre-life and after-life, we have to engage ourselves in philanthropic undertakings and good deeds; those are the tenets of Buddhism that my mother and grandmother hold. Though I am, at least at the present time, an atheist, I have undergone constant struggle as I have tried to strike a balance between its influence on my life and the impact of science.

I am totally aware that being over-obsessed with the potency of some imaginative figure or resigning ourselves to our destiny mapped out by a fortune teller is absurd and highly detrimental as that might result in a pessimistic worldview. Nevertheless, strangely enough, each time I have achieved something or whenever I have had some very hard time, I would spontaneously make some connotation as some unseen power might manipulate all the things that happen to me. I would under some circumstance, when I am extremely unhopeful, lost or depressed, resort to Buddha and pray though I know exactly it is of little avail. Thus, I think I am very much affected by my mother and my grandmother and some Buddhist tenets and thoughts have already become one part of my cultural background.

Three watersheds that divide my generation and my parent's or grandparent's generation are the reform and opening up policy and the information age and globalization. The former one, which unleashes productivity and brings about unprecedented economic benefits is by no means parsimonious in its impact on my cultural context. Compared to my parents who are more traditional and a bit invulnerable to change and adaptation due to the immense influence of Confucian thought, I, like my peers, tend to be more flexible and receptive to fresh things or phenomenona. Improvement of life, diversity of goods, consumption economy, swollen pockets: all these factors strongly transform our lifestyles, outlook of the world, and they corrode some traditional virtues such as thrift and integrity.

Unlike my parents who still prefer a relatively self-restrained lifestyle which features "saving for a rainy day" and not wasting money on luxurious goods, I tend to favor hedonism and am more willing to purchase brand names. In addition, waste, either food or money, is acceptable as far as I am concerned. For instance, if I really loathe the food or the food goes bad, I will refuse to eat it and I make great efforts to urge my parents to give up some unhealthy lifestyle such as eating the leftovers, buying cheap, poor quality products or using expired daily necessities . Another case in point is that I always have a heated argument or debate with my parents whenever we go shopping as I like to buy the brand names such as Nike or Adidas but they are very reluctant to spend money on those expensive clothes for they think cheaper ones will also do. When my friends and I hang out, we like to go to Starbucks, KFC or some upscale restaurants to dine, and we always frequent KTV or some other entertainment venues to have fun and to socialize. My parents are quite against all of these deeds which they deem as a deterioration of moral codes and extravagancy.

The second and third factors that divide my generation and my parents and grandparents' generations culturally are the information age and globalization. A large number of novel words, phrases, epithets and things pop up. Facebook, MySpace, Twitter, ICQ, MSN, QQ, iPod, 3-G, netizen, on-line shopping, cyber love and so on. All these novelties profoundly affect our socializing forms, behavior, linguistic competence, viewpoints, way of thinking, relationships and communication patterns. In contrast to some temperaments that my parents favor such as reticence, unassuming demeanor or humility, the surviving know-how of the new millennium is eloquence, aggressiveness and dominating. Introverted temperament is out of date and for us extroverted disposition is very desirable. Blogs, BBS, passion for democracy, decency, social responsibility and individuality make my generation more vocal and voluble to express ourselves, to show great concern on the inequality or dark side of the society and to gather momentum for change. All of these seem very appalling and frightening to my parents for they more than once have warned me to have restraint and not be involved in freely expressing my opinions on line and with my peers. The rapid pace of globalization not only brings in western goods, but also imports western thoughts and ideologies which sometimes are in great conflict with their Chinese counterparts.

Fast food, indulgency, loose relationships between opposite sexes, self-centeredness: all of these factors have immensely challenged traditional Chinese virtues which my parents' generation holds. However, though these new changes might not always be beneficial, they are here, they are my generations' as well as my cultural context and there is no way to reverse globalization. I love freedom, resent rules and restrictions, and I prefer a simple, individual lifestyle in which I can enjoy more privacy. I am fascinated about new things, metropolitan prosperity, and I am voracious for new knowledge. Unlike my parents who pay undue importance to family members, I consider friendship more important and I want that more attention should be directed to me. I correspond with my friends with emails, short messages or on socializing web networks, while my parents still prefer to make phone calls. My peers and I are interested in pop stars, Hollywood's big budget movies, extreme sports and online games while my parents are less receptive to these things. In terms of my future career, my parents want me to take a stable job in the government or some public institution, but I want to be employed by some top 500 multinational corporations and do some really creative and rewarding tasks.

In a word, it is really difficult to fully summarize my cultural background in this increasing diversified world in which numerous factors interact with each other in constituting my specific cultural context. Nevertheless, the above mentioned characters, Confucian thought, the Cultural Revolution, Buddhism, the reform and opening up policy, the information age and globalization do approximately generalize my cultural background by offering a panorama view of who I am.

4.   Reflections on My Identity and Personality

Sabrina Yang
Shanghai International Studies University, Shanghai, China

Before I came to the "Intercultural Communication" class (in the Master's program in intercultural communication at the Shanghai International Studies University), I never thought about my identity. It seems to be self-evident to me. But when I sat down and asked myself who I am? I find it is not an easy question to answer. So I reflected on my past and sorted out stories that helped to form my personality today.

I want to begin my story with identifying myself. Now I earn my living by being a college teacher in the city of Jiaxing (I moved from a university in Huhhot, Inner Mongolia to Jiaxing Autonomous Region last year.) I am also a daughter and a sister of two younger brothers. I have a happy family now and last year I became a happy mother. My son is only 16 months old. Before my son was born, being a college teacher was the most important identity for me, but after the birth of my son, being a mother has become more important. It is my son who changed me a lot though he is just learning to walk now.

I had discussed the question "what kind of person am I?" with my friends years before. I am a very kind and warm-hearted woman. I am sympathetic to others' misfortunes and like to help those in need. I will come into tears when reading sad stories or watching tragedies on TV. I don't think I am a very easy-going person though I have always been dreaming of being a person like that. I am somewhat introverted and reserved, but I really like to be with people. I don't have a good many friends, but I really have several intimate friends who can share my tears, laughter and secrets. To the students, I am a strict teacher in class but I am also their friend after class. They like to talk about their troubles with me and they can often get some suggestions from me. I am an impetuous person. So sometimes I finish one task too quickly, to have to regret as I might have done better. Both my parents and my friends agree that I have a fatal weakness. They said I am apt to believe in people easily and quickly. My husband often tries to teach me to be more rational but he is often disappointed. As for me I don't think it necessary to improve my "weakness". I'd like to believe that the world is full of love and beauty.

Talking about how I grow into a person like this, I have to mention three things – my family, my college education and my summer camp (cultural program) experience.

I was born in a very common family. My father was a civil servant and my mother took care of the family at home. But I learned a lot from my parents, especially from my mother. It was my mother who taught me the value of hard work and how to love people. It is so important to me that even today I still value these two virtues and I often think of my mother whenever I am in difficulties. What she taught me years ago can often encourage me to go on and on in today's world.

It was a turning point for me to get the chance to study in the university. I transformed myself from a shy, timid and introverted girl into a mature, optimistic and self-confident woman today. College education provided me the opportunity to broaden my knowledge. More importantly, it guided me to look at the other side of this world. I became open-minded and learned to be in harmony with the society.

I want to put much emphasis on my summer camp (cultural program) experience because it was in this camp that I first encountered intercultural communication in real life. And I learned to get along with different people and deal with different situations. I became mature after the program. The program was launched in the year 2000. My college decided to accept 20 American college students to hold a cultural camp. So during the summer vocation about 20 American college students, who came from different colleges in America, would come to stay in my college for one month. And 20 Chinese students would be chosen to accompany them. The Chinese and the American students would live, eat, study, travel and hold different activities together. One Chinese student and one American student would live in the same dorm. They tried to help each other to learn languages, get to know a different culture and develop understanding and love between two countries. We gave lectures, held discussions and went out to visit some scenic spots. As the advisor/supervisor of the Chinese side, I saw many conflicts between the two different cultures. Fortunately, when problems appeared, we tried to communicate with each other to find where the problem was and tried to find the solutions. So when the program came to an end, all of the students became good friends and kept contact with each other for a long time. Here I want to tell one incident which impressed me deeply.

We Chinese are hospitable, so we like to persuade our guests to eat more to show our hospitality and concerns. Our hospitality brought a lot of headaches to the American students. The Chinese students preferred to pick the "delicious food" for their American friends and persuaded them to finish it. There was an American girl who was tall, but quite skinny. She was very extroverted, friendly, considerate and easy-going, so she became good friends of many Chinese students. She ate very little during the meal and the meal time became miserable for her. Her Chinese friends decided that she ate too little and this would be harmful to her health, so several of them would sit around her and persuade her to eat more. They put "nutritious" food in her bowl and watched her to finish all the food. At last, she was out of patience and became angry. She complained to me about that and asked me to "save" her. I was aware of the problem and tried to explain the cultural difference to her. I also tried to make my Chinese students realize that their kindness had become a heavy burden to their friend. I saw this kind of conflicts all too often during the whole month, which made me increasingly aware of the cultural diversity. This program gave me a chance to get in touch with another culture and I learned to be broad-minded and appreciate cultural diversity after the program.

Another story is also quite interesting. We know that Chinese girls like to walk hand in hand with each other and the boys like to hug each other's shoulders when walking to show their good relationship. This horrified the American students when they first saw this. They thought these Chinese students were homosexual, so when the Chinese students intended to be close to them, they escaped. When I found this, I held a party and explained this cultural difference to the Chinese and American students. I asked the Chinese students to respect the personal space of the Americans. And I told the American students that being very close to each other among the same sex didn't mean they were gay; it was just a way of showing their good relationship. When the camp was going to end, I was surprised to find that some American students walked with their Chinese friends, hugging each other's shoulders.

After attending the intercultural communication class, I have begun to be further aware of the influence of Chinese culture on me. I will try to evaluate myself from the view of culture and try to improve myself from now on.

5.   Western Culture Is My Culture

Frank Zhang
Ocean University of China, Qingdao, China

I come from an ordinary small village in Henan Province. Our village neither is enclosed in cols, nor whatever kind of economic development zone in the outskirts. Not extremely backward, not rich. Perhaps the reality is that from the children out of the mountains, in the face of the wide world they will feel free to fly when the well-being might have been had the experience of major aspects of society's children, will be familiar with the big cities in the face of naturally poised surroundings. Well, me? We came to this county rather than the city of a thousand times better. I feel complete freedom, neither flying nor having an inexplicable fear of helplessness. My general appearance, general scholarship, common relationships, plain and moderate may be the inherent characteristics of my heart.

Knowledge systems are based on an individual's culture which is a subjective understanding of the world system, with a strong disciplinary nature, constituting a basis for rapid development of people in the future. From the knowledge of the targets, knowledge can be divided into natural science, social science, knowledge of human knowledge and thinking. As an undergraduate student of engineering expertise a solid knowledge of natural science has always been my strong suit. My childhood dream of being an inventor of all natural science and technology expert, I am very enthusiastic about. In a variety of disciplines I have participated in many competitions in mathematics, physics, biology and in other disciplines. I have also been successful in the race results.

Natural science knowledge to me means the viability of a strong material that people always understand the nature and transformation of nature in the understanding and find their great potential. The concept of culture from the individual in terms of natural scientific knowledge is more satisfactory with my own aspect of a solid cultural foundation for the discipline that I am very confident in. Of course, my goal now is to master the advanced learning methods to improve the capacity for lifelong learning. Social sciences and humanities for me are an aspect of relatively weak background.

At school, I have read various Chinese and foreign masterpieces, but realistically speaking, most of the books are a kind of a busy life way to relax and adjust, so a sudden epiphany, like the kind of people always feel from the delay in the ultimate has not yet come to me. Many times I have a book review to write about famous people, but the overall feeling to my mouth then, but the thought is blocked. This is the direction I want to go in the humanities and social sciences as they have been gradually consolidating their base and further developing their own arts and science skills to cultivate good human qualities. Ethnic Chinese were brilliant for five thousand years of civilization as I grew up with my great masters of culture; Confucius, Mencius, Laozi and Zhuangzi, such as the impact of national cultural treasures, like all other Chinese people deeply affected me. I am firm that a national culture has of its own beliefs. Chinese culture, in a variety of philosophical theories to deal with people, are my sources.

In the external culture, Western culture is my culture and the relative degree of openness in foreign countries is improving, the European and American culture is also more fully known in China. The role of the media with information on the reflection of films makes the European and American culture widely recognized for me. But for me, Africa, South America and the Middle East cultures are always in my mind as a big blank, and referring to them, such as my mind can only emerge out of the desert, oil and the like vocabulary. In the future I want to be more extensively studied, to fill this vacancy. I am not religious but its culture is also a well-known area. Near my home is a temple, plus there has always been a strong influence of Buddhism, so I quite understand it. As for Taoism, Islam, and Christianity, I can only get from books occasionally fragmentary knowledge. I read part of the "Bible," but I just also 'kick the tires"; maybe in the future I will be able to find people who really share these religious beliefs and their experiences with me.

A system is a subjective concept of the aesthetic system of the world, including architecture, painting, sculpture, music, dance, literature, theater, film and art appreciation for life, work, study, appreciation of beauty and kindness. Bo Yang in the "Ugly Chinese" had this to say: 'If we change our ugly image of the Chinese people, and only from now on, everyone wants a way to train themselves into connoisseurs." For me, the idea of the system is to allow people to enjoy a higher quality of life elements. I like music and I like movies, but I am also willing to accept other forms of art, whether Eastern or Western, and I can stop and enjoy it. I think that while there is music, no art of life is boring, and material life at the same time, appreciation of art, and the quality of life will be higher.

Systems handle the main way people ask "how" or "why" a question is the subjective world of the operating system. In this regard, I emphasized that for "truth" in the real world, there are often subjective and objective contradictions, but in the face of these contradictions, the spirit of truth is very important. To solve the problem, to explore the true law of things is very important. Seeking truth from facts is the primary objective world we face in our attitudes. In this regard I have a lot less truth, because my life experiences are not enough to deal with some issues when the time attitude seems to be a lack of objective truth. I would like to increase with age and experience, along with future work and to live in society when I am more mature and able to face all kinds of things with the pragmatic facts.

This is the story of my culture so far.

6. The Story of My 30+ Years

Jacky Zhang
Dezhou University, Dezhou, China

Complicated feelings filled my mind for I had to look back at my life carefully and seriously. I was born in the 1980s, the period for China to start the "One Family One Child" policy. In China, we young people born in the 1980s are called the "Post-80s Generation." Most are the only child who usually stress self-value, pursue their own personality and enjoy love from their family members, but lack the ability for self-care and a sense of social responsibility. In many people's eyes, we are the "spoiled" generation. Unfortunately, I am one of the "spoiled" group. Fortunately, I have a younger sister, and many cousins, so my childhood was not so lonely as the only child of most families. Actually, I don't think I was spoiled.

My grandparents were not rich when I was born, living in a rural area in Shandong Province. My father told me that life at that time was poor. My grandparents had 3 sons and 2 daughters, and 5 grandchildren already before me. As a result, I haven't ever received any gifts or red envelopes from my grandparents. But I haven't complained because they still loved me very much, especially my grandmother who died in my junior middle school period. I have to show my great appreciation to my parents because they made a great decision as soon as I came into this beautiful world that they would do whatever they could to support my education. My mother told me her greatest wish when I was an infant was that I could enter the best university of China one day. I didn't let my parents become disappointed. I entered a good university, although not the best one in China. Later, I entered Shanghai International Studies University (SISU) to pursue the master's degree in international relations from 2006 to 2009 and completed my thesis, entitled: "USCC's Cognition on China and Its Influence on Sino-US Relations." I also taught English at the Overseas Development Center to a group of high level Buddhist monks. My experience in SISU changed my life again because I met my lasting teacher and friend Michael H. Prosser who brought me abroad to experience the colorful world and culture.

A wonderful cruise trip opened the curtain for me to experience various cultures. Michael and I went to Australia and New Zealand, visiting ten different cities. I am still excited when I think of the trip. All the things in the cruise are as clear as if I am still enjoying it. After arriving at our Sydney hotel, later we visited the Sydney Museum and the world-famous Opera House. At the Bondi Beach I swam while Michael talked to two beautiful young Indian women. I wanted to get stuffed kangaroos, koala bears, and Tasmanian devils for my roommates and nephew, but we soon realized that all of them were made in China as were most souvenirs or clothing. This really makes me happy for China and being a Chinese. We watched the biggest Chinese Lunar New Year parade outside of the Asian continent, with many schools and other groups participating.

We boarded the Holland America Line ship MS Volendam for the fourteen days cruise where many guests appeared to be in their sixties, seventies or older, and from several different countries including Australia, Canada, ten from China, Japan, and the United States. So I felt so honored to have Michael as my best friend helping me to have an international view and think broadly. We travelled to Melbourne and Tasmania and through the Tasmanian Sea, the roughest sea in the world, to New Zealand, another fantastic experience. Both New Zealand and Australia left me deeply impressed. What I thought most about is when China could have as clear a sky as those two countries. Particularly, China still has a long way to go in environmental protection.

Back in Shanghai, we planned to go to Japan in September 2009 to attend the 15th International Association for Intercultural Communi¬cation Studies conference. We met in Fukuoka, Japan, and surely another cultural experience awaited me. I did better than in my first trip outside of China because I had become more mature in international travel. Different from the first one, the Japan trip meant more to me. Since this was my first time to attend a formal international academic conference outside of China, I learned a lot in writing my power point presentation for the conference. I made a cultural mistake about cross-cultural communication as I wore a black tie the last day of the conference. But when I walked into the auditorium, some Japanese stared at me surprised, confusing me by the looks on their faces. At that moment, the conference leader kindly told me that a black tie in Japan is only for funerals. Realizing my mistake,

I apologized and I didn't wear the tie in the closing ceremony. Then we traveled to several places in southern Japan where the clean environment impressed me greatly. I noticed something similar in Japan as what happens in China as the Japanese children are very shy when they say hello to western people. A lot of Japanese we met couldn't speak very fluent English which surprised me.

After the Japan trip, Michael and I developed another trip to Thailand in November 2009. So the unique and traditional Thailand culture filled my mind closely. On our seventh day in Thailand, we went to Cambodia, staying there for three days and two nights. The strong contrast between Thailand and Cambodia touched me greatly. Cambodia is such a poor country and the basic construction is underdeveloped. But the poverty couldn't stop people to pursue a better life. Our young Cambodian guide at Angkor Wat, a UNESCO World Heritage spot, told us that most Cambodians live a satisfactory life. I didn't know how to describe my feelings when I wandered in the ancient castle and Hindu temples. This wonderful place caused a very strong sense of history to occupy my mind.

Life is always a mystery. We will never know what will happen tomorrow. But one thing we could do is to be ready to the presentation from life. In 2012, I got a chance to go to Taiwan to attend the 2012 annual conference. Taiwan is a legendary place for us who live in mainland. Taiwan is an inalienable part of China. But the people living on either side of the Taiwan Channel are separated for a long time because of the political problem. So we all have a dream that we could go and see Taiwan one day.

During the 2012 IAICS annual conference in Taiwan, I could talk with the scholars from all over the world. Interestingly, I had a dinner with another 4 presenters one evening. One is from Iran, a faraway country from us. The other two are from Japan. The other is from America but married to a Japanese. And I am a Chinese. So we exchanged a lot over the dinner. We talked from our "Taiwan impression" to "Chinese culture"; then we mentioned China's policy toward Taiwan and Japan's influence on Taiwan. And suddenly the relationship between Iran and the United States caused our attention. So after 5 minutes' talk about the relation, the topic was changed to the similarity among Chinese, Japanese, English and Persian people. For example, we shared the expression how to congratulate the other in each country's culture. We found the result interesting. We found Persian most diversified in expressing congratulation to others. We found more similarity between China and the United States than between China and Japan in expressing congratulations to others. That surprised me and the two Japanese because China and Japan belong to the same civilization – Asian civilization. Anyway, the conversation moved freely and smoothly. Thinking, laughing and discussing were filled during the 2 hours' conversation.

Another topic should not be avoided. That is how the youth consider the relationship between the mainland and Taiwan. The impression is that most older and middle aged people in Taiwan know little about the mainland. Some think that the mainland was still as poor as before. Others think that the quality of the population in the mainland could not catch up with Taiwan. But young people know more about the mainland than their parents. I talked with many local young people there. Generally speaking, the visitors from the mainland are not so welcome because the mainlanders are noisy in public areas. Besides, they don't care so much about politics. They even don't care which Taiwanese party is in power. They just care whether they could live a good life and whether they could earn enough money to buy a house in Taipei, a high consumption city of Taiwan. So I do find common ground with the young people in Taiwan.

All the travels contribute directly to my teaching. I knew Michael Prosser's favorite secular quote is from Socrates: "I am neither a citizen of Athens, nor of Greece, but of the world!" That's a good goal for my future (and yours). At the very beginning, I didn't understand its significance. But after travelling in the world, I DO understand the meaning of it. As an individual among all the human beings, what he or she should do is not only being a citizen of his or her country but being an international citizen of the world. Especially, as a Chinese youth, how I look at my country and how I face the problems in China or how I face the gap between China and other countries is always in my mind. So when I came back to my university for teaching, I have been trying to bring the sense of globalization and international citizenship to my students. It works well in influencing the young students. Everytime when they give presentation or answers, they could combine the book knowledge with the world reality. From this aspect, we could share a lot with people from different countries. Culture should be dynamic and diversified, which makes the planet colorful and worth exploring. However, communication could bridge the gap among cultures to reach peace and freedom.

I know that the world is full of variety and mystery. But my cultural experience outside of China strengthens it. All of my international travels make me better and better and let me think more globally. I love the world and I love more the people who made everything become more interculturally real for me.

7. FROM THE MINI UN TO THE REAL UN, THE UNITED NATIONS, 2010

Jing Zhang
The United Nations, New York City, New York

Before I came to the United States, I studied at the Beijing Language and Culture University (BLCU), whose nick name is "the mini United Nations" as it has international students from more than 170 countries. I enjoyed studying and living in this pretty campus for three years. This was the place where I made many international friends and experienced cross-cultural communications by exchanging languages and going out together. This was also the place where I heard about a small European country called Moldova for the first time.

Now I am a Public Information Assistant at the Department of Public Information at the United Nations (UN) headquarters in New York City. UN is such a multicultural organization. Take my office for example, my colleagues are from 5 continents. One Italian lady had studied Mandarin at BLCU before! What a small world! One day I even came across my high school math teacher from Shenzhen. You never know whom you will meet next! At the UN not only do I have opportunities to work with people from different cultures, but I also have opportunities to meet visitors from around the world. I have noticed that Asian people like to take photos a lot, while Europeans tend to want to know more about the organization. French and German people are critical and always have questions. I have met people from places such as Kosovo, Palestine, and the Democratic Republic of the Congo, where the Security Council has deployed the peacekeeping operations.

My most unforgettable experience at the UN was to work for the 64th General Assembly (GA) in September, 2009. This is the time once a year that the New York Police Department blocks the road up to the Second Avenue as heads of state and heads of government attend the General Debate. I was lucky to work for three different departments during the week of the General Debate. Working for the Meeting Service Department enabled me to hear speeches from many big-wigs such as President Hu

Jingtao, Barack Obama, and Nicolas Sarkozy. I came across famous ladies like Hillary Clinton and Carla Bruni just by randomly walking inside the building. Of course I should say the security was very tight; not every staff member could enter the General Assembly building and you need a special pass besides the work ID. I also experienced some unique moments such as seeing Muammar Gaddafi make the second longest speech in the UN history (the longest speech was made by Fidel Castro for more than 4 hours); witnessing the voting whether to let the so-called president of Madagascar to speak in the GA or not as they had a coup and apparently the voting result didn't recognize the current government.

Working for the Media Relations Department made it possible for me to attend press conferences and meetings hosted by Tony Blair, Al Gore, and Hugo Chavez. Moreover, I once escorted a FOX news reporter to interview Iranian president Mahmoud Ahmadinejad. We had argued where to wait for him: the reporter thought we should wait at the elevator as Ahmadinejad was going to the 38th floor to meet with the Secretary General. I didn't agree with him as no one else was waiting there and suggested that we should wait at the Delegates' Entrance. I was right. He showed up on his way to meet the SG. We had been waiting for him for more than 2 hours, but in the end he only talked to an Iranian reporter in Persian when he left. My third duty was to work at the Bilateral Meetings. During my tenure, I witnessed many agreements that were reached as a result of the meetings or negotiations.

As I am new and still learning the ropes, I feel proud to work for such a great organization which has gone so far since its creation in 1945. At the same time, I feel that I have responsibility to let more people know about the work of the UN, because it's our world.

8. OFFICE OF THE SPOKESPERSON FOR THE UNITED NATIONS SECRETARY GENERAL, BAN-KI MOON, 2011

Jing Zhang
The United Nations, New York City, New York

I have been working at the Office of the Spokesperson for the Secretary-General (OSSG) for about two months (May-June, 2011) and have been totally enjoying what I am doing. There's no typical day at OSSG. Every day I work on different shifts and each shift has its own responsibilities. Therefore, sometimes I'm at work as early as 7:30am and sometimes on a late shift I might leave the office at as late as 9pm. For the early shift, the first 45 minutes are crucial as I need to prepare the newsfeeds for the Secretary-General (SG) and the Deputy Secretary-General (DSG). Not only do I read the news but I also need to highlight any information that I think important for the SG and DSG to know. The newsfeeds are usually from various wire services such as Xinhua, Agence France-Presse (AFP), Associated Press (AP), BBC, CNN, Reuters, etc. In the past I only heard those big names above, but now I get to know more major news agencies in other languages. For example, Al Jazeera is a major Arabic and English language news agency and DPA is a major German one.

Since our office mainly produces SG related products such as statements, remarks, readouts, and press encounters, we work closely with media and press. We always fight with time as one of the most important things we do is to send out the SG's statement immediately to the journalists and post it on our website. I often have calls from CNN and Fox news reporters asking for SG remarks and speeches. It's fun to work with reporters but of course sometimes we have to roll with the punches.

I feel lucky to be in the center of international affairs and be a witness of important world history such as Secretary-General Ban Ki-moon's re-election and South Sudan's coming independence on July 9 and which might soon be the 193rd member state of the UN. I had a chance to work closely with the SG's office and Media Accreditation and Liaison Unit to arrange interviews with the SG after his re-election. So far I assisted to coordinate interview requests from Xinhua, CCTV, FAZ, RTR, KBS, etc.

I have also been working closely with reporters who will travel with the SG to South Sudan in regard of logistics.

One of the reasons that I enjoy working in this office is that I often use four (Chinese, English, French and Spanish) of the six UN official languages at work! I answer inquiries from offices within the UN, Permanent Missions to the UN and of course our main clients who are the reporters by using different languages. Sometimes people are very patient with me and encourage me to continue speaking in French or Spanish when I try to switch back into English.

9. DOTS CONNECTED: BACKWARDS AND FORWARD

Grace Liang Xiaoxue
Shanghai International Studies University, Shanghai, China

Cultural Roots – My Family

The reason why we become who we are is highly correlated with our past. When I search my soul and try to figure out my cultural roots, the answer falls undoubtedly on my family. My family features a strong sense of old-fashioned style, so does the education I have received. Since my birth, I was expected to be cultivated as a true "lady" even before I made out what this word meant. This is not at all weird given my family background. Dating back to the generation of my grandparents, the overwhelming majority of our extended family members are teachers (five of them hold doctoral degrees). Thanks to these "teachers" (from elementary school teachers to university professors), I was taught to read and write at an early age. By twelve, I had perused scores of masterpieces of both Chinese and western classics. I could reel off with emotion almost any poem of Dream of Red Chamber; my eyes moistened when Jane Eyre demanded to be treated as an independent human being and when Scarlet O'Hara promised that "tomorrow is another day". Books read during my childhood left an indelible mark on me, which shaped my initial judgments about beauty, truth, and justice.

My education also consists of other important aspects. The traditional Chinese culture sets a high standard for a "lady", that she must be a master of four basic skills: playing Guqin (a kind of musical instrument), Chinese chess, calligraphy, and painting. My father taught me chess. I was also required to practice calligraphy on dated newspapers, and learned painting in an art training center. Unfortunately, all these big plans lasted for only a short while due to my lack of interest. Later, my mother watched on TV her favorite actress gracefully playing the violin, she announced that I should follow suit. Such wishful thinking of parents unavoidably goes against the child's natural playfulness. Each time I was forced to undergo the boring practice, I played one piece of music called "Sonata Pathetique" to convey my displeasure. That piece later became my specialty, and I was often asked to play it in front of the home guests. They never knew, however, that it was played well because it contained the player's real emotion.

When I was thirteen, we moved from the extended family to a downtown block built specifically for the local university faculties. Our apartment building was mostly for senior professors, and their children grew up in a way more or less similar to mine. In such an academic environment, parents competed with each other not in terms of power or wealth, but whose son got the first prize in a math competition, whose daughter passed the highest professional level of accordion, or whose child was offered the full scholarship to study overseas. Martin Luther King, Jr. once said: "I am not afraid of tension... there is a type of constructive tension which is necessary for growth." Living under such pressure awakened competitiveness in me, for the last thing I wanted was to let my parents down. I began to strive for excellence in whatever I do. I managed to maintain my academic record within the top three in class; got elected as the president of the Students' Union; I devoted my spare time to learning swimming and skating and piano...

Looking back, those years set the tone for my future development: I enjoyed the feelings of making plans and seeing them achieved; I recognized that competition and pressure are good so long as they bring out my inner strength and potential; I realized that happiness is not derived solely from our own accomplishment, but also the happiness of those people we love. Knowing why and for whom I am fighting makes my life more complete.

Yet a big challenge came soon when I was about to depart from my warm family nest to a remote and strange city, where I would start a new journey.

Growing Pains – My College Life

Once I came from north-western China to south-eastern Shanghai, everything seemed to have changed. The physical environment (food, weather, unfamiliar dialect) was relatively easy to deal with, but psychological accommodation painfully took time. I began to live and study with people from all parts of China, whose background, customs, habit, and personality were distinctly different from my own.

I was raised in an academic environment, and that had never occurred to me as something special. But when I talked with my new friends, they all responded: "Oh, you are from a scholarly family (Shu Xiang Men Di, a favorable term to describe a family whose members are highly-educated and well-cultivated), how lucky!" Since southern coastal China has been traditionally leading the economic development, people here are more driven by doing business and making money while paying less attention to political and cultural affairs than in the north. This is clearly demonstrated in observed preferences and pursuits. There were times when I mentioned Freudian psychoanalysis or Verdi's Aida, and was surprised that none of my roommates had ever heard of them. Compared with reading books and newspapers, they were more interested in watching Japanese cartoons and the latest Paris fashion show.

At first this was disturbing, for I had to make hard attempts to explore our common interests and shared dimensions. But gradually I recognized that students from the coastal areas have another side of advantages. They are more open and flexible about new things, are good at financial management, show more knowledge in technology, and demonstrate more confidence and aggressiveness. We learned from each other local dialects, made jokes and above all, tried to understand and accommodate to each other's uniqueness. Though during the process I encountered numerous cultural shocks and underwent a series of identity frustrations, my tolerance capacity was enlarged inch by inch: I became more patient when answering questions like "do children in your hometown ride camels to go to school?" recognizing that each person has his/her limitations, not to mention that I myself had many aspects of ignorance; I developed a clearer image of my own strengths and weaknesses, beware that we all have our own cultural contexts and social discourses which could not be judged by a generalized set of standards; I grew less self-conscious, realizing that what counts most is not to be wrapped up in one's own cultural identity, but to gain another way of thinking or point of view.

The interesting thing was, once my cultural tolerance had been improved, life itself seemed to be more diverse. I became better at balancing the two forces within me – the Dionysus self and Apollonian self (applied by the German philosopher Friedrich Nietzsche). The former welcomes spontaneity, passion, intuition, rebellion, and excess; while the latter tells me to get moving, stop stalling, do what I know needs to be done. My world had been widened. College life taught me that don't be trapped by one's small world, and don't let the noise of prejudice or bias drown out the truth, otherwise we would miss many breathtaking sceneries along the way.

Developing and Maturing – Social Experience

My working experience as a student intern lasted only a year, but much of what I stumbled into by following my curiosity turned out to be priceless later on. I was fortunate enough to get an internship at a Fortune 500 American company. My title was HR & Administrative assistant, but in fact, I only served as a secretary of JJ, the HR executor of Asian-Pacific region. The job sounded fairly easy, but the amount of work lay heavily on a novice.

Once more I was confronted with another emergent psychological transition: from a carefree school youth to a professional office lady. Each time I was summoned to JJ's office, I felt butterflies in the stomach. She seemed to be determined to forget the fact that I was still a student with no previous working or on-board training experience. My daily work began by scanning thousands of resumes from the talent pools, picking out the most promising ones and making candidate reports; during the process there were other constant demands to arrange meeting rooms, confirm appointments, book plane tickets and hotel rooms, handle express delivery, translate various legal documents, manage PowerPoint or Excel forms and other numerous trivialities. As if all these jobs were not enough

to exhaust my nerves, I had to bear the bad temper and sometimes irrational fastidiousness of JJ, who appeared to be a "Devil in Prada" in reality.

When once more I forced myself to choke back the tears after returning
from her office, I began to ask myself: where was that shining girl who
had been the pride of her parents and the role model for all the neighborhood children? Where were her courage and confidence? Was she so
easily beaten? Little by little, I calmed down and came back to my normal
senses. I started to reflect how I had performed those days, realizing that
what had made me lagging behind was the sub-conscious of not being
able to adjust myself to the new identity. Whenever confronted with challenges, my inner voice said: "Take it easy, you are just a student intern,
not a formal employee." In other words, I was not at all engaged in this
new environment. Instead of accommodating to the new role, I wrongly
positioned myself as an outsider. Such careless attitude was definitely
detrimental to my performance.

Once steering myself to the new direction, I modified the work plan,
took notes of do's and don'ts, learned from other experienced colleagues,
and observed carefully how things worked. I even consulted JJ about her
suggestions on my work and asked for ways to improve. Gradually, I
found myself getting involved, gained more pleasure in what I was doing,
and developed a respect for the company's profound history, motivated
corporate culture, and its mature management system. By the time I left
the company, JJ complained to me that she would find it hard to find a
more competent and devoted intern than me.

Edward T. Hall wrote in 1959: "When I talk about culture I am not just
talking about something abstract that is imposed on man and is separate
from him, but about man himself, about you and me in a highly personal
way." My cultural story has few dramatic events to commend, but different stages in life have acted on my well-being as a magic wand. The
striving for excellence – a heritage from my family runs deep in my blood,
influencing every direction I choose; college life teaches me to explore
and appreciate my own cultural identity as well as those of others; the
brief yet fruitful working experience unveiled the cruelty as well as the
opportunities of the outside world, noting the significance of balancing
different identities in various discourses.

That is how dots are connected in my life. By now I am fully convinced that everything happens for a reason. Our past, present and future are strongly linked. Things that are happening now may well have their far-reaching influence in one way or another. Every decision we make will have its consequences. Looking from a particular vantage point confirms the truth made by Steve Jobs at the beginning of this article. I can now say that his approach has never failed me, and it has made huge differences in my life.

10. THE BIBLICAL ELIJAH: PERSISTENCE AND COURAGE

Elijah Tang
Ocean University of China, Qingdao, China

I was born in 1990, so I belong to the generation of after 90s, which is called "the brain disabled generation." Speaking of my cultural story, it's made up of many" unfortunatelies."

First of all, I want to talk about my oldest ancestor, the first emperor of China (5,000 years ago). He was called Yao. Or you can also call him Tang Yao. Unfortunately, when he retired, he didn't deliver his power to one of his sons .A young man called Shun with no blood relationship took his power. His sons had no chance to be princes, one of them moved to a place called Tang (south of Shanxi Province today), where my family name comes from.

Then time went to 618A.D when Li Yuan and his sons established a great dynasty called Tang (618~907).because they were raised up in Tang. In other words, they were my ancesters' close neighbors.

My family had a good start, but,unfortunately again, everything changed in the 1400s.There were rarely people in Shandong as a result of the war; thus the emperor compelled people of south Shanxi to move to Shandong, and my ancestor was one of them.He moved to the mountainous centual Shandong, and started a new, poor and peaceful life. He chose a wonderful place to live, with beautiful mountains and a river. Now, it is a big village with more than 3000 people. I'm the 23th generation. We were poor peasants in more than 18 generations since then.

My great-grandfather changed this. He was a diligent man; he acquired some land and cattle. He employed people, which means that he was a small landlord. Landlords were a superior part of China for more than 2000 years until 1949. Unfortunately, my great-grandfather was a landlord ,and that was the end of his landlord life. The Communist Party confiscated all of his land , fortune and house. So we became poor peasents again.

In 1966, the great Cultural Revolution came. As an offspring of a landlord, my father didn't get the chance to go to school. My family was pushed aside in these ten years.

There was much breaking news in 1990: the disintegration of the Soviet Union, Li Denghui became the president of Taiwan, Margaret Thatcher stepped down as Prime Minister. I swear to god that my birth has nothing to do with this. However, that means a lot for my family. And it's my turn to take the mission of changing my family's destiny. I'm always passionate because I know that I'm living not only for myself but also for my whole family. The tragedy of the past made me responsible and academically strong. Destiny means nothing to me. I can hardly think of any romantic plot in my cultural story. I'm a rebellious man. There may be not much sunshine in my life, so I should be more optimistic to create sunshine myself. Perhaps god didn't smile to me; thus I'm humorous enough to make god smile.

I chose Elijah from the Old Testament as my English name because I appreciate his persistence and courage. The Bible related that he denounced the foreign cults and defeated 450 prophets of Baal in a contest on Mount Carmel. In doing so, he earned the enmity of King Ahab and his consort, Jezebel, who forced him to flee into the wilderness. Adversity reveals genius, fortune conceals it. I appreciate all the misery that afflicted my ancestors but my family think that I have a better destiny for them. Let's wait and see.

E) Book Reviews Related to China

Michael H. Prosser
University of Virginia, Charlottesville, Virginia,
Shanghai International Studies University, Shanghai, China

1. Chang, Hui-Ching, Clever, Creative, Modest: The Chinese Language Practice (2010)

Shanghai: Shanghai Foreign Language Education Press, 294 pp (Chinese Foreword and Introduction. References – pp. 275-289; Endnotes – pp. 290-294; No index).

Taiwan-born, Hui-ching Chang, Ph.D., Professor of Communication at the University of Illinois at Chicago, has been actively researching and publishing scholarly work about Chinese language, communication patterns, discourse, and Chinese relationships since the early 1990s. Among her earlier scholarly papers and articles there are the following: "A Taoist View of Language and Communication" (1991); "A Popular Culture View of Chinese Romantic Relationships: Nature and the Self" (1991); "Language and Words – Communication in the Analects of Confucius" (1997); "The 'Well-defined' is 'Ambiguous': Indeterminacy in Chinese Communication" (2001); "Harmony as Performance: The Turbulence under Chinese Interpersonal Communication" (2001); "The Concept of YUAN and Chinese Conflict Resolution" (2002); and "Serious Play: Chinese Artistry in Verbal Communication" (2003). Beginning in the mid-1990s, she and her husband, Richard Holt, Ph.D., Professor of Communication at Northern Illinois University, and an expert in the dialogical aspects of the Internet, have coauthored more than a half-dozen more articles on related subjects. To the best of my knowledge, this is her first scholarly book on these studies.

Chang's book is indeed a significant study of Chinese language practices and deserves reputation and wide distribution among those scholars and students interested in this topic. Having grown up in Taiwan, teaching, making conference presentations, and traveling both within Taiwan and the Chinese mainland, she is a foremost authority on ancient Chinese texts relating to Confucius, Mencius, and Daoism, as well as contemporary Chinese language practices. The book's title is most interesting, and identifies much of the development of the book itself in the three main chapters. Beginning in Chapter III, "The Artistic Chinese Speaker," Chang introduces the context of the Chinese language (101-108) which would have been helpful in the beginning of Chapter I "The Myth of the Silent, Restrained, and Humble Chinese."

Chapter II, "The Manipulative Speaker" discusses "Some Cultural Foundations of Interpersonal Skills," "Interpersonal Connections as Social Resources, ""Manipulating Interpersonal Ties via Talk," and "'Outside People,' Outside Category." In this chapter, she clearly demonstrates the contradictions in Chinese language practices, where the Chinese are viewed stereotypically as uncaring about people who are not in the "in group" such as in kinship, close friends, and professional relations on one hand, and as hard-working, competitive, intelligent and members of a highly developed civilization on the other hand. Chang notes that while the Western scholars tend to compare and contrast cultures bipolarally, calling the West consisting primarily as individualists and the East, including specifically Chinese, primarily as collectivists, thus overgeneralizing. In this chapter, she articulates an alternative perspective, first by asking a number of rhetorical questions and then responding throughout the chapter and later as the book proceeds to them. Earlier writers such as Robert T. Oliver in his 1971 book, Communication and Culture in Ancient India and China, emphasized that the role of communication was embedded in the philosophy of these countries' early communicative and rhetorical development, but it was clearly not studied for direct action as it had been in the early Greek society. Chang's treatment of this broad topic throughout her book articulates how the Chinese, over many centuries, and today, can be viewed in three contradictory perspectives as the book title suggests. This focus demonstrates the multi-dimensionality of the subtle and often highly indirect framing and formatting of communicative patterns. She points out in her book that often the Chinese are conflicted in whether they should be or not be clever, while at the same appreciating artistic language, and also demonstrating a sense of modesty.

Basically, she indicates that the Chinese see almost all interpersonal connections as social resources for both present and future relationships, but especially within the framework of "Preferences for One's Own People" where emotional ties are also expected to be utilitarian. In this way, she claims that the Chinese are constantly balancing the debts of human feelings and relationships, and thus often appearing to exhibit a manipulative nature either among those in the relationship, or going through an intermediary. "Outside people" are typically not accorded the same sense of close feelings and relationships. Chang states: "For Chinese, harmonious relationships engender not simply cooperation, but utility, practicality, and manipulation."

In Chapter III, having discussed the Chinese language itself, Chang demonstrates how "High Culture", including artistic and poetic expressions, has moved over the centuries and today into "Folk Wisdom" for the ordinary Chinese people. Much of the current tendency among the Chinese toward self-reflection and reflection of others has its origins in the witty and humorous turns of phrases established in classical Chinese books, treatises, and poems: "Whether it is high culture or folk wisdom, life evolves through continual reflection on others and the self; on the struggle engendered as a result of moral and human indignities, and on the contradiction between the elevated and the mundane. It is within these boundaries that one contemplates the meaning of life and integrates oneself with the universe through words varying in their subtlety" (p. 115). In this chapter, Chang discusses words as art and signs of wisdom, the Chinese philosophy of language, the role of indirectness in language, and metaphors and analogies, which not only were the substance of much of classical Chinese writing, but also have become a part today of the ordinary Chinese mentality. Chang gives many examples of artistic expressions, including poems, matched couplets, chengyu (idiomatic expressions) and other forms. These linguistic usages are often common to ordinary contemporary Chinese, even with small children being taught to memorize such expressions and thereby being brought into the culture linguistically at a very early age. Basically, she says that the progression in Chinese society has moved from solemnity, to playfulness, to humor which are all useful in social occasions and relationships.

Chapter IV: The Humble Chinese Speaker" introduces (again) the intro-spective, self-reflective Chinese character. But, Chang argues that "while this image may represent a 'partial truth,' to fully appreciate the humble Chinese speaker requires us to probe into their philosophical ideas about life and the universe, as well as the emotion they feel for relational others. Philosophy can be said to be part of Chinese everyday life and ordinary action, with theory and practice inseparable" (p. 187). This perspective, then, incorporates "words and life: the moral universe and the need for self-inspection." Although Chang does not mention this aspect as a major influence in the Great Proletarian Cultural Revolution (1996-1976), it was clearly a part of that period of Chinese cultural history, where most members of the nation, including many of the leaders, were required to do both self-inspection and self-criticism.

However, this tendency had a long cultural heritage in Chinese society. As Confucianism, Daoism, and Buddhism formed a major part of the Chinese civilizational culture's development, words have been seen, over time, as evoking both a spiritual and moral requirement, though not a particularly religious emphasis at least in Confucianism and Daoism. Still, she feels that words are an imperfect means for describing the universe, but at the same time, the Chinese typically reason with the universe through words, and therefore the world or universe is fundamentally interconnected and emotionally implemented through words. In Igor E. Klyukanov's 2010 book, A Communication Universe: Manifestations of Meaning: Staging of Significance, he remarks that "no communication concept, including the concept of communication itself, can be fully understood if we forget – or rather fail to remember its ancestory. Even history in general 'viewed reflexively, is communication history '" (p. 8). Chang has certainly provided an ample history of the development of Chinese language practices, and thus her book has a broad and historical importance in its study and that of the Chinese communicative ancestors , bringing them fully and creatively into the present.

In her final chapter "Epilogue: Multidimensionality of Chinese Lan-guage Use," she reflects on how contemporary communication channels and devices are changing the current Chinese language usage, moving conversations from collective events to private interactive conversations. Chang discusses sincerity as the foundation for interpersonal transactions, which many young Chinese say is one of their most important values, while at the same time, both in China and the West, because of the new media, plagiarism and cheating are rampant. In this final chapter, she concludes: "Like a kaleidoscope that continues to yield different displays of combinations of colors, Chinese speakers have configured a richer and more abundant linguistic repertoire to construct their interpersonal lives" (p. 273). Throughout her book, Chang provides numerous practical examples to illustrate her arguments, which make the book more lively to read than if it would only be abstract and theoretical. Personally, I have enjoyed very much reading it, despite my lack of clear knowledge and understanding with many of the Chinese terms articulated in the book. It definitely is highly academic, but also a very strong description and analysis of both ancient and modern language practices.

As much of her interview research was conducted in Taiwan, and many of the cited authors are speaking of conditions in Taiwan, we can ask whether her analysis also fully covers the language practices in the mainland, but with her wide background in both cultures, I am assuming that it does. Nonetheless, though the Chinese in the mainland and in Taiwan share many cultural similarities, it would seem that both also can be seen as separate cultures, with the mainland Chinese being identified as the dominant culture and Taiwan Chinese as a co-culture. Certainly, it is well known, as she identifies, with Mandarin and Cantonese as the leading two different forms of Chinese language practice, that there are many different spoken dialects in China, united however by a reasonably common written language. Even then, the Taiwanese written Chinese system is more likely to resemble the more classical written Chinese while the mainland Chinese system has simplified its written Chinese into a pinyin format that has helped to bring more than 100 million rural mainland Chinese into literacy, and also out of abject poverty.

Published as the eleventh book in the Shanghai Foreign Language Education Press' "Intercultural Communication Series" most of which were intercultural communication text books published originally in the United States, and reprinted by SFLEP for Chinese university students, it is the first which is not really a traditional intercultural communication text book in the series, despite the fact that there are certainly significant intercultural dimensions in her approach. Although it is not identified as a book either fitting within the context of socio-linguistics, it is my impression that it clearly belongs in that academic study. At the same time, very few of her quoted references deal directly with socio-linguistics. Perhaps, with its highly philosophical nature, and linkages to interpersonal communication, rhetoric, and conflict resolution, it can be seen as multidisciplinary and transcending specific disciplinary boundaries. However, since with only five chapters, including three very long chapters, for example, Chapter II covering pages 21-99, Chapter III covering pages 101-186, and Chapter IV covering pages 187-266, and no indication in the book itself that it is indeed intended as a text book, it would seem that it should have been published within the aegis of the Shanghai International Studies University's "Intercultural Research" series under the sponsorship of the University's Intercultural Institute, rather than with the ten earlier republished Western intercultural communication text books. It is possible, of course, that by becoming one of the books in the SFLEP "Intercultural Communication Series," it will be read more widely in China. The high academic quality of the book suggests, however, that it should have a much wider influence than just in China itself, as the first ten books in this series were first published outside of China and then republished in China, where her book is first being published in China but perhaps will not also be published outside of China. Since many English departments and colleges in the Chinese university system have sociolinguistics as one of their main branches or programs, hopefully it will be a great success for scholars and students whose major study is in the field of sociolinguistics. And ideally, it will find its way to interested scholars and students outside of China.

2. Gallo, Frank T. (2011). Business leadership in China: How to blend best western practices with Chinese wisdom.

When Professor Li Mengyu and I were planning our intercultural communication text book for Chinese university students, Communicating Interculturally (2012) at Higher Education Press in Beijing, we agreed early that there should certainly be a chapter on intercultural business communication. Since both of us have spent our professional careers in academic institutional settings, neither of us have had much special expertise on developing such a chapter. Starting each chapter of the book with a dialogue among imaginary Chinese university students, an imaginary Professor Zhang, and myself, in this case it dealt with intercultural business communication. For the basic context of the chapter, we included brief essays about Chinese media billionaires; organizational and advertising theories; an invited essay from an international banker about business and international communication; an essay from an American teaching in China about intercultural business communication; an essay from an internationally recognized Canadian author in intercultural training; a somewhat misplaced Chinese-authored essay on intercultural education in Urumqi in China's far west; and essays by four educated young Chinese, three of whom were working for managers from France, Brazil, and Italy (but missing illustrative essays for young Chinese working for German and American companies), and the fourth, who had some brief intercultural training in the United States and was teaching in a Chinese business college in Shanghai. The chapter concludes with a case study on "the McDonaldization of Society." While we consider it a good chapter, but only "scratching the surface," within the context of our book about intercultural communication for Chinese university students, we hope that it will be very useful for these young Chinese who will enter State Owned Enterprises (SOEs), local domestic companies, and those involved either with international trade, business, or training.

At the time of our writing, however, neither of us were aware of Frank T. Gallo's book, Business Leadership in China, which could have greatly enriched the focus and content of our text book's chapter, "Intercultural

Business, International Trade, Training, and Education." Widely praised by more than a dozen foreign and Chinese experts, and a bestseller, several of its endorsers call it a "must read" for foreigner managers and leaders wishing to conduct business and international trade in China, and also for Chinese leaders and managers. Gallo notes that there is an ever enlarging emerging talent development in China, but many of the Chinese managers are quite young compared to those in western countries, without appropriate mentoring, and relatively inexperienced in business and international trade and management. Many of those who might be midlevel executives today were caught in the ten year time warp of the Cultural Revolution, often forced to work in the countryside, and were unable to begin even undergraduate programs on the basis of merit until the opening up policies of Deng Xiaoping in 1978 and 1985, together with his designation of special economic zones for China.

Additionally, many senior level executives were products of the Communist reward system after having served in the People's Liberation Army or Communist Party of China hierarchy, or the State Owned Enterprises where a manager's primary goal was to please the demands of his or her superiors, to meet the needs of a Soviet-oriented economy, and to advance in the ranks of the Party rather than considering the demands of a market economy and the needs of the lower employees, as is now the necessary rational for producing a profit to remain viable among private companies in China. Today, Gallo notes that more and more young people in China are enrolled in MBA programs or have studied abroad, but the number of competent young managers and business leaders who are able to combine best Western practices with Chinese traditional wisdom is still relatively small. Most of them need about ten years of practical experience to be highly successful in combining these Western and traditional Chinese practices. However, young Chinese business people and entrepreneurs are moving into leadership roles far more quickly than would be typical in most of the Western countries, and the very rapid advancement of those entering the middle class creates an important threshold for not only advancement but also wise and empowered leadership.

Gallo identifies four major goals for his book: how to respond to the complex challenges of leading a firm or a division in China; what the major differences are in activities such as a team; working and decision-making;

and where misunderstandings can arise. There are three main parts of his book, suited for a very easy reading style: Part I: "Understanding Leadership in China Today:" with eight chapters; Part II: "Making It Work in China:" with eleven chapters; and Part III: "What Do We Do Now?" with three chapters. In each chapter he offers an introduction, quotes by some of the twenty major leaders in Chinese businesses and industries whom he has interviewed extensively; a transition to the following chapter; and a succinct "Executive Summary." The first appendix provides the biographies of each of these twenty leaders, some foreign and most Chinese; and the second appendix defines twenty-three special Chinese terms which help to explain the traditional Chinese perspectives that relate to his discussion of the central aspects of his chapters.

Gallo notes that perhaps the most impressive book dealing with leadership is the 2002 third edition of Leadership Challenge by James Kouzes and Barry Posner, which was a bestseller with more than one million copies sold: "The authors espouse a leadership model that has become famous around the world. Their model states that there are five practices for exemplary leadership. They label these as follows: (1) model the way; (2) inspire a shared vision; (3) challenge the process; (4) enable others to act; and encourage the heart" (214). Gallo states that in a questionnaire to more than 100 Chinese managers on their model in 2004 by Elizabeth Weldon, she found that when Kouzes and Posner propose that the leader help others to succeed (enable others to act), Chinese managers believed that this aspect was only of secondary importance, and in their responses to the Kouzes and Posner proposal to challenge the process, the Chinese managers in her study were "much less willing to experiment and take risks than the Kouzes and Posner model calls for" (214). Gallo suggests:

Successful managers in China achieve their success by proving their abilities and setting the pace for good and hard work. So, practice one, "model the way," works very well in China. "Inspiring a shared vision" is also something that Chinese leaders can identify with, although they may inspire others more by what they do, than what they say, as many Westerners might. The idea of a "shared" vision especially rings true in China, as it implies a collective ownership rather than one which seems to come from an individual leader.... The next three practices would need modification, however. "Challenging the process" is not at all a Chinese practice.... Chinese leaders are generally more conventional and accepting of the status quo than their Western counterparts.... The concept of enabling (or empowering) others is Western and is based on the assumption that individuals want to be empowered. In China, many employees are still not as comfortable with empowerment as Westerners are.... The final practice in the model, "encouraging the heart," can have mixed success in China.... The China approach almost always celebrates team success and rarely focuses on individual excellence.... I have used their model here as an example because I view it asperhaps the most famous in the West (or at least in the United States). But as great as it is, it still needs to be modified to be fully applicable in China.... Best Western leadership practices cannot be introduced in China without some modification (214-216).

Personally, Gallo's emphasis on blending best Western practices with Chinese traditional wisdom seems to be a very significant contribution of his book to the understanding of Chinese business and trade leadership patterns. His use throughout the book of specialized Chinese terms, many coming from Confucianism or Daoism to explain his major concepts has been enriching for me, particularly as in my recent past conference presentations or papers, I have frequently used a small number of these expressions, sayings, and proverbs to develop a greater understanding of Chinese culture. Like Gallo, I first came as a foreign expert, in my case as a university teacher, in 2001 when China was on the cusp of many extraordinary educational, social, and business breakthroughs. Having spent about the same amount of time as Gallo in China, but as a teacher in various universities, I recognize through his book many characteristics of my own individualism versus the Chinese collectivism that I encountered among administrators, fellow Chinese teachers, and my students. As he says, nonetheless, the young Chinese are increasingly more individualistic.

Like Gallo, I have emphasized a number of Confucian concepts in my writing, lecturing, speaking and teaching, while in my case still being very American in most of my approaches, but as he indicates, "there is not yet a model (at least that I am aware of) that incorporates the best practices from both the East and West and that could be followed by anyone who aspires to be a great leader in China" (218-219). I consistently tell my own Chinese university students that they are "the future of China," but beyond that general and encouraging statement, I have yet to learn specifically how they should maximize their Western learning, conducted generally in English, with the traditional aspects of Chinese culture, to become future Chinese leaders. Happily, Gallo, while disclaiming that his book is the last word on business leadership in China, as he concludes: "The findings here, plus those to come from other sources, will be the foundation for the development of a unique Chinese model of leadership" (218-219).

3. Li Mengyu's and Michael H. Prosser's Communicating Interculturally (2012)

Mansoureh Sharifzadeh,
Ministry of Education, Tehran, Iran

Dialogue: To Enhance Positive Cultural Communication

As an Iranian English language teacher and a 'public thinker,' it is an invaluable opportunity for me to write a commentary on Communicating Interculturally. Li Mengyu's, and Michael H. Prosser's textbook can answer numerous questions in the field of communication to the people of any nation, although it is basically written for the people of China. Communicating Interculturally can be used as a reference including a series of extensive significant topics that the world is facing at this crucial stage of the history.

One day, on Professor Prosser's blog, www.michaelprosser.com , Ali, a Muslim student from Xi'an attracted my attention. Soon I realized him as one of the 40 students of the class being involved in a dialogue, while Michael was demonstrating a good model for teaching in general. Michael calls Ali brave since he is the first to introduce himself and the teacher implies his act as a ''good self-disclosure.''

The method of teaching, especially the creative, happy and friendly atmosphere of the class in addition to Michael's character as a wise, patient, respectable, thoughtful, flexible leader and an organizer as well as a mentor is admirable. What captivates me is his main aim in motivating and involving the students in the class discussions to empower the process of teaching and the art of thinking together while being critical.

The book reflects the world. It is noticeable that special information is sorted with the most understandable literature to define the concepts brightly. China and the United States have been compared in different aspects. Important facts have been mentioned about some other nations too. The variety of given information is stunning and ties the content of the book to all nationalities and ideas. Mentioning different ideologies as well as religious beliefs provide the reader with fundamental awareness. The book is educational for everybody.

In the present history of the world, China has occupied the world market and is pioneer and holds the central focus on trade and production of all sorts. As a result, all nations are interested in knowing more about this hard working country with a history of more than 400 years. China has always been of great importance with the highest population in the world. In this book the readers can get enormous information about many different aspects of this country including life style, ideology, literature, tourism, trade and market, art, history, politics, geography and much more.

This book is spectacular with deep insight while exploring peoples' minds through case studies. The astonishing feature of the case studies is focused on the personal experiences of the writers. Variety of writers with different interests and perspectives make the readers more interested and their everyday life issues of all sorts are invaluable experiences which are shared with the readers.

Dialogues shape the stunning dimension of the book. They are imaginary writings while revealing Professor Prosser's ability as a skillful playwright that gives useful information in all areas related to communication and its history. The wit tone brings joy and satisfaction and excludes the boring side of the books of this type. Prosser's personal experiences add more attraction to the book as it is not very usual for the Iranian people to share their privacy so openly with the public. The simple and short sentences of the experienced writer engage the reader with the most intimate method.

The real situation of the class atmosphere brings the reader to a more pleasing process. I compare this imaginary class of Michael with the Iranian high school classes where the textbooks encourage the teachers to be the core of the exam-oriented educational system to present the whole text on their own. In this class, Michael is the leading character that brings up different ideas and leaves them to the students to get involved and participate in the class discussion so as not to be neglected.

By going through the lines, one can easily imagine Michael as a very kind teacher whose main aim is to be a contributor rather than a lecturer. Michael's main aim is to demonstrate the learners as the main educational purpose whose capacity and talent should not be neglected. He involves the learners in the process of teaching through the most skilled technique. The students express their ideas freely and critically. The systematic approach in this process shows the students should not learn in isolation and out of context. Professor Prosser reminds the teachers of the fact that the students might even know more than the teachers as he reads "one undergraduate knew far more than I".

Considering the present situation of the world and the rapid progress in every aspect of life which is mainly related to technology and interest in it, and the role of media, the need for dialogue becomes more and more crucial among different nations. To gain the goal some of the ideas that lead to communication breakdown must be recognized. For instance, some points might seem to conflict, but if it comes to face to face conversation this can be solved and real intentions be revealed: "Other conflicts in the Middle East, plus nuclear technology and weaponry in Iran and North Korea, the spread of HIV/AIDS and malaria, and terrorism, which continues to be a menacing global threat and the source of major communication breakdowns."

In the world today, the media create stereotypes and the need for dialogue and communication becomes more serious. In a research the Iranian students illustrated the Americans as vampires, opportunists, demolisher, main terrorists, torturers, arrogant oppressors. The American students demonstrated the Iranians as terrorists and drew all of them as Arabs. (The Visual and Artistic Rhetoric of Americans and Iranians of Each Other Impacted by Media: Professor D. Ray Heisey, Mansoureh Sharifzadeh). The drawings were trying to verify the other nation negatively. They would appear to show how the media of both nations reflected both nations in a stereotypical fashion to create phobia. The mentioned points bring up the importance of direct communication.

In 2001, President Mohammad Khatami proposed "Dialogue Among Civilizations" and the United Nations proclaimed the year 2001 as the United Nations' Year of Dialogue Among Civilizations, on Khatami's suggestion. In 2006 President Mahmood Ahmadinejad sent an open letter to President Bush and to the American people hoping for genuine dialogue on issues of mutual concern. Later on, Barack Obama wanted to turn the page with Iran. Neither of the decisions have given way to a prosperous consequence so far. By dialogue, collective thinking gives way to individualistic considerations.

Nowadays the world is witnessing fundamental changes especially in the Arab world. In this book, Michael demonstrates the role of leaders that should show the way and trust others to reach the target by themselves. 'Communicating Interculturally', implicitly insists on dialogue which can be a final solution for better relationships in the world today in all aspects, from the smallest units like the family life to the biggest one which is relationship among the civilizations. Then the value of dialogue, mediation, and arbitration and face to face communication that distinguishes human beings can be discovered. The mentioned points broaden our understanding, perspective, and acceptance of others and the contribution they can make to our lives, if we but open our eyes and minds.

A verse from the holy Qu'ran, Chapter Al Imran, :103, reads: "And hold fast, all of you together, to the Rope of Allâh and remember Allâh's Favour on you, for you were enemies one to another but He joined your hearts together, so that, by His Grace, you became brethren and you were on the brink of a pit of fire, and He saved you from it". The mentioned verse is the most significant verse of the Quran in terms of binding and communication. And we shall keep wishing to extend our hearts for each other in a hope that no one extends the arms with arms for the others.

And also Jesus reminded the Pharisees, "out of the overflow of the heart, the mouth speaks." Jesus reminds us that the words we speak are actually the overflow of our hearts (Matthew 12:34-35).

Communicating Interculturally, presents a strong model for teaching as well as communication in different aspects. This book can be considered as a good example for the Iranian experts in the field of communication. As Iran is concerned about 'cultural invasion' and intends to provide the Iranians with the noble Islamic Iranian culture, a book can be edited with the base of Iranian culture with respect to other nations' values. Iran's history goes back to more than 2500 years ago. Now, Iran consists of 31 provinces with different dialects and customs that can attract not only the Iranians but also the world. Iranians like communication and having relationship with other nations as their hospitality is unique especially to foreigners.

The value of communication is highly respected in Iran as Prophet Mohammad Peace Be Upon Him, suggested "going to China in quest of knowledge". This proves the value of communicating with other nations even if they are from other beliefs or very far from us.

Communicating Interculturally is a measureless book and in my opinion a masterpiece. It is a sweet textbook which is easy to digest while the strongest message can be perceived through the act of dialogue.

Blessings and salaam to Li Mengyu and Michael H. Prosser and congratulations on their fruitful effort.

PART III

CROSS-CULTURAL COMMON GROUND IN THE MIDDLE EAST AND IRAN

A) Essays

1. Discourse on the Middle East for New Intercultural Under-standings

Michael H. Prosser
University of Virginia, Charlottesville, Virginia,
Shanghai International Studies University, Shanghai, China

Introduction

Both rhetorical analysis and discourse analysis offer useful perspectives on reading discourse on the Middle East with the goal to create new intercultural understandings or "a dialogue among civilizations" rather than the "clash of civilizations" as proposed by Samuel P. Huntington in his provocative book in 1996. The rhetorical analyst considers not only the speaker/author/rhetor as a chief source of understanding, who according to Aristotle must properly use ethos (credibility, good will for the audience and knowledge of the author), proper logos (correct reasoning, based on the probability of the proposition's likelihood of success and evidence for the proposition), and pathos (appropriate emotional appeals to the audience), but also an understanding of the persuasive message itself, or in modern rhetorical studies the role of language as sermonic, the channels through which the message is delivered, and the audience being addressed. In a complementary fashion, the more modern development of discourse analysis, while utilizing some of the aspects of rhetorical analysis, focuses primarily in a descriptive manner, basically on the message, but placed in its contextual setting, and in the case of this article on the history of the Middle East peace process, in the context of this discourse development over the past 105 years, between the Israelis and Arabs, the Israelis and the Palestinians, and between these actors and the Western world.

There are a number of useful axioms relating to the application of both rhetorical and discourse analysis. Plato, through his Socratic dialogues, called upon rhetoric and dialectic to promote truth, goodness, wisdom and the good life for humans, and Aristotle developed this idea further by urging the rhetor to not only promote these principles, but also to lead one's audience towards happiness.

As the late Kenneth Burke argued, human beings are symbol makers, symbol users, symbol misusers, the creator of the negative, and tool makers of tools that can make tools (such as the modern computer, for example). Burke and other rhetorical scholars proposed that the purpose of effective rhetoric is to create understandings out of misunderstandings. Michel Foucault emphasized that discourse provides us with an understanding of "the archeology of the mind" and is always bound by power relationships, where one interlocutor has superior standing over others. Jurgen Habermas sees the need for the creation of a "universal audience" for understanding messages. Burke tells us that "language is the soul of culture," and with Aristotle's dictum, Marshall McLuhan acknowledged that the "metaphor is the soul of language." In the Middle East, for example, we are aware that highly expressive metaphors often exaggerate contexts, such as Saddam Hussein's "the mother of all wars" metaphor. All discourse is naturally contextual, set in a specific time and place. Certainly, as has often been the case in highly explosive discourse in the Middle East, we are aware that the greatest communication breakdowns often lead to intercultural mistrust, conflicts, wars, and geographical destruction. The former UN Secretary General, Kofi Annan, postulated that the greatest human rights violations are war and abject poverty, which is often the result of war and the displacement of millions of vulnerable people.

As Ray T. Donahue and I have articulated in our book, Diplomatic Discourse: International Conflict at the United Nations (1997) where we discuss both the importance of rhetorical and discourse analysis as means of understanding international discourse and conflicts, the discourse and conflicts in the Middle East are extraordinarily complicated and tortured, with both Israel and the Palestinians deeply mistrusting the other side in the negotiations. We include the 1988 address of PLO Chairman Yassir

Arafat to the United Nations Security Council in which he loudly protests Israel's harsh rhetoric and treatment of the Palestinians. Also, in my article for this Journal on Obama's outreach to the Arab world in his June 4, 2009 Cairo address, I discussed the Israeli attacks on Gaza as a contextual bridge between the Bush and Obama administrations.

There also are many familiar axioms related to the Middle East, for example, the often repeated Jewish quote from Genesis 15: 18-21 as a basis for greater Israel: "The Lord made a covenant with Abraham saying: Unto thy seed have I given this land from the river of Egypt to the great river Euphrates," which is often challenged by Arab and Palestinian leaders. The term "Middle East" is essentially a modern linguistic concept, originated only in 1902. "Eretz Yisrael – the Biblical land of Israel" is often linked both by Jews, Christians, and Muslims by the usage of the term, "Holy Land" referring to the birthplace for all the Abrahamic monotheistic religions – Judaism, Christianity, Islam, and the Baha'i faith. The various religious groups consider the "Holy Cities" as Jerusalem, Hebron, Safed, and Tiberias. Additionally, the Christians identify both Bethlehem and Nazareth as holy sites; and the shared monotheistic "Holiest Sites" include the Foundation Stone, Temple Mount, and Western Wall. The "birth of political Zionism" in 1896 is attributed to Theodore Herzl's article "The Jewish State" in which he argued that with growing antisemitism in Europe a new Jewish state was required in Palestine. In 1897, the first Zionist Congress ''called for the establishment of a home for the Jewish people in Palestine secured under public law.''

These two persuasive but widely dismissed discourses began the more than a century-long development of the modern readings on the Middle East discourse to the present time. In 2011, Israel ranks the highest in development in Middle East countries on the UN Development Index. Presently, Israel's population, including many of the Jews who came from Eastern Europe, stands at 7.7 million, with a Jewish population of 5,8 million and non Jewish minorities (Muslims, Christians, Christian Arabs, and Druze) of 1,6 million.

Middle East Discourse and Conflicts from 1906 to 1977

When Chaim Weizmann and Lord Arthur James Balfour met in 1906, Balfour suggested a Jewish homeland in Uganda. Dr. Weizmann replied: "Mr. Balfour, supposing I was to offer you Paris instead of London, would you take it?" "But Dr. Weizmann, we have London." "That is true," Weizmann said, "but we had Jerusalem when London was a marsh." Balfour asked: "Are there many Jews who think like you?" Weizmann answered: "I believe I speak the mind of millions of Jews whom you will never see and who cannot speak for themselves." It is widely believed that this somewhat humorous but persuasive exchange led Lord Belfour and others in the British government to proclaim "The Balfour Declaration" on November 2, 1917: "His Majesty's government views with favour the establishment in Palestine of a national home for the Jewish people, and will use their best endeavours to facilitate the achievement of this object, it being clearly understood that nothing shall be done which may prejudice the civil and religious rights of existing non-Jewish communities in Palestine, or the rights and political status enjoyed by Jews in any other country." Considering the exchange between Weizmann and Balfour and the 1917 declaration descriptively and contextually "what is" from the point of view of discourse analysis, as well as persuasively from the perspective of rhetorical analysis "what ought to be," when following the Versailles Treaty at the end of World War I, Great Britain had the British Mandate for Palestine. This declaration greatly increased Jewish immigration to Palestine and gave an increasing emphasis on securing a Jewish homeland in Palestine. In 1947, Great Britain turned the Mandate over to the UN, which in 1947 adopted Resolution 181, partitioning the land into two states, Arab and Jewish. As this resolution was the first one passed in the United Nations on the Middle East peace process, it had the basic persuasive symbolic strength of an international law on this subject.

The 1947 UN Palestine Partition Plan's final report of the Commission in the United Nations Special Committee on Palestine (UNSCOP) recommended for the region in 1947: the partition of Palestine into a Jewish state, an Arab state, and UN-controlled territory (around Jerusalem). Resolution 181 was adopted by the UN General Assembly on November 29, 1947. The

Jewish community agreed, but Arab countries and Palestinian Arabs did not, resulting in the 1948 Arab-Israeli War. On May 14, 1948, Israel became a state, a day celebrated annually in Israel, and also regularly denounced by many Arab countries. In a highly symbolical celebratory discourse, Israel's first president, David Ben-Gurion, proclaimed the Israeli state, standing below the large portrait of Theodor Herzl, thus linking rhetorically and discursively to Herzl's 1896 call for a Jewish state in Palestine and the first Zionist Congress in 1897.

In 1956, under the leadership and persuasive rhetoric of Egyptian President Gamal Nasser, the Suez Canal crisis (also called the Tripartite Aggression) erupted on July 26. The Egyptian government nationalized the Suez Canal Company; all its Egyptian assets, rights and obligations which Nasser transferred to the Suez Canal Authority. At the UN Security Council, we can read the contrastive discourse on the crisis taking a very strange diplomatic turn, as in an unusual example of jointly promoted US-Soviet rhetoric, the US and USSR stood together on one side of the debate with Egypt while France and Great Britain supported the other side with Israel, and against their ally, the United States. The United States had promised to build the Aswan Dam for Egypt at the same time that Egypt was establishing closer ties to the USSR and had recently recognized the PRC when a possible war between the Mainland China and Taiwan was being widely debated and feared. Diplomatic pressure from the United States and the USSR at the UN and elsewhere forced France and Great Britain to withdraw from the area. Following the planned invasion of the eastern Sinai by Israel, on October 29-31, 1956 to April, 1957, when the Suez Canal was blocked to shipping, and the later French and British occupation of the Suez Canal Zone, on December 22, 1956, the Canal Zone was restored to Egyptian control, following the French and British withdrawal, and the landing of UNEF troops through the acceptance of Egypt. Israeli forces remained, however, until March 1957 which both symbolically and literally prolonged the crisis.

In November 1966, Syria signed a mutual defense agreement with Egypt and the Israeli Defense Force (IDF) attacked the city of Samu in the Jordanian-occupied West Bank, with the Jordanian units engaging the Israelis quickly beaten back. Jordanian King Hussein harshly criticized Egyptian President Nasser for failing to come to Jordan's aid, and "hid-ing behind UNEF skirts." On June 5-10, 1967 "Six-Day War", following inflammatory rhetoric by the Arabs, Israel took control of the Gaza Strip and the Sinai Peninsula from Egypt, the West Bank and East Jerusalem from Jordan, and the Golan Heights from Syria. At this time, the United States hesitated from immediately calling for a ceasefire until Israel had achieved its military objectives. In a testy exchange between USSR leader Alexei Kosygin to President Lyndon B. Johnson meeting at Glasboro State College in New Jersey, Kosygin said: : "If you want war, you will get war." One of the most important and later the basis for the fundamental UN and international discourse on the Middle East, UN Security Council Resolution 242 in November, 1967 called for an "Inadmissibility of acquisition of territory by war," "Peaceful and accepted settlement," "Withdrawal of Israeli armed forces from territories occupied in the recent conflict," "Termination of all claims or states of belligerency," "Every state has the right to live within secure and recognized boundaries free from threats or acts of force," and "Just settlement of the refugee problem." Much later, following the Oslo Accords, the PLO leadership accepted this Resolution in its "Declaration of Principles."

During the surprise Arab attack on Israel in the 1973 Yom Kippur War, Syrian forces overran much of southern Golan Heights, before being pushed back by Israel. Israel and Syria signed a ceasefire in 1974 with almost all the Heights in Israeli hands. East of the 1974 ceasefire line lies the Syrian controlled part of the Heights, an area not captured by Israel, 500 square kilometers. The Golan Heights have been under military administration since 1967. In 1981, Israel passed its Golan Heights Law, which applied Israeli ''laws, jurisdiction and administration'' to the Israeli occupied Golan Heights. Then Prime Minister Golda Meir's reflections on the Golan Heights stated: "The Syrians seemed bent on an escalation of the conflict; they kept up an endless bombardment of Israel's settlements below the Golan Heights ,and Israeli fishermen and farmers faced what was sometimes virtually daily attacks by snipers. I used to visit the settlements occasionally and watch the settlers go about their work as though there was nothing at all unusual in plowing with a military escort or putting children to sleep – every single night – in underground air raid shelters."

Discourse about the Middle East Peace Process, 1977-1993

On November 9, 1977, Anwar El Sadat startled the Arab world by announcing his intention to go to Jerusalem. Ten days later he arrived for the groundbreaking three-day visit, which launched the first peace process between Israel and an Arab state. The Sadat visit came about after his Cairo speech stating that he would travel anywhere, "even Jerusalem," to discuss peace. The Begin government declared that, if Israel thought that Sadat would accept an invitation, Israel would invite him. In Sadat's Knesset speech he talked about his views on peace, the status of Israel's occupied territories, and the Palestinian refugee problem. Symbolically, it was the most important discourse for a renewed peace process since the founding of Israel in 1948. Through President Jimmy Carter's 1979 Camp David Accords, Israeli Prime Minister Menachem Begin and Egyptian President Anwar Sadat signed the first Israeli-Arab peace treaty. The other Arab states refused to endorse or participate in it. And the Arab League moved its headquarters from Cairo and most members broke ties with Egypt, ushering in nearly a decade of Egyptian isolation in the Arab world. Sadat was assassinated by Egyptian fundamentalists in 1981. President Carter moved to rejuvenate the Middle East and to replace bilateral peace talks with a comprehensive multilateral approach. Carter visited Anwar El Sadat in Egypt, King Hussein in Jordan, Hafez al-Assad of Syria, and Yitzhak Rabin of Israel as a part of his personal diplomatic and persuasive endeavor to achieve a Middle East process. King Hussein refused to take part in the process fearing isolating Jordan from the Arab world and provoking Syria and the PLO. Syrian President Hafez al-Assad only agreed to meet Carter in Geneva.

Nonetheless, these meetings gave Carter a basic plan for restarting the peace process based on the Geneva Conference and presented three main objectives for Arab-Israeli peace: "Arab recognition of Israel's right to exist in peace, Israel's withdrawal from occupied territories gained in the Six Day War and to ensure that Israel's security would not be threatened; and securing an undivided Jerusalem." The 1978 Camp David Accords was signed by Begin and el Sadat, following thirteen days of secret negotiations at Camp David. Two framework agreements signed at the White House, were witnessed by President Carter. "A Framework for the Conclusion of Peace Treaty between Egypt and Israel," led to the 1979 Egypt-Israel Peace Treaty, and resulted in Sadat and Begin sharing the 1978 Nobel Peace Prize. The long-term importance of the Camp David Accords signaled persuasively and descriptively that the joint discourse had resulted in a very important Middle East peace conference; the view of Egypt within the Arab world changed; Egypt had more power than any of the other Arab states to advance their interests; the Camp David Accords ended a united Arab front in opposition to Israel. And the Accords were supported by most Egyptians and Israelis.

The discursive success of Begin, Sadat, and Carter at Camp David demonstrated to other Arab states and entities that negotiations with Israel were possible. Because of the Iranian hostage crisis, President Carter was often vilified as a weak leader, but late in his only term of office, his accomplishments clearly included his efforts for the Israeli-Arab peace process; his return of the Panama Canal to Panama; and the US-PRC establishment of full diplomatic recognition by the United States for the PRC. Also, in my opinion, the release of the US hostages in Iraq also was a direct result of his diplomatic efforts, but credit was given improperly to newly sworn-in President Ronald Reagan as he was being inaugurated on January 20, 1981. In 2002, President Carter received the Nobel Peace Prize for his work "to find peaceful solutions to international conflicts" and he has been active since his Presidency in helping to negotiate many international conflicts.

During early January 1981, I was a member of a US faculty study delegation of 26 participants in Lebanon, Jordan, and the occupied territories of Israel while the PLO controlled much of Lebanon. We met with Chairman Arafat, many local delegations, and the outgoing US ambassador in Beirut, as well as with the Jordanian Council of Foreign Relations and various delegations in the West Bank of Israel and the Gaza Strip. Publically, US officials were restricted from meeting with Chairman Arafat, but secretly negotiations continued between the US government and the PLO under Arafat's leadership, who labeled himself as "a stateless person," required to travel internationally through a UN passport, and who called for open negotiations with the American and Israeli governments and the PLO. In 1982, several American and British negotiators were taken hostage in

Lebanon and held for a long period. When we were in southern Lebanon in Tyre, our entire delegation was forced into an underground air shelter, and the Israeli shelling was reported by The International Harold Tribune the next day. In Israel, government officials refused to meet with our delegation because we had met with PLO officials and Chairman Arafat. Thus in this case, Israeli discourse was harsh, but without an actual opportunity for it between Israeli leaders and the American professorial delegation.

During the Presidency of George Herbert Walker Bush, the 1991 Madrid Middle East Peace Conference was convened on October 30 under the sponsorship of Spain and co-sponsored by the United States and the USSR. As the last conference co-sponsored by the US and USSR, before the Soviet system collapsed, it was an early, but unsuccessful attempt by the international community to start a peace process through negotiations involving Israel and Palestinians as well as Syria, Lebanon, and Jordan.

Discourse about the Middle East Process, 1993 to 2011

In the Israeli-Arab Peace process in Oslo 1993 during fourteen secret meetings, in cooperation with the Norwegian government, Israeli Foreign Affairs Minister, Shimon Peres sent the highest-ranking non-political representative and a military lawyer to continue the negotiations. Israeli and Palestinian delegations in Norway lived in the same residence, with meals at the same table, and ongoing friendly discussions in contrast to the Madrid conference where the delegations met only in the formal sessions. In August 1993, the delegations reached an agreement, signed in secrecy by Peres while visiting Oslo. The Palestinians and Israelis had not yet agreed on the Accord's wording, with the PLO to acknowledge the state of Israel and pledging to reject violence, while Israel would recognize the (unelected) PLO as the official Palestinian authority, and also allowing Arafat to return to the West Bank.

In relation to the Oslo Accords, Benjamin Netanyahu's comments provided an interesting view of what was supposed to be private discourse. In a 2001 video, Netanyahu, reportedly unaware that he was being recorded, said: "They asked me before the election if I'd honor (the Oslo accords)...

I said I would, but (that) I'm going to interpret the accords in such a way that would allow me to put an end to this galloping forward to the '67 borders. How did we do it? Nobody said what defined military zones were. Defined military zones are security zones; as far as I'm concerned, the entire Jordan Valley is a defined military zone. Go argue." Netanyahu then explained how he conditioned his signing of the 1997 Hebron agreement on American consent that there be no withdrawals from "specified military locations," and insisted he be allowed to specify which areas constituted a "military location" - such as the whole of the Jordan Valley. He asked rhetorically: "Why is that important? Because from that moment on I stopped the Oslo Accords."

The Jordan-Israeli Peace Treaty of 1994 normalized relations between the two countries and resolved territorial disputes," discursively as an end to the age of wars." The conflict had already roughly cost $18.3 billion. The treaty was closely linked with efforts to create peace between Israel and the Palestinian Authority. The signing ceremony occurred at the southern border crossing of Arabah on October 26, and made Jordan only the second Arab country, after Egypt, to normalize relations with Israel.

The 1998 Wye River Memorandum negotiated between Israel and the Palestine Authority to implement the earlier Interim Agreement was moderated by the United States at the Aspen Institute Wye River Conference Center near Wye River, Maryland and signed on October 23, 1998. President William Jefferson Clinton opened the summit at the secluded Wye River Conference Center on October 15, 1998 and he returned at least six times (and perhaps more secretly) to the site to press Israeli Prime Minister Benjamin Netanyahu to overcome remaining obstacles with Chairman Arafat. Clinton invited King Hussein to join the talks.

Earlier in March 2000, Pope John Paul II made the second historic and highly symbolic papal and interreligious visit to Israel (the first having occurred by Pope Paul VI.) Expectations grew considerably about the likely conclusion of the ongoing Israeli-Palestinian peace process. At the July 2000 Camp David Summit, President Clinton moderated meetings between Palestinian leader Yassir Arafat and Israeli Prime Minister Ehud Barak. Barak reportedly offered the Palestinian leader approximately 95% of the West Bank and Gaza Strip, as well as Palestinian sovereignty over East Jerusalem, and proposed that 69 Jewish settlements (which comprised

85% of the West Bank's Jewish settlers) would be given to Palestinians. He also proposed "temporary Israeli control" indefinitely over another 10% of the West Bank territory – an area including many more Jewish settlements. At the Camp David Summit, Arafat rejected the treaty but surprisingly made no counter proposals. Thus, the raised symbolic peace process and ongoing discourse between the Israelis and Palestinians was once again halted. It might be called a "discourse of silence."

Although Israel unilaterally withdrew troops from southern Lebanon, Prime Minister Sharon's visit to the Temple Mount initiated the second Intifada which temporarily ended negotiations between the PLO Fatah leadership and Israel, causing most of the earlier supportive. Israelis to lose confidence in much of the on and off again Israeli-Palestinian peace process. At the Beirut Arab Summit Endorsement of Arab Peace Initiative, March 2002, a comprehensive peace initiative, first proposed in 2002 at the Beirut Summit of the Arab League by then-Crown Prince, and later King Abdullah of Saudi Arabia, and re-endorsed at the Riyadh Summit in 2007, to end the Arab-Israeli conflict, which meant normalizing relations between the entire Arab region and Israel, in exchange for a complete withdrawal from occupied territories (including East Jerusalem) and a "just settlement" of the Palestinian refugee crisis based on UN Resolution 194. At this time, Israel was not willing to negotiate with this major Arab initiative for the Middle East peace process.

In June 2002, the "Roadmap for Peace" was articulated by President George W. Bush, to resolve the Israeli-Palestinian conflict and proposed by the "quartet": the United States, EU, Russia, and UN. It was considered a new starting point for a "Palestinian state living side by side with Israel in Peace". Although this "roadmap" is still an aspect of the rhetorical and discursive framework, to date it has produced no concrete results. After suicide bomb attacks, ending in the "Passover massacre" in 2003 Israel launched Operation Defensive Shield and Prime Minister Sharon began constructing tall barriers around the West Bank, segmenting Palestinian settlements from each other. When the January 2003 elections were held for the Knesset, the right-wing Likud Party won the most seats. In December 2003, Prime Minister Sharon announced that he would consider a unilateral withdrawal from parts of the occupied territories. Disengagement from the Gaza Strip was completed on September 12, 2005. Most Israelis and Palestinians agreed on a two-state solution.

President Bush hosted the Annapolis Middle East Peace Conference on November 27, 2007, at the US Naval Academy. Forty countries were invited including China, Middle Eastern states, the Arab League, Russia, the EU, and the UN. This conference marked first time that the reality of a two-state solution was internationally articulated in an agreed upon outline to address the Israeli-Palestinian Conflict based on the "Roadmap for Peace." Palestinian leader Mahmoud Abbas' major quotes over several years suggest his contrasting visions of the ongoing discourse: in 2003, "There is absolutely no substitution for dialogue," In 2005, "The little jihad is over, and now we have the bigger jihad – the bigger battle is achieving security and economic growth," and 2005: "I renew my commitment to continuing the road he (Arafat) began and for which he made a lot of sacrifices, until the Palestinian flag flies from the walls, minarets and churches of Jerusalem." Although Israel had unilaterally withdrawn from Gaza in 2005, a major event occurred when because of ongoing rocket strikes into southern Israel from Gaza, Israel engaged in an "Unrelenting/uncompromizing War" toward the Gaza leadership and population in a surprise air attack by the Israel Air Force against Gaza. Israel was widely criticized by many human rights groups for using heavy firepower and dropping phosporous on the population from the air. Israel's aggressive part in the conflict echoed criticism through both the Israeli NGO "Breaking the Silence" and a special report by Israeli filmmaker Nurit Kedar shown on Israel's Channel on January 4, 2011.

In April 2009, President Barack Obama gave a major Middle East address in Turkey, and then on June 4, 2009 he delivered his major Cairo address to the Middle East: "A New Beginning" in which he called for improved mutual understanding and relations between the Islamic world and the West and said that both the Muslim world and the west should do more to confront violent extremism. However, it was Obama's call for peace between Israel and Palestinians that provided the highest profile. Obama reaffirmed America's alliance with Israel, calling their mutual bond "unbreakable", but also described Palestinian statelessness as "intolerable" and recognizing their aspirations for statehood and dignity as legitimate – just as legitimate as Israel's desire for a Jewish homeland.

The speech had 7 parts: violent extremism, the Israeli/Palestinian dispute, nuclear weapons (with a reference to Iran), democracy, religious freedom, rights of women, and economic development.

Benjamin Netanyahu had been the Israeli Prime Minister in 1996-99; and was elected again in 2009. On June 14, 2009, Netanyahu gave a seminal address, broadcast live in Israel and across parts of Arab world, on the topic of the Middle East peace process. He endorsed for the first time the notion of a Palestinian state along side Israel. This was a remarkable discursive development in the long and seemingly unending discourse about a sustainable Middle East peace process. In 2010, the British magazine, New Statesman, listed him as the eleventh among the most influential world figures in 2010."

Roger Cohen, writing in the New York Times on May 3, 2011, about the capture and death of Osama Bin Laden, made the following points: "From Bin Laden to the transformation and fast-forwarding of the Arab world toward pluralism and self-expression, we need to make America's closest regional ally, Israel, understand that a changed Middle East cannot be met with unchanging Israeli policies. Palestine, like Israel, must rise to the region's dawning post-Osama era of responsibility and representation." As Cohen says, only when the" dialogue among civilizations" places discourse and not conflict and war as the first priority, can a greater intercultural and international understanding be developed.

As a discursive initiative, even before the Egyptian, Lybian, Jordanian, and Syrian protests, social media began to play an important role discursively. Facebook appears to have had a pivotal role in engaging young Middle Easterners to call for a change to the decades long leadership in the region, to be replaced by "power to the people." In the autumn of 2011, a major rhetorical proposition gaining traction among UN delegations is to declare Palestine a state, something which Arafat contemplated but never achieved. Prime Minister Netanyahu is facing his own form of social networking protests in Israel. So we have potential positive discourse between Israel and Palestine, a potential symbolic announcement of Palestine as a new state, and clashing discourses throughout the Middle East away from decades long rule in the Arab states moving toward their own uncertain patterns of democracy, and within Israel an increasingly divided population over many social issues. Will the ongoing rhetoric lead toward pragmatic solutions or a communication breakdown? It is presently slightly too early to tell, but many changes can be anticipated in a matter of months rather than years now: leading to more "clash of civilizations" or "a dialogue among civilizations."

Selected References

Arafat, Y. (1900: May 25). In United Nations Security Council redord. S/PV/2923. Pp. 3-55.

Benson, T.W. & Prosser, M.H. (Eds.) (1969). Readings in classical rhetoric. Boston, MA: Allyn and Bacaon, Co.

Bishop, P. (1990: May 26). Arafat tells UN of war threat in Middle East. The Daily Telegraph. [online: Lexus Nexus].

Bloomfield, D. M. (1990: May 26). Going over the edge at the summit: The Jerusalem Post. Op-Ed [online: Lexus Nexus].

Cowell, A. (1990:May 27). Arab anger at Israel: Has Mubarak caught it too? New York Times [online: Nexus Lexus].

Donahue, R.T. & Prosser, M.H. (1997). Diplomatic discourse: International conflict at the United Nations. Grenwich, CT: Ablex.

Dullforce, W. (1990: May 26). Arafat presses UN to take action: Security Council in Geneva hears demand for West Bank emergency force. Financial Times [online: Lexus Nexus].

Elsner, A. (1990; May 23). US told Arafat it would reject visa request from him. Reuters. [online: Nexus Lexus].

Huntington, S. P.(1996).The clash of civilizations and the remaking of world order. New York, NY: Penguin

Lewis, P. (1990: May 26). Arafat in Geneva, calls on UN to send force to occupied areas. New York Times [online: Lexus Nexus].

Prosser, M.H. (2012). Universal human rights as universal values: A historical perspective. In S.J. Kulich and M.H. Prosser (Eds.). Value Frameworks at Theoretical Crossroads of Culture. Intercultural Research, Vol. 4. Shanghai, China: Shanghai Foreign Language Education Press.

Siegel, C. (1990: May 26). Palestinians applaud Arafat, Israel says he exploited tragedy, Reuters [online: Lexus Nexus].

The Times. (1990: May 26). Israelis hit back after Arafat plea for UN protection. Overseas news [online: Lexus Nexus].

United Nations (1992) Prospects for peace in the Middle East: An Israeli-Palestinian dialogue. Helsinki encounter. New York, NY:

United Nations (1994). Promoting a culture for peace in the Middle East: An Israeli-Palestinian dialogue. New York, NY.

United Nations (1995). Preresquisites for peace in the Middle East. New York, NY.

Weizman, S. (1990: May 27). Israel-US relations headed for crisis, ambassador says. Reuters [online: Lexus Nexus]

2. Damavand College, Tehran, Iran, a Path to "Intellectual Openness"

Mansoureh Sharifzadeh
Ministry of Education, Tehran, Iran

In 1979, the Islamic Republic of Iran replaced the Pahlavi Dynasty and the Iran-Iraq war broke out. The relationship between the USA and Iran became pale and dreams of cooperation seemed to find their way to an everlasting frustration.

In 2008, an unexpected message of the second last president, D. Ray Heisey, of Damavand College was thrilling. For preparing a presentation on what had happened to graduates of Damavand, he appreciated hearing from me. The information gave life to some invaluable details that were recorded in "The Persian Jewel: Damavand College, Tehran" by Professor D. Ray Heisey [later condensed and published in the January 2011 issue of The Journal of Middle Eastern and Islamic Studies (in Asia)].

The continuation of a 4 year constant contact brought the most prosperous memories and awareness that emphasized the importance of dialogue between the two nations that have been considering each other as the 'Axis of Evil' and the 'Great Satan' during the last 3 decades.

Our profound belief in a peaceful relationship between the two countries is the main concept of our joint paper, 'The Visual and Artistic Rhetoric of Americans and Iranians of Each Other Impacted by Media" in which a sobering issue has been brought up.

The invitation of me as an Iranian teacher to the Kent State University can be marked as one of the most spectacular efforts of Dr. Heisey. The arrangement of 6 presentations at KSU in the form of dialogues was demonstrating not only the common aspects of the two cultures but also the harmony which exists between Islam and Christianity.

As Professor Heisey's last international guest, I was asked to attend a worship service at the Kent Presbyterian Church and talk with the Faith and Life Class on the 'Islamic Faith in my daily Life' while showing my Iranian Hijab to the audience. This mentioned point was a giant step in the path of an 'Intellectual Openness' that had its origin in Damavand College principles. Attending the Islamic Community center of Kent Service on Friday is the highlight point, while Professor Heisey watched the ritual for the first time in his life.

He did his utmost effort in respecting my beliefs. He showed me the right direction to Kaaba and permitted me to say my prayers in his home. His ultimate hospitality was beyond words.

And as the last step he changed the hotel schedule to let me be more punctual about saying my last noon prayer in the USA.

An American, Dr, Heisey, and I, an Iranian woman, serve as a model in breaking the rules and let's never forget that, "Blessed are the peacemakers, for they shall be called the children of God." [St. Matthew, Sermon of Jesus on the Mount] Blessings. Salaam.

3. IRAN–AMERICA POSITIVE INTERCULTURAL COMMUNICATION

Mansoureh Sharifzadeh
Ministry of Education, Tehran, Iran

When Professor. D. Ray Heisey, my lifelong mentor and I started a new research project "The Visual and Artistic Rhetoric of Americans and Iranians of Each Other Impacted by Media" [Proceedings of Phi Beta Delta, Volume 2, No. 1 May 2011], I didn't expect such a painful consequence.

To find out how the youth of both nations conceive each other, we invited them to draw a picture of people who were considered foreigners to them. In this process American teenagers demonstrated their individualistic perceptions of Iranians, whereas the Iranian teenagers viewed Americans as a collective nation doing something rather than as individual Americans.

American teenagers illustrated the Persians as Arabs. They drew the females covered in full Hijab from head to toe except for the eyes and saying "Allah" (which is written next to the drawings). The men were portrayed as terrorists dressed in Arab clothes with beards, looking mean and holding machine gun or handgun saying the words "For Allah." One of the drawings illustrated a man flying to bomb Obama and as a terrorist ready to go to America to point his nuclear bomb toward the American flag.

Iranian teenagers illustrated the US government's activities in the Middle East and conveyed their message collectively. They focused on Iraq, Afghanistan and Palestine where the United States and Israel have been involved in war. Totally they portrayed the United States as a powerful nation while using its authority in creating war and taking advantages of the invaded countries' resources.

The Iranian students demonstrated the Americans as "Great Satan, Demolisher, Unreliable, Torturer, Main terrorist, Arrogant and Opportunist oppressor that has dominant desire, Exploitative colonialist, Conductor" and finally as a nation that is trying to enhance the world's condition.

The student drawings were trying to verify the other nation negatively. They would appear to show how the media reflected both nations in a stereotypical fashion to create phobia.

The consequence was unexpected because of my own experience. The peaceful and positive presence of the Americans in educational spheres of Iran before 1979 can never be neglected. The new generation of Iranian teenagers is in conflict because of what they study at schools related to the US government activities related to the Muslim world since 1979 and later on after September 11th, 2001 attacks to the twin towers of NYC and the US Pentagon. I would hope they might seek to know some other things about the United States, such as, food for the hungry, life enhancing medical care, education for those who want to learn, a bright sky for those who want to serve others, and a known future for those who believe in themselves. All countries, if we are honest, have a dark side and a light side and the United States is no exception.

The American teenagers' idea about Iranians as Arab terrorists is painful and disappointing. Most Muslims, and in our case, Iranians are not terrorists, while the phenomenon might appear in any society at any rate.

Sir John Chardin, a French traveler recorded his observation in Travels in Persia 1673-1677, describing the Iranians as the most lavish and civilized people of the east who clothe themselves richly. He described them as kind and hospitable to strangers, very honest in matters of religion, adding that the Persians never fight and all their anger being not blustering, and they reverence God's name at any case. Justin Perkins, the first American who visited Iran in 1833 and lived there for 7 years writing in his book Missionary Life in Persia described the intellectual Iranians as lively, imaginative, social, and fond of discussion and literary people.

Seeing is believing, and in 4 verses of the Qu'ran God asks the prophet of Islam, "say: travel in the earth… " In this regard a quote from the prophet of Islam, Mohammad (P.B.U.H) can be mentioned that reads, "Go in quest of knowledge even to China." With having these entire views in mind, we can discover the value of dialogue, mediation, and arbitration and face to face communication that distinguishes human beings. The mentioned points broaden our understanding, perspective, and acceptance of others and the contribution they can make to our lives, if we but open our eyes, ears, and hearts.

In October 2010, in my visit to the United States, I got invaluable awareness about Americans although my family was in a distinct conflict with me warning me not to take the trip to a country that threatens Iran and can't have a positive respect to our values. What I was seeking was the truth and finding out the American reactions to my presence as a Muslim Iranian in their country. The outcome was quite beneficial. I found them quite friendly and helpful, although I discovered that unlike our teenagers who know a lot about the United States, many American teenagers had never heard anything about Iran. Of course, at the university level the students were more familiar with Iran.

To have a positive intercultural communication between Iranian and American intellectuals, the barriers of politics and policies must be left to the governments and the intellectual communication should be done by individuals, and as Dr. Heisey emphasized, to show more respect and deal with each other with mutuality and dignity and not treat each other as inferiors. We must listen more, engage more, dialogue more, and try to see the other side more. It allows us to hear and see what the other nation hears and sees to become more aware and therefore more understanding of where we are in our thinking and perception and experience.

4. CASE STUDY IN USING IMAGINATION TO TEACH ENGLISH IN IRANIAN PUBLIC SCHOOLS

Mansoureh Sharifzadeh,
Ministry of Education, Tehran, Iran

and

D. Ray Heisey (d. May 20, 2011)

Introduction

Considering the present situation of the world and the rapid progress in every aspect of life, which is mainly related to technology and interest in it, the need for learning English as an international language becomes more and more crucial. "English is the dominant international language for communications, diplomatic relations, business, and science."

In Iran, the United States and Britain are seen as great powers imposing their determination on the people of the world, so English language teachers may seem to be among those who are imposing foreign educational and cultural values on the youngsters. They [the textbooks] depict the USA and the West as the enemy. (Heisey& Sharifzadeh, 2011).

"Since our nation has been sacrificed for the needs of super powers and imperialism through the past 200 years, some negative attitudes toward learning a foreign language may exist that must be changed" (Haddad Adel, 1364/1985, pp. 6-11). This change must occur not only by the system of teaching English in Iran but also by the teachers who have a key role in teaching and educating the students. So it is necessary to teach English language in a way to not only maintain Iranian cultural and spiritual values, but also give awareness about the importance of learning English in the world today.

This paper aims at emphasizing the importance of free writing which can be encouraged by empowering the imagination. In this paper, first the role of English in the world today, second using imagination as a tool, third writing attitude, fourth the role of literature, fifth essays and composition writing, and finally, the value of using drawings, and letters, to inspire the imagination will be described. Some examples of Iranian students' writings and drawings will be presented, too. To conclude, the results will be stated.

Literature Review

Different researches prove that teaching English for the purpose of communication in the public high schools of Iran has not been successful. In 2002 a research done under the supervision of the Ministry of Education of Iran stated that, "In Iran English is taught as a foreign language from the first grade at public junior high school. Public high school students are required to study English three hours a week and the number of students in one class is about 35. Compared to other countries, high school English is more grammar based and the teachers put more stress on teaching grammar rather than on teaching reading comprehension and communicative skills.

Lack of language labs, tapes, pictures and other facilities makes the students unmotivated and different level of students with different English knowledge in one class make the teachers tired and unable to do what is necessary. The method of teaching is grammar translation and teaching is usually provided with the help of mother tongue. At schools no special supplementary reading is suggested, so the teachers decide for the extra studying which is not paid much attention to because of the shortage of time. The text books which are authorized by the ministry of education don't convey the culture of the target language, and it makes the books without any sense to the students.

At public schools no attention is paid to the needs of the learner, what looks necessary to the government is usually practiced during the years. Evaluation of the students is usually based on written and oral tests, while more value is given to the final written exam." (Javadi, 2000)

Sharifzadeh's 32 years of personal teaching experience reflect the fact that at public schools students are not highly motivated to learn English, as they feel no need to learn it and their goal is to pass the so called "slaughter house" of Konkoor, (entrance examination of the universities). And after 7 years of studying English at public junior high schools and high schools, they are not able to engage in simple social conversations, make practical requests, doing some kind of activities like shopping, travelling and other routine daily uses of English. The most important reason is that the English courses which are offered at public junior high schools and high schools are not reasonably well planned, efficiently executed and don't have the characteristics of current communicative language teaching methodology.

Based on the current English language teaching system of public schools of Iran and the argues of the so far done researches we can list such points as:

Textbooks

"Teachers don't have the freedom of choice. Teachers are servant of the course books while they should be master. The print of the textbooks is awful so students are not motivated." (Birjandi, Parviz, 2000).

Students

"The learner is neglected in Iran's english language teaching of Iran. And they don't know why they should learn English" (Toosi, B, 2000).

Instruction

"English instruction is wide-spread in our schools, it typically doesn't lead to a high degree of proficiency, my judgment is that oftentimes we have not adopted systematic approaches and are mostly tired to solve our problems in isolation and out of their contents" (Tahririan, M. H, 2000).

Method of Teaching

"Research studies indicate that there are severe limitations on the way of importing Communicative Language Teaching in the English as a Foreign Language context. In Iran there are some barriers on the way of implementing the CLT approach in the high school context, which are learning strategies of Iranian students, the very nature of the EFL environment, as well as the wash back effect of the university Entrance Examination and finally, the communicative approach needs a very strong ability of language teachers and students participation." (Maftoon, Parviz, 2000)

Why should English be included in the educational system of Iran?

The reason is that, English is the dominant international language. "Today, Chinese is spoken by 999 million people, Hindustani 457, Spanish 401 and Russian by 280." (Iwasaki, 2002, P.3).

"More than 600 million people speak English as their first or second language. It is the common language around the world. Academics around the world must publish their materials in English; the textbooks in universities are in English. English is the language of international business, research and science. More than three-fourths of the world's mail is written in English. More than three-fifths of the world's radio stations use English. More than half of the scientific and research journals are in English. English became the international language because by 1900 the UK had several colonies in different parts of the world so the people had to learn its language. Then after World War II the United States became more powerful and even more people had to learn English. English is a good international language since it has more words than any other language with a simple grammar although difficult spelling."

The mentioned points create the basic reasons for English to be the dominant international language which makes it necessary for the current educational system of Iran to include that in the curriculum.

English in the public schools of Iran

Based on the earlier points, learning English for many students cannot be a choice, but a necessity. Of course, the only purpose of learning English, for the majority of the students, is passing the exams and only a few see English as a valuable supplementary skill. And for a few it may look as a means of getting a better job. Also, for some others, English language can be considered as a useful tool for international communication.

In Iran, English language textbooks which are the core of the teaching program, mainly focus on reading, some writing, little speaking and nearly no listening with a lot of emphasize on the grammar. Heisey believes that, "The Grade One lessons in English (English Book 1 - 1386) are very good with building vocabulary and using writing exercises in various ways. They use the interactive method of engaging the student in asking questions. They also build on what has gone before and they use the same pattern of constructing the lessons, beginning with new words and going on to the reading and speaking out and reviewing vocabulary, etc. Using the same sequence of activities from lesson to lesson helps build the self-confidence in the student. The reading assignments are chosen to acquaint the student with ideas and information from different sources even outside the students' lives, like the Newton story. However, even though the lessons are positive in the above ways, the one deficiency is that there is no emphasis on composition writing to encourage the creativity of the students."

The high school textbooks have been edited in the early 1990s. The subject of the texts usually is not of interest to the students. Sharifzadeh believes that the Iranian English language textbooks neither convey the Iranian culture nor that of the west. They seem quite impassive. "English is a language that can be used in any culture, for instance, Indians, Australians, Singaporeans, Africans and others employ English language in a way to convey their own cultural values" (Sharifian, 2004).

In order to motivate the students to learn English for the long term, especially when it is not seen as important for their immediate needs other than to pass the examination, teachers have to engage them in a condition to use their knowledge practically. "Arabic and English will be taught more practically and according to the need of the learner." (Haji Babayee, 2011) "In Iran, English should be taught according to the Iranian culture. Reading and writing should be prospered. Speaking and listening skills should be taught according to the concepts that are commonly used in everyday life without being integrated with the culture of the west." (Sharifian, F, 2004)

Drilling the students with continuous grammatical exercises, makes them pooped. "Although the drill-and-practice approach has some advantages in language teaching, it does not help students master the language in the long run" (Hussin, Maarof & D'Cruz, 2001, p. 1). Teachers need to find creative ways to teach the language and increase the student's motivation. Of course, it is very important for the teachers to use different approaches in their teaching process, but "it is more important for teachers to know what the most appropriate approach to teaching the language in that environment is and what activities are suitable for a given group of learners" (Hussin, Maarof, & D'Cruz, 2001, p. 1).

Discussion

Iranian English language experts have different ideas about the current system of teaching EFL in Iran. In Nov 2000, there was a three-day "Seminar in Foreign Language Teaching in Iran" in the city of Tehran. Several experts along with Professor Jack Richards expressed their ideas and findings which are listed below in brief.

"The barriers on the way of implementing the Communicative Language Teaching approach in the Iranian high school context" were emphasized by Maftoonon:

- o the broad category of milieu
- o the framework context of teaching English in Iranian educational systems in which students can not actively use English
- o the learning strategies of Iranian students which is based on memorization
- o the very nature of the EFL environment where sometimes 40 students are in a class
- o the wash back effect of the university entrance examination which is basically based on reading and comprehension
- o the fact that any curriculum change should be sensitive to cultural values and pedagogical beliefs in order not to influence the learning process
- o "Reza does not Learn English" by Tahririan stated that, although English instruction is widespread in our schools, it typically does not lead to a high degree of proficiency due to the fact that systematic approaches have not been adapted and have mostly tried to solve our problems in isolation out of their contexts.
- o Farhady presented a research with the title of , "Evaluation of students achieved in Iranian Junior High Schools" based on the following facts:
  - o The subject included around 3000 male and female students in grade 2 and 3 of the junior high schools of Tehran.
  - o The students' had positive attitude and high motivation to learn EFL while being in grade 2.
  - o A decline in both attitude and motivation as the students move toward higher degrees.
- o The title of Birjandi's research was "Evaluating and selecting EFL materials". His findings were based on such facts as:
  - o Teachers don't have the freedom of choice about the textbooks.
  - o Teachers are facing the shortage of time in their classes.
  - o The budget is not enough.
  - o English is taught for no purpose.
  - o There is a lack of equipment.

- o   Cultural values bring problem in teaching foreign language.
- o   Professor Jack C. Richard's lectures were on 'Reflective teaching method in the new millennium', 'The principles of effective teaching', and 'Exploring teacher expertise in Language teaching'. Meanwhile he was emphasizing on using the books as:
    - o   a source book rather than a course book
    - o   "SOAR-ing" with the book, i.e. supplement, omit, adapt, re-organize
    - o   not a tool for teaching
    - o   In summary, the findings of the seminar were based on such categories as:
    - o   The students don't equip the necessary 4 skills of language learning after 7 years of learning in the public junior high schools and high schools.
    - o   Culture is the neglected element in the present system of Iranian EFL.
    - o   The textbooks don't contain such materials that are relevant to the needs and interests of the learners.
    - o   The textbooks need to be revised and improved.
    - o

Seminars like this may be enlightening, although they have never been able to create a fundamental change in the process of teaching English in Iran. So, the teachers might be more capable to bring a change in the area of their teaching due to the direct connection with the students. As a solution, the authors decided to empower the imagination of the students to motivate them to make them write their ideas and use their language knowledge in a more effective way as an extra activity.

The present method of teaching English as a foreign language in Iranian schools, is based on reading and some writing. The authors think by empowering the imagination of the students their writing ability must be enhanced to use their language knowledge in a more effective and practical way as an extra activity. Teachers can play a significant role in giving shape to the behavior of the students in learning English. "English is one of the most important means for acquiring access to the world's intellectual and technical resources" (Talebinezhad & Aliakbari, 2001, p. 1). And also, since "it is an international auxiliary language" (Smith & Rafiqzad. 1979, p. 1) and "English as a world Language" (Nunan, 1999/2000, p. 1), teachers must find ways to not only motivate the students but also attract their attention and stimulate them to learn it more eagerly. Among the motivational techniques, free writing can be an effective way of encouraging the children to put down their ideas and expand them in order to be heard and read by others.

Using Imagination

"I am imagination. I can see what the eyes can not see. I can hear what the ears cannot hear. I can feel what the heart cannot feel" (Zarlegna, 1997). As the Encyclopedia Americana (1962, p. 706) mentions, "In the classical psychology of Thomas Hobbes (1650), imagination denotes the arrival of faint copies of sense impressions. It is a reproductive process which takes place in the brain. Originally, all experiences arise from stimulation of sense organs, but the effect tends to persist." The first step to every production is imagination. Webster's Dictionary (1974, p. 700) defines imagination as, "the act of or power of forming mental images of what is not actually present." It makes us feel alive, because it gives the power of production.

Heisey thinks that imagination is the spark that ignites the mind to see and experience what it has not seen or experienced before. As a result, Sharifzadeh thinks that one of the most effective ways of teaching English for the purpose of long-term learning is to encourage imagination to motivate the students to use their creativity through their writings and the presentation of their ideas. A painter imagines, then creates the image of a rainbow, and brings it to existence, even to those who have never viewed a rainbow. A designer first imagines, and then gives life to a new brand of car or a building. A writer or poet is the same: he/she first imagines, then pens and brings the words and ideas up. But, most people must find opportunities to create new ideas and produce words and write meaningful paragraphs. Children must learn and be encouraged to do so. Everybody lives with his/her own thoughts and ideas.

Usually, people have new ideas, but they assume themselves incapable of expressing them, which is a result of a lack of self-confidence. They think only certain types of people are capable of expressing their ideas and thoughts. This behavior can be minimized from the earlier stage of schooling. The main aim of education is to enable the people to think clearly and as Joseph Campbell (1995) says, "The job of an instructor is to make the students see Vitality in themselves."

Writing Attitude

In Iran, English language textbooks are essentially based on reading with the aid of grammar. The usage of writing is limited to short sentences (see Appendix 2), and the style of final examinations relies on the power of memorization rather than acquisition. The mentioned form doesn't make the students keep the materials in their mind and makes them bored with the books. "Writing is an act of faith, not a trick of grammar" (White, 1997).

Writing provides the students with opportunities to be productive. Producing the sentences for the purpose of bringing up their ideas into existence may give pleasure and encourage them to rely on their abilities and find self-confidence. Jn addition to that, writing should happen for several reasons as:

1. Language is a productive process.
2. Language must be practiced.
3. Language must be used practically.

In the present textbooks the students find the opportunity of sentence writing but not essay writing. For instance, in the pre-university textbook there can be some instances of creative writing. Heisey mentions the two lessons on exercise and health as good models which have pre- and post-reading sections that focus on the main points of the lesson, but it includes questions for the students to answer with their partners and with the class as a whole. It includes activities for creative thinking and answering. Another lesson on giving a speech also has creative activities for the students to think through what they have read and apply questions about the effects on an audience of good speech qualities. It asks the students to apply this to their teacher and to give their own ideas of giving a good speech. In both lessons the students are asked to apply what they have learned on the topic to the issues of grammar used. In these lessons, the grammar and vocabulary elements are included as part of the topic under discussion, such as physical exercise and giving a speech.

By writing, we don't mean a very complicated process. As Brown (2001, p. 341) mentions, there are "thirty-odd types of written language forms." What we are concerned about is using the language through written forms by bringing up the ideas in a composition. If students use words and grammar in a passage-based writing, they may keep the usage of the used words and grammar in their long-term memory. Meanwhile, they must be encouraged not to be overly concerned about their errors, but just try to write whatever comes to their minds related to a specific subject based on their culture. "Writing is an act of faith, not a trick of grammar" (White, 1997).

Brown (2001, p. 350) implies their ideas should not be judged and they should not be worried about their spelling and grammar mistakes. This process is called free writing.

The purpose should not be evaluation but production, writing down the result of thinking and being taught in order to get fluent in English, or writing down whatever they are interested in – an idea or a plan or a memory. In this way, the students are given a chance to bring out ideas and are encouraged in their thinking process. The role of a teacher at this stage is "to be a facilitator and coach, not an authoritative director and arbiter" (Brown, 2001, p. 340).

"In the 1970s many English second language program writing classes were, in reality, grammar courses. Students copied sentences or short pieces of discourse, making discrete changes in person or tense" (Reid, 2001, p. 28). In the early 1980s, as teachers became more aware of current practices in NES (Native English Speaking) composition, there was a shift from strictly controlled writing to guided writing. Writing was limited to structuring sentences, often in direct answers to questions, or by combining sentences–the result of which looked like a short piece of discourse. In the 1980s, writing was taught as a process of self-discovery; writers expressed their feeling in a climate of encouragement. This approach later on entered the classroom as the "process movement," a concentration on personal writing, student creativity, and fluency (Zamel, 1982, p. 29).

Students must be encouraged to produce sentences to learn and practice English practically. "If a child can't learn the way we teach, maybe we should teach the way they learn." (Ignacio Estrada). Teachers going through some specific materials which are provided in a text book cannot help the students master a language. "Focus must be on the learner by giving choices to learners over what to learn, how to learn, and responsibility for learning." (Richards, 2000) Learning a foreign language is different from learning other subjects. Learning a language is not only a skill but also a process of self-discovery. So, teachers "must provide a supportive learning environment by addressing affective concerns as well as academic ones" (Richards, 2000).

Reid (2001, p. 29) argues that today we discover that tests of writing, including the standardized tests of English Proficiency, such as TOEFL Test and IELTS writing sub tests, are partly based on writing, too. So, thinking and writing are both very necessary even in the international exams. Besides, Iranian culture is very rich in the field of literature and it is one important part of most of the Iranians' thoughts and ideas. Iranian teenagers are basically fond of literature and are eager to read and write it.

By encouraging the students to imagine and write on their favorite subjects, they produce new sentences and think about the usage of the words and practice grammatical points. In this way they create new ideas and give variety to their learning materials.

Young people usually have interesting thoughts and ideas which need to be encouraged to come into existence. This means that they have them in their minds, and are willing to be heard and enjoy being mentioned in order to be approved and encouraged. They can easily write down their dreams, imaginative characters, religious ideas, politics and natural phenomena, if they are stimulated properly. So, "as a successful language teacher, each of us must have competent preparation leading to a degree in TESL, a love of the English language, critical thinking and a feeling of excitement about our work" (Allen, 1980, p. 429).

Method

Based on the mentioned points the authors decided to motivate the students to express their ideas in the form of essay, letter writing, and drawing. Since writing composition is not included in the present system of teaching English in the current curriculum of Iran, we decided to convince the students to devote extra time to think in order to write compositions.

At the beginning, it was announced that they were free to write about whatever they liked, e.g. their hope, disappointments, successes, failures, and experiences. Meanwhile it was noticed that they needed to be given ideas. As a result they were provided with some literature background.

With having the role of literature in language teaching in mind, and remembering that all of the great writers, poets, thinkers, philosophers and intellectuals, started to record their ideas by very simple sentences and ideas called essays and compositions, maybe at school, we provided them with a short poem from Mark Strand (2009) which reads, "Ink runs from the corner of my mouth. There is no happiness like mine. I have been eating poetry." Then the poem of Sohrab Sepehri (1928-1980) (1384/2004, p. 80) one of the greatest contemporary Iranian poets, was presented to them. They enjoyed reading and knowing that the well known poet's poems have been translated into English.

Rain

Washed the sides of tranquility,
I was playing with
The wet sands of departure
Dreaming of the colorful journeys.
I felt like
Missing Something.

The students realized that the poet uses his very deep imagination about an unknown condition which is death.

This method based on encouragement, paved the path to obtain many essays, letters and drawings from the students. Out of 200 students about 30 students tried their best and wrote on different topics.

When they were asked to draw their ideas about the United States, they encountered a tangible subject that could easily be thought about. "Iranian students study the US actions in such textbooks as history, sociology, Persian literature, Islamic Culture and religion throughout different levels of elementary and high school education." (Heisey & Sharifzadeh, 2011).

Letter writing to President Obama was of great interest to them. The feeling of writing a letter to the president of a large country as the United States gave them a special feeling of self-determination, capability and self-importance. So they welcomed the ideas and as we dealt with the subjects very properly the outcome of the research was quite satisfactory and those students who voluntarily did the task enjoyed it. And we left a good model of EFL teaching in the current educational system or at least in the mind of our students.

Using Literature: Using Essays and Composition Writings

Of course, when it is said that literature must be included in the high school text books, it doesn't mean that all of the students must be fond of prose and poetry and use them very properly, but the goal is to bring up our culture through our literature in teaching English, too. Many of the great Iranian writers' and poets' writings have been translated into English. So why shouldn't we include them in our teaching program to empower our culture, too? "This central role of literature was carried over into TESL/TEFL in the early part of the twentieth century. In many parts of the world, such as India, it remains integral to the teaching of the language to this day" (Maley, 2001, p. 180).

Iran is an old country with a very ancient civilization. Iran can be considered as the richest country in literature. Famous poets like Hafiz, Saadi, Babataher, and others are always in the minds of the Iranians and many other nations. Their works are repeatedly published and usually people like to read them over and over eagerly. The younger Iranian people are fascinated with this rich culture and it is as if love of literature and poetry is in their blood. Many of the high school students read poems, write stories and pen poems. Students can easily be attracted to the literature of other cultures, too, so I think it's our duty to give them a chance to go through literature in the English language, as well. Exploring the sentences and ideas may empower their imagination in this case.

There are some reasons for using literature in teaching EFL as:

- o   Literature gives awareness
- o   Literature improves understanding
- o   Literature brings variety
- o   Literature refreshes soul

Writing compositions and essays requires certain types of evaluation and categories which must be considered. There are some advantages and disadvantages related to them which are:

Advantages

- o   "Essays allow for student individuality and expression. They are a medium in which the 'best' students can distinguish themselves.
- o   Essays can reflect the depth of student learning. Writing freely about a topic is a process which demonstrates understanding and grasp of the material involved.
- o   Students are used to writing essays. In many disciplines, essays represent the form of assessment which students are most familiar with. However, mature students often admit that the medium of assessment which worries them most is essays.

Disadvantages

- o   Essay-writing is very much an art in itself.
- o   Essays take time to write (whether as coursework or in exams).
- o   Essays are demonstrably the form of assessment where the dangers of subjective marking are greates." (Race, 1995, p. 3).

So, regarding the disadvantages, our intention was not marking, so no anxiety happened, otherwise we should have informed them of the exact evaluation measurement for the examples of student writings:

Using Political Cartoons

Another form of creative expression is inviting students to draw political cartoons that show how their imagination can work. In February 2009, Iranian high school students in Tehran, Iran were asked to draw pictures of what they thought Americans looked like (Heisey & Sharifzadeh, 2011). To illustrate the work of imagination by these students, some of these drawings are reproduced here. The following are four examples of these drawings along with the description of what the drawings mean to the students as written by the students.

Regarding the President Bush cartoon created by a student, she writes, "After Sep. 11, President Bush got very worried about terrorism so he decided to knock it down. To reach the goal, since then he has been preparing himself to threaten the world with creating wars in different Muslim countries as Iraq and Afghanistan. He is holding a giant bomb tightly enough not to lose control over it. He seems to be very worried because he might be attacked, without the bomb. Ordering a worldwide sanction against Iran's uranium enrichment in 2008 has been a result of his distress in this regard. So he is the Main Terrorist."

In the second drawing, for the bombing of Iraq, the student explains, "The US is bombing Iraq to get more oil and the man in the middle is the head of a media and is happy for the war progress because it makes his ratings higher while the anchor woman represents a US or UK official who is taking advantages of the condition to increase her country wealth. The US is an opportunist."

For the puppet drawing, the student writes, "These two puppets represent different nations which are at the service of the US, but they have no freedom to do anything. The US conducts their actions"

Regarding the cowboy drawing, the student states: "The US is riding Iraq as its prisoner/slave/donkey, while expressing extreme happiness and satisfaction. The US officials take advantages of the conditions and ride nations to double their property and wealth boorishly. The US is an opportunist oppressor."

These drawings by Iranian high school students illustrate how their artistic imagination sees America or Americans. As Heisey & Sharifzadeh (2011) argue, these negative perceptions of America can be attributed to what they read in their school textbooks about America's history and role in the world and to what they see in their media. Their written explanations of what the drawings mean offer a further opportunity to express in English their images of Americans.

Using Imaginary Letter Writing

Letter writing is another form of using imagination to learn English as a second language which was used in the Tehran high school. As part of an extracurricular activity, in November 2009, two Iranian high school students were also invited to write imaginary letters to President Obama to describe the Iranian people and the country of Iran. These letters follow.

In the first letter Mina Korrani writes:

Dear Mr. Obama; I've been informed that you are interested in getting familiar with my people and that you would welcome anyone who can help you. I'm not sure whether I can be of any help since I'm only 18 and I see the world and people from the sight of a teenager and sometimes a little more than that. I'll try to tell you as much as I can.

First, my people have a great Persian hospitality and kindness towards every one. They care about people around them and people's lives. People and everything connected to it is of great value to us. Ergo we won't pass by if we see someone dying in front of us in the streets. People of my country are mostly very clever and bright. They analyze every thing very perfectly. Comfort in life is very important for us. In many ways Iranians are like the British people. They use lots of idioms and ironic words when they talk to each other and just like the British people you can never guess from the expression on our face, eyes and head what we are going to do next. We may sometimes seem very complicated. Mostly, Iranians never lie but it's easy for them to do so whenever needed and unfortunately they are good at it. They can never tolerate the power of tyranny on their lives and they'll protest against it. That's why they have a truly people selected government. They are really ambitious ergo they always have a bright look for the future. They have extreme self-confidence which sometimes cause the problems. That's all I could tell you. In the end I would like to thank you for giving me the chance to introduce my people to you and the world.

Sincerely yours Mina Korrani

The second letter is from Elnaz Fazeli and it consists mostly of questions about her way of expressing herself in English:

In the Name of God, communicating to all corners of the world is getting easier and easier, we live in a global village. But how well do we understand each other and knowing 'What is Freedom'? Hello Mr. Obama; We are Iranians. Iran with Cyrus the Great, Iran with Persepolis, Iran with Damavand, Hafiz, Sa'di, Ferdowsi and much more historical backgrounds. I am a student, an Iranian student. I would like to ask you a question, what is freedom? What is the meaning of freedom in your society? I just know the dictation of freedom. Does it mean to challenge other countries? Is it to kill the innocent people? Different nations recognize freedom well, but they don't have any experience in it. I think freedom is the only thing that each person must have. Elnaz Fazeli

The first letter writer above was asked also to write an essay describing America from her point of view. She wrote the following:

America? The only thing that pops into the mind of an Asian child is this: Blood, death, prison, dark sky, unknown future.

America? America is someone who has no idea what a war is like. He has no idea how it feels like to sleep with the fear of not being able to see the sky tomorrow. To be afraid that you may not be able to see any of your family members anymore just in the near few moment. To be afraid of thinking about the future.

America is known as the country of nations. The country of liberty. Isn't the liberty statue supposed to mean so? Is liberty a symbol or does it really exist in the US? No it does not exist. The government defines freedom and peace like this: Killing a lot of women and children every day in Palestine, Iraq, Afghanistan, ... It is to just destroy, to see dead bodies which had been cut into pieces. It means to support a vampire government named Israel who kills children in the name of fighting against terrorism. Are children really killers? How can US government give itself the right to forbid someone from living. They get people's house and they call them thieves. They make people homeless and call them you don't have the right to live. Americans live in news censorship without even knowing how this PEACE! is in the world. American people are nice but their government is a killer. But I ask you this question: Aren't Americans the one who choose this government?

These letters from Iranian high school students offer an additional insight into how their imaginations can be used to write in English about a subject that is part of their lives. American readers don't get the opportunity to read what ordinary Iranians are thinking about them. These letters are sobering because of the way in which they express cultural attitudes.

Conclusion

These essays and drawings show how the minds of the Iranian students imagine stories, letters, and their perceptions of Americans. Writing these imaginary accounts gives them an opportunity to express in English how they feel and think about the chosen subjects. They can be effective in the learning process as they relate to the lives, thoughts and interests of the students themselves and not some theory in the textbooks.

Teachers must consider the capabilities of their learners. Learners must not be assumed as empty vessels that knowledge must be poured into them. They must be given a chance to explain their ideas, imagination and skills. Students should be trained to create ideas. Teachers must maintain a more flexible attitude toward their teaching and not be too concentrated and dependent on text books and the school program, which are usually exam oriented. Literature is a means by which the students can read different types of writings and can write composition to bring out their favorite subjects and ideas. Empowering the imagination and giving the opportunity to the students to empower the imagination may lead us to teach English language according to our cultural values, too.

English language teachers are responsible to motivate the Iranian students to learn the language according to their needs. Students must be given self-confidence that their ideas are highly valued to the class and to the teacher, and, as a result, to the society.

References

Allen, H. B.(1980). What it means to be a professional in TESOL. Lecture presented at the conference of TEXTESOL, April. In H. D. Brown, (ed.), Teaching by principles. An interactive approach to language pedagogy, Second Edition (2001). Reading, MA: Adison Welsey Longman. Inc.

Brown, H. D.. (2001). Teaching by principles. An interactive approach to language pedagogy, Second edition. Reading, MA: Adison Welsey Longman. Inc.

Campbell, J.. (1995). Quotes for teachers compiled by R.D. Zakia. Retrieved January 26, 2009, from http://people.rit.edu/andpph/text-quotations.html

Dewey, J.. (2008). Quotes For teachers: Be inspired!. Retrieved January 26, 2009, from http://www.theeducatorsnetwork.com/quotes/2.php

Einstein, A.. (1997). Education – quotes. Retrieved January 26, 2009, from http://www.etni.org.il/quotes/education.htm

Encyclopedia Americana (1962). Vol.14, p. 706.

Encyclopedia International (1973). V. 9, p.155.

English Book 1 - 1386

Goldman, E. (2009). Retrieved January 12, 2009, from http://www.brainyquote.com/quotes/authors/e/emma_goldman.html

Haddad A.G. (1364/1985). The need for learning foreign languages. Roshd, The Foreign Language Teaching Journal. 2:5, 6-11.

Heisey. D. R. & Sharifzadeh, M. (2011: May). The Visual and Artistic Rhetoric of Americans and Iranians of Each Other Impacted by Media. Proceedings of Phi Beta Delta, Volume 2, No. 1.

Hussin, S., Maarof, N., & D'Cruz, J. V. (2001: May). Sustaining an interest in learning English and increasing the motivation to learn English: An enrichment program. The Internet TESL Journal, 7:5 (May). Retrieved January 12, 2009, from http://iteslj.org/.

Iwasaki, S. (2002). The role of English Language teaching: Linguistic imperialism orlnguistic empowerment? TESL-EJ Forum. 6:1. p.3. Retrieved January 12, 2009, from http://tesl-ej.org/ej21/f1.html

Joubert, J. (1997). Imagination – quotes. Retrieved January 26, 2009 from http://www.etni.org.il/quotes/imagination.htm

Kabilan, M. K. (2000: June). Creative and critical thinking in language classroom. The Internet TESL Journal, VI, 6 Retrieved January 12, 2009, from http://iteslj.org/

Le Guin, U. K. (1997). Imagination – quotes. Retrieved January 26, 2009, from http://www.etni.org.il/quotes/imagination.htm

Maley, A. (2001).Literature in the language class. In R. Carter& D. Nunan, The Cambridge guide to teaching English to speakers of other languages (pp. 180-185). Cambridge, United Kingdom. Cambridge University Press.

Mays, B. (2009). Retrieved January 12, 2009, from http://www.motiva-teus.com/teach29.htm

Nunan, D. (1999/2000). "Yes, but is English?" TESOL Matters, p. 3. Retrieved January 12, 2009, from http://iteslj.org/Articles/Talebinezhad-EIL.html

Race, P. (1995). The art of Assessing, SEBA Publication the New Academic, 4:3 Retrieved January 12, 2009,, from http://www.londonmet.ac.uk/deliberations/assessment/art-of-assessing.cfm

Reid, J. (2001). Writing. In R. Carter & D. Nunan, The Cambridge guide to teaching English to speakers of other languages, (pp. 28 -33). Cambridge, United Kingdom. Cambridge University Press.

Ruskin, J. (2006). Quotation. Retrieved January 26, 2009, from htttp://thinkexist.com/quotation

Sepehri, S.. (1383/2004). The traveller (Selected poems), Translated by A.Zahedi from Farsi to English. Tehran, Iran: Zabankaded Publication, 1383.

Sharifian, F, Persoanl Interview, 2003-2004 by Sharifzadeh

Smith, L.E. & Bisazza, J.A. (1982). The comprehensibility of three varieties of English for college students in seven countries. Language Learning, 32: 2. Retrieved January 12, 2009, from http://iteslj.org/Articles/Talebinezhad-EIL.html

Smith, L. E. & Rafiqzad.(1979). English for cross-cultural communication: The question of intelligibility. In L.Smith, (1983). Readings in English as an international language. Pergamon Press. Retrieved January 12, 2009, from http://iteslj.org/Articles/Talebinezhad-EIL.html (City etc. have not been mentioned in the webpage that the case has been adapted from.)

Socrates. (1997). Education – quotes. Retrieved January 26, 2009, from http://www.etni.org.il/quotes/education.htm

Starr, R. V.. (2007). Retrieved January 26, 2009, from www.saidwhat.co.uk/quotes/favourite/ralph_vaull_starr/dream

Strand, M. (2009). Brain candy poetry and songs, pieces of great poetry, beautiful words from poems. Retrieved January 12, 2009, from http://www.corsinet.com/braincandy/miscpoem.html

Talebinezhad, M. R.& Aliakbari, M.. (2001), Basic assumptions in teaching English as an international language. The Internet TESL Journal, 2: 7, (July). Retrieved January 12, 2009, from http://iteslj.org/Articles/Talebinezhad-EIL.html

Webster's new world dictionary of the American language, Second edition (1974).

White, E. B. (1997). Grammar – quotes. Retrieved January 26, 2009, from http://www.etni.org.il/quotes/grammar.htm

Zamel. V. (1982) Writing: The process of discovering meaning. TESOL Quarterly 16:2, 195-209.

Zarlegna, P. N. (1997). Imagination – quotes. Retrieved January 26, 2009, from http://www.etni.org.il/quotes/imagination.htm

5. The Dignity of Iranian Women

Mansoureh Sharifzadeh
Ministry of Education, Tehran, Iran

Introduction

Each nation consists of a set of rules and values that has been obtained through different eras impacted by various events. Those values set up cultural norms that become the main principles and integrated in the life of the people as the backbone of the values of their nations.

Culture is defined as: the customary beliefs, social forms, and material traits of a racial, religious, or social group; also: the characteristic features of everyday existence (as diversions or a way of life) shared by people in a place or time. (Merriam Webster Dictionary)

In this essay my main aim is to argue that the Iranians' cultural and religious background is so fixed that it is not very likely for it to be invaded by any other cultures. In other words, the religious and cultural values of the Iranians are the base of their lifestyle which has shaped the dignity of the Iranian women before and after the revolution which happened in 1979.

Before the revolution, the ruling systems supported by the West neglected the Islamic and cultural identities of the Iranians and since then the West is still following its old policies. Before the revolution, the neglected facts led to the collapse of the Pahlavi dynasty in 1979. After the revolution the neglected facts have led the West to have problems with Iran. The Islamic Republic of Iran that has found its independence and freedom since 1979, aims at categorizing the dignity of the Iranian women based on the teachings of Islam. We believe that the traditional nature of Iran supervised by the Islamic laws is the key point to identify and support our dignity as Iranian women. Historically, when the rest of the world, from Greece and Rome to India and China, considered women as no better than children or even slaves, with no rights, whatsoever ("Women in Islam"), Islam acknowledged women's dignity through different Surah's.

In this essay the main intention is not to prove that Iranian women are treated exactly in the same way that the holy Qu'ran suggests but to demonstrate the actual right of a Muslim woman and the efforts which are taken in this regard. In Iran, since the collapse of the Pahlavi dynasty in 1979 and the establishment of the Islamic Republic of Iran, both the government and the true Muslim women have been trying to make the nation aware of our actual rights as Muslim Iranian women. Of course, the Qu'ran in 8:53 reads, "Allah has never changed a favor which he has conferred upon a people until they change their own condition." As is mentioned, Iranian Muslim women have to discover their rights based on the teachings of the Qu'ran which will enable them to defend themselves against those who try to overlook their dignity.

My main focus in this essay is the dignity of the Iranian women based on the guidelines of the holy book of Quran. To get to this goal, I discuss, the role models for the Muslim Iranian women, equality of men and women in the realm of Islam, Iranian women and the rise of the Islamic Revolution, the condition of Iranian women after the Revolution, the Iranian women's movement, Iranian Islamic wearing of Hijab, the women's status during the Qajar and Pahlavi Dynasty, Iranian women and the rise of the western cultural values, contributions of the West on the education of the Iranian women, the ancient historical facts about the Iranian culture, and finally I will present my personal conclusion.

The Role Models for the Muslim Iranian women

In the world of Islam, there are some great women who are of significant importance. Four of them are Hazrat Fatima Zahra (Upon whom be peace), Hazrat Khadija (Upon whom be peace), Hazrat Zeynabi (Upon whom be peace), and Hazrat Maryam (Upon whom be peace).

Hazrat Fatima Zahra (Upon Whom be Peace) was the divine daughter of the prophet of Islam. The noble Prophet (s. a. w.) said: "Fatima is the best of all women of the world (Sayyidatu Nesae Al A'lameen), and a role-model for all Muslim women." (Hazrat Fatima (S. A.)). Ayatollah Khamenei says: "A multi-dimensional human being, a brave warrior in the way of Islam, a knowledgeable lady who at the same time played her role as a house wife and affectionate wife and mother, to perfection – such was Hazrat Fatima-Zahra (s. a.). Her life was very simple, and she had very frugal needs or expectations." (Hazrat Fatima (S. A.) is the role-model). The anniversary of the birthday of Fatemeh Zahra (S. A.) marks the women's day in Iran.

Hazrate Khadija (Upon whom be peace), was the noble wife of the prophet of Islam and mother of Fatima Zahra (S. A.); and the first lady who accepted Islam.

Hazrat Zeynab (Upon Whom be peace) was the brave granddaughter of the prophet of Islam and the daughter of Fatimah Zahra (S.A.). Imam Khomeini calls her the one who "stood against the tyrannical rulers" ("The position of women from the view point of Imam Khomeini," Autumn 2001, p. 28). The anniversary of the birthdate of Hazrat Zeynab is called the Nurses' Day in Iran.

Hazrat Maryam (Upon Whom be peace) is an everlasting beauty whose son; Jesus Christ, is a symbol of peace and toleration. It is a blessing to always keep the image of the Virgin Mary and her beloved baby Jesus in one's own heart. Her pure and innocent look is inspiring and brings an unknown perception which is both heartbreaking and pleasing that emphasizes chastity and righteousness. Hazrat Maryam (Upon whom be peace) is so dignified that her name has become the title of the 19th Surah of the holy book of Qu'ran. The Surah of Maryam (Upon whom be peace) consists of 98 verses that includes some divine personalities as: Zakariya (Zachariah), Yahya (John), Ibraham, Ishaq (Isaac), Ya'qub (Jacob), Harun (Aaron), Isma'il (Ishmael), Moses, Idris (Enoch), Adam, Nuh (Noah) and Maryam. In this Surah the virgin Mary has been placed in the highest stance because of her toleration, virtue, modesty, integrity which led to the endless kingdom of Jesus Christ.

In the Qu'ran 3:42, God reads, "Behold, the angel said: Oh Mary! God hat chosen thee and purified thee, chosen thee above the women of all nations." In this regard, Imam Khomeini reads, "They revealed to her (virgin Mary) the knowledge of the unseen". (The position of women from the view point of Imam Khomeini, Autumn 2001, p. 30)

In the holy book of Qu'ran, a number of Surahs contain guidelines for the women; among which An Nesa (Women), the 4th Surah, and Maryam the 19th Surah, as well as Al-Kauther (Aboundance) the 108th Surah that is dedicated to Hazrat Fatima (Upon whom be peace) can be highlighted.

In many Surahs we can find numerous verses that defend the women in case of misapprehensions, as in 24:4, "And those who launch a charge against chaste women, and produce not four witnesses (to support their allegation) — flog them with eighty stripes: and reject their evidence ever after: for such men are wicked transgressors." This verse gives awareness to those men whose pride and prejudice mislead them in doing fair judgments.

In some more Surahs, God gives advice to the Muslim women. For instance in 24:31, "And say to the believing women that they should lower their gaze and guard their modesty; that they should not display their beauty and ornaments except what (must ordinarily) appear thereof; that they should draw veils over their bosoms and not display their beauty except to their husbands, their fathers, their husbands' fathers, their sons.... " The meaning apparent to the Arabic reader is that in the presence of men who are not mahram to a Muslim woman, she should wear a head cover that extends long enough to cover the bosom, not that only the bosom is covered." ("Hijab... a Must, Not a Choice," 2012)

Mohammad (Peace Be Upon Him) said, "Paradise lies at the foot of the Mothers." Such a promise has never been given to the fathers. This of course, means that true mothers have certain very good characteristics which are inspired by their divine role models.

Equality of men and women in the realm of Islam

The equality of men and women is what Islam is concerned about. In Islam each one of them has her/his own stance that must be accepted by the followers. Islam is derived from the Arabic root "Salema": peace, purity, submission and obedience. "In the religious sense, Islam means submission to the will of God and obedience to His law." ("The Meaning of Islam"). A true Muslim must observe the rules mentioned in the holy book of Qu'ran. In Islam the advancement of humanity is of fundamental importance.

In the holy book of Qu'ran, the equality of men and women has been emphasized in a unique way. For example, in 33:35 their equality is mentioned like this, "For Muslim men and women - for believing men and women, for devout men and women, for true men and women, for men and women who are patient and constant, for men and women who humble themselves, for men and women who give in charity, for men and women who fast (and deny themselves), for men and women who guard their charity, and for men and women who engage much in God's praise, for them has God prepared forgiveness and great reward." And in 2:187 it reads, "they (wives) are your garments and you (Husbands) are their garments." "That verse implies that they are for mutual support, mutual comfort and mutual protection on fitting into each other as garment fits the body in respect of natural rights of husbands and wife equally" ("Qu'ran Emphasizes on Gender Equality"). Further on in 2:228; The Qur'an reads "Women have rights similar to the rights against them." This means that women can compensate in the same way that they are treated and that right is not limited to the men. Muslim women can refer to the Qu'ran and defend themselves in various cases but the most important point is that they should know their Islamic rights to process their claim.

In the case of equality between men and women, Imam Khomeini said: "The history of Islam is witness to the immense respect that the Prophet (Peace Be Upon Him) had for Hazrat Zahra (s. a.) which also powerfully reflects on the importance of women in society. If they are not superior to men, they are definitely not any inferior." ("Hazrat Fatima" S. A.)

Some of the verses of the holy book of Qu'ran need clarification. For instance Professor Michael H. Prosser brings up this idea: In Surah 4: Section 34, "An-Nisa: The Women," the Holy Qur'an states: "Men are the protectors and maintainers of women, because Allah has given the one more (strength) than the other, and because they support them from their means. Therefore, the righteous women are devoutly obedient, and guard in (the husband's) absence what Allah would have them guard. As for those women on whose part you fear disloyalty and ill-conduct, admonish them (first), (next), refuse to share their beds, (and last) chastise them (lightly); but if they return to obedience, seek not against them means (of annoyance): for Allah is Most High Great (above you all)." More and more young women coming from various religious traditions in different societies seek full equality with the men, and even with their husbands. How does a traditional Islamic society like Iran deal with such a modern contradiction to the prescriptions of the Holy Qur'an?

My answer is: Some verses of the holy book of Qu'ran may bring contradictions as in Surah 4: section 34. "Each verse has been revealed to the prophet of Islam under a certain circumstance which must be taken under consideration. In the ancient times, Arab men often hit their wives for no good reasons. The women came to Mohammad (Peace Be Upon Him) and complained. Then, this verse was revealed to give advice to the men." ("Religious Ambiguities and Political Beliefs"). However, although the west has just recently set up organizations to support the women in this case and reduce gender based violence against them, Islam has set it up more than one thousand four hundred years ago.

"In 1993, the United Nations General Assembly defined violence against women as "any act of gender-based violence that results in, or is likely to result in, physical, sexual or psychological harm or suffering to women" (United Nations, 1993). In real terms this includes violence in domestic and inter-personal relationships; many forms of sexual violence including rape and sexual assault; systemic, institutional and culture based forms of violence (rape in conflict settings, preventing girls from attending school by threat of violence, honor killings); and new emerging forms of harassment and stalking based in modern technology." ("Engaging Men and Boys to Reduce and Prevent Gender-Based Violence")

Nowadays, in the marriage books of the Islamic Republic of Iran, there are new trends to support the women better, and no reason is acceptable for a woman to suffer, unless she herself wants to neglect her Islamic rights. The equality of men and women is not the case. Islam has given so much dignity to the women that, they are thought to be spiritually of a higher rank. Women are wives, mothers and the main managers of their homes. In this society all women can pursue their education to the highest degree and have jobs with an equal salary as the men. They can be educators, nurses, police officers, pilots, physicians, or researchers and involved in politics, while all of the goals must be based on the Islamic values.

Women can own different sectors as publications and any form of ownership. Women can drive; while they are never street waste collectors but can work as attendants and very often as waiters in restaurants.

Meanwhile the Qu'ran stresses the equality of men and women in the realm of God. In this verse, God reads, "And among His signs is this: that He created mates for you from yourselves that you may find rest and peace of mind in them, and He ordained between you love and mercy. Certainly, herein indeed are signs for people who reflect. [Noble Qu'ran 30:21]. In the sense of the equality of the men and women the Prophet Muhammad (peace and blessings be upon him) said: "The most perfect in faith amongst believers is he who is best in manners and kindest to his wife."(Muslim Marriage in the light of Holy Qu'ran [Book of Allah] and Ahadees")

Iranian women may need more freedom and privacy, but may never claim equality with men as Islam has given them so much value and protection that, they feel themselves in a higher position in the realm of God than the men.

Iranian Women and the Rise of the Islamic Revolution

In 1979 the Iranian people, especially the women, who had been deprived of their human rights for many centuries were addressed to take part in the process of revolution and play an active role in bringing the collapse of the Pahlavi dynasty. The leadership of Ayatollah Khomeini was based on involving all of the people especially the women whom he treated very respectfully and kindly and tried to dignify and encourage them to regain their rights and find a higher status through their Islamic values. All of the women either from the rural or urban areas participated to have a share to defeat the active role of the west in Iran that had caused "a sense of loss of national and cultural identity" (Moore 1988 p. 34). Imam Khomeini said "The woman has a great role in the society; she represents the realization of human ideals." ("The Women's Role in the Society")

The women's involvement in the rise of the Islamic Revolution was the defeat of the western ideology about the enhancement of the Iranian women. Later in 1979, in his visit to Iran, President Jimmy Carter called Iran the 'Island of Stability' whereas the prologue of instability had been formed in the earlier decades and he didn't know that the fire was under the ashes. In the 1960s when Imam Khomeini had been exiled from Iran for his opposition with Mohammad Reza Shah, the explosion of the Revolution had already started. ("Iranian Revolution")

The Condition of Iranian Women after the Revolution:

Following the 1979 Islamic Revolution, giant steps have been taken by all of the women based on the Islamic laws. Today 9% of the Iranian Parliament members are women, while the global average is 13%. In the 9th Islamic Consultative Assembly of 2012, among 288 representatives, 9 members are women. ("A chart of the number of the female members in the 9 elections of the Islamic parliament"). The election of the first Islamic parliament was in 1980/1359 when there were 327 members among whom 4 were women. (Ibid.)

"Today, women make up almost 30% of the Iranian labor force, and the percentage of all Iranian women who are economically active has doubled from 6.1% in 1986 to 13.7% in 2000" (Islam and science) "27.1% of the ministers in government are women (ranks 23rd out of 125 countries) and 3.4% og parliamentarians are women (140th out of 157 countries)" ("Where Are Iran's Working Women?"), which needs improvement.

In 2009 Fatemeh Bodaghi became Vice President for Legal Affairs and a top advisor to President Mahmoud Ahmedinejad. Maryam Mojtahidzadeh who runs the Women's Ministry was also selected as an advisor to the president. However, Zahra Eshraghi; the granddaughter of Imam Khomeini demands more steps and believes that: "The constitution my grandfather approved says that only a man can be president, we would like to change the wording from 'man' to 'anyone', though. (Zahra Eshragi)

In the social sphere women have gained more rights after the Revolution in comparison with the former regimes. For instance by 1999, Iran had 140 female publishers. In 2005, 65% of Iran's university students and 43% of its salaried workers were women. In 2007 nearly 70% of Iran's science and engineering students were women. This growth is a result of the growing rate of literacy for the women. "Before the revolution 35% of the women were literate whereas this growth has reached to 80% after the revolution." (The Identity given to the Role of the Iranian Women.) Literacy Movement Organization was established in 1979 to enhance the people's literacy especially of the women. The literacy rate in 1976 (two years before the revolution) was 28.7% which rose to 85% by 2005. (Khas Ali, 2010, p. 6)

In the Islamic Republic of Iran's legislation, women have always been legally supported, although based on the traditional cultural values; men have assumed themselves superior to the women in the family life which has created problems. In order to change the perspectives Ayatollah Khamenei addresses the women as "the supreme character or the highest position in the family." (Islamic Republic of Iran State TV)

Since more than 2500 years ago, Iranian men have been considered as having the highest position. For instance, the last king of Iran, Mohammad Reza Shah, had 3 marriages. His first wife was with Fawzia from Egypt. "They married in 1939 and divorced in 1948. They had one daughter, whereas the throne should only be inherited by a son, so they divorced" (Fawzia). His second marriage was with Soraya Esfandiary-Bakhtiari who was divorced after 7 years in 1957 as she was barren. His third marriage was with Farah Diba who was 20 years younger than him and bore 4 children. The first child was a boy that apparently brought them a stable life until the collapse of the Pahlavi dynasty. So in a patriarchal society likes Iran, it is not very probable for the changes to happen very rapidly for the women, although during the last 30 years, the changes have been satisfactory with a better image for the future.

An Iranian woman either with a job or not is responsible for all of the family affairs, including cooking, washing, shopping and totally every-thing. She is the absolute manager of the house. The man pursues the traditional formula and earns money for the family. Sometimes what the man earns is not enough for the expense then the woman is of great help.

It is necessary to mention one important point, the employed Iranian women are not obliged to provide any expense for the family or even for themselves. They can save their money to spend as they wish. This means that the husband is responsible for the expense of the family including the food, clothes, shelter, and education of the children and so on.

The involvement of the women in both the family affairs and their job usually brings them immense tiredness. The above mentioned point may create problems between the couples too, but what makes them have jobs is to be independent in the case of coming across a serious conflict with the husband."The statistics show that 11% of the Iranian women have a job and more than 80% are homemakers." ("Women's employment in the mirror of statistics")

Iranian Women's Movement

The Iranian women's movement emerged some time after the Iranian Constitution Revolution in 1910, when the first women's journal was published by women during the Qajar Dynasty. The movement lasted until 1933 in which the last women's association was dissolved by Reza Shah's government. Between 1962 and 1978, the Iranian women's movement gained tremendous victories: women won the right to vote in 1963 as part of Mohammad Reza Shah's White Revolution, and were allowed to stand for public office, and in 1975 the Family Protection Law provided new rights for women which tried to reduce polygamy which has not been successful in an Islamic traditional society like Iran even up to that day. The Iranian women's movement heightened again after the Islamic Revolution of Iran (1979). ("Women's rights movement in Iran")

During the past few years 'Nasrin Soltankhah' (Nasrin Soltankhah) has been head of the Center for Women and Family Affairs (September 25, 2005 to now) and Maryam in the government for the women's organization. Currently what is quite evident is that any activity related to the people including the women in Iran should be under the guidelines of the Qu'ran; otherwise it is not acceptable.

In Iran the term of feminism is not used. As, "Among the women's rights activists in Iran, feminism means different things. Furthermore, the word feminist itself has a non-positive connotation among conservatives. It is perceived as advocacy for gynecocracy, lesbianism and other perceived radical agendas." ("Women's rights movement in Iran")

The feminist movement (also known as the Women's Movement, Women's Liberation, or Women's Lib) refers to a series of campaigns for reforms on issues such as reproductive rights, domestic violence, maternity leave, equal pay, women's suffreage, sexual harassment and sexual violence. The movement's priorities vary among nations and communities and range from opposition to female genital mutilations in one country or to the glass ceiling in another. Having the whole concept in mind, it is necessary to mention that the term is strictly avoided in Iran since the concept of homosexuality is forbidden in Islam as a great sin. So, when President Barack Obama frankly defended same sex marriage in 2012, ("Obama's Switch on Same-Sex Marriage Stirs Skepticism"), the world of Islam feels more hatred towards the US officials as being a means by which our perceived sense of corruption in the marital state is demonstrated as an ordinary human relationship. Professor Michael H. Prosser explains,"Most feminists would not consider the movement to be solely associated either with lesbianism or homosexuality." (Prosser, Michael H., 2012)

Iranian Islamic Wearing of the Hijab

Hijab in Arabic means "barrier" or "screen" and thus it appears in various Qu'ranic verses, referring to many things besides the woman's head cover. For example:

Allah Almighty says in the Qu'ran that 'He only talks to humans from behind a hijab'. (42:51) Or in another place it reads, The Virgin Mary worshipped behind a hijab: (19:17). It means she placed a screen [to screen herself] from them.

In the west, Hijab is known as the scarf but actually it is beyond that in Iran. When we say some one is in Hijab or without Hijab or in a bad Hijab, it refers to women with different sorts of hijab. A 'bad Hijab' refers to someone who partially exposes her hair. Based on Islam, true Muslim women must consider her Hijab in front of non-related adult males. In Iran, the women are free to wear Chador (Veil) or scarf or both of them as a complete Hijab in public. The traditional Iranian veil has a history rooted back in the political condition, which is of special importance.

Based on the Qu'ran, the Hijab should be considered by both men and women for the establishment of morality in a society. Today, in some Islamic Arab nations as the Kingdom of Saudi Arabia, the men maintain

Hijab as strictly as the women do. In 24:30 -31, the holy Qu'ran states: "Say to the believing men that they cast down their looks and guard their private parts; that is purer for them; surely Allah is aware of what they do. And say to the believing women that they should lower their gaze and guard their modesty; that they should not display their beauty and ornaments except what (must ordinarily) appear thereof; that they should draw veils over their bosoms and not display their beauty except to their husbands, their fathers, their husbands' fathers, their sons...). What the Qu'ran mentions is not only the bodily Hijab but also the Hijab of thought, heart and 'nafs/self' as well. In other words based on the Islamic values, virtue should be in association with every single act and thought of a Muslim.

In 1936, based on the new policy which was from the West i.e. the UK, King Reza ordered the abolishment of wearing the Hijab by force, although "Unveiling at the time of Reza Shah and political repression that dominated our society caused most of the women to be unable to participate in the whole social activities."(Kar, 1977, p. 23).

Wearing the Hijab has not only been our religious convention but also a cultural value since ancient times. The visual arts indicate that before the Pahlavi dynasty both the men and women, either Muslim or Zoroastrian, wore a Hijab and some pictures dated back to 1910 show the mentioned point and the historical monuments are good reasons to prove the claim.

Based on the international perspectives, wearing the Hijab may be a challenge for the Iranian women, whereas it is a religious obligation. Some observers claim that, "In Iran, Hijab is superficial as the women don't seem to care about the actual covering of the hair." ("Countries in which HIJAB is compulsory by Law") while the mentioned claim might be relevant to some women but not all. Vice President of the State TV in women affairs, Parvin Salihi says, "based on a recent poll, about 70 percent of the Iranians aged between 19 to 40 are advocates of the Hijab." ("Seventy percent of the people feel a need for Hijab")

Wearing the Hijab is not a big deal for an Iranian Muslim woman whose country gained its freedom with the devotion of thousands and thousands of the youths whose aim was to bring Islamic theology and independence to Iran. (Mehdi Tahanian)

"The Memoir of the Youngest Iranian Captive", the youngest (13 years old) Iranian captured by the Iraqis during the Iran-Iraq war in 1982, refused to be interviewed by an Indian reporter who had no Hijab. When the reporter took the scarf out of her hand bag and covered her hair, he gave amazing answers to her questions.

All of the Iranians believe in the religious and cultural values of Iran. They attend their rituals and perform their religious and traditional duties willingly. For instance, there are many shrines dedicated to the grandchildren of different Shi'a Imams in Iran. Those holy places are called "Imam Zadeh" as a descent of an Imam, i.e. religious leader. In those holy places, young girls perform their religious rituals even with a half Hijab. Nowadays some commercial programs of the communication satellites tend to invade the Iranian cultural values. The cultural invasion was what Imam Khomeini gave awareness about in the 1980s.

The Hijab is considered to be a sign of virtue in Islam and virtuous women are respected. The performance of religious values is merely up to the individuals and it doesn't mean that in all of the Islamic nations, the people treasure their Islamic identities and women are not an exception in this case. "There are currently four countries, including France (since 2004), which have banned the wearing of all overt religious symbols, including the hijab in public schools and universities or government buildings. Currently Tunisia since 1981, and Turkey since 1997 are the only Muslim-majority countries which have banned the Hijab in public schools and universities or government buildings, while Syria bannedface veils in universities from July 2010 as a result of the political condition there. In Morocco there have been some restrictions or discriminations against women who wear the hijab. The Hijab in these cases is seen as a sign of political Islam. ("Hijab by country")

Since 1984, wearing the Hijab has become compulsory in Iran and many Iranian women feel more secure with it. The Hijab gives the true Muslim women a sense of freedom and protection which brings perfection and enables her to fulfill her duties in a Muslim society. Of course there are some controversial ideas related to the Hijab in Iran too; for instance Zahra Eshraghi wants "the wearing of headscarves to no longer be compulsory." (Zahra Eshragi)

The women's Status during the Qajar and Pahlavi Dynasty: Women's Status in the Qajar Dynasty (1785-1925)

Until 1906, the system of the Iranian government in the period of Qajar was of a monarchical type, and the social structure of Iran was rather traditional. The women's main responsibility was being a wife to look after the children and do the housework. Men were permitted to divorce and polygamy was practiced. Education for the people was reading of religious texts such as the Qu'ran in "Maktakhaneh", which was the primary school. Patriarchal norms continuing even to this day have made the women less active in having a major share in their families or social decision-making.

Nevertheless, some very limited numbers of women have always had a share in social and political activities too. "For instance Mohtaram Eskandari (1895 – July 27, 1924), was the first leader of feminism and publisher of its journal for women" (Mohtaram Eskandari). Zahra Khanoum Tadj es-Saltaneh (1883 – 25 January 1936) was a Persian princess and a daughter of Nasser a-Din Shah. She was one of the defenders of the Iranian Constitutional Revo–lution and a prominent member of the Anjoman Horriyyat Nsevan ("The Society of Women's Freedom"). (Zahra Khanom Tadj es-Saltaneh)

In 1890, the Iranian women had a very active participation in the movement of the Boycott of Tobacco (Tobacco Protest). According to Delrish (1996), the role of the Iranian women in the tobacco movement was significant, but traditional views and patriarchical culture did not allow women to improve their situation in society.

"Women also played a significant role in the Constitutional Revolution in 1906". (Persian Constitutional Revolution) For instance, the bodies of 20 women who disguised themselves in men's clothing and took part in the fights were found among the revolutionary martyrs in the area of Azerbaijan. After the mentioned revolution the urban middle- and upper-class women were allowed limited social and political participations. However, the educational system was designed in such as way that it provided opportunity only to the rich and the urban few (Keddie & Richard, 1981).

Women's status in the Pahlavi Dynasty (1925-1979)

Reza Shah (1925–1941) and his son Mohammad Reza Shah (1941–79) tried their best to bring to Iran a cultural value that was accepted by the West, i.e. France, the United Kingdom and the United States which brought the collapse of the Pahlavi Dynasty.

Although he made a great contribution in the area of education, one of the biggest mistakes of Reza Khan was the abolishment of wearing the veil in 1936 as all women could not appear in the society unveiled. In 1935, i.e. the year after Tehran University was founded, women were given permission to enroll in it which was a great achievement for the women. The circumstances under which the girls attended the university were far from ideal, but their presence was nevertheless noteworthy (Chaido, 2006).

Even with the reforms undertaken by Reza Shah, however, "no substantial social or political reform or emancipation was envisaged" (Beck & Nashat, 2004, p. 95). In general, women in Reza Shah's era, as in the Constitutional period, were denied political rights, and could not claim their rights based on the principles of democracy in the strangulation political atmosphere (Chaido, 2006). Therefore, it should be pointed out and noted that "unveiling at the time of Reza Shah and political repression that dominated on society caused all women to be unable to participate in the whole social activities" (Kar, 1977, p. 23).

Mohammed Reza Shah became the king of Iran from 1941 to 1979. However, two important events happened for the Iranian women; in 1963 they gained the right to vote and in 1967 the Family Protection Law was enacted. The achievements were wrapped in the project of westernization which led to increasing social differentiation and "it encouraged western values and lifestyles and inculcated among the masses a sense of loss of national and cultural identity" (Moore, 1988, p. 34).

However, these reforms helped only a few women from the upper class citizens to achieve their social rights. Maknun (2000) states that "women's political activities during the monarchy of the second Pahlavi were not spontaneous or independent and could be identified as immature, dependent on the government, unbalanced and non-localized" (p. 189). In fact, the presence of women in politics in this period should be considered not an actual political participation, but a deliberate propaganda. Thus, the political presence of women in a mass movement did not occur during the Pahlavi Dynasty; on the contrary, their widespread participation beside men came about during the process of the Islamic Revolution in the form of their protests against the Pahlavi Monarchy.

Iranian Women and the Rise of the Western Cultural Values

Since the foundation of the Pahlavi dynasty in 1925, Reza Shah Pahlavi (1925–1941) and Mohammad Reza Shah Pahlavi (1941–79) ruled more than 50 years in Iran. During those years, the United Kingdom and the United States were actively involved in imposing their cultural values and identities on the Iranian people, especially the women. Dr, Rebeccah Kinamoon writes, "When I went to Iran in 1974 to teach English Literature at Damavand College, an American-style college for women, I found young women awakening to the same kind of possibilities as their American counterparts thousands of miles away. In the poems, stories and novels selected for discussion, they read about Western women asserting their independence of thought and action, and they found kindred spirits. They were just beginning to discover their own capabilities and to consider wider possibilities than just marriage and family" (Kinnamon Neff). Different plans and policies including the abolition of wearing the Hijab in 1936 during the reign of Reza Shah were all targeting the society's cultural and religious beliefs.

In 1928, the wife of the Shah, Reza Khan, and some of his daughters appeared unveiled on one of the balconies of the Saida Masuma shrine in Qum, where a large number of people had gathered to see in the new solar year. This greatly angered the clergy, in particularly Ayatollah Bafqi, who shouted at them: "If you are Muslims, you must wear the Hijab, and if not, you must leave this place." This outburst landed him in prison and then condemned him to exile. In 1934, with the British drawing up detailed plans to take over and control religion in Turkey and Iran, Reza Khan visited Turkey and conceived the intention of adopting the policies of the British, with Ataturk as his role model. (Khas Ali, July 2010, pp. 5-6)

The prologue of what Imam Khomeini called a 'cultural invasion' was started in the 19th century with the presence of the American missionaries in some cities of Iran to establish a center for Christianity and maintaining a Western civilization in Iran. Justin Perkins' Missionary Life in Persia (1893) is a good evidence in this case.

During 1925 to 1979, the West was mainly interested in enhancing the life and ideas of the royal family and the upper class with a main focus on the women, whereas the population of Iran in the 1970s was about 34 million people. Except for a certain elite class the rest of the women were neglected for different reasons, among which their illiteracy might have been the most important negative factor.

Contributions of the West on the Education of the IranianWomen

During 1975- 1978, studying at the unique American woman college in Tehran was a good opportunity for me to get familiar with the culture of the Americans and study in an American college. It was a good chance for me to compare the American schooling system with the Iranian's. The United States had employed all of its facilities to create the best opportunity for the Iranian women to enhance both their education and life.

The educational system was based on encouragement which was absent from the Iranian schooling atmosphere of those years. The American system brought me self reliance which was vital for a girl brought up in a traditional society. There, I found myself among the students who were from upper classes and westernized families and mostly native speakers or very fluent in English. To my surprise, the professors never discriminated and basically were paying attention to our challenges to learn with love and authenticity.

Damavand College had no opposition with the students' personal religious attitudes, although whatever we were taught was from the West and Christianity. The regime and the West were underestimating the religious and cultural values of the people and that was what was being practiced in Iran since 50 years earlier.

D. Ray Heisey expressed himself about the religious and cultural values of the Iranians as this:

One example of how this emphasis (unveiling of women) on women's advancement in Iran came into conflict with the traditional values represented by the rising fundamentalist Islamic movement may be seen in an event that occurred at Damavand College in February 1978 as discussed by the President, Dr. D. Ray Heisey. The Damavand College Women's Institute held a celebration of the unveiling of women instituted by the Shah's father in 1936 by holding a conference of workshops and lectures by prominent leaders in Tehran. There was a demonstration for the students of what the old-fashioned chador looked like on a current student. They invited the founder of Iran Bethel School for Girls, Jane Doolittle, to speak about how far the advancement of women had come in the fifty years that she had been in Iran and to show the young women how the chador in previous years had looked. A photograph appeared in the local newspaper the next day of the event. My [Heisey's] Iranian assistant received a phone call the next day from a mullah who threatened to close down the College if an apology did not appear in the paper for what he had interpreted as an insult to religious values.

As Professor Heisey said, the College was supported by the government, and he contacted the office of the Minister of Science and Higher Education, under whose auspices we operated, to get advice. They did not want any apology given to the religious leaders because it would make the Shah's regime look like it was caving in to the fundamentalists. The threat was not idle, however, because in other cities unrest and violence had also been going on between the government and the religious leaders. Heisey notes that "We had to go back and forth with government officials on the sensitive matter in order to get agreement on language that would satisfy both sides." Professor Heisey said "We finally arranged to use language that apologized for the misinterpretation that had occurred in relation to the publication of the photo that was celebrating the role of women in society." ("That Damavand College was caught in the middle": 2001: pp. 24- 25)

To give a very brief review of the past events, "in 18th-19th centuries Iran fell under the increasing pressure of European nations, particularly the Russian Empire and Great Britain. The discovery of oil in early 1900s intensified the rivalry of Great Britain and Russia for power over the nation". (History briefly stated)

When the Pahlavi Dynasty came into power in 1925, Reza Shah introduced many socio-economic reforms, reorganizing the army, government administration, and finances. To his supporters his reign brought "law and order, discipline, central authority, and modern amenities – schools, trains, buses, radios, cinemas, and telephones" (History of Iran).

Dr. Rebeccah Kinnamon Neff writes, "The wider world began to open to Iranian women during the reign of Reza Khan, who in the 1920s introduced a period of modernization and secularization, including eliminating the required wearing of the veil. His son, Mohammed Reza Pahlavi, who succeeded him, continued this elevation of women in Iran, and in 1963, women won the right to vote and to run for public office. Enlightened parents encouraged their daughters' education and entrance into careers, and women began to move into roles beyond the scope of the family" (Kinnamon Neff).

However, his attempts of modernization have been criticized for being "too fast" and "superficial", and his reign a time of "oppression, corruption, taxation, lack of authenticity" with "security typical of police states." Many of the new laws and regulations created resentment among devout Muslims and the clergy. For example mosques were required to use chairs; most men were required to wear western clothing, including a hat with a brim; women were encouraged to discard the hijab; men and women were allowed to freely congregate, violating Islamic non-mixing of the sexes. Tensions boiled over in 1935, when bazaars and villagers rose up in rebellion at the Imam Reza Shrine in Mashhad, chanting slogans such as 'The Shah is a new Yazid.' Dozens were killed and hundreds were injured when troops finally quelled the unrest. Reza Shah was forced to abdicate in favour of his pro-British son Mohammad Reza Shah Pahlavi, who ruled Iran as an autocracy with American support from that time until the revolution in 1979.

Ancient Historical Facts about the Iranian Culture

Iranian women have always been playing the most fundamental role in the life and dignity of their nation. In the family life, they have been doing everything with no expectation but a reward from the creator. This has a deep root in our culture and the teachings of Islam. The mentioned point can bring the most tragic story of mankind that no one can imagine except for those who are involved in. Iranian culture is associated with forgiveness and devotion which in many cases has caused the women to overlook their rights. O'Shea (2000: 101) maintains that for Iranians "aberu or honor is a powerful social force. All Iranians measure themselves to a great extent by the honor they accumulate through their actions and social interrelations."

Sharifian (2011: 99) translates 'aberu' as 'face'. He thinks, "Speakers of Persian may use words such as 'honor', 'reputation' or 'face' in their use of English much more frequently than speakers of American English." Sometimes 'aberu' brings the highest obligation for a woman who must try her best not to lose 'face' among the people especially relatives and friends. An Iranian woman devotes herself to her children. She ignores herself to keep the family life for the 'aberu' of her children. Her cultural perception brings her such a painful tolerance that is breathtaking. In the Iranian families the girls have always been encouraged to observe 'aberu' more than the boys.

The cultural background of any nation can be studied through the visual arts which I refer to very briefly as not being an expert in this case. Persian arts or Iranian arts are one of the richest art heritages in world history and encompasses many disciplines including architecture, painting, weaving, pottery, calligraphy, metalworking and stonemasonry. The Persian rug, painting and miniature, pottery and ceramics, music, literature, architecture, Persian gardens, calligraphy, tile work, metalwork including; Khatam-kari, Mina-kari, relief and sculpture, and in the modern days cinema can be the main Iranian arts. (Iranian Art). What differentiates Persian art from those of the West is the style in which humans should be presented with more covering. What I mention has found its origin in more than 2500 years of the history of Iran.

"The classical art of the west proves the people to be very realistic while bringing the human body and face in its natural shape, whereas the Persian art brings shelter especially to the women. This has a base in ancient history and since the manifestation of Islam this aspect has become stronger. With respect to veiling, it has a long history in ancient Mesopotamia and Mediterranean cultures. In the first known reference to veiling, an Assyrian legal text of the thirteenth century B.C., it is restricted to respectable women and prohibited for the prostitutes and lower class women. In some of the seals, statues and figurines found at Persepolis, women are pictured fully clothed with partial veils while in others, they are dressed and even crowned but with no veil. The aristocratic and royal women very likely used the veil in public as a sign of their higher status. But veiling as an institution to subjugate, control and exclude women from public domain originated after the Islamic conquest." (Women in Ancient Iran)

Based on the archeological evidence the women of Achaemenid times discovered at Persepolis (509-438 BC) both men and women worked and received payment and also powerful women managed their wealth. They enjoyed economic independence, and were involved in the administration of economic affairs, traveled and controlled their wealth and position. Mothers have been of high importance as the mother of the kings had the highest rank. Different titles were used for the different members of the royal women.

Fortification texts reveal that royal women traveled extensively, visited their estates, and administered their wealth individually and at times with help from their husbands. We know that divorce existed but we have no information on details. There has been polygamy too.

History proves that the Iranian women have always been quite active not only as the homemakers but also in the social activities or political sphere. "But it is worth remembering that over two thousand years ago Persian women enjoyed rights that American women fought to gain as recently as the last century. ' (Ancient Persia's Remarkable Women).

Conclusion

In this essay I have argued that the cultural and religious background of the Iranians is the base of their lifestyle and should not be neglected. The Islamic Republic of Iran aims at categorizing the dignity of the Iranian women based on the teachings of Islam.

We believe that the traditional nature of Iran supervised by the Islamic laws is the key point to support the dignity of the Iranian women since Islam acknowledges women's dignity through different Surahs.

Islam should be viewed as a religion that had immensely improved the status of women and had granted them many rights that the modern world has recognized only this century. Islam still has so much to offer today's woman: dignity, respect, and protection in all aspects and all stages of her life from birth until death in addition to the recognition, the balance, and means for the fulfillment of all her spiritual, intellectual, physical, and emotional needs.

Iranian women have been playing a central role in their country through different stages of history. They have played their role as Iranian Muslim women maintaining their traditional values. Enhancing the Iranian women condition should be first based on the Islamic values and second our cultural identities, otherwise the plans will find no way except for another crash. Iranian women have no problem with the law of God but with those who cannot apprehend the laws of God and neglect their dignity. The true Muslim Iranian women stand firm to gain the satisfaction of their creator and dear Islam.

References

A chart of the number of the female members in the 9 elections of the Islamic parliament, article code Number 169329; author's translation from Farsi into English, See: http://www.hamshahrionline.ir/news-169329.aspx

Beck, L., & Nashat, G (2004). Women in Iran: From 1800 to the Islamic Republic .Urbana, IL: University of Illinois. From: Women in Politics: A case Study of Iran, see: http://us-iran.org/sites/default/files/webform/userarticle-submissions/women_in_politics-iran.pdf

Countries in which Hijab is compulsory by Law, see: http://www.sunniforum.com/forum/showthread.php?5848-Countries-in-which-Hijab-is-compulsory-by-Law

Delrish, B. (1996). Women in Qajar period. Tehran: Islamic Development Organization. From: Women in Politics: A case Study of Iran, see: http://us-iran.org/sites/default/files/webform/userarticle-submissions/women_in_politics-iran.pdf

Engaging Men and Boys to Reduce and Prevent Gender-Based Violence, Prepared by: White Ribbon Campaign www.whiteribbon.ca; Prepared for: Status of Women Canada and the Public Health Agency of Canada. Adapted from http://whiteribbon.ca/issuebrief/pdf/wrc_swc_issuebrief.pdf

Fawzia, See: http://en.wikipedia.org/wiki/Mohammad_Reza_Pahlavi#Fawzia

Hazrat Fatima (S.A.) is the role-model for women throughout history and for all, See: http://www.imamreza.net/eng/imamreza.php?id=4726

Hijab… a Must, Not a Choice, (2012), See: http://www.onislam.net/english/ask-about-islam/ethics-and-values/muslim-character/166177.html

Hijab by country, see: http://en.wikipedia.org/wiki/Hijab_by_country

Heisey, D. R,(2011). Reflection on a Persian jewel: Damavand College, Tehran

History briefly stated, http://sitara.com/iran/history.html

History of Iran, http://en.wikipedia.org/wiki/History_of_Iran

Iranian Revolution, see: http://novaonline.nvcc.edu/eli/evans/his135/Events/Iran79.htm

Iranian Art, http://en.wikipedia.org/wiki/Iranian_art

Islam and science, see: http://www.nature.com/nature/journal/v444/n7115/full/444022a.html From Women in Iran, See: http://en.wikipedia.org/wiki/Women_in_Iran#cite_note-52.

Islamic Republic of Iran state T.V. 14th Tir/ July, 1391/2012

Keddie, N. R. & Richard, Y. (1981). Roots of revolution: an interpretive history of modern Iran. New Haven, CY: Yale University Press. From: Women in Politics: A case Study of Iran, see: http://us-iran.org/sites/default/files/webform/userarticle-submissions/women_in_politics-iran.pdf

Khas Ali, A. (July 2010). Iranian Women After The Islamic Revolution, Conflicts Forum. Beirut ,Lebanon: see: http://conflictsforum.org/briefings/IranianWomenAfterIslamicRev.pdf

Kinnamon Neff, R. Observations on Roles of Women in America and Iran, See: http://www.michaelprosser.com/2012/06/rebeccah-kinnamon-neff-ph-d-observations-on-roles-of-women-in-america-and-iran-june-14-2012-post-497/

Mahram, See: http://en.wikipedia.org/wiki/Mahram

Maknum, S. (2000). Feminism in Iran. Tehran: The office of human Science Research Center. Women in Politics: A case Study of Iran From:, see: http://us-iran.org/sites/default/files/webform/userarticle-submissions/women_in_politics-iran.pdf

Marriam Webster Dictionary – Culture 1- An on line dictionary, See: http://www.merriam-webster.com/dictionary/culture1

Moore, G.E. (1988). Principia ethica. New York, NY: Prometheus Books., from: Women in Politics: A case Study of Iran, see: http://us-iran.org/sites/default/files/webform/userarticle-submissions/women_in_politics-iran.pdf

Muslim Marriage in the light of Holy Quran (Book of Allah) and Ahadees, see: http://www.ezsoftech.com/omm/marriage.asp

Nasrin Soltankhah, see: http://en.wikipedia.org/wiki/Nasrin_Soltankhah

Obama's Switch on Same-Sex Marriage Stirs Skepticism, Adapted from: http://www.nytimes.com/2012/05/15/us/politics/poll-sees-obama-gay-marriage-support-motivated-by-politics.html

O'Shea, M. (2000). Culture Shock: Iran. Portland, OR: Graphic Arts Publishing Company. From Cultural Conceptualization by Farzad Sharifian. Persian Constitutional Revolution, see: http://en.wikipedia.org/wiki/Persian_Constitutional_Revolution Prosser, Michael H., (2012), Personal Interview

Qur'an emphasizes on gender equality, see: http://www.yahind.com/articles/directory.php?id=40

Religious Ambiguities and Political beliefs, a translation from Farsi to
English, See: http://www.ebhamat.blogfa.com/post-49.aspx

Sharifian, F. (2011). Cultural conceptualization and Language. Amsterdam, The Netherlands, John Benjamins Publishing

Seventy percent of the people think Hijab should be compulsory, See: http://fararu.com/fa/news/118301/70-
%D8%AF%D8%B1%D8%B5%D8%AF-
%D9%85%D8%B1%D8%AF%D9%85-
%D8%AD%D8%AC%D8%A7%D8%A8-%D8%B1%D8%A7-
%D8%B6%D8%B1%D9%88%D8%B1%DB%8C-%D9%85%DB%8C-%
D8%AF%D8%A7%D9%86%D9%86%D8%AF

The Identity given to the tole of the Iranian women in the society by the
Islamic Revolution, authors' translation from Farsi into English, see:
http://www.whc.ir/articles/articles/view/16020

The meaning of Islam, http://www.barghouti.com/islam/meaning.html

The memoir of the youngest Iranian captive in Iraq to be compiled, see:
http://iranbooknews.com/vdcciiqp.2bqss8y-a2.html

The position of women from the view point of Imam Khomeini, (Autumn
2001) See: http://www.iranchamber.com/history/rkhomeini/books/
women_position_khomeini.pdf

The Women's Role in the Society (Wise Sayings of Imam Khomeini), see:
http://www.tebyan.net/newindex.aspx?pid=208016

Tobacco Protest, see: http://en.wikipedia.org/wiki/Tobacco_Protest

Where Are Iran's Working Women? See: http://www.payvand.
com/news/09/feb/1110.html From Women In Iran, See: http://
en.wikipedia.org/wiki/Women_in_Iran#cite_note-54

Women in Islam, Islam's women Jewles of Islam, See: http://www.islams-
women.com/articles/women_in_islam.php

Women's employment in the mirror of statistics, 1390/11/25 – 2012
http://zanan.irib.ir/web/guest/48?id=750&CMD=hozehNewsView

Women's rights movement in Iran, Adapted from: http://en.wikipedia.
org/wiki/Women's_rights_movement_in_Iran

Women's rights movement in Iran, See: http://en.wikipedia.org/wiki/
Women's_rights_movement_in_Iran

Women in ancient Iran, http://www.cais-soas.com/CAIS/Women/
women_ancient_iran.htm

Zahra Eshraghi; See: http://en.wikipedia.org/wiki/Zahra_Eshraghi.
Zahra Khanom Tadj es-Saltaneh, see: http://en.wikipedia.org/wiki/
  Zahra_Khanom_Tadj_es-Saltaneh

6. FASTING: A SPIRITUAL AND PHYSICAL UPGRADING IN UNITY AND COMMUNICATION

Mansoureh Sharifzadeh
Ministry of Education, Tehran, Iran

These days more than 1.5 billion Moslems all over the world are celebrating the holy month of Ramadan that occurs in the ninth month of the Islamic Calendar. It is the 'feast of God' in which the host expects the voluntary guests to observe the fast and cut down from some of the worldly desires from dawn to dusk for 30 days. The host compels the guests to practice self–control and purify the soul through patience by abstinence from food to control appetite to recreate health once a year. Those who are invited to this feast are females above nine and males older than fifteen years old.

In ancient times, Socrates, Plato, Aristotle, Galen, Paracelsus, and Hippocrates all believed in fasting as a form of therapy. Further on in the Bible, Moses, Elijah, Daniel and Jesus suggested fasting for the sake of spiritual purification by complete abstinence from food and drink as a means of communication with God even for one day in a year. In the Bible it is mentioned that Jesus warned his followers against fasting only to make others admire them. He provided practical steps on how to fast in private (Mathew 6:16- 18). Of course it is performed differently based on the New Testament.

In some beliefs as Hinduism, Buddhism, Baha'i's and others, the followers fast in one way or another. For instance Zoroastrians do that, by not eating meat on 4 certain days of each month and don't kill any animals during those days.

Later on, the holy Qur'an which was revealed to Mohammad Peace Be Upon Him in Ramadan, mentions: O you who believe! Fasting is prescribed for you as it was prescribed for those before you, in order that you attain piety. (Al-Baqarah/ Cow 2:183).

For Muslims, fasting is an act of faith to perform what is mandated by the Qur'an. In Ramadan, it is permitted to drink and eat from dusk to dawn. Quran reads: And also Eat and drink until the white thread of the light of the dawn appears to you Distinct from the black thread of the night; then complete your fast till the night falls. And do not associate with your wives ... .even do not draw near thought of violating them. Thus, does Allah Make His words of revelation clear to Mankind, detailed and well explained, so that they may become pious. (Al-Baqarah / Cow 2:187).

Muslims are recommended to study and interpret one of the 30 chapters of the holy Book of Qur'an every day in Ramadan to analyze the words of God and perform them in real life. In this way the whole book can be completed by the end of the 30 days of Ramadan. The goal is to purify our deeds and review the words of God to gain spiritual and physical upgrading.

Ramadan is a time of contemplation. The Muslims get up before dawn; eat a light morning meal based on their appetite. When the call of prayer is heard, eating must be stopped and a 16 hour of fast starts in hot summer days of Iran.

In Iran during Ramadan the working hours are reduced and summer schools are usually closed to give more opportunity to the children to rest and avoid the long hot days. At the end of the day, people invite their friends and relatives to Iftar (supper) and enjoy meeting each other while having their evening supper together. Many wealthy Iranians, set tables in the streets and host the people with foods at dusk. The state officials announce a decrease in criminal and violent actions in Ramadan.

In Ramadan, TV and radio programs are produced to refresh, educate and entertain the audience. At nights, shows, serials and discussions are programmed on the 8 channels of the state TV. People can get together in the parks to enjoy the happy programs which are organized by different sectors as well. Since Iran is a Muslim Shiit country and the martyrdom of the first Imam, Imam Ali (A) took place in this month, the last 10 days of Ramadan cannot be happy and the mourning ceremonies are held to cherish the anniversary of the event. It is necessary to mention that observing the Islamic values and producing amusement for the people is not an easy task in this Islamic country, but is being done anyhow.

As the Muslim calendar shifts every year, the month of Ramadan happens in different seasons and every 33 years reaches to its previous point. When Ramadan occurs in a season like summer with long days and hot weather, performing a 30 day ritual gets tougher. Islam gives complete freedom in this case, though. The sick and women are exceptions in some cases to avoid the harmful effects of the ritual. In trips, all people can break their fast, unless it takes more than 10 days. Those who break their fast as for what has been mentioned must pay atonement to the poor. And no one is permitted to break ones fast for no good reason.

Although not eating and drinking for several hours may have risky results for some, extended fasting has been recommended as therapy for various conditions by health professionals of most cultures, throughout history, from ancient to modern.

Ramadan ends with Eid-al-Fitr or the Festival of Fast-Breaking. On that day Muslims attend a community prayer in the morning and based on their means give money to the charity organizations.

Some of the targets of fasting in general are: focusing on our inner self, thinking about creation, respecting the creator of the whole universe. 'Fast' makes us start changes in 'ourselves' while pursuing God's commands. The main objective of 'fast' is to give a chance to the individuals to cut from some of the earthly values for a while. Concentrating on the actions and communicating with God to discover the strengths and weaknesses of bodies and souls and finding out the depth of patience and tolerance is what one gets through this process.

It is substantial that fasting is common in essential religions and some beliefs. This brings unity and harmony among different cultures. Although it is a big challenge but conveys the goal of creation which is nothing but correcting our own behavior to create peace and love in a better world. By concentrating on one's own actions a better universe can be shaped with the help of God's Commands. Let's pray for peace and unity in any communication among different cultures and ideas of the world. Amen

7. THE IMPACT OF COMMON GROUND IN THE IRAN – IRAQ RELATIONSHIP

Mansoureh Sharifzadeh
The Ministry of Education, Tehran, Iran

People of different nations with the same belief come to a higher understanding about each other, although there might be probable risks as a result of certain circumstances. Such unity brings the individuals into a condition that they tend to overcome all the dangers that may threaten their security.

In April and Oct. 2011, I took two trips to my neighboring country, Iraq as for a pilgrimage. Each of them lasted for about 8 days. The first one was a land trip and took about 30 hours and the second one was by air, about 12 hours including a 6 hour land trip to get to the destination. Flights from Imam Khomeini airport in Tehran to Baghdad last about one and a half hour. I was in a group of 40 pilgrims in both trips. Since Saddam's decline the Iranian government has been organizing the trips to give a good opportunity to the Iranians to undertake pilgrimages to the holy shrines of Imam Ali (AS) in Najaf and Imam Hussein (AS) in Karbala. Every month about 40 thousand Iranian pilgrims visit the holy shrines in Iraq. Needless to say that nothing can stop them from reaching their goal which is nothing but holding enshrines of the Imams. More than 95 percent of the Iranian population is Shiite which makes Iran the largest Shiite country in the world. Shiites believe in the 12 Imams, the first of whom is Imam Ali (AS) who is believed to be the successor of the holy prophet of Islam, Muhammad Peace Be Upon Him, although he is respected by all Islamic believers of the world.

Iraq is in the post-war era and the withdrawal of the American troops has been completed by 2012 after about 10 years. The Iraqi troops and military forces are actively present in all areas to cope with those who agitate sedition. Although security is almost being maintained in this country, sometimes massive explosions scare both the inhabitants and the visitors. The Shrine of Imam Ali (AS) is in the city of Najaf and as both Shiites and Sunnis respect him, the city is in less danger. It can be said that the city of Samara where the 10th and 11th Imams are buried, is the most hazardous city at the moment. For example during the past 3 weeks several deadly explosions have happened in Samara. During my second trip, there were 3 blasts in the city of Basra.

Pilgrims of land trips have a one night stay in the border city of Mehran that is an Iranian county. In May 1986, during the Iran – Iraq War, Iraqi forces captured Mehran. The occupation lasted only one month, and Iranian forces recaptured Mehran and drove off the Iraqis. Now, this city is not populous enough and war has left a desolated atmosphere in that area. The facilities are of poor quality for the pilgrims that have to spend the overnight collectively based on gender in separate rooms to rest after a 12 hour trip to regain energy for the next day to go to the border and find the opportunity of entering the land of their dreams to do their pilgrimage.

All through history, the people of these two countries have been restrained with walls that are put away by the will of people. Some may think what 40 thousand Iranians do each month in welcoming the dangerous condition of Iraq might be pure madness, whereas for the Shiites this is an ethnic reaction that can be defended by some Sunni clerics too. It is necessary to mention that Iraqis enjoy the presence of the Iranians in their countries as the pilgrims buy souvenirs and help the poor financial system of the country to enhance. Iranians are actively involved in construction especially related to the shrines and other projects. The history of both countries which shows the inner satisfaction of both nations in this communication is of the greatest value.

For me it started as an idea to know more about my neighboring country that has the longest border with Iran in comparison with other neighbors, i.e. Afghanistan, Pakistan and Turkey. The length of its border is not the main significance, as in 2003 my mind moved towards it. Saddam was captured in the same year and a new white page was unfolded in the history of the Iran – Iraq relationship. My deep affection was directing me to discover and learn more about this mysterious country where the beloved generations of my beloved prophet are buried in to bring the Shiites the most hazardous memory of the human communication. What I wanted to explore was out of respect and love for my prophet, Mohammed Peace Be Upon Him. So nothing could stop me from pursuing my decision and fear seemed meaningless.

For the Iranians, Iraq is the most important and the greatest neighbor, not as for the population and quantity, because in those cases Pakistan can be considered the first. However, there are some religious and historical links between these two countries. Iraq is a very important country for us as any changes in it can shake both the West and the East. Baghdad is one of the oldest cities of the world. It is a city that has been occupied several times and each time a new change has happened in the management of the world. Iraq has some special characteristics which are a result of the presence of different tribes and beliefs in it. In this country different nations as Iranians, Turks and Arabs are actively involved in the realms of thought, culture and art. So as our knowledge about Iraq improves, our diplomatic features become more authentic and less risk-taking. Iran intends to have both a relationship with the West and the East as well and Iraq has always been a measure for this relationship. Iranians and Iraqis have always been eager to have a good relationship with each other as for the holy shrines of Imams both in Iraq and Iran with the 8th Imam. This has been a strong reason for both countries to ignore some of the facts and pursue their interest to perform their religious rituals and go as pilgrims to the shrines of their beloved prophets.

In 1920, Iraq was formed as an independent country. The years of the Iran-Iraq war (1980-1988) brought such a deep separation between the two countries that left about 1 million victims from both sides. Now the people of both countries are wounded. Both have lost their family or relatives. A great number of veterans injured in the war are still alive and there can't be found any family in these countries that doesn't live with a victim from chemical warfare.

The mentioned points above may make the people think of each other as enemies but with great surprise, the people of both countries communicate and take advantages of visiting each other's countries and enjoy themselves. Some documents prove that even during the Iran-Iraq war the people of both countries never stopped passing the borders and the presence of our Imams has always been a strong link between these two nations.

Our common belief brings us a unity that might seem strange but the truth is what I unbelievably observed and a stronger relationship has been shaped. Now I like to visit my neighboring country more than ever as peace is not possible unless the nations ignore the negative facts to enhance Iranians' positive relationships among themselves as God writes in the Holy book of Qu'ran, "And hold fast by the covenant of Allah all together and be not disunited, and remember the favor of Allah on you when you were enemies, then He united your hearts so by His favor you became brethren; and you were on the brink of a pit of fire, then He saved you from it, thus does Allah make clear to you His communications that you may followthe right way".(3: 103). Salaam and blessings to all of the true followers of peace and unity.

8. Creating Wars and International Solutions

Mansoureh Sharifzadeh
The Ministry of Education, Tehran, Iran

The Washington Post writes that Tehran Polls opened on Friday March 2, 2012. There are more than 48 million eligible voters to elect 290 new members of Parliament. Results are expected Sunday, March 4 for larger cities and Monday for rural areas. Iran's supreme leader, Ayatollah Ali Khamenei, was one of the first to cast his ballot early on March 2. State television quoted him as saying that a high turnout will "safeguard" Iran's reputation and security.

Election for the Iranian people means having a share in the destiny of their country and to cope with the threats of the United States and Israel. Some people elect people to solve such problems as high inflation, foreign currency prices, housing, and unemployment. People vote to obey the leader to challenge the United States and Israel. In the Province of Hamedan a 100 year old man cast his ballot and died shortly after casting it. In Gonbad Kavoos which is a city of Golestan Province, an alleged 145 year old man cast his ballot too.

Three hundred and fifty correspondents from such countries as Germany, Austria, Spain, USA, Ukraine, Italy, Brazil, Belgium, Turkey, Czech Republic, Russia, Japan, France, Finland, Qatar, Canada, South Korea, Colombia, Lebanon, Venezuela have been reporting on the event. They not only witnessed the people in long lines to take part in the poll and have a share in their country's fortune for the next 4 years, but also talked with them whose main aim has been to obey the leader.

Four million youngsters over 18 have been eligible to give their vote for the first time and one of them told a correspondent that he voted to prove to the United States and Israel that Iran is not Iraq or Afghanistan, and can't be challenged easily.

In an interview President Barack Obama warned that he was not "bluffing" about attacking Iran if it builds a nuclear weapon. Obama also warned the United States ally Israel that a premature attack on Iran would do more harm than good.

Something which is noticeable is that President Obama is quite aware of the billboard quotes in Tehran that it was mentioned that "Obama is bluffing on Iran" and the distance between Tehran and White House has given way to a closer relationship in awareness and understanding about Iran. So it can be said that conflicts can bring relationships, closeness and awareness too.

We hope that the governments of both nations come to mutual understanding about each other and try to solve the problems and perspectives related to nuclear power in friendly talks and debates as wars have proven not to be a means to solve any difficulty except for creating more problems for the people of both nations.

Recently Asghar Farhadi, the director of the movie 'The Separation" who won an Oscar prize for the best foreign film, invited the nations to work for peace and avoid war. He brought the fragrance of unity by his "Separation" even though it seemed inevitable.

The late Professor D. Ray Heisey, who served as President of Damavand College in Tehran from 1975-78, described his idea about war as "I personally believe that going to war to solve problems is immature, inhumane, animalistic, and intolerable. Disputes between nations should be resolved by the human behaviors of dialogue, mediation, and arbitration."

As Sohrab Sepehri reads, "You have to wash your eyes, you have to see the world differently."

Blessings and salaam to all of the peace makers.

9. Nowruz, the Iranian New Year Is Associated with the Spring, Harmony, and Communication

Mansoureh Sharifzadeh
The Ministry of Education, Tehran, Iran

Tonight is Chahārshanbeh Suri which precedes the last Wednesday of the current Iranian year of 1390.

These days Iranians are preparing themselves for the arrival of the New Year, 1391 based on the Solar Calendar. In Iran the New Year starts on the first day of spring i.e., 20 or 21 of March. The prologue to this great celebration starts, during the last month of winter in Esfand. People do their utmost effort to clean the entire house as if they were to "shake the house." New clothes and household materials are bought to welcome New Year with complete preparation and cleanliness. In the Islamic culture it is quoted from the prophet of Islam that "Cleanliness is an icon of Faith". Ancient Iranians were concerned about constructive thoughts, words and deeds. Purification of soul, action and the beauty of thought is the central idea of the Zoroastrians. So the custom of cleaning the houses before the New Year has been practiced since ancient times. Up to this day, Nowruz is the most important holiday in Iran which lasts for 13 days.

Nowruz starts on the first day of spring in association with the "rebirth of nature." Implicitly everything must find new birth including the relationship among the people. During the Nowruz holiday, people of the same family and friends meet each other and try to forget any former conflicts and tighten the future relationship. This is a time for re-union and bringing good wishes for each other for the year ahead. New Year holiday is a time for communication and visiting each other even for a short period of time. During the visits, the hosts serve their guests with sweets, candies, fruits, dried nuts and tea to bring freshness and happiness to their short visit.

On New Year's Day, families dress in their new clothes and start the twelve-day celebrations by starting their visit with the elders of their family who offer gifts, especially money which had been left among the leaves of the Holy Book of Quran. The given money is believed to bring blessings along with pockets full of money and more income in the year ahead.

As a child my grandparents gave me different gifts as dolls, purses, stockings and even a 10 Rial Coin that made me proud and happy. Nowadays, my parents gift me with money too and I give gifts to the younger ones. Iranians believe gifts bring faithfulness and satisfaction.

The people visit all of their relatives and friends too. During the Nowruz holiday all of the people of the same family meet each other. Sometime, people visit each other several times during the holiday in different houses. And finally on the thirteenth day, families leave their homes and picnic outdoors in the nature.

Visiting the others has been stressed in Islam as 'Seleh Rahem" which literally means "Communication with the Relatives." Of course, different perspectives might be of interest but the main point is 'to communicate with each other in order to contribute in others' "problems and happiness." The core of the idea brings unity and friendship.

The last Wednesday of the year is called Chahārshanbeh Suri. 'Chahrshanebeh' means Wednesday and 'Sur' means feast, party or festival in Persian. This festival is the celebration of the light (the good) winning over the darkness (the bad); the symbolism behind the rituals are all rooted back to Zoroastrianism. The tradition starts when people go into the streets and alleys to make bonfires, and jump over them. While jumping over the fire they sing, "My yellowness is yours, your redness is mine." The main message is "My paleness (pain, sickness) for you (the fire), your strength (health) for me." Serving different kinds of pastry and nuts is a way of giving thanks for the previous year's health and happiness.

Haft Sīn or the seven 'S's is a major traditional table setting of Nowruz. The 'haft sin' table must be set at the time of the New Year. That includes seven specific items starting with the letter 'S' or Sīn (س) in the Persian alphabet. These seven items are Sabzeh – growing in a dish – symbolizing rebirth. Samanu – a sweet pudding made from wheat germ; symbolizing affluence. Senjed – the dried fruit of the oleaster tree; symbolizing love. Sīr – garlic; symbolizing medicine. Sīb – apples; symbolizing beauty and health. Somaq – sumac berries; symbolizing (the color of) sunrise. Serkeh – vinegar; symbolizing age and patience.

In addition to the mentioned items, Mirror symbolizing 'Sky', Candles symbolizing 'Fire', Golab or rose water symbolizing 'Water', Goldfish symbolizing 'Life', Painted Eggs symbolizing 'Humans and Fertility' are placed too. The Holy Book of Qu'ran and Divan of Hafiz have a special place on this table.

The family sits at 'Haft Sin' table, recites some verses of the Holy Book of Qu'ran at the time of the renewal. It is conventional to recite a 'Du'a' which is known as 'Ya Moghalebal Gholoob " that reads, "Thou, Director of hearts and eyes – Oh mastermind of the Night and Day. Oh reformer of hearts and minds; Transform our condition to the best in accordance with your determination."

The traditional herald of the Nowruz season is a man called Hājī Firuz. His face is painted black (black is an ancient Persian symbol of good luck) and wears a red costume. Then he sings and dances through the streets with tambourines and trumpets spreading good cheer and heralds the coming of the New Year a few weeks ahead of the New Year.

New Year dishes are Sabzi Polo Mahi which is rice with green herbs served with fish. Reshteh Polo which is rice cooked with noodles which is said to symbolically help one succeed in life and finding the best way. Kookoo sabzi which is Herbs and vegetable soufflé, traditionally served for dinner at New Year.

Sizdeh Bedar is the thirteenth day of the new year festival. Figuratively it means "Passing the bad luck of the thirteenth day". This is a day of festivity in the open and at the end of the celebrations on this day, the sabzeh grown for the Haft Seen (which has symbolically collected all sickness and bad luck) is thrown into running water to exorcise the demons (divs) from the household. It is also customary for young single women to tie the leaves of the sabzeh before discarding it, so expressing a wish to be married before the next year's Sizdah Bedar. Another tradition associated with this day is Dorugh-e Sizdah, literally meaning "the lie of the thirteenth," which is the process of lying to someone and making him or her believe it.

These days Iran is facing sanctions and the result is inflation which affects the people's lives especially those of middle class. Policy can bring logical results in order to create a better condition in solving the common problems. President Barak Obama usually sends New Year greeting messages to the Iranians. Constructive messages to the rulers can bring the long term conflicts to an end to prevent the people from more damages and hardships. Anyhow, the Iranians are preparing themselves for another New Year celebration as it is the main aspect of the profound culture of Iranian Identity.

Happy New year to the people of Iraq, Turkey, Afghanistan, and Syria and the world. Seasonal greetings to all and hope for a world without boundaries and borders integrated with peace and harmony for the year ahead.

B) Public Conversations on Iran

1. Perspective on Iranian Communication Studies

D. Ray Heisey (d. May 20, 2011)

Interview on Communication and Intercultural Communication in Iran

with

Ehsan Shahghasemi
University of Tehran, Iran

D. Ray Heisey: 1. Which universities in Iran have departments of communications?

Ehshan Shahghasemi: The University of Allameh Tabatabaei, University of Tehran and College of IRIB are academic institutions within which communications is taught. Imam Sadegh University also has a Faculty of Islamic Knowledge, Culture and Communications. Imam Sadegh University is like a seminary within which modern humanities are also taught. One other Institute is the University of Sooreh which has a Department of Communication and Culture. The University of Baqer ol-Oloom of Qom offers an MA program in Promotion and Communications which is exclusive of the students of the seminary. There is an Islamic Azad University in Iran which has hundreds of branches inside or even outside Iran. I know that some branches of the Islamic Azad University have departments of communications. Branches of, Oloom va Tahghighat, Tehran Markaz, Arak, Bandar Abbas and Jahrom are among them.

D. Ray Heisey: 2. Which of these are considered the top 2 or 3 in quality and size?

Ehshan Shahghasemi: In size, Allameh Tabatabei is the biggest. In fact, it is Faculty of Communications at Allameh Tabatabaei University and other universities – except Imam Sadegh University – have only a department of communications. It is also the oldest in Iran and offers BA degree in three majors of Journalism, Public Relations, and Communication and Information Technology Studies. It has three MA programs in Journalism, Media Management and Social Communication Studies. There is one PHD program in Communications at this Faculty. There are 10 faculty members at this Faculty and also some guest professors who help them in teaching. There are about 750 BA students, 110 MA students and 48 PHD students at this Faculty.

The Department of Communications at the University of Tehran is second in size. It has BA, MA and PhD programs in Communications. It also has an MA program in Media and Cultural Studies. There are about 200 BA students, 50 MA students and 7 PhD students at this department. It is about 15 years since this department has been established. There are 8 faculty members at this department in which some guest professors help them teaching students. The Faculty of Islamic Knowledge, Culture and Communications at Imam Sadegh University with about 160 students is third in size. It has a 6 years MA program. High school graduates after hard exams and strict religious and political evaluation, directly enter this program. There are three Departments at this Faculty. The Department of Communications and Culture offers PHD program in Communications and Culture, MA program in Islamic Knowledge and Culture, and an MA program in Communications and Culture. The Department of Communications and Religion offers an MA program in Guidance. There is also a Department of History and Culture at this Faculty.

I really prefer the University of Tehran's approach towards communications. This is a pioneer department in that its students perceive a global approach for themselves. The amount of academic production of faculty members and students is incomparable to other similar institutions. But, as I have an affiliation to this University, perhaps a third party person can offer a more plausible account.

D. Ray Heisey: 3. Which universities have an emphasis in intercultural communication?

Ehshan Shahghasemi: The University of Tehran and University of Imam Sadegh are more active in this discipline. Nevertheless, this field still needs more attention. Professor Saied Reza Ameli and Professor Mehdi Mohsenian Rad are two well-known professors in Intercultural Communication Studies in Iran. Professor Hassan Bashir presents courses on Intercultural Communications at the University of Imam Sadegh. Professor Masoud Kousari from the University of Tehran also presents a course on Intercultural Communications for BA students of the Department of Communications at this University.

D. Ray Heisey: 4. Is there a professional association in Iran that consists of professors, students and researchers of communication? If so, what is its title and how often does it hold a conference?

Ehshan Shahghasemi: Yes, there are many of them. But, they are not so active. In fact, the lack of financial support is a big problem. I would contextualize it in the wider context of the Iranian politicians' approach towards Social Sciences. In my country, little is paid for the Social Sciences because the tangible effects of Social Sciences could hardly be seen without a passionate eye. In fact, people never offer a design for a power plant but almost all of them perceive themselves as Social Science experts. The same view is held by many of our policy makers.

The Iranian Association of Communications and Cultural Studies is one of the most active associations in Iran. It is located at the Department of Communications at the University of Tehran but professors and students from other academic institutions including those outside Iran are also included in it. Naturally, it has a gathering every three months.

The Iranian Association for Studies in Information Society is another active institute which is devoted to studying Iranian cyberspace. Many famous academic figures including Professor Kazem Motamed Nejad, Professor Shahindokht Kharazmi, Professor Younes Shokrkhah and Professor Mehdi Mohsenian Rad are members of the board of this association. This association holds frequent meetings on Information Society and their focus is on Iran.

The Center of Cyberspace Studies at Faculty of World Studies, University of Tehran is also active in studying the Iranian cyberspace. Professor Saied Reza Ameli, founder of this center tries to link the theory and action. This center has accomplished several projects on virtual cities, virtual services, cybercultures, and dual spaced cyber interactions.

The Institute for Social and Cultural Studies is another institute which is directed by Iranian Ministry of Science. They are active in publishing works in Communications research.

The Media Community Center is active in holding gatherings on communications issues. This is operated by the municipality of Tehran. So, financial support of the municipality helps them to serve communications better.

The Bureau of Media Studies and Planning is another institution which was established about 20 years ago to cover the communication and media studies issues. This bureau offers some training programs for media and communication practitioners but its activities are mostly concentrated on publications and tens of translation projects have been sponsored by this institute. Moreover, Resaneh (means "Media"), which is a peer-reviewed Journal and is published every season, is directed by this Bureau.

The Hamshahri Centre for Media Research and Training which is a part of Hamshahri institute is another active institute in the field of communication and media studies. This center has recently been established by merging two pre-existing institutes. The website of this center considers "Intercultural Communications" as one theme of interest. Recently, this center has bought thousands of articles in Farsi and put them on its website to be used by students and researchers in communications for free. This centre is directed by Professor Hassan Namakdoost.

The Center for Cyber Journalism Research is another institute in this field which is managed by some scholars from the Islamic Azad University. Professor Hamid Ziaei Parvar is the founder of this Center and Professor Soltani Far is the current Head.

D. Ray Heisey: 5. Is there a journal or newsletter devoted to communication studies and how frequently is it published and by whom?

Ehshan Shahghasemi: Yes, there are some in Iran. The Global Media Journal is a famous online journal at the University of Purdue which has a Persian version edited by Professor Hamid Abdollahyan and Professor Alireza Dehghan from the Department of Communications at the University of Tehran. Communication and Culture is another peer-reviewed journal which is directed by Iranian Association of Communications and

Cultural Studies and its office is also located at the Department of Communications at the University of Tehran. Namey-e Sadegh is another Communication journal which is published by Imam Sadegh University. Professor Yahya Kamalipour and Professor Omid Ali Masoudi are editors of this journal. Communication Research is another peer reviewed journal which is published by IRIB. Cultural Research is another communication journal which is published by the Institute for Social and Cultural Studies. Rasaneh, which is being published by The Bureau of Media Studies and Planning is another peer-reviewed journal in the field of communications. All of these journals are being published each season except Global Media Journal which is published every 6 months.

D. Ray Heisey: 6. What would you list as the top 5 or 10 books in Farsi with titles translated into English on communication theory or practice from an Iranian perspective?

Ehshan Shahghasemi: The most common books which Iranian students in Communications read are translations. In fact, translation in Iran is very rampant. So, few textbooks are written by Iranian scholars. On my opinion these are the top five: 1) The Law of the Press by Professor Kazem Motamed Nejad who is also known as the Father of the Iranian Communications. Professor Motamed Nejad is a distinguished professor at the Faculty of Communications, Allameh University. This book is an overview to Law of the Press in the Iranian history of Journalism. It also reviews the history of legislation on journalism in other countries. Finally, Professor Motamed Nejad delivers his own suggestions in order to fit the laws of Iran with the principle of freedom of speech; 2) Communicology by Professor Mehdi Mohsenian Rad from Imam Sadegh University. This book is highly Iranian! In general, the works of Professor Mohsenian are highly contextualized in the Iranian culture, history and geography. Although this book still sells well, Professor Mohsenian is supposed to update it. 3) Electronic Public Relations by Professor Saied Reza Ameli from the University of Tehran. The nobility of this book lies in its approach. Professor Ameli shows how using new communication technologies helps PR practitioners to work better and act in a more responsible way. He also shows how these new facilities help people to have better life. 4) New Journalism by Naem Badiei and Hossein Ghandi. This book is a practical handbook for Iranian young journalists to get involved in the real scene of Journalism. 5) Cultural Studies, Cultural Consumption and Everyday Life in Iran by Professor Abbas Kazemi. This young professor of the University of Tehran puts the Iranian everyday life in the Cultural Studies tradition and describes its features.

D. Ray Heisey: 7. Please answer the same question, except list those published in English.

Ehshan Shahghasemi: 1) Globalization, Americanization, and British Muslim Identity by Professor Saied Reza Ameli. I chose this book because of its approach. The academic and communicative approach of this book helps Professor Ameli to talk about a problem without falling in the pitfall of two poles of self-centrism or self-denial. 2) Media, Culture and Society by Professor Mehdi Semati from the Department of Communication at Northern Illinois University. This is an edited book within which some well-known communication scholars study the Iranian communicative sphere. New media and their impact – particularly on the youth – are covered in this book as well. 3) Global Communication by Professor Yahya Kamalipour, head of the Department of Communications and director of the Center for Global Studies at Purdue University Calumet. The nobility of this book is in its historical approach. This edited book starts with the history of global communications and finishes by some suggestions about the future of the world and global communications. 4) Iran Encountering Globalization: Problems and Prospects by Professor Ali Mohammadi who is Reader in International Communication and Cultural Studies at Nottingham Trent University. Taking a communicative approach, this edited book considers a wide range of issues regarding the Iranian society, culture, economy and politics. 5) Nonverbal Communication by Professor Albert Mehrabian, Professor Emeritus of Psychology, UCLA. The importance of this book is in its depth of analysis. As a result, many debates have been held about this book. This book has also been reprinted several times.

D. Ray Heisey: 8. Which ones of these would be considered intercultural communication studies?

Ehshan Shahghasemi: None of them! Though these books have chapters on understanding, cognition, systems of shared meaning and knowledge, global communication etc., unfortunately, Intercultural communication still needs more attention in my country. Perhaps, since we have no serious cultural or racial difference in our society, the need for this discipline cannot come to the forefront. Nevertheless, there are some other aspects of intercultural communications such as intercultural communication at the political level (e.g. relationships between religious and non-religious people at the political and even at the societal level) have important implications and have attracted the attention of the Iranian academia.

D. Ray Heisey: 9. If there is none from an Iranian perspective, which texts in English have or are being translated into Farsi for use as a text.

Ehshan Shahghasemi: Most of the texts which are taught are in English. For example, Professor Ameli introduced Communicating Across Cultures at Work by Maureen Guirdham as his favorite textbook. I also found Intercultural Communication by John V. Thill which has been translated into Farsi but, I couldn't identify the source among Thill's books in English. Perhaps, the translator has changed the name.

D. Ray Heisey: 10. What would you list as the top 5 or 10 journal articles on Iranian communication theory and/or practice? and Intercultural communication theory and/or practice?

Ehshan Shahghasemi: This is a hard question to answer because I haven't seen all of the articles by Iranian scholars. But, among those I have read are 1) "Acculturation, communication, and the US mass media: The experience of an Iranian immigrant" by Professor Flora Keshishian; 2) "Globalization, Culture and Message Bazaar" by Professor Mehdi Mohsenian Rad; 3) "Dual Globalisations and Global Society of Anxiety" by Professor Saied Reza Ameli; 4) "Internet and Social Changes in Iran" by Professor Mehdi Montazer Ghaem; 5) "Iran-China Relations: A Historical Profile" by A. H. H. Abidi; 6) "Dialogue of Civilizations for Peace" by Professor Majid Tehranian; 7) "Some Words on National Epic of Iranians and Armenians" by Professor Mir Jalal-e-din Kazazi; 8) "Communication media and globalization: An Iranian perspective" by Professor Yahiya Kamalipour; "Methodology and Analysis of Ideology in Newspapers' Texts in Iran" by Professor Hamid Abdollahyan; 9) "Glocalization, Towards and Iranian-Islamic Bricolage" by Professor Masoud Kousari; 10) "National Identity and Interaction in Cyberspace" by Professor Behzad Dowran.

D. Ray Heisey: 11. Who would you list as the top 10 leading Iranian scholars in Iranian communication?

Ehshan Shahghasemi: This is also a hard question to answer because of two reasons. First, I have affiliation to the University of Tehran so my opinion could not be impartial; and, second, I do personally know only some of professors and I know others through their works and activities. Anyway, I list these people as top ten leading Iranian scholars: Professor Saied Reza Ameli from the University of Tehran; Professor Kazem Motamed Nejad from the Faculty of Communications, University of Allameh Tabatabaei; Professor Mehdi Mohsenian Rad from Imam Sadegh University; Professor Mehdi Semati from the Department of Communication at Northern Illinois University; Professor Yahya Kamalipour, head of the Department of Communications at Purdue University Calumet; Professor Ali Mohammadi from Nottingham Trent University; Professor Albert Mehrabian, Professor Emeritus of Psychology, UCLA; Professor Mehdi Montazer Ghaem from the University of Tehran; Professor Parviz Piran from University of Allameh Tabatabaei; Professor Abbas Kazemi from the University of Tehran. I would like to add two other people to this list. The first is Professor Hassan Namakdoost, who in 2006 was dismissed from the University of Allameh Tabatabaei. Alireza Ketabdar, MA graduate in Communication and a media expert from the University of Allameh Tabatabaei who passed the scientific exam and was accepted in the PhD program but was rejected because of his ideas. Professor Namakdoost and Mr. Ketabdar are now working for Hamshahri Institute.

D. Ray Heisey: 12. Who in Europe or the United States or Asia have had the biggest impact on Iranian communication study? Who has influenced Iranian scholars the most?

Ehshan Shahghasemi: As most of scholars in the Iranian Communication Society are graduated from universities in different continents, they have been affected by different schools of thought. So, no special discipline is dominant in the Iranian communication society. Like what we have witnessed in the academic world, older scholars more or less believe in quantitative methods and younger ones more like qualitative methods. As a result, the correspondent figures of each camp are popular in Iran. Generally, leftist approaches are more popular in my country. So, Marx, Gramsci, Althusser, and Žižek's ideas – particularly their ideas on sociology of cognition – are taught at the communication departments. The Frankfurt School has its proponents and their works counted among some of the most widely read in my country. Among them, Habermas is the most popular and he had a travel to Iran in 2002. Manuel Castells also is popular and he has traveled to Iran in 2006. Michael Foucault, Stuart Hall, Roland Barthes and Jacque Derrida also enjoy popularity and most of their works have been translated into Farsi. I personally like Umberto Eco and Zygmunt Bauman. They are known to Iranians but their ideas are not still so popular in my country.

Cultural Studies as a discipline has got a big thrust by recent years. Many of the works of Williams, Hall, Hougart and Thompson have been translated to Farsi and as you see, all of this figures are from the British tradition of Cultural Studies. Feminism also is a growing field of interest as currently about 65 percent of the Iranian students are women and they want to push the academic intellect to a different kind of understanding.

D. Ray Heisey: 13. List the leading MA theses and PhD dissertations (titles translated into English) at the University of Tehran in intercultural communication.

Ehshan Shahghasemi: 1) Psychological Pressures, Stresses, Challenges and Techniques for Coping in Human Communications: The Case of Intercultural Couples by Maryam Asghari; 2) Globalization and Intercultural Sensitivities: The Case of Intercultural Communications Between Sunis and Shias in Golestan Province by Hamideh Molaei; 3) Studying Intercultural Communication Between Iran and the US Emphasizing Theory of Intercultural Sensitivity and Schema Theory by Farnaz Ahmad-Zadeh-Namvar; 4) Ethnic Globalism and Media Consumption; The Case of Media Consumption of TV Among Jargalan's Turkamans by Somayeh Karimi-Tararani; 5) Glocalization and the Kurdish Identity: The Case of Mahabad by Mustafa Ahmad-Zadeh; 6) The Iranian World View in Dual Spaced World by Hadi Khoshnevis; 7) Comparative Study of Kurdish Identity Representation in Works of Kurdish and Non-Kurdish Film Makers by Behzad Garmroudi; Studying the Relationship Between Communicative Rationality and Intercultural Sensitivity (The Case of Suni and Shia Students at the University of Tehran) by Laya Yarahmadi Khorasani; 9) Globalization Discourses in the Eyes of the Iranian Elites by Goudarz Mirani; 10) The Cross-Cultural Schemata Iranians Have for Transsexuals by Hosna Masoumi.

D. Ray Heisey: 14. In the intercultural communication course at the University of Tehran, what is the title of the text or texts and what are the main topics in the course syllabus?

Ehshan Shahghasemi: I have described the first part of the question in #8. Generally, they teach intercultural communication based on their own pamphlets. Professor Masoud Kousari teaches the course for BA students, Professor Saied Reza Ameli also has his own powerpoint presentations for MA students. Elsewhere at the University of Tehran, Professor Mehdi Mohsenian Rad uses his own pamphlet to present intercultural communication course for PhD students in the Social Problems major.

D. Ray Heisey: 15. What would you say is the most important factor needed in advancing the study of intercultural communication in Iran today?

Ehshan Shahghasemi: The first thing that will help Iranian academia to be more acquainted with intercultural communication is to include more professors in this field. Iran has no major in intercultural communications. Therefore, students in Communications perceive intercultural communications as merely a course among others. The second solution is to encourage students to present their works at international conferences. This will help them to see other people in person. Iranians already use diverse media sources and see the differences but that's not enough to encourage the Iranian students to work in the field of intercultural communications. Iran is an historical country and has many things which international tourists will find interesting. But, we have a totally poor tourism industry and the personal contact with different people in my country is very limited. Participating in international conferences will be helpful. As you know, the number of papers on the subject of intercultural communications presented by the Iranian students at international conferences is ever increasing. Here, at the University of Tehran, our professors encourage students to participate in international events and I think this has been effective in empowering intercultural communication studies in Iran. The third way to empower the discipline is to encourage instructors to include more materials regarding intercultural communications. This will help the students of Communications to shape their intercultural interests. The fourth way to help this discipline is to fund projects for translating textbooks of intercultural communications into Farsi.

D. Ray Heisey: 16. What would you say is the most effective way Iranian scholars in intercultural communication could make their views known to Western and Asian scholars?

Ehshan Shahghasemi: The best way is to present their works in more world-known languages. As a personal experience, I have understood that people outside Iran are highly curious about Iranian culture. Iranian communication scholars should take this opportunity and make their works global. And, for those who like to continue to work in Farsi, international conferences in other Farsi speaking countries such as Afghanistan, Tajikistan and even India would be helpful. Connecting scholars in other countries and working on joint papers will also help the Iranian scholars. As you have said elsewhere, "Whether in teaching opportunities or in research projects, if a door begins to open, give it a push and see what awaits you for growth, understanding, and learning."

In size, Allameh Tabatabei is the biggest. In fact, it is Faculty of Communications at Allameh Tabatabaei University and other universities – except Imam Sadegh University – have only a department of communications. It is also the oldest in Iran and offers BA degree in three majors of Journalism, Public Relations, and Communication and Information Technology Studies. It has three MA programs in Journalism, Media Management and Social Communication Studies. There is one PhD program in Communications at this faculty. There are 10 faculty members at this faculty and also some guest professors who help them in teaching. There are about 750 BA students, 110 MA students and 48 PhD students at this faculty.

The Department of Communications at the University of Tehran is second in size. It has BA, MA and PhD programs in Communications. It also has an MA program in Media and Cultural Studies. There are about 200 BA students, 50 MA students and 7 PhD students at this department. It is about 15 years since this department has been established. There are 8 faculty members at this department in which some guest professors help them teaching students. The Faculty of Islamic Knowledge, Culture and Communications at Imam Sadegh University with about 160 students is third in size. It has a 6 years MA program. High school graduates after hard exams and strict religious and political evaluation directly enter this program. There are three departments at this faculty. The Department of Communications and Culture offers a PhD program in Communications and Culture, MA program in Islamic Knowledge and Culture, and an MA program in Communications and Culture. The Department of Communications and Religion offers an MA program in Guidance. There is also a Department of History and Culture at this Faculty.

I really prefer the University of Tehran's approach towards communications. This is a pioneer department in that its students perceive a global approach for themselves. Of the amount of academic production of faculty members and. to this university, perhaps a third party person can offer a more plausible account.

2. ELEVEN QUESTIONS ON PROFESSIONAL TOPICS

Michael H. Prosser
University of Virginia,
Shanghai International Studies University

Mansoureh Sharifzadeh
Ministry of Education, Tehran, Iran

Public Conversation with Mansoureh Sharifzadeh as an Iranian
Teacher of English, Ministry of Education, Tehran, Iran

Michael H. Prosser: 1. Your connection to Damavand College when
Professor D. Ray Heisey was the second last American President there
(1975-78) led you later to develop a close intercultural research collaboration with him relating to the attitudes of Iranian youth towards American
youth and the reverse. Can you describe the process which you developed
together to test these attitudes?

Mansoureh Sharifzadeh: On February 17, 2009, Professor D. Ray Heisey
invited me to join him in a little project "How foreigners are perceived."
The reason was that he had been asked to give a talk at a monthly Lyceum
Series by a local organization that he was a member of. In this regard his
main interest was in obtaining the Iranian and American teenagers' ideas
about each other through drawings. The outcome was some drawings that
were done skillfully.

On March 6, 2009 he presented the drawings to the organization with
the title of "How We See Each Other." The next day he wrote, "I was very
pleased with the reception my slide show got from the audience. The
drawings by your students received great praise. The audience was very
impressed with the quality of the drawings and the depth of insight and
perceptiveness of the artists. In fact, one of the men in the audience is a
professor of art at Kent State University and he said to me, "Those drawings
by the Iranian students must be by students who have had special training in art classes." I replied that I don't know if they have had or not, but
the identification at the top of the drawings with the names I believe says

"Math." Then he added "They are fantastic. I am delighted with them." I'm glad to know my own response is supported by my friends who saw them."

He sent me the American students' drawings too and wrote, "You will notice of course that their perceptions are influenced by our American media, which is unfortunate." The drawings were trying to verify the other nation negatively. They would appear to show how the media reflected both nations in a stereotypical fashion to create phobia.

Later on he considered presenting the drawings at a conference in Ohio in October of the same year, and he asked if I and my students were interested in participating in this way or not. We did agree and this was the first step in accepting constructive criticism to explore the others' ideas about ourselves to obtain as much awareness on the perspectives of the people of both countries as we could.

Then Dr. Heisey decided a new title for the paper, "The Visual and Artistic Rhetoric of Americans and Iranians of Each Other Impacted by Media." In May 2010, he presented that at the Phi Beta Delta Honor Society conference in Philadelphia too. Two years later, the paper was published in Proceedings of Phi Beta Delta, Volume 2, No. 1 May 2011.

Michael H. Prosser: 2. What were your joint findings about the attitudes of the Iranian and American youth?

Mansoureh Sharifzadeh: As Dr. Heisey concluded, Intercultural communication efforts, such as this one, can in a small way initiate more positive attitudes toward others as we obtain more information and consider the perspectives of others.

President Seyed Mohammad Khatami argued for dialogue among civilizations. Even the current President Mahmoud Ahmadinejad sent open letters in 2006, first to then President Bush and then to the American people, hoping for genuine dialogue on issues of mutual concern. The new approach is consistent with the words of the current American President Barack Obama who wants to turn the page with Iran and has asked for open minds and open hearts and the use of fair-minded words when people of different views communicate with one another on controversial topics. This paper has presented the visual rhetoric that American and Iranian school children have in their perceptions of each other's culture and nation. Through the drawings this paper elaborates on how the political impact from the textbook and other media, the socialization process of growing up, along with that of the new technology of the Internet, and from their understanding of their history and of the history of the other culture, can influence how they view the other culture in personal behavior and in collective, national behavior. The drawings clearly show the impact of prejudice socialization in these adolescent young people. Parents and peers receive information from such sources and become in turn influential in the drawers perceptions about other cultures.

Visual rhetoric, as is verbal rhetoric, is constructed from political and historical understandings of reality. This reality is seen more fully when it is interpreted by scholars who are from different cultural backgrounds. What seemed obvious to one interpreter was seen differently by another when America's history was brought into the discussion. The understanding of the drawings was made more complete by a cross-cultural dialogue. One is reminded of Kenneth Burke's well-known statement that language is the dancing of an attitude.

Michael H. Prosser: 3. Generally speaking, it is my assumption that American secondary school students may either have a very neutral or somewhat biased opinion about Iranian high school students. In your joint research with Professor Heisey, did you find that both Iranian and American young people were biased toward the other group when you began your research? How did this develop after they did their perceived drawings of the other group, and toward the end with your use of art to provide a different understanding of the other group?

Mansoureh Sharifzadeh: Yes, we could predict such a result as other research had examined Iranian American perception of each other. Tadayon (1982), World Public Opinion Organization (2007), Ehsan Shaghasemi, D. Ray. Heisey, Goudarz Mirani (2009) as well as being citizens of such nations that have been in conflict for over the last 32 years, since the collapse of the Iranian Pahlavi Dynasty and the establishment of the Islamic Republic of Iran. Media of both countries have actively been trying to depict the other nation negatively.

Both groups were biased towards each other. While the American students' drawings proved they had limited knowledge about Iran and Iranians, as they seemed not to know the difference between the Iranians and Arabs. Visiting two high schools in the United States confirmed to me that the American students were not having precise knowledge about Iran; many of them were not familiar even with the name of 'Iran', and 'Iraq'.

In Iran, all of the people recognize the US government but not the people. The Iranian students study about the US activities in their sociology and history textbooks. In Persian literature textbooks, there are narratives, descriptive writings, poems and reports on such countries as Palestine, Afghanistan and Iraq where the United States has actively been involved in wars. The students learn about the US activities in Iran during the Pahlavi dynasty in many details.

The Iranian students drew the US government's activities in the Middle East. They pursue the thoughts of Ayatollah Khomeini who called the United States 'the Great Satan whose teeth must be crushed in its mouth while not being capable of doing anything.' And, 'Kill us, more awakening will be brought to the nation and it is an honor for all of us to be martyred in the path of Islam.'

The textbooks as well as the national events as the Quds day and the 22nd of Bahman/11th of February (Victory of the Islamic Revolution of Iran) tend to bring the most awareness about the US activities.

When the paper was published in the United States, the Iranian students showed a different reaction. One of them said, "American intellectuals are quite aware of their government's mistakes and wrong actions in the world. Their movies demonstrate their falsehood. The American citizens know that their government lies, but they are not decisive enough to take action to improve the ruling system of their country. The publisher has been willing to disclose the Iranians' ideas to the world. I think that the content of the article has been pleasing as it brings more awareness to the people and is an eye opener for their government."

Michael H. Prosser: 4. You have taught English to young Iranians for several years. What are their attitudes toward learning English? In many cases, students learn grammar and vocabulary, but are unable to carry on any lengthy conversations in English. Since Iran is presently rather isolated, and English may not be the common second language, how do you see this developing in your own teaching experience?

Mansoureh Sharifzadeh: Although Iran seems to be isolated, the Iranian students are of very high potential and understanding about the importance of learning English in the world today. They know that in the later stages of their education they must comprehend different courses in English at the university; they know that it is necessary for them to deal with computers and they finally know that English is a means by which they can get a better job. In addition we are living in a global village so the Internet or satellites can transfer cultural and informational values in one way or another.

The importance of learning English is not limited to the mentioned points. In an article, Civilian Death and Injury in Iraq, 2003-2011-Neta C. Crawford, Boston University, September 2011, a Lebanese Broadcasting Corporation journalist, Burhan Fasa'a who entered Fallujah during the siege reported that he personally witnessed that "Americans did not have interpreters with them, so they entered houses and killed people because they didn't speak English! They entered the house where I was with 26 people, and shot people because they didn't obey their orders, even just because the people couldn't understand a word of English. Ninety-five percent of the people killed in the houses that I saw were killed because they couldn't speak English. Soldiers thought the people were rejecting their orders, so they shot them. But the people just couldn't understand them!"

Not being in direct contact with an international audience makes the Iranian students less motivated. Although reading and writing is compulsory at the high school level, most of them don't like to learn it due to the present weak system of teaching English system at public high schools.

The national curriculum for Teaching English language at public schools needs to be revised. In 2000, Professor Jack C. Richards made several presentations on "Issues in Foreign Language teaching in Iran". But there has never been any direct reflection on that yet.

In 2002, Dr. Mohammad Jafar Javadi presented a research in a conference at the Ministry of Education of Iran, in the Persian language. I interpreted it from Farsi to English and referred to it in one of my papers An Overview of Teaching English as a Foreign Language in Various Countries and comparing them with that of Iran, which was published in The Selected papers of the first Conference on English Language Teaching, 7-9th December 2005 in Hamedan- Iran, that will come in the following paragraphs.

In Iran two different systems of Teaching English as a Foreign Language (TEFL) are presented. One is the system which is taught at the private language centers and the other one at government schools.

There are two types of schools, private schools and government/ public schools.

Private schools try to maintain the system of private language centers such as Kish, kanoon, Milad, Shokooh, etc., integrated with the teaching system of English Language planned at the Ministry of Education. I tend to write about the public schools and private Language centers and finally comparing them with each other.

In Iran English is taught as a foreign language and it starts from the first grade at junior high school. At high school level the students are required to study English three hours a week and the number of students in one class is about 35. Compared to other countries, high school English is more grammar based and the teachers put more stress on teaching grammar and vocabulary rather than on listening and speaking.

The lack of language labs, tapes, pictures and other facilities makes the students unmotivated and different background knowledge of the students makes the teachers tired and unable to do what is necessary. The method of teaching is grammar translation and teaching is usually provided with the help of mother tongue. At schools no special supplementary reading is suggested, so the teachers decide as for the extra studying which is not paid much attention to because of the shortage of time.

The text books which are authorized by the Ministry of Education don't convey the culture of either the target language or the national identity. This makes the books unattractive.

Teacher Training Courses aren't usually performed very effectively. Evaluation of the teachers is not done very carefully and whether a teacher does her/his job satisfactory or not makes no difference in terms of her/his salary.

At schools, no attention is paid to the needs of the learner. What looks necessary to the government is usually practiced during the years. Evaluation on the students is usually based on written and oral tests, while more value is given to the final written exam.

Students are not highly motivated to learn English, as they feel no need to learn except for passing the entrance examination of the universities.

And after 6 years of studying English at junior high schools and senior high schools, they are not able to engage in simple social conversations, make practical requests, do some kind of activities like shopping, travelling and other routine daily uses of English. And the most important reason is that the English courses which are offered at junior high schools and senior high schools are not reasonably well planned, efficiently executed and don't have the characteristics of current communicative language teaching methodology.

On the other hand at the language centers, students study English sometimes up to 10 hours a week according to their needs; the number of students is usually about 10 to 15 in each class. And the syllabus appeals to the student's level.

At the mentioned English language centers, the communicative method is stressed and the textbooks are standardized. TTCs are performed both theoretically and practically; and teachers are paid according to their ability of performing their job. The final exams are both written and oral with exactly the same value. The students from different ages experience the pleasure of learning English at the English language centers.

Seminars and conferences are enlightening, although they have never been able to create a fundamental change in the process of teaching English in Iran. As "English is one of the most important means for acquiring access to the world's intellectual and technical resources" (Talebinezhad & Aliakbari, 2001), "it is an international Auxiliary Language" (Smith & Rafiqzad. 1979), and "English is a world Language" (Nunan, 1999/2000) teachers might be more capable of bringing a change in the area of their teaching due to the direct connection with the students. As a solution, I sometimes empower the imagination of the students to stimulate them to write their ideas and use their language knowledge in a more effective way as an extra activity.

Among the motivational techniques, free writing can be an effective way of encouraging the children to put down their ideas and expand them in order to be heard and read by others.

Teaching a foreign language needs patience. In my teaching experience, I usually remember my professors' teaching methods at Damavand College. When I started my education at Damavand College, my English was poor. Little by little I tried to improve myself and the good method of the professors encouraged me in learning the language. The effect still remains and has made me a long life learner as I am not in an English language speaking environment.

Michael H. Prosser: It seems possible that young Iranians may have very different attitudes towards the American government and the American people. If this is true, how would you characterize each set of attitudes?

Mansoureh Sharifzadeh: As it is explained in the third question, the youngsters usually have a common idea about the US government, but not the people since they are not in contact with any American in person. The US war actions in the region have left negative impacts on the minds of the people. Iranian media, especially the radio and TV, which have more audience, magnify and focus on the most destructive actions of the United States.

Youngsters are highly motivated about the United States through the textbooks. When it comes to the qualified students who apply for the American universities for higher education, more attention is paid to the constructive features of the United States. Otherwise the United States is considered as an everlasting 'Great Satan', As Ayatollah Khomeini suggested.

One more point is that, either positive or negative attitudes towards the American government and the American people, war actions are of great disgust. In nature, Iranians like peace. As our ancestors Zoroastrians believed in "good thoughts, good words, good deeds" (Humata, Hukhta, Hvarshta as is mentioned in Avesta), and as Muslims, the followers of Muhammad Peace Be Upon Him, and advocates of Justice and the Straight Path of Allah.

Michael H. Prosser: 6. You have had the opportunity to attend one or more conferences in the United States and to be a guest in the home of Professor and Mrs. Heisey. You have indicated that they were very kind to you and had deep respect for your own cultural and religious beliefs. How do you see the differences and similarities that you experienced in the United States and in the Heisey home in Kent, Ohio between professional Iranians and Americans, and as friends?

Mansoureh Sharifzadeh: Dr. and Mrs. Hesiey were just like my parents and quite familiar with the Iranian culture. Dr. Heisey had a broad understanding about Islam. When I was planning to go to the United States, he asked me to have my veil to wear during my stay in the United States, I told him that Hijab was enough. He respected my religious ideas. He showed me the direction towards Ka'ba to perform my prayers even at his home. He took me to the Islamic Community Center of Kent to attend the Friday Service and he himself was in the men's praying hall and observed the ritual. The Heiseys did their utmost to bring comfort to me and were very hospitable and liked their guest to feel at home.

Dr. Heisey remains an endless legend for me. I am very happy to have found the chance of knowing him more through my trip.

During my short stay in the United States, I was very pleased with the personnel of the Detroit international airport, Holiday Inn Express, Kent State University, Kent Presbyterian Church, Cuyahoga Valley Christian Academy and RHS School – Code: 362778. College and High school students paid close attention to my lectures and I didn't notice any negative attitude towards myself. Everything was fantastic and left me the best memory of my life. People were kind and friendly with me and looked at me with smiles and I was the same in return. Face to face communication brings more awareness.

Of course there was one harmful action by me. Based on Islam, shaking hands with the opposite gender is considered a sin. One day at the church a professor whom I had rejected his offer criticized me and in return I apologized and told him that the rules of Islam prohibits us from doing that. Further on Dr. Heisey told him that he himself had reminded me of not doing so as it was considered a sin.

Studying at Damavand College gave me a good opportunity to not only take advantages from my dedicated professors but also to find my best friends. They encouraged me to improve my self confidence. I can never forget my professors at Damavand College and they remain as my best friends and I have not found better friends than them.

Michael H. Prosser: 7. You have also had the opportunity to attend conferences and to meet professional teachers, researchers, and scholars from various countries. What do you see as the most common similarities and differences you have found in these different cultural and professional settings?

Mansoureh Sharifzadeh: Conferences are eye openers, the atmosphere is educational and the intellectuals gather to exchange ideas especially when it comes to the people of different countries. In Iran the topics are more oriented and not many discussions follow and usually they are forgotten and not much debate or attitudes are expressed afterwards. In the United States, there is more freedom in the case of expressing ideas. For instance when I was in the United States, I was prohibiting myself to mention Israel during my presentations, as I was thinking it would bring a negative reaction. I mentioned it and no negative response was received. In Iran, it is wiser not to focus on the political features or personalities openly. Self censorship is observed which might be the base of many differences.

Michael H. Prosser: 8. You have had opportunities to undertake religious pilgrimages in various Middle Eastern countries, such as Saudia Arabia and Iraq, and to share your worship experiences with Muslims from different points of view. What are the cultural features that these Muslims share which provide you with a greater understanding of such cultural representatives of Islamic traditions?

Mansoureh Sharifzadeh: Faith is the key to human solidarity and brings equality and unity. All religions establish a higher spiritual understanding. When the minds focus on the Lord and the messengers, such differences as sex, age, race, wealth, position, nationality are discounted.

In any religious pilgrimage the pilgrim finds her/himself in a spiritual domain and separated from the worldly values to bring tranquility and peace. In the pilgrimage places, Muslims meet each other, with the same goal. West and East come to unity with the people of Africa. The variety of ethnicities, races and nationalities give us a deeper understanding about the power of Islam. People seem to become more sincere and passionate; since they have been invited to Allah's Banquet.

Although people don't understand each other's language, they communicate with simple words as Salaam (Peace) and Eltemase Du'a or at least a simple smile. Sometimes people speak in English and exchange ideas about their country and wishing each other to come back again. Among the pilgrims, those from the Philippines or China are very calm and in harmony with beautiful dress. Indians dress beautifully and all Muslims are reminded to keep the Islamic values in all cases.

During the Hajj, Shiite and Sunni find a good opportunity to forget the differences and hold fast to the rope of Allah. Sunnis pay close attention to daily prayers and following the Sunni Imam of the two holy mosques bring us a deeper unity and brotherhood.

In the Hajj pilgrimage thousands of people from all over the world circumambulate a sacred structure at the center of the earth; all pursue a common purpose of praising Allah, yet each is engaged in private reflection oblivious of any other, with tears. Every few minutes, with a new group of people there is a fresh burst of energy. It seems the footsteps of the beloved Prophet Muhammad (Peace Be Upon Him) is pursued – he trod the same path some 1400 years ago declaring the oneness of God and Muslims do it now – the message is as pure as it was when it was first delivered. Hajj is a journey to the heart of Islam, and is called the Greatest Islamic Congress.

In Saudi Arabia, 54 degree celsius hot, it is nothing and even the hotness adds to the satisfaction.

In Iraq, Muslims pilgrimage include the shrines of the martyred Imams who sacrificed themselves for maintaining freedom and liberty in the world.

History can be touched in these areas and one finds a better reason to live. Contemplation is the least that can be gained in these trips. People talk with Allah as if He were there and listening to them. Today there are 1.2 to 1.6 billion people in the world who are Muslims and the number is increasing. These pilgrimage places are the best place to pray for the peace and tranquility in the world and reconciliation of the governments with each other.

Michael H. Prosser: 9. Despite tensions between the Iranian, European, and American governments, what steps can be taken to create greater cultural understanding and empathy at the level of civic discourse among both the well educated elites and more ordinary citizens in these countries?

Mansoureh Sharifzadeh: Communication and dialogue bring positive steps in the case of understanding and enhancing our relationship, as what we are doing now. Taking trips is another way to open our eyes.

The United Nations called 2001, the year of 'Dialogue Among Civilizations.' President Seyyed Mohammed Khatami had introduced the idea, although the term was initially used by Austrian philosopher Hans Köchler who in 1972, in a letter to UNESCO, had suggested the holding of an international conference on the "dialogue between different civilizations".

As Dr. Heisey mentioned, 'Disputes between nations should be resolved by the human behaviors of dialogue, mediation, and arbitration.' I think that dialogue and presenting ideas can be the only solution to the problem; otherwise more people will be the victims of the battle of the governments.

Cross-cultural research is a good means and brings the people to a deeper understanding about each other. Books, movies and cultural items can be of great help. The nations must know the cultural values of each other. The nations must want to have a relationship with each other. The governments must learn from the outcome of cross-cultural researchers. The people must be of value to the governments.

When I was collecting drawings for our joint paper with Dr. Heisey, I thought it would be better to collect drawings from the elementary boy school children too, since all of the present drawings are from the high school girls. So I referred to an elementary boy school in my area. In Iran, boy's and girl's schools are separated. And the women are not permitted to teach at boys' high school. When I brought up the issue to the principal he did refer me to the administration office of the Ministry of Education to explain my intentions. This happened since there is a stereotypical attitude towards the United States. I didn't pursue the case, as it would bring problems for me.

Michael H. Prosser: 10. What are several contributions that both elite and ordinary Iranians and Americans can undertake to provide greater intercultural awareness and competence in dealing with each other?

Mansoureh Sharifzadeh: Cross-cultural research helps the nations to understand each other. The result of the research must be presented to the governments and they should consult with the researchers in the field of communication to come to a better understanding about other nations.

Dr. Heisey's view was, 'We want America to show more respect and deal with others with mutuality and dignity and not treat others as inferior. We want to listen more, engage more, dialogue more, and try to see the other side more. That is what your letter is accomplishing. It allows me, an American, to hear and see what you hear and see and to take notice so that I become more aware and therefore am more understanding of where you are in your thinking and perception and experience.

Mahmood Ahmadinejad, the Iranian president, in the UN, Sep 20 2011 said, "There is no other way than the shared and collective management

of the world to put an end to the present disorders, tyranny and discriminations worldwide."

One of my students was very displeased with the walkout during the
president's speech on the 20th of Sep 2011, and said, "Our president keeps
presenting his ideas in the American universities and the U.N., although
he is never respected as a president in that country. The US authorities are
never willing to share their ideas with him face to face. The United Nations
is supposed to be a place for the leaders of the world to exchange ideas
and have dialogue on different issues to maintain peace on the earth. They
themselves can't listen to each other and the problems remain without any
change. Dialogue can be the most effective way in solving the problems
of the world". Peoples must come to a higher understanding about each
other's values even in wars.

In Iraq, a journalist wrote, "I watched American snipers shoot civilians so many times. I saw an American sniper in a minaret of a mosque
shooting everyone that moved." So, the governments must learn to be
fair even in wars, while dealing the innocent people. News of this sort is
heartbreaking indeed.

Michael H. Prosser: Do you have any additional thoughts which you
would like to share?

Mansoureh Sharifzadeh: I really enjoy your thoughtful questions, I
thank you for giving me the chance of expressing myself. I hope the people
of the world come to a deeper understanding about each other through
dialogue and exchanging ideas which is the base of any relationship.

Michael H. Prosser: Thank you.

3. Ten Cultural and Personal Questions for Mansoureh Sharifzadeh

Michael H. Prosser
University of Virginia,
Shanghai International Studies University

Mansoureh Sharifzadeh
Ministry of Education, Tehran, Iran

Michael H. Prosser: 1. In Roger Scruton's foreword to Robert R. Relly's 2010 book, The Closing of the Muslim Mind, he asks the question: "Why is it that this (Islamic) civilization, which sprang up with such an abundance of energy in the seventh century of our era, and which spread across North Africa and the Middle East to produce cities, universities, libraries, and a flourishing courtly culture which has left a permanent mark on the world, is now in so many places mute, violent , and resentful? Why does Islam today seem not merely to tolerate the violence of its fiercest advocates, but to condone and preach it?" Would you consider these to be reasonable or unreasonable claims? If you were to offer an alternative view for readers of my blog, what would be the main arguments and evidence to support your perspective?

Mansoureh Sharifzadeh: Roger Scruton's foreword to Robert R. Reily's 2010 book, The Closing of the Muslim Mind, seems quite logical to me. He has reasonable understanding about Islam and our religion with the base of politics in some case. He is a well known philosopher in Iran while many of his books are translated into Farsi.

Today the Arab nations lack a truthful leading management. In 2011 and 2012, the people of Egypt, Yemen, Lybia, Syria, decided to replace their ruling system. Muammar al-Gaddafi of Lybia, Husni Mubarak of Egypt, Ali Abdullah Saleh of Yemen were considered as dictators by the majority and overthrown. In Tunisia, the government was changed by the will of the people. Yet, a true leadership cannot decide to establish new governments that the people approve in Egypt, Yemen and Lybia. The interference of such countries as the USA, Israel, the UK and other superpowers doesn't let the nations decide for themselves and live at peace in order to think about other advancements in the realm of the rich Islamic knowledge, philosophy and education which the world is quite familiar with.

Let's consider Iran as an example. The reason that the Revolution of Iran gained victory was because of the strong and so called divine leadership of Ayatollah Khomeini whose ideas and perspectives were understood and followed by the majority. His commands were the main reason for Iran's victory over Saddam Hussain who brought us the most painful moments in 1980-1988. Although Islam has pervaded state politics and the Islamic Republic of Iran has always been trying to advance this country in cultural and scientific aspects, it has always been facing numerous pressures from the anti-Iran activists. The pressures are either financially or psychologically along with threats to create problematic spheres.

Sanctions, assassinations of the most sincere nuclear energy scientists are just a portion of their threats. So in this case, how can this nation be expected to have great advancements in the cases that Roger Scruton expects based on the history of the Islamic nationality?

In the case of individuals or nations, advancements find ways under the shadow of peace and tranquility. The world knows that Iran or many other Islamic countries treasure the most talented students who leave their country and are absorbed by the scientific centers of the west while 'Muslim' must be wiped out in order to be accepted by those organizations.

Some say, as long as we are Muslims and own oil, we will never experience peace and the achievements that Roger Scruton mentions. Superpowers must consider the right of all nations as equally as theirs. September 11, 2001 happened to prove power, it was a challenge and an accomplishment to show the ability of those who have been let down by the global arrogance.

Roger Scruton is right; but Muslims must discuss and exchange ideas with those who value their ideas and have ears to listen and eyes to see the right of all nations.

Michael H. Prosser: 2. In Zhang Shengyong's and my essay, "A Comparative Review: 2010 Middle East Books" in the September 2010 issue of the Journal of Middle East and Islamic Studies (in Asia), we state that "Reilly indicates that the mind of many Muslims throughout the world frequently has not closed intellectually and suicidally, ... but that too many of the two billion current Muslims accept the flawed concept that only what Allah wills or does not will incomprehensively have any authority in all matters of human existence. A key question for Reilly is how so many current intelligent Muslims blindly can accept these earlier arguments over the nature of Allah that since Allah only wills or does not will, nothing that humans do can occur except in obedience or defiance of Allah's will." Reilly's book was philosophical, historical, and political. Do you agree or disagree with these arguments and why?

Mansoureh: Sharifzadeh: As a Muslim, I do agree with what the Qu'ran teaches and I always refer to it to find the best answers. Several verses explore the fact that we are engaged in Allah's will while some more indicate our freedom in decision making and choosing the best alternative. The will of God for us is to go through the actions which are considered right in the realm of Islamic guidelines. For me it means taking action and even encounter risks to gain the goal, but if I come across an obstacle, I assume it has not been right for me and it has been the will of God to change the path. We have been thought that the will of God is always in our favor as God is the compassionate and merciful. Even we assume the problems as a means to be tested. This perspective helps us in trouble and makes us more patient. A verse from the Qu'ran indicates that 'we are from God and will return to him'. ان ا لله و انا عليه راجعون.

In the following verses, the Qu'ran focuses on the power and will of God and the domination of Allah's power in different aspects of our lives.

1. In the 97th Surah of Qu'ran, Al-Qadr, Allah reads: "Indeed, We sent the Qur'an down during the Night of Decree. And what can make you know what is the Night of Decree? The Night of Decree is better than a thousand months. The angels and the Spirit descend therein by permission of their Lord for every matter. Peace it is until the emergence of dawn."

2. In the 3rd Surah of Qu'ran i.e., Aale – Imran – verse 47- 48, Allah reads: "She (Mary) said: "O my Lord! How shall I have a son when no man hath touched me?" He (the angels) said: "Even so: Allah createth what He willeth: When He hath decreed a plan, He but says to it, 'Be,' and it is! And Allah will teach him the Book and Wisdom, the Law and the Gospel."

In the 15th Surah of Qu'ran, i.e. Al – Hijrverse – verse 21, Allah reads; "And there is not a thing but that with Us are its depositories, and We do not send it down except according to a known measure."

3. In the 67th Surah of the Qu'ran. i.e. Sūrah al-Mulk in verse 1-2, Allah reads; "Blessed is He in whose hand is dominion, and He is over all things competent - [He] who created death and life to test you [as to] which of you is best in deed – and He is the Exalted in Might, the Forgiving."

4. In the 74th Sura of the Qu'ran, i.e. 'Sūrat al-Muddaththir, in verse 38, Allah reads: "Every soul, for what it has earned, will be retained."

5. In the 91st Sura of the Qu'ran, i.e. 'Shams', in verse, 8, Allah reads, "Then He showed him what is wrong for him and what is right for him."

In this regard, Muslims believe that there is freedom of choice to take action but in the limitations of the Islam guidelines. A Muslim must take those actions that are free of sin and confirmed in the Qu'ran. Otherwise he/she goes beyond the borders of Islam and is sinful.

What are the 'wills' of God? Those which are mentioned in the Holy book of Qu'ran. One must avoid what is against the will of God which is nothing but unrighteousness and corruption. Of course, I am not a scholar in this field and whatever I say is based on my general understanding.

The following Chapters from the holy book of Qu'ran, imply the freedom of Muslims in taking action and choosing the best way, as they are the main decision makers. God shows the ways and people must choose the best whereas several ways are ahead.

Eight times a day, the Muslims recite Surah Al- fattehe the 1st Surah of Qu'ran, while saying their prayers. In the 5th and 6th verses of this Surah, it reads; "Guide us to the right path. The path of those upon whom thou has bestowed favors, Not of those who thou has cursed once nor of those who have gone astray."

In this way Muslims beseech Allah not to leave them to themselves. This doesn't mean that they sit and wait for occults, but they take actions with complete awareness of being right.

On the other hand, there are numerous verses that tell us to do, and not wait for the divine to do everything for us. Some examples are mentioned in the following lines:

1. In the 13th Sura of the Qu'ran, verse 11, it reads, "surely Allah does not change the condition of a people until they change their own condition." There are many interpretations related to this Surah that are of important consideration.

2. More examples in this regard can be found in these chapters of Qu'ran. 2:286; 5:105; 6: 104,113, 130, 131; 8:42; 10:42, 43, 44, 108; 41:40; 53:36, 37, 38; 2: 286; 4: 79.

So, I can say that the will of God is what is considered the best by Allah and those who can realize the best way are the representatives of the prophet of Allah; i.e. clergies and ruling system of any Islamic nation that are considered the best decision makers who must be followed by the people.

The Islamic Republic of Iran has been approved by the majority of the Iranian population. The claim can be proved in different occasions as the Quds day, elections for the presidency and Parliament of Iran and more national occasions that people rally in the street to confirm their government.

Michael H. Prosser: 3. In Surah 4: Section 8, "An-Nisa: The Women," the Holy Qur'an states: "Men are the protectors and maintainers of women, because Allah has given the one more (strength) than the other, and because they support them from their means. Therefore, the righteous women are devoutly obedient, and guard in (the husband's) absence what Allah would have them guard. As for those women on whose part ye fear disloyalty and ill-conduct, admonish them (first), (next), refuse to share their beds, (and last) chastise them (lightly); but if they return to obedience, seek not against them means (of annoyance): for Allah is Most High Great (above you all)." More and more young women coming from various religious traditions in different societies seek full equality with the men, and even with their husbands. How does a traditional Islamic society like Iran deal with such a modern contradiction to the prescriptions of the Holy Qur'an?

Mansoureh Sharifzadeh: In Surah 34: section 8, 'An Nisa', is one of the verses that usually bring disputes in different Muslim nations too. One must know that, each verse has been revealed to the prophet of Islam under a certain circumstance. The circumstance must be taken under consideration otherwise it is not easy to digest and understand the case and it might be misunderstood.

The story is that, in the ancient times, Arab men often hit their wives for no good reasons. The women came to Mohammad (P. B. U. H) and complained. Afterwards, this verse was revealed to the prophet to give advice to the men and guide them. Nowadays, Muslim men don't do such an action whereas in the west it may happen more, as there are organizations to support the women in this case.

Besides, in the Marriage Books of the Islamic Republic of Iran, there are new tips to support the women more. Women can claim dowry and husband must pay right away, but Iranian women don't do it lest it may weaken the emotional relationship, as marriage is not an investment.

Equality of men and women is not the case; women are thought to be of a higher rank. Women are wives, mothers and the main manager of their home. In this society all women can pursue their education to the highest degree and have jobs with an equal salary as the men do. Women can have different jobs as men do as being educators, nurses, police, pilot, physician, researcher, Parliament representatives, and ministers and so on. The only thing that women are prohibited to do publicly is singing, dancing, doing such sports as swimming as for athletic results. There are some halls where women can attend to enjoy their favorite women singers' performances. There are halls where the models demonstrate fashion only for the women.

Women can own different sectors as publications and any form of ownership. Women can drive; while they are never streets waste collectors but can work as attendants and very often waiters in the restaurants.

The only case is the importance of their dignity and maintaining their chastity. Women are free to choose their Hijab. Some wear chador (veil) and others don't while wearing hijab (scarf) is compulsory. Virtues of women are respected in Islam and in this society chastity must be kept to bring the ideas of Islam into existence.

In "Separation" a film by Asghar Panahi, which won the Oscar prize in 2012, a typical Iranian woman is clearly defined. In the last episode, the woman is shown in a more limited condition in comparison with her husband, whereas both wait for their child to make the last decision and that's the reality of the Iranian family lives.

Anyhow, Iranian women may afford more, but never claim for the equality with men as we feel we are in a higher position. It is necessary to quote Mohammad (P. B. U. H), "Paradise lies at the foot of the Mothers." Which of course, true mothers have certain characteristics.

And finally I suggest this document that might be of interest: http://www.iranchamber.com/history/rkhomeini/books/women_position_khomeini.pdf

Michael H. Prosser: 4. There are 41 references in the Holy Qur'an to the concept of Jihad or the struggle to strive to live in union with Allah. From Wikepedia, we learn that: "According to the authoritative dictionary of Islam Jihad is defined as: "A religious war with those who are unbelievers in the mission of Muhammad ... enjoined especially for the purpose of advancing Islam and repelling evil from Muslims.... An accurate interpretation of the concept of Jihad is provided by the BBC about how Muslims describe three different types of struggles: A believer's internal struggle to live out the Muslim faith as well as possible, the struggle to build a good Muslim society, Holy war: the struggle to defend Islam, with force if necessary." How do Iranian Muslims see these different dimensions of the BBC interpretation and what implications do they have for the current Iranian conflict with the Western nations over Iran's nuclear policies?

Mansoureh Sharifzadeh: Some news agencies try to create conflict and bring up some points that are never focused on in this era. Honestly, this is the first time that I read such a thing. As I see, today, superpowers attack Islamic nations in order to keep them on their seat.

Iran has never attacked any nation but has defended itself in case of attacks. I read, "The United States, Israel and their allies accuse Iran of trying to build nuclear weapons. While Washington has repeatedly threatened Tehran with the "all potions" mantra, Tel Aviv openly speaks of a military strike against the Islamic Republic. Iran, a member of the International Atomic Energy Agency (IAEA) and a signatory to the Nuclear Non-Proliferation Treaty (NPT), refutes the allegations, saying its nuclear energy program is peaceful in nature. Iranian officials have vowed a crushing response to any act of aggression against the country.   (http://www.islamtimes.org/vdcjvhevouqexaz.92fu.html).

I include only one of the Surah of Qu'ran, 3:62; which brings unity between all of the believers, [3:65] Say, "O People of the Book! come to a word equal between us and you – that we worship none but Allah, and that we associate no partner with Him, and that some of us take not others for Lords beside Allah. But if they turn away, then say, 'Bear witness that we have submitted to God.'" (Book means the holy books of the former prophets, i.e. The Bible and Torah.).

The above verse emphasizes a unity between all of the followers of God, either Christians or Jews or Muslims. Muslims, believe in the former prophets and as much as I know, they never attack any nation for being non-Muslim, this won't happen in the future as it is quite unreasonable. Ayatollah Khamenei said; "The nations must think differently and know that any attack will be answered with the same measure."

Michael H. Prosser: 5. In his very sensational and highly polemical New York Times best-selling 2010 book, The Grand Jihad, Andrew C. McCarthy's book promotion asserts that: "The real threat to the United States is not terrorism. The real threat is the sophisticated forces of Islamism, which have collaborated with the American Left not only to undermine US national security, but also to shed the fabric of American constitutional democracy – freedom and individual liberty … and how it has found the ideal partner in President Barack Obama, whose Islamist sympathies run deep." How should those of us who believe that a dialogue among civilizations is far better than a clash among civilizations react to such arguments and convince other intelligent people in Iran and the US to accept our premises rather than McCarthy's?

Mansoureh Sharifzadeh: The first and last words in this regard have been expressed by Imam Khomeini about the United States. He saw no need to do any sort of dialogue with the United States. Ayatollah Khamenei in one of his speeches on Friday 5 June 2009 09:59 said: "The nations in the region hate the United States from the bottom of their hearts because they have seen violence, military intervention and discrimination. The new US government seeks to transform this image. I say firmly, that this will not be achieved by words, speeches and slogans. "They have done things that have deeply hurt the nations in the region … things are not going to be changed by speeches. He (Obama) has to do it in practice. Even if he delivers hundreds of speeches and talks very sweetly, there will not be a change in how the Islamic countries perceive the United States." Imam Khamenei also accused the United States of "lying" about Tehran's nuclear program. "They lied about our intention; they concealed the truth about it. They stood against the legitimate rights of our nation. We have said several times that we want the nuclear energy for industrial and peaceful purposes. But they continuously say that Iran is seeking nuclear bombs. By doing this, they are hated by our nation. For many years, our nation and its officials have repeatedly said that we do not want nuclear weapon, it is Ḥarām (forbidden) in Islam. Even if they pay us to have it, we do not want it, but in order to justify their allegations they continue accusing us. They bomb innocent civilians in Afghanistan. What is the difference between this killing and killing by terrorists? He said in Iraq, the United States was "supporting the Baathist elements", in reference to members of Saddam Hussein's Baath party, many of whom are returning to government jobs in the new regime of Iraq. He (Obama) has to change these things."

Of course dialogue among the intellectuals has not been condemned in any one of the speeches, so it is safe, I assume. And I think the governments must come to a better solution than wars as the history proves it to be the worst way in solving problems while a lot of destructions remain and hatred increases among nations.

Michael H. Prosser: 6. Steven Kinzer's 2010 book: Reset: Iran, Turkey and America's Future argues that "Iran is the big country in the Middle East ... The United States should shape its policy not by emotional past insults by Iran, or by a cool calculation of self-interest. ... The tragedy of America's long estrangement from Iran is that it has undermined America's own interest." Kinzer proposes that the United States should have to recognize Iran as an important power with legitimate security interests while remembering that a nuclear armed Iran would cause a major security threat to the entire Middle Eastern region. "Iran is the only Muslim country in the world where most people are reliably pro American. This pro-American sentiment in Iran is a priceless strategic asset for the United States." How would you assess Kinzer's arguments in light of a potential reconciliation between Iran and the United States?

Mansoureh Sharifzadeh: The United States must stop its cruel actions in the region. During the past 30 years it has been moving from one country to another one and actually has been trying to surround Iran. The bloodsheds have left vicious memory about the United States in the mind of the Iranians. Even the younger generation never accepts any reconciliation with the United States with the present condition. Kinzer has a good understanding about the Iranians and the 8 year war with Iraq has proven a lot. Now Iran is more powerful than in the 80s and has established a stronger defense system while 60 percent of the population of Iran is under 30 who will voluntarily take part in any clash.   (http://www.slate.com/articles/news_and_politics/explainer/2009/06/the_iranian_baby_boom.html)

Michael H. Prosser: 7. Joe Klein, writing in the March 5, 2012 Time Magazine comments: "Any unprovoked war with Iran would be crazy. It is a real country – not a cobbled-together colonial whim like Iraq – with strong national pride, a great historic culture and probably the best educated populace in the region, outside of Israel. An attack on Iran would unify the populace ... The US military and intelligence services oppose such an effort."

In your recent post on my blog, "Creating wars and international solutions," you write: "Something which is noticeable is that President Obama is quite aware of the billboard quotes in Tehran and the distance between Tehran and White House has given way to a close relationship in awareness and understanding about Iran. So it can be said that conflicts can bring relationships, closeness and awareness too." Can you elaborate further about why you believe that "conflicts can bring relationships, closeness and awareness too"? How can these relationships, closeness, and awareness help the international situation between Iran and the Western countries?

Mansoureh Sharifzadeh: I always think that those whom we love or hate the most can never be forgotten. This act means "not forgetting" brings us unity and closeness. This gives the people of extremes a tighter relationship. They always remain in each other's mind. Enemies try to find ways to attack each other, so they look for more features to find a deeper understanding about the other side. I see that the intellectuals of the United States are trying to go deeper into the mind of the Iranians, if Iranians were mute, the intellectuals were never so interested as they are today about them.

It was very interesting for me to know that President Obama knows that on the billboard in Tehran, the word bluff has been written. This proves that, Iranians are paid attention to, so this brings closeness and awareness for both of our nations. Iran and the US relationship is finding a legendary story.

The United States likes Iran which is our beautiful country with a cat shape map. Cats are nice as long as no one harms them, but as soon as they feel danger they paw to defend. Iran never attacks but defends and that has been its strategy as long as I remember in my life time.

Separation always brings misunderstandings. When people communicate, they find more positive features in each other's personality or at least they become familiar with the true intentions of each other. In this process a lot of problems might be solved. For instance, nowadays, many countries own nuclear energy, but when it comes to Iran, the world shakes and thinks that the only purpose is producing nuclear weapons and can never accept that producing Nuclear energy as for creating wars is considered Ḥarām in Islam.

Michael H. Prosser: 8. In the March 5, 2012 Time Magazine, Babak Dehghanpisheh says: "Iran is in the midst of a vicious economic crisis…. The value of the currency, the rial, has dropped by nearly half against the dollar in the past month, the price of meat has tripled to nearly $30 per kilo, and the price of tea has doubled." Writing in the March 19, 2012 Time Magazine, Massimo Calbresi and Jay Newton Small state: "For the past six months, Obama's Iran strategy has been gaining force and credibility, as international sanctions have finally begun to bite…. The results have been crippling; the rial, the Iranian currency, has lost 75% of its value, and the country is suffering from hyperinflation…. Iran has never before been so alone." Historically, sanctions have been seen to have both positive and negative effects, but especially negative on the ordinary people of the country being sanctioned. Quite apart from the intergovernmental implications, can you reflect on how you see these sanctions are negatively affecting ordinary citizens financially in Iran at the present time?

Mansoureh Sharifzadeh: In the message of the leader of Iran, Ayatollah Khamenei as for Nowruz, 1991/2012, he warned the people of being more cautious about the economic situation by these words: "'Economic' Jihad, which was the slogan of the previous year, is never-ending, adding that one important aspect of economic issues is 'domestic production.'" He added, if domestic production prospers, most of the enemy's efforts will undoubtedly fail. And the prosperity of national production is the key to resolving the problems of inflation and unemployment and will strengthen domestic economy. (http://now-ruz.com/portal/en/tabid/138/articleType/ArticleView/ articleId/423/IR-Leader-1391-year-of-National-Production.aspx)

One of the most important characteristics of the people is adapting themselves to the new condition. People have been through war and are familiar with this problem. Yes, it is difficult for the people, but they increase their working hours and Iranians are very good at saving money as they have been through ups and downs all through the history.

Michael H. Prosser: 9. Thanks to our mutual friendship with the late Professor D. Ray Heisey (d. May 20, 2011), there are now already more than a dozen posts on my blog, starting with your project together in inviting young students to talk and draw pictures about their images of each other in Iran and the United States; several of your own thoughtful posts on various issues of interest internationally from your Iranian perspective; and most recently our ten question intercultural dialogues. Even though we are separated by thousands of kilometers and come from potentially hostile governmental attitudes toward each other, if we had an opportunity to coauthor a book together on Iranian-US relations as a dialogue between civilizations, what would be some of the major concepts that we should consider?

Mansoureh: Sharifzadeh: In 2000, when I heard about the internet, I decided to learn working with the computer to find my former professors at Damavand College. Now I find a lot of advantages as being in contact with different people especially Dr. Heisey who taught me a lot and opened many closed doors and left me to push them wide open to come to a better understanding about the world and people around. With his departure, you were born in this virtual world and I am grateful to his memory that brought me deeper understanding.

And finally, anything that brings a better understanding among the nations especially Iran and the USA. When I was in the United States, I was noticing many youngsters not knowing anything about Iran or any other country far from them. I sometimes imagine a society where all of the people know the beauty of existence and friendship. It is depressing for me to find people unkind to each other. God is beauty and kind and expects us to be the same, why not?

Michael H. Prosser: Is there anything else that you would like to add?

Mansoureh Sharifzadeh: I wish the people of the world a much greater understanding about the purpose of creation which is nothing but knowing our creator and ourselves to enhance this temporary center of life and prepare ourselves for a better condition which is waiting for us hereafter. Amen. And thank you.´

Michael H. Prosser: Thanks for continuing our Iranian-American inter-cultural dialogue.

4. TEN PROFESSIONAL QUESTIONS FOR PROFESSOR FARZAD SHARIFIAN

Mansoureh Sharifzadeh
The Ministry of Education, Tehran, Iran

Professor Farzad Sharifian
Monash University, Australia,
Author of Cultural Conceptualizations and Language

Biography: Farzad Sharifian

Farzad Sharifian (PhD.) is a leading linguist with a multidisciplinary background in cognitive science, anthropology and education. He is a pioneer of cultural linguistics. He has made theoretical advancements including a theoretical model of cultural conceptualisations and language. This theoretical model and its applications in the areas of intercultural communication, cross-cultural pragmatics, second language learning, and political discourse analysis are the subject of his monograph entitled Cultural conceptualisations and Language (John Benjamins, 2011). Farzad Sharifian is also the founder of the academic program of English as an International Language within the School of Languages, Cultures, and Linguistics, Monash University. He is the Editor, (with Prof. Ning Yu, Oklahoma University) of Cognitive Linguistic Studies in Cultural Contexts, book series, John Benjamins [flyer]. In 2011, he was the Chair of the 17th conference of the International Association of World Englishes (IAWE) at Monash University (November, 23-25, 2011).

The interview refers to Chapters 8- 14, emphasizing the Farsi language. Amsterdam, The Netherlands, John Benjamins, 2011.

Mansoureh Sharifzadeh: 1. Could you please tell us in your own words what the book is about?

Farzad Sharifian: The book is about the relationship between language, culture, and conceptualisation. Over the last two decades, cognitive linguistics has offered a new approach to the study of language by exploring the relationship between language and conceptualisation. However, the role of culture in shaping our conceptualisation of the experience, I believe, has not been adequately explored in cognitive linguistics, and this is what I have tried to focus on over the last ten years. So the book covers the result of over a decade of my research into the investigation of the ways in which conceptualisation interacts with culture and the reflection of this interaction in language. The book also covers research that shows how I have drawn on the model of cultural conceptualisations and language that I have developed, to explore aspects of intercultural communication, language learning, cross-cultural pragmatics, and political discourse analysis.

Mansoureh Sharifzadeh: 2. In Cultural Conceptualizations and Language, in chapters 8 to 14, Iranian cultural habits that tend to honor the whole process of communication are brought up. There are such cultural schemas as 'sharmanedegi', 'hormate kalam', and 'ghedasate kalam', which bring a sacredness and chastity of speech as you say. In your different articles, you focus on the cultural values of Iranians in communicating with others through their language. How would your writings and these cultural measurements help in bringing awareness to the people of the West about Iran and vice versa?

Farzad Sharifian: I didn't really just mean to increase awareness about the Iranian cultural norms of communication among the people in the West, but for anyone who is interested in learning about the relationship between language and culture. In particular in those writings that you refer to I explored certain cultural concepts that significantly impact language use among speakers of Persian, just to provide examples of the ways in which meanings are embedded in cultural conceptualisations. I think having the knowledge of those concepts would reduce chances of intercultural miscommunication between speakers of Persian and non-Persian speakers, from any national background.

Mansoureh Sharifzadeh: 3. Chapters 8-11 are committed to such concepts as 'adab', 'shekastenafsi', 'aberu', 'ta'rof', 'nafs', the beautiful concepts of 'del' with its wide and poetical notions, while in chapters 12 to 14, we encounter the translators that don't consider our cultural background and with the usage of their words bring the political conditions into clash. How could these sorts of interpretations be avoided not to lead them to neglect profound Iranian cultural background?

Farzad Sharifian: I don't think it is simply a matter of interpretation and knowledge. I think the discourse of politicians, both Iranian and non-Iranian, are often intentionally mistranslated/misrepresented to achieve certain political agendas. In the writings that you refer to I try to show specific examples of this mistranslation/ misrepresentation in action.

Mansoureh Sharifzadeh: 4. In Cultural Conceptualisation and Language, there are many Farsi sentences and words as those on pages 141, 143, and some more that have been written with the aid of English alphabets which is referred to as 'finglish' in Iran, rather than phonetic symbols, which would make the pronunciations more appropriate for nonnative Farsi speakers. What I mean is in the long term, doesn't this create a risk of bringing our written language into the state of Turkish language that uses the English alphabet?

Farzad Sharifian: I don't think all readers of my work would be able to read phonetic symbols, and that is why I, and many others, use English words to write the Persian words for non-Persian readers. It is really not my writings, but the use of the new technology, including mobile phones for text messaging, and computers for emailing and chatting etc that has led to this kind of usage, I mean the use of 'finglish' as you call it. This is a major problem, but I guess the increasing use of Persian fonts in the new technology is battling that.

Mansoureh Sharifzadeh: 5. In several cases as on pages 153 -154, it has been brought into consideration that culture is of a higher importance than language. How should the Iranians living in other parts of the world preserve their culture and transfer it to their next generation? And how important is it to maintain Iranian cultural values wherever we are?

Farzad Sharifian: That is a difficult question to answer. A lot depends on what you mean by culture, material aspects of culture, such as food, dress, etc or cultural norms, as for example reflected in language use? It is really not up to me to mandate how my fellow Iranians should preserve our culture, but in general I think our fellow Iranians living outside Iran have got the chance to learn about many other cultures and then reflect on their own cultural norms and habits, and I think this is empowering. The other aspect to this question is the fact that naturally many Iranians become more aware of their cultural identity, and try to protect it when they start living in societies other than Iran, and that is natural and is observed among many other ethnic backgrounds. A lot of Iranians living outside Iran regularly get together, for example for poetry nights, to enjoy and reinforce certain aspects of their cultural heritage.

Mansoureh Sharifzadeh: 6. On page 144, Beeman (1986) compares personal relations in Iran to an art that requires sophisticated verbal skills. On page 145, Taghavi compares 'tarof' with a war. As a person who has been living in the west since July 1998 and in direct contact with different nationalities and cultures, how can you compare our cultural values with theirs? What can be considered the best or the worst? Please give some examples. What is the best cultural values of the people of the West that you deal with?

Farzad Sharifian: I really don't evaluate cultural norms, they are what they are, cultural norms and values. Personally I have been interacting with many people from a large variety of cultures and I have really enjoyed them, because I learn about other cultures and in learning about other cultures I learn about our own culture and my own share of the Iranian culture. I can say that in general exposure to other cultures have expanded my horizons and my attitudes towards many aspects of my life.

Mansoureh Sharifzadeh: 7. In Cultural Conceptualisation and Language, as a psycholinguist, you explore the daily and routine words that are exchanged among the Iranians. Couldn't we consider language as a habit oriented skill rather than conscious rules and pre-planned intentions?

Farzad Sharifian: I don't think language is just one of them, it is both and much more. We underestimate the significance of language in our lives. It is the main tool that we use to express our emotions, thoughts, personality traits, etc. Certain aspects of language are more habitual and certain aspects lend themselves more to conscious choice and reflection.

Mansoureh Sharifzadeh: 8. In this global village that the nations can easily get in touch, would it be predictable for the peoples to come to such a unity that a unique worldwide culture establishes?

Farzad Sharifian: I really don't believe in the emergence of a unified worldwide culture, unless what you mean is for all the people around the world to come to watch the same movies, wearing similar clothes, etc. As I said before, as people come to live and work closer together, many people become more conscious and protective of their cultural values and norms than before. However, what I see happening is people adopting values and norms from several cultures. Many people now live intercultural and multicultural lives. Globalization and trans-cultural/trans-national mobility has made the notion of 'culture' very complex for many people.

Mansoureh Sharifzadeh: 9. There are numerous notions that are used by the World English speakers, how could an English language teacher of Iran bring the same cultural values of the target language into her/his class atmosphere while the texts never tend to convey the culture of the target language?

Farzad Sharifian: I am not sure what you mean by "the culture of the target language." English is now associated with many cultures and not just one. The whole point is that English language teachers in Iran, and elsewhere for that matter, should raise awareness among their students about the fact that English is a multicultural language and during international communication in English speakers from different cultural backgrounds draw on various systems of cultural conceptualisations. So what we really need to focus on more and more is developing intercultural communication skills in our students.

Mansoureh Sharifzadeh: 10. On page 146, Speaker A says, 'Na jooneh to ...', how important is it to highlight such colloquial parts of speech?

Farzad Sharifian: Some colloquial expressions are associated with what I have called cultural conceptualisations and they are likely to impact and surface in intercultural communication. I have tried to highlight and analyze some of those in my writings, such as cheshmaatun ghashang mibineh meaning "your eyes see beautifully" in response to a compliment.

Mansoureh Sharifzadeh: Do you have any additional thoughts which you would like to share?

Farzad Sharifian: I would like to stress that my main aim in putting together all the work that I have done during the past decade in that book is to show how language and culture are inter-related through conceptualisations that are culturally constructed, or what I have called cultural conceptualisations. I have not found this link in a laboratory or through experimental research but as a result of living in a multicultural society for about one and a half decade. I have closely witnessed during everyday of my life in the last 14 years how language, culture, conceptualisation, and identity are interwoven and how each one is complex in its own right. I took the chance of writing this book to share my experiences with others, and I hope the readers find it helpful in encouraging them to reflect on their own experiences.

Mansoureh Sharifzadeh: Thank you.

C) Cultural Stories

1. The Iran Youth Is Getting Older

Mansoureh Sharifzadeh
Ministry of Education, Tehran, Iran

The collapse of the Pahlavi dynasty in the late 1970s gave birth to an infant named the 'Islamic Republic Of Iran', with the purpose of transforming the history of the monarchy of Iran into an everlasting Islamic conclusion.

The early Iranians began training their children as infants, so the new born baby was being raised, but with the purpose of having no trace of its late Zoroastrian ancestors. The baby was being given enough commands to digest the guidelines of a true Islam that was accepted by its ancestors about 1400 years ago while being mixed with the former beliefs.

As a toddler it was given special attention not to be pretentious with the degraded ideas of the East and the West. it should become powerful enough to cope with the assaults of the Western neighbor, Iraq that broke an eight year war attack from September 1980.

In 1980, the Cultural Revolution Committee was formed to issue rules for nourishing the kid's school days with Islamic and desired national and international values. New identities were given to the textbooks as the main media to expose the kid with the pure guidelines of accurate Mohammadan Islam and worldwide politics. The main idea of the textbooks were derived from the quote of the founder of the Islamic Republic of Iran, Ayatollah Khomeini: "The Muslims must use the power of the Islamic Republic of Iran for crushing the teeth of this domineering government (USA) in its mouth and observe the flower of freedom, Tohid (oneness of God) and Imamah (leadership) that will blossom out in the realm of the Messenger of God." After his departure on June 3, 1989, his commentary has been adapted by the second leader; Ayatollah Khamenei to give awareness to the school children about the enemies.

During the school years all students were segregated by sex, and the kid got familiar with the history, geography, and literature of Persia as well as the world in brief and general. The kid was given some information about the Persian kings in the sociology textbooks too. In the literature textbooks, the noble poets and writers of Iran such as Sanaee Ghaznavi, Gheisar Aminpoor, Hafiz, Morteza Avini, Martyre Morteza Motahari, Salman Harati, and many others were introduced as well as some works of Tagoor, a Palestinian poet – Nazar Ghabani, Victor Hogue, Antoine de Saint-Exupéry's The Little Prince, Robert Fisher's story and some less known writers and poets. In the theology textbooks, the religious identity of the kid was being shaped as a correct Muslim.

In the fields of science and mathematics adequate knowledge was being taught by the hard working teachers. The kid was witnessing that although the founder of the ISRI Ayatollah Khomeini said, "Teaching and learning are both devotions" and "Tutorial is the profession of the Prophets", the teachers were held in very low respect and were not paid enough as the other sectors of the government. Ayatollah's respected ideas motivated the teachers not to demand higher salary so as to satisfy God.

The teachers were exposed with a method that urged them to keep the new school child with memorization that was forming the heart of the educational system. The kid was getting tired of having demanded more details by its teachers. So the curriculum tried to upgrade the quality of the educational system at all levels, and develop appropriate programs of vocational training. [1]

It is necessary to mention that the commands of Islam and Zoroastrianism had taught the parents to pay special attention to the education of the kids, so they were supposed to spend all of their time on instruction based on the new trends. This form of education provided the youth with both individual and public learning.

During the high school years, the kid started learning two foreign languages; English and Arabic at the same time. This made it confused and the lack of communicative method made it unmotivated. Not being in direct communication with the native speakers and just relying on the textbooks without any variety in method of teaching materials, made it bored and didn't reveal why a foreign language should be learned.

During this period it got more familiar with the history of the world and other topics. Its political and literal awareness was in the way of improvement. Meanwhile it was realizing sex discrimination in different textbooks i.e., more concentration was given to the boys.

By the end of its high school education it got familiar with a new device – Computer – that associated it with the Internet and as a result to the world. This was the first step to a new awareness that the global village needed means of communication and dialogue. The world of Internet, chat rooms, DVDs, politics and satellite TV opened its eyes to a new world.

While being university students, it understood that there were approximately 92,500 public Iranian educational institutions at all levels, with a total enrollment of approximately 17,488,000 students. [13]

In 1997, there were 9,238,393 pupils enrolled in 63,101 primary schools, with 298,755 teachers. The student-to-teacher ratio stood at 31 to 1. In that same year, secondary schools had 8,776,792 students and 280,309 teachers. The pupil-teacher ratio at the primary level was 26 to 1 in 1999. In the same year, 83% of primary-school-age children were enrolled in school.

And according to the CIA World Fact book, from information collected in 2002, 83.5% of males and 70.4% of females over the age of 15 were literate, thus 77% of the population was literate. [14]

In 2007, the majority of students (60%) enrolled in Iranian universities were women. [11] According to the UNESCO world survey, Iran has the highest female to male ratio at primary level of enrollment in the world among sovereign nations, with a girl to boy ratio of 1.22 : 1.00. [15]

University education was an eye and mind opener for it in many cases such as knowing about the fact that Iran currently has 54 state operated universities, and 42 state medical schools. There are 289 major private universities operating as well. [12] In addition there are over 40,000 students engaged in masters programs and 20,000 students in PhD programs. In all these schools, except for private universities such as the Islamic Azad University system, tuition and room and board, are mostly paid for by the government. The universities themselves largely operate on state budgets. There are also institutes like Payame Noor University that offer degrees remotely or online. Of course, very recently the President of Iran has announced that many college courses taught by Iranian Universities are too westernized and do not comply with Moslem law. Those courses may be changed radically to comply with Moslem law – or they may be completely eliminated.

Now it is a 33 years old matured Iranian with a job. Although many of its friends have left the country or a few are being attracted to an irrelevant carrier or unemployed, it still loves its country that has a population of about 75,330,000 and with the total area of 1,648,195 km2 (18th). The culture and the height of Mount Damavand and Alborz mountains are of its complete attraction. It loves a country that consists of 31 districts with various climates in the same season. The kid loves taking a 1 hour air flight from Tehran to Kish or Qeshm Island to enjoy the mildest weather in winter and swim in the clean water of the Persian Gulf. it enjoys travelling to the beautiful North of Iran to enjoy the cool and pleasing weather of Sabalan in the midst summer hot days of Tehran.

It enjoys listening to different accents and dialects of the people as well as the traditional Persian music, although females are not permitted to sing songs individually as it has been restricted by the commands of Islam.

It still loves the 'Islamic Republic' as a young nation, with 35 percent of its population between the ages of 15 and 29, one of the highest shares in the world. Although complete Islamic rights are not being seriously practiced about the females, it hopes for a day that the words of the founder of the Islamic republic of Iran will soon be practiced. He said, "We are proud that our women, young and old, regardless of their status, are present and active, side by side with the men, often more active than men, in all scenes including cultural, economic and military areas. They strive, sometimes more effectively than the men".

It demands the world, especially the United States, to create more opportunities for the cross cultural activities and as for its country a freer atmosphere in which activists, such as students and journalists, can express their ideas about the management performance more openly without any fear which is the base of any democracy. It desires for an intercultural relationship with the intellectuals of the world to come across a better model for the young and to present a model to the young Americans to become more familiar with Iranians and their culture.

Khoda Negahdar (God protects you!)

(The identified notes come from Wikipedia, "Education in Iran.")

2. THE SAME CULTURES DON'T BRING THE SAME INTERESTS: MY CULTURAL STORY

Mansoureh Sharifzadeh
Ministry of Education, Tehran, Iran

My first image of life is sitting on the laps of my paternal grandmother reading the Qur'an while leaning against a cushion. Her rare blue Iranian eyes with long braided pepper and salt hair seemed spectacular to me. I listened to her murmur reading the verses with interest. Later on, I found myself playing in a yard with a pool at the center with my cousins. We all were living in an old house.

When I was four, we moved to our new houses and grandmother decided to live with her youngest son. In the following years I remember the monthly religious assemblies at grandmother's house on a specific day which was for the women. The relatives and friends of about 50 sat on the carpets leaning against cushions, around a big room and exchanged the past month's events and shared their news with each other. My cousins and I at the age about 13-18 were happy to meet each other and were welcoming the guests. Several preachers came one after another, sat on a chair to preach and finally got fees and left. My grandmother was sitting next to a Samovar and poured tea for the guests and we served it with sweets.

One hot summer afternoon, lying down on my bed reading Her Eyes by Bozorg Alavi, my mother came and said, "Ms. X has sent a message and asked for our positive reply for your marriage with her son, Mr. Hossein." Ms. X and her daughters were one of the distant relatives who always attended the assemblies. For a second I went numb; I was sixteen and a high school student. I anxiously replied, "No, No, I don't want to marry." Then I pulled the sheet over my head and repeated that again. "She is not ready for any marriage, leave her on her own," my brother who was a civil engineer university student said.

In Iran spring is short and so was my childhood. Subsequently I seldom attended the assemblies and the only shield was studying harder. The following year, I ranked the first in the class and after that obtained my high school diploma. Although in the university entrance exam I wasn't accepted in medicine, which I was longing for, I didn't give up. The probability of our marriage was getting stronger, but marriage for me was the death of any achievement at eighteen.

In 1974, the same year, fortunately I passed the Damavand college entrance exam and gave a stronger negative reply to their request. He (my intended husband) left Iran the same year and went to the United States for his post graduate education. For me it was a sigh of relief.

The Damavand days were the most fruitful period of my life. Although my English was rather poor, I gradually could communicate with different students and professors of various cultures. My first trips to Europe happened in that period and brought me a deeper perception about other cultures.

Those beautiful years came to an end in a blink and I graduated in 1978. One of my professors received my application from Kent State University when I was engaged with Mr. Hussein as he returned from the United States and his family insisted on our marriage. The application was ignored. The storm of the revolution started blowing and Tehran University where I was a post graduate student was closed. At the same time I was teaching English at two schools, too.

After the collapse of the Pahlavi dynasty in 1979, the universities were closed for about 2 years, I think. We married in 1979 and, in 1980 the Iran-Iraq war broke out. My first son, Vahid was born in the same period. I couldn't attend the university anymore as I had a baby and my husband was opposed to the continuation of my education. I didn't give up my job although he didn't like me to do so. I continued it as a part time teacher as an employee of the Ministry of Education. In 1988, with the war's ceasefire, my second son was born. I taught for about 32 years and retired in 2010, while still tutoring at home.

Vahid left Iran about 10 years ago and has been living with his Russian wife in the Ukraine although before his marriage he asked our opinion about her. Nowadays, Amir 24, a mechanical engineering graduate, is asking me to look for a wife for him. My answer always is, "You yourself must find a wife for yourself as you are the one who must live with her."

All through the past 32 years, my husband and I both have been trying to enhance each other in the way that we think is correct. We come from different perspectives and backgrounds although the layer of our beliefs might be the same. Our marriage proved a lot; people of the same cultures don't have common interests. Those assemblies were just a means to make decisions for future generations with no knowledge about the depth of the importance of the seat of our thoughts.

3. GROWING UP IN EGYPT

Aliaa A. Khidr
University of Virginia, Charlottesville, Virginia

Growing up in Egypt provided me with a sense of community, respect of elders, and independence. Both of my parents were born in the 1930's and by 1960, when I was born, they both had finished their higher education in Cairo University, the leading Egyptian Higher institute of education. Both of my parents came from middle class families, my father from a rural village in Egypt, and my mother from Cairo. At that time, higher education was only a privilege for the elite rich and a handful of high achievers who were able to earn scholarships that granted them a free university education. Both my parents were among that group. Not only that but right after their graduation they worked for a few years, then started their master's degrees in education, becoming junior faculty at the university. As I was finishing my elementary education, they were finishing their doctoral education.

Life during that period had a soothing rhythm. Winter, spring and fall were school time, while summer was vacation time. School days were mostly the same: wake in the morning to the radio with the music of a famous program called "kelmeteen we bas" (only two words) that discussed social issues, followed by morning news and excerpts of famous Egyptian songs. I can still hear my dad's voice singing along and holding my hands in dance like steps, and smell dates, eggs and butter from the kitchen as mom was preparing our daily breakfast and school sandwiches. We each had two home-made sandwiches, the first was always cheese and the second varied from "halawa" (a type of sweet spread) to jam or dates spread. "Belila" (organic wheat and milk) was another daily item for breakfast, which is a totally organic based cereal.

In elementary school years, dad used to drive us to school, but as soon as we started middle school we started taking the metro on our own. Every day my brother and I would walk to the metro accompanied by all the kids in our neighborhood, each going to a different school. We could tell schools by the uniforms: public schools had overall brown uniforms, while each private school had suit uniforms for girls or pants, shirts and ties for boys. Inside the metro all of us bundled up standing waiting for our station to come and get out because the seats were always reserved for the grown ups. So even if we found an empty seat, we would sit in it until a grown up came by, where we would usually get up saying "tafadal" (please have this) and the grown up would accept and reward us by a huge smile, a pat on our backs and a lengthy prayer for our happiness, success and health. It almost felt like reserving the seat for the morning good-luck prayer. The conductor would come by calling us "ebney " (my son) or "binty" (my daughter); we usually would give him ticket money or show him our seasonal pass addressing him as "amou" (uncle). Once each group arrived at its station the doors would open and tens of short and tall kids would get out and start running in different directions to their schools.

Afternoons on school days started with a short nap, followed by an hour or more of playing with neighborhood kids on our street. We had to make up new games to keep ourselves engaged. Not only that but we had to keep modifying the rules of the games to get everyone engaged. We also made up plays and took our roles very seriously. We almost never had adults sit down to watch our plays, but they would come by every now and then give us homemade cookies or drinks. Looking back, that must be part of why we were happy to see them come out. Sunset was the official time to come back to dinner followed by homework until bed time. Television had little role in our lives at that time; the radio was our main source of news and entertainment.

Summer vacations were always luscious and long. We spent two months in Cairo and one month on one of Egypt's fascinating beaches. Most of the middle class families did the same. It was always the most anticipated adventure of the year. We had a whole month to spend with our family as well as a lot of new people of all ages. Those usually ended up being our new group of friends.

Nowadays the middle class majority has disappeared and is being replaced by economically sound families or economically challenged families. The former group is more and more visible on the streets, in the sport clubs, in the malls and in the media. Public schools that were a respectable choice in the past are only selected by those who cannot afford a private school. Private schools in turn range from "affordable ones "to "totally outrageous ones" where tuition is paid in US dollars. Obviously those who graduate from the latter schools tend to attend one of the many foreign universities in Egypt. Accordingly the youth experience growing up in Egypt now totally depends on their economical level. The metro and the buses are no longer used by everyone.

Most of the "well to do" youth have never experienced using any public transportation. Private cars and personal drivers would be the only transportation they would be willing to try. Kids waiting for the metro today are no more taking pride in being independent and part of a "nationwide family like community." And most kids waiting for their private school's buses have never had a chance to meet, greet, or do any activity with other kids less privileged than themselves. Their community is limited to their socio-economic compatible peers. Even food choices differ along those lines; homemade sandwiches and healthy whole grain "affordable" meals become an unwelcomed destiny of the poor, while unhealthy snack style meals and fast food become the norm for those who can afford it and the dream for those who can't. Playing on the street with the neighbors is only reserved for the poor, while private sports clubs and malls are mainly populated by the rich. Kids end up not knowing their peers from their own neighborhood and having no contact whatsoever with anyone outside their family and parents' network. Similarly, summer vacations which now have been shortened to one week depend on the family's income. The rich spend their vacation in expensive private resorts where their kids complain about what they are not enjoying, and the poor spend it on one of the many beautiful public beaches wondering how would it feel like being in a resort.

But one very positive feature of Egyptian youth today, is that regardless of their socio economic status, they all thrive on technology; they make it their job to understand every new gadget inside out, whether they are cell phones, desk top computers, laptops, satellite dishes, a motor cycle , a fully equipped car, truck or airplane. They discuss and analyze the differences between different technologies as if this were their field of expertise. It doesn't matter whether they own one or not and it doesn't matter if they could even afford one in the future or not. Not only that but they follow up closely all global developments of different products, and brag about whichever nation or company has become the new leader in the technology discussed. This can be linked directly to the nationwide affordable access to the internet through phone lines and internet cafes as well as international and local satellite channels. The youth have become the experts on using technology for communication, research, and networking and even have gone a step further. Many active young Egyptians are finding a new way to express their opinions and report uncensored live events. They have become experts in using video streaming and uploading to different blogs and facebook networks to rally public support on different issues as well as to expose corruption.

These advantages have made Egyptian youth more bold than before, more trusting in their own opinion, and more daring in the way they are expressing themselves. They are feeling more connected to the outside world and keep sizing themselves up against other nations' youth hoping they can use different experiences to help them deal with their own challenges.

4.   Egyptian Youth Nowadays Are a Mystery

Edmaad M. O. Abdel Rahman
University of Virginia, Charlottesville, Virginia

Though I am not considered a youth any longer, I still remember those days. Things were different. There are things that changed to the better, others took a nose dive! My teenage years were in the early 1970s. Egypt was witnessing a major change in directions. After being ruled by President Gamul Nasser for close to two decades, President Anwar Sadat came to power. The major shift from the socialist regime led by Nasser to the open market regime led by Sadat was affecting every aspect of our lives. In the late 1960s and early 1970s, we had television, black and white, with only two channels. Programs started at 5:00 p.m. and ended by 11:00. It was only on during our weekend days, On Fridays, programs would go on until after midnight, with a late night movie. Only three newspapers were available. While this limited our source of information as well as entertainments, it allowed us more family time. Another benefit was that we shared with our peers the same entertainment. A new movie would be seen by everyone, and would be the topic of our next day discussions.

Our days were simple. Coming from a family where both my parents were working parents, my brother, my sister and I would go to school in the morning and return around 2:30 pm. By 3:00 pm my parents would be back from work and we, as a family, would sit together for our main midday meal. A couple of hours of napping would freshen us up. If the weather permitted, my brother and I would go down to the street and play soccer. No traffic was there, with limited cars in Cairo at that time. After sunset came homework time, followed by a 30 minutes of watching television with the family. Days were simple with no worries. Weekends were the days to go to the sporting club and occasionally a movie theater.

By the mid to late 1970s, changes were apparent. Now the television had color with more channels and longer hours of programming. The Cairo streets were seeing more cars. Working opportunities were opening in the rich gulf countries and families were starting to separate. Progress continues!! This was then. Things have changed dramatically now, and I can see that just by looking at my nieces and nephews. The information technology explosion had its toll on everything. Satellite dishes, cable, Internet, cell phones, while adding a lot, took away a lot. Youth nowadays are more informed and more entertained. This came at a price. The family fabric has shattered. Playing in the streets in Cairo is no longer an option. Just crossing the street has become an adventure. On the positive side, the youth are becoming more independent and "free" as well as computer and technology-savvy.

Youth nowadays are a mystery. They are a heterogeneous bunch of people. They range along the rainbow colors, mirroring the huge spectrum that Egypt now is witnessing. The division that occurred in the community has been happening at many levels; maybe the most evident cutting line, though by no means the only dividing line, is the line that separates the "have" and the "have nots." The youth in Egypt nowadays can encompass the teenagers who just are old enough to get a driver's licenses who are roaming the streets of big cities driving recklessly in the car that their parents bought them, without the least concern for their safety or the safety of others. It also can encompass those who stand for hours waiting for the public transportation, to go to work to support their families at a very young age. Youth can be highly educated, mastering more than two foreign languages to illiterate young men and women unable to read and write.

Whether then or now, youth is youth; the vibrant time of our lives. The mixture of the illusion of one's own immortality with the uncertainty of what the future has in store. During my youth, the solidarity of family and community ties was our main support system. For today's youth, this has been replaced by the confidence of knowledge and the ability to connect to the outside world through modern technology.

5. Life as a Teenager in Egypt

Ali E. Abdel-Rahman
Montecello High School, Charlottesville, Virginia

Nowadays in Egypt we have more and more youngsters and teens conforming to western (American) life. Westernizing, they eat fast food such as KFC, McDonalds, Taco Bell, and Pizza Hut instead of what they used to eat; traditional Egyptian/Arabian food and fresh fruits and vegetables. The new generation of Egypt is also listening to mostly all American music and watching western television instead of famous all time Egyptian singers like Umm Kalthum or Abdel Halim Hafez. If you asked them their favorite food/song/television show, over half of them would say American/western things. And yes, that means that almost all of them speak some English. The rich kids in private English schools can hold conversations in English, and the not so rich still learn English as a second language starting in elementary school and can say many meaningful phrases.

I personally think that Egyptian youth are feeling down because of the current limitations in job positions and resources. They dream about enjoying a highly paid job in a rich society like the United States, and think that by dressing, eating and acting like Americans they are a step closer to living like them. With that said, there are still a lot of youth who live by old-fashioned Egyptian principles and really want to be good people; they are willing to lend a helping hand even to people they have never met before; they will go out of their way to have a nice conversation with you to make you feel good, and will show a lot of respect to their parents, grandparents as well as any elders.

D) A Comparative Review: Three 2010 Middle East Books

Kinzer, S. (2010). Reset
McCarthy, A. C. (2010). The Grand Jihad
Reilley, R. R. (2010). The Closing of the Muslim Mind

reviewed by

Zhang Shengyong
Dezhou University, Dezhou, China

Michael H. Prosser
University of Virginia, Charlottesville, Virginia,
Shanghai International Studies University, Shanghai, China

Introduction

Samuel P. Huntington (1996) shocked the West in his book The Clash of Civilizations and the Remaking of the World Order, identifying this "clash" as representing mostly the Judao-Christian West versus the Islamic Middle East/Northern Africa and the Hindu/Confucian/Taoist/ Buddhist Asia. Martin Jaques' book When China Rules the World: The End of the Western World and the Birth of a New Global Order (2009) argues that modernity for Asia has an entirely different meaning than the concept of Western modernity. Jacques offers rather little importance to Asian religions, but clearly they are of great significance in terms of Asian (and Middle Eastern) modernization. The three books being reviewed in this article (Reset: Iran, Turkey and America's Future by Stephen Kinzer; The Grand Jihad: How Islam and the Left Sabotage America by Andrew C. McCarthy, and The Closing of the Muslim Mind: How Intellectual Suicide Created the Modern Islamic Crisis by Robert R. Reilly) all place special importance on religion, particularly Islam, as a major force in shaping the current Middle East.

Edward W. Said, in his book, Orientalism (1978), called academically for "a dialogue among nations," as did Mohammad Khatami when he was elected President of Iran in 1997. However, neither President Clinton nor Khatami at that time was brave enough to make an effort worthy of restructuring the difficult and tense relations between the United States and Iran. "Iran and the United States remained frozen in hostility, awaiting some lightning bolt that would change everything. It came on September 11, 2001. The September 11, 2001 attacks gave reconciliation between Washington and Tehran an urgent political logic. Iran and the United States found themselves facing a common foe (The Taliban and al Quaeda)." Unfortunately, President Bush's 2002 State of the Union address linking Iran, Iraq, and North Korea as "the axis of evil" again froze the potential cooperation between the Iranian and American governments (Kinzer, 125).

In Yong Yu and Peng Fan's article,"Five Keys to the Middle East Issue: A Review of Middle East Politics and Society" by Lian Wang (2009) they provide multiple sources relating to the modern issues relating to the Middle East. In the Prologue to the book, Weilie Zhu notes: "In order to apprehend the labyrinthic situation in the Middle East, we must be aware of three keys, i.e., desert culture, Islam and oil resources" (Zhu, 2009). The five keys by Wang to the Middle East issue identified by Yu and Fan include: the concept of the Middle East in 24 countries; Muslims and Arabs in the Middle East; conflicts, revolution and the greater Middle East; and the interrelation between the Middle East and oil (75-80).

Among books about the Middle East and Islam in 2010, three have considerable potential significance: Stephen Kinzer's Reset; Andrew C. McCarthy's The Grand Jihad; and Robert R. Reilly's The Closing of the Muslim Mind. Kinzer is the author of Overthrow: America's Century of Regime Change from Hawaii to Iraq; All the Shah's Men: An American Coup and the Roots of Middle East Terror, and Crescent and Star: Turkey between Two Worlds. McCarthy is the author of Willful Blindness: A Memoir of the Jihad. Reilly was a former director of the US Voice of America.

High praise for Reset has been offered by such well-known and objective Middle East experts as Andrew J. Bacevich, author of The Limits of Power: The End of American Exceptionalism; Thomas K. Pickering, former

US Ambassador to the United Nations; Karl S. Meyer, coauthor of Tournament of Shadows and Kingmakers: The Invention of the Modern Middle East; and Juan Cole, author of Napoleon's Egypt and Engaging the Muslim World. Meyer calls Reset "fluent, timely and provocative" and Pickering compliments Kinzer on his "deep knowledge of the Middle East" with "his historical perspective and trenchant analysis" (back flyleaf).

Conservative writers William J. Bennett, and Mark R. Levin, author of Liberty and Tyranny both give strong recommendations for McCarthy's The Grand Jihad. Both the title of McCarthy's book and quotes by such very conservative media stars in the United States as Rush Limbaugh, indicate the highly conservative, sensational and alarmist "Iran threat" direction of the book. Limbaugh has stated: "Our freedom is under assault as never before. For years, we've known about the Left's campaign to undermine our constitutional liberties and about radical Islam's campaign to destroy our way of life. What we now see, thanks to Andy McCarthy's piercing eye and gripping narrative, is that these campaigns work together, seamlessly." (endorsement in the book).

Reilly's The Closing of the Muslim Mind has received strong endorsements from a variety of liberal and conservative Middle East experts, including Roger Scruton, author of The West and the Rest; Vice Admiral John M. Poindexter; Patrick Sookhdeo, the Director of the Institute for the Study of Islam and Christianity; Paul Eidelberg, President of the Foundation for Constitutional Democracy (in Jerusalem); and Tawfik Hamid, Chair for the Study of Islamic Radicalism at the Potomac Institute for Policy Studies. Poindexter's endorsement is illustrative, "This meticulously researched book provides the historical context that has given rise to violent Islamism, and explains why the ethos of multiculturalism in the West is a largely misguided response to this violence." (back flyleaf). The conservative Michael Novak writes in his endorsement: "For some fourteen hundred years, Islam has been both intent on making the West Islamic and also in deep turmoil about its own identity and incapacity to govern itself. Reilly offers an intelligent person's guide to both of these longtime struggles" (back flyleaf).

Overview of the Three Books

1.   *Stephen Kinzer's Reset*

Historically oriented, Kinzer skillfully and analytically counter-balances the movement of Turkey toward a secular democracy and Iran toward an Islamic republic, and their effects on such countries in the Middle East as Iraq, Israel, and Saudi Arabia as well as their impact on relations with the United States. With eight chapters (274 pages), 20 pages of notes, and a generously cited bibliography, Kinzer's four parts concludes in which he offers new proposals for easing the Middle East crisis.

Reset's first five chapters compare and contrast Turkey's modernizing progress with Iran's systematic retreat from modernism. He features three major Turkish figures: Mustafa Kemal Ataturk, although the father of modern Turkey, he helped set the stage for its movement toward a secular democracy, but he did not by himself establish the modern Turkish emphasis on secular democracy (See Mango, 2002); Turgut Ozal, Prime Minister from 1983 to 1989 and President from 1989 to 1993, who actually did move a very traditional and conservatives state toward modernization and westernization, as well as potential European Union membership; and Istanbul Mayor Recep Tayyip Erdogan who was convicted, accused of promoting an Islamic state over a secular one, and jailed because of his recital of an ancient poem . After release from prison, he established a new political party, Justice and Development, a genuine grassroots movement, which swept to power. Kinzer notes "That such a dramatic victory could be won through the ballot box showed the strength of Turkish democracy. Immediately after taking office, Erdogan set off a whirlwind of reform unlike any the Turks had seen since Ozal" (134). Erdogan vigorously sought European Union membership, which Ozal had initiated in 1987, but during the 1990's both Turkish and EU sentiments toward Turkey's membership in the EU had faded. Still, at the 1999 Helsinki summit, EU leaders indicated their intention to move Turkey toward membership (but it remains today in an ambiguous status) (135). Although the military feared the creation of an Islamic fundamentalist state under Erdogan's leadership, he called new elections and again won a sweeping landslide victory. Kinzer remarks: "for the first time in modern history, a country was led toward democracy by a political party with roots in Islam.... The success of Erdogan and his AKP (Justice and Development Party) does not represent the triumph of Islamist politics in Turkey, but precisely the opposite: its death. Democracy has become Turkey's only alternative" (137-138).

In the same first five chapters, Kinzer compares and contrasts Turkey's clear movement toward democracy with Iran's process in becoming a fundamentalist Islamic republic. Kinzer asks: "In the years after 1980, both the Turks and the Iranians became disillusioned with their authoritarian regimes. They sought a way back to democracy. The Turks found one; the Iranians did not. Why?" (138).

Answering his own rhetorical question, Kinzer responds: "[Turkey] has been able to change with the times.... In Iran, the opposite happened. [The Shah, Reza] Pahlavi absolutism suffocated the natural development of democracy.... Reza became obsessed with family power.... In Iran, the democratic hero Mohammad Mossadegh was elected Prime Minister.... What threw Iran off track was foreign intervention. The Iranians, like the Turks, grasp the essence of democracy.... Their spontaneous uprising after the disputed 2009 election was proof of their democratic passion.... Turkey and Iran are then the only Muslim countries in the Middle East where democracy is deeply rooted" (139-141). Major figures in Iran's development, identified by Kinzer, have been the Shah Rezi Pahlavi, and after he was forced to flee, Iran became the setting for the establishment of an extremist fundamentalist Islamic Revolution under the leadership of the formerly exiled Ayatollah Rukollah Khomeini and the hostage-seizure of 52 American diplomats by a student mob in 1978. Since that time, the tensions have been very great between US governments and Iran, with periods where tensions seemed eased, and then intensified, particularly under the current leadership of President Mahmoud Ahmadinejad. Kinzer indicates that President Obama's outreach to the Middle East, especially to Turkey, and in a more constrained manner with Iran, has proven unsuccessful as late as 2009. With the UN Security Council's 2010 resolution to tighten sanctions on Iran because of its nuclear technology development, which is assumed to be directed toward the creation of nuclear weapons, further American-Iranian steps toward reconciliation seem to be less of an option.

Kinzer's Chapters Six and Seven are directed both toward the US-Saudia Arabian partnership, initiated secretly by President Franklyn D. Roosevelt a month before his death in April 1945, with King Abul-Aziz ibn Abd al-Rahman, based on the US need for a close Middle Eastern partnership and its increasing need for Middle Eastern oil, on one hand, coupled with the King's claim that compared to the European powers, America was "so very far away"; and the pressure placed on Roosevelt's successor after his death, President Harry S Truman, on the other hand, for the creation and protection of the state of Israel. In the former case, the United States accepted a monarchial, dictatorial and highly conservative fundamentalist Islamic regime as its major partner in the Middle East. In the latter case, both Jews from Europe and the United States, through Truman's best friend, Eddie Jacobson, and a whole host of Jewish mob figures, pushed Truman to accept a Jewish state in Palestine, causing several Middle East wars, in which Israel was increasingly victorious, but more and more isolated in tandem with successive US presidents. Kinzer argues that the continuing lack of peace between Israel and Palestine can be solved only in the following ways: "It is the essential precondition to security in the world's most explosive region. Although it seems very far away, even unachievable, in fact the opposite is true; it is within reach; It will not be reached if the warring parties are left to shape it themselves" (186). Still, Kinzer recognizes all of the problems that a peace imposed from outside the region, such as a bold American president might impose, but with both positive and negative results in the region externally.

2.   Andrew C. McCarthy: The Grand Jihad

Written in rather casual, newsy, folksy, often non-scholarly language, with multiple metaphorical clichés, alarmist views toward "the Iran threat," very conservative and sensationalistic, his 18 chapters (435 pages) nonetheless appear to be carefully researched and have very helpful extensive notes (pages 377-436), but surprisingly no specific bibliography or references. Already a best-seller with his earlier "Iran threat" book Willful Blindness, The Grand Jihad has the potential of also being a best seller for fearful Americans, intrigued by "the Iran threat" as exemplified by the front flyleaf endorsement by Steven Emerson, bestselling author of Jihad: The Terrorists Living among Us: "Once I opened the first page, I could not put it down. McCarthy has produced an unparalleled masterpiece that every American must read." (See also Cordesman & Kleiber, 2007; Hitchcock, 2006; Jafarzade, 2008; Kiesbye, 2010) or the same sort of Americans who are immersed in "China threat" best-selling books (See Agarwala, 2002; Burman, 2009; Elwell, Labonte, & Morrison, 2008; Geertz, 2002; Menges, 2005; Peerenboom, 2008; Storey, 2009; Timberlake& Triplett, 2002; Yee and Storey, 2004; Yee, 2010). McCarthy's early chapters, "With Willing Submission," "Islamism: A Triumph of Hope over Experience," "Jihad Is Our Way," "Eliminating and Destroying the Western Civilization from Within," "We Will Conquer America through Dawa" all build up the Islamist threat toward America. McCarthy defines dawa as "the Islamists primary method of undermining Western values and American constitutional society" (43).

McCarthy exhibits a continuing very strong disdain for socialism, "the Left, ("Islam is lined up with the Left,"185) and Barack Obama and his Kenyan communist-leaning father.. McCarthy consistently equates "the Left" with Islam and socialism/communism, and President Obama, as a highly successful but untruthful politician with "the Left" as well as Islam, and therefore also leaning toward the Marxist and radical training of Sol Alinsky, and his own Kenyan father's explicit following of communism. Through a close reading of The Grand Jihad, it seems obvious to McCarthy, and other conservative writers, that since the Muslims believe that Islam is the "only true religion" which follows Allah's guidance in the Qur'an, Mohammed the Prophet, the early caliphs, and more recent wise political/religious leaders, their goal always has been, and must continue to be, to convert others to Islam, in order to make the perfect umma, or perfect society. Therefore, they are also required morally to conduct a Jihad against all nonbelievers, and moving when possible to the shar'ia or Islamic law over democratic constitutional law.

McCarthy begins and ends his book with rather sarcastic assaults on President Obama, first discussing the indeed somewhat curious public and reverential deep bow to Abdullah bin Abdul Aziz, King of Saudia Arabia, at the Buckingham Palace 2009 G 20 Summit, while being almost hostile and inappropriately impolite to Prime Minister Gordon Brown of the United Kingdom, America's closest ally, in the same celebratory gathering. Denouncing the "Obamamedia's" 2007-2008 election coverage of Obama, particularly the very gingerly but generally positive treatment given him in a long feature essay by the Boston Globe during the 2008 presidential campaign, McCarthy spends several chapters "exposing" Obama's bias toward Islam, his general untruthfulness, and constant shifting of his story. In the final chapters, Chapter 23 "Isolated Extremists" and "Epilogue," McCarthy returns to his subtheme of demonstrating Obama's leftist/socialistic leanings in the context of US Army Major Nidal Malic Hasan's rampage in which he murdered 13 Americans, including 12 US troops, and wounded another 38 at Fort Hood, Texas on November 5, 2009. McCarthy argues that despite Obama's pious platitudes about religion and Islam specifically being peaceful, he has been an enabler for such Islamicist diatribes and violence against the American public and constitution.

In the Epilogue, McCarthy not only castigates Obama's weakness toward Islam, but also President Clinton's Justice Department creation of an "infamous" wall in pretending that terrorists should be treated as citizens with full transparent and fair privileges in a US criminal court. In the case of Obama's chief advisor on homeland security and counterterrorism John Brennan, he assured Islamic law students at New York University that "Obama was "determined to put America on a strong course" – meaning a course that would correct the Bush administration approach to counterterrorism that had been so "over the top" and "excessive" (373-374). McCarthy concludes his book: "If you didn't know better, you'd think Islamists had developed 'a kind of grand jihad in eliminating and destroying the Western civilization from within and 'sabotaging' its miserable house. Why, it's almost as if they now had a government that was helping them do it." (p. 376) The Grand Jihad does have much serious thinking about the development of Islam, Islamists, and the role of extremists in creating modern obstacles to the development of other religions and political thought and action. However, because of its right-wing conservative bias against the modern media and political leaders such as Presidents Clinton and Obama, one has to consider the potential bias of the strongly conservative, anti-Left positions which McCarthy and other "Iran-threat" authors espouse. Essentially, based on our reading of his book, McCarthy appears to be anti Left, anti Islam, anti Obama, and anti main stream media's Obama election campaign coverage in 2008. It is reasonable to say that while The Grand Jihad seems to offer a comprehensive and well-researched view of its subject in terms of his quoted resources in his notes, extremist writers on the Left or Right with a polemical agenda have the potential of creating justified suspicion about their total objectivity.

3.   Robert R. Reilly: The Closing of the Muslim Mind

In a very philosophical, politically, historically-oriented and objective scholarly book of nine chapters (244 pages), with ample reference notes (pages 207-227) and brief "Further Reading" (pages 229-231), Reilly makes extensive comparisons between Greek Hellenistic thought about the nature of logic and reason, Christian theological perspectives about the First Cause, reason, and natural morality, including in the treatises of Thomas Aquinas, and the early medieval opening of Muslim philosophical thought with references to ancient Greek philosophy's approach to reason. Through the Islamic discovery of the Greek Hellenistic arguments by Socrates, Plato, and Aristotle through their contributions to the understanding and appreciation of logos (logic – reason) we note ("Chapter 1: The Opening: Islam Discovers Hellenic Thought," then the partial acceptance by the Mu'tazilites of this logic, almost sensing a dual nature of Allah (Allah the unknowable and Allah the all knowing). However, the Mu'tazilites suffered increasingly very hostile attacks on them by the Ash'arists and by the seminal and most revered Islamic thinker after Mohammed, al-Ghazali, with his eventual mystical experience with Allah, after overcoming his flirtation with Hellenic thought. Reilly claims that by incorporating their denunciation by these Islamists, later the closing of the Muslim mind by the acceptance of their wide-spread condemnatory-view toward the value of the human will in favor of a Divine will by Allah that is not only the

First Cause, but the only cause of all actions occurred: (Chapter 2: "The Overthrow of the Mu'tazilites: The Closing Commences," Chapter 3: "The Metaphysics of the Will," Chapter 4: "The Triumph of Ash'arim," Chapter 5: "The Unfortunate Victory of al-Ghazali and the Dehellenization of Islam," and Chapter 6: Decline and Consequences." Writing in the Foreword, Roger Scruton ponders the disappearance of the logical Western "cause-effect" in Muslim society:

Why is it that this (Islamic) civilization, which sprang up with such an abundance of energy in the seventh century of our era, and which spread across North Africa and the Middle East to produce cities, universities, libraries, and a flourishing courtly culture which has left a permanent mark on the world, is now in so many places mute, violent, and resentful? Why does Islam today seem not merely to tolerate the violence of its fiercest advocates, but to condone and preach it? (ix-x).

Reilly describes the moral and intellectual crisis of Islam in the ninth to eleventh centuries of Islam "when it turned its back on philosophy and took refuge in dogma" especially in the rise of the Ash'arite sect in the eleventh century. Al Ghazali, who died in 1111 (CE), was their most powerful voice, proclaiming that reason was the enemy of Islam, particularly through his well known treatise The Incoherence of the Philosophers. Despite the efforts of Averroes (Ibn Rushd) in his treatise, The Incoherence of Incoherence, to refute al Ghazali's arguments, the Ash'arites sent him into exile, ending any support for the concept of human reason in human actions, and thus continuing until today as a widespread understanding among many Muslims, including Muslim intellectuals, that the issue of reason versus the sometimes contradictory will of Allah is a closed issue (Scruton, x-xi).

Reilly indicates that the mind of many Muslims throughout the world frequently has not closed intellectually and suicidally, which seems to be a different more nuanced perspective than that offered by McCarthy, but that too many of the two billion current Muslims accept the flawed concept that only what Allah wills or does not will incomprehensibly has any authority in all matters of human existence. A key question for Reilly is how can so many current intelligent Muslims blindly accept these earlier arguments over the nature of Allah that since Allah only wills or does not will, nothing that humans do can occur except in obedience or defiance of Allah's will (3). Reilly states that terrorism, or support for it, by Islamic extremists and fundamentalists, is not the only problem for modern Islam, but that it includes the loss of even basic Islamic science and philosophy, as well as indigenously developed democratic constitutional governments, in favor of Islamic law, shar'ia, over democratic legislative law: "the Arab world stands near the bottom of every measure of human development.... How much of this is Islam and how much is Islamism? Is Islamism a deformation of Islam?"(6). McCarthy would certainly agree with Reilly in his own denunciation of Islamism.

Reilly compares "The First Struggle: Qadar (Man's Power to Act) versus Jabr (Fate/Compulsion)"; "The Second Struggle: 'Aql'(Reason) versus Naql (Traditional Faith). He highlights the primacy of reason and reflection; the objectivity of morality: knowing the good; the goodness and justice of God; and the unity of God as Hellenic and Christian philosophical orientations. He argues that the created Qur'an contrasts Islamic differing beliefs in whether it was created in time and thus subject to further interpretation, leading to free will, or as coequal with God, and thus unchangeable with an emphasis on jurisprudence rather than the questioning that is normally a part of philosophy and theology. Thus, the demotion of reason in Islamic intellectual thought became the standard for much Islamic thought that has been a major force in Islam today (15-33, 48). In the earlier and later manifestations of Ash'arite views, "because "God is unknowable, if God is pure will, then He is incomprehensible.... Nothing is like Him.... If the world cannot be understood by reason, how possibly could its Creator?" (54). As the Christian view of God is that he created man (woman) in his own likeness, and that the Gospel of John begins "In the beginning was the Word (Logos-reason), and the Word was with God and the Word was God"; thus in this way, Christianity believes that God's creation has ordered and logical consistency and Islam says that since God is unknowable, as pure will, he can say "Be," or "not be (without logical inconsistency). Thus, in this way, the two religions are incompatible (56-58). Reilly claims that from this belief, Islam has lost causality, any sense of epistemology, an objective morality, a sense of justice, and even a loss of individual freewill, leaving only jurisprudence and potentially despotism, without a relation to justice or precise morality (60-90).

In Chapters 6: "Decline and Consequences," 7: "The Wreckage: Muslim Testimonials," 8: "The Sources of Islamism," and 9: "The Crisis," Reilly provides numerous examples from Islamic media (See also Said, 1981) and Islamic leaders who denounce the logic of the Western world, modernity, freedom, and democracy. He offers the question: "The great crisis that has seized the Islamic world poses the question to Muslims: 'Can we enter the modern world and also retain our faith?'.... One answer to the question above has been provided by the Islamists and Osama bin Laden. His answer is no; we cannot retain our faith in the modern world. Therefore, we must destroy modernity" (197).... The answer of Islamism is grounded in a spiritual pathology based upon a theological deformation that has produced a dysfunctional culture" (197). Reilly concludes: "As was seen in the blood-soaked history of the twentieth century, the 'priority of the irrational' – even if embraced only by the radical few – can inexorably lead to limitless violence, because of primacy of the will, whether in God or man, knows no bounds. The recovery of reason, grounded in Logos, is the only sentinel of sanity.This is imperative for the East as well as the West" (205).

Major Conclusions and Contributions by the Three Authors

Kinzer focuses his comments about Turkey and Iran and their importance to the United States, as well as to other Middle East countries, such as Iraq, Israel, and Saudia Arabia. In his last concluding chapter "Part Four: The Door is So Wide Open," Kinzer offers the following conclusions and proposals. When Nobel Peace Laureate President Shimon Peres spoke in 2007 to the Turkish Grand National Assembly, he proposed "Turkey instills trust" (195). Kinzer emphasizes that "instilling trust has become Turkey's global mission.... Turkey has been a political and military ally of the United States for more than half a century.... Turkey has taken on the role of mediator, conciliator, and arbitrator.... Foreign Minister Ahmet Davuto-glu's grand concept, which he calls 'Strategic Depth,' envisions Turkey as a hyperactive peacemaker" (195-197). Turkey has remained a close ally of the Persian, Arabic and Israeli nations, though this relationship with Israel was seriously strained during the 2008-09 Gaza crisis (See Prosser, 2009: September). Kinzer's book had not yet been published when in April 2010 the Israeli Navy and Air Force intercepted the humanitarian aid flotilla seeking to break the Gaza water blockade, where nine Turkish citizens were killed by the Israeli military. This event caused a great outrage by Prime Minister Erdogan and the near breaking of Israeli-Turkish relations.

Kinzer argues that just as the Middle East needs Turkey as a model nation in the region, it would be foolish for Turkey to reject Israeli-Turkish relations and to further isolate Israel with only its American ally. At the same time, he insists that the United States must also maintain its friendly and cooperative relations with Turkey. Additionally, Turkey must continue to support its possible accession to the European Union and to maintain friendly relations with Europe: "Not only Arabs but Muslims everywhere place great hope in the Turkey-EU relationship." Because of the cooling of interest in the European Union for Turkish admission, Kinzer believes that this could cause Turkey to look elsewhere – with more relations with the Middle East to the detriment of the European Union and the United States.

Offering concluding arguments about Iran, Kinzer notes that "Iran is the big country in the middle" (205); See also Fuller, 2007; Morris, (2006). Thus, Kinzer argues that in this case the United States should shape its policy not by emotional past insults by Iran, or by a cool calculation of self-interest. The tragedy if America's long estrangement from Iran is that it has undermined America's own interest" (206). Kinzer lists ten realistic objectives that the United States should seek to improve its relationship with Iran (208). To achieve these goals, he proposes that the United States would have to recognize Iran as an important power with legitimate security interests while remembering that a nuclear armed Iran would cause a major security threat to the entire Middle Eastern region (208). Ideally, then a far reaching accord is needed between the United States and Iran: "Iran is the only Muslim country in the world where most people are reliably pro American. This pro-American sentiment in Iran is a priceless strategic asset for the United States" (p. 212). Kinzer concludes by noting that the 1972 Shanghai Communique was not itself an accord between China and the United States, but set the stage for later significant cooperation and accords between the two countries. He believes that this communique might serve as a model for later agreements between the United States and Iran.

McCarthy makes a number of major assumptions about how the Grand Jihad sabotages the United States. Beyond a "wake-up" call to his readers to accept that Islam, Islamists, and many Muslims have as their goal to undermine and sabotage American values and constitutional freedoms, as he claims has happened in several European countries, and indeed in many potentially more moderate Muslim countries, he is strongly focused as well on the crisis dangers that the Left socialistic leaders have created for American freedom and constitutionality, including the current administration of President Obama. The book's promotion argues: "The real threat to the United States is not terrorism. The real threat is the sophisticated forces of Islamism, which have collaborated with the American Left not only to undermine US national security, but also to shred the fabric of American constitutional democracy – freedom and individual liberty.... and how it has found the ideal partner in President Barack Obama, whose Islamist sympathies run deep" (front flyleaf). Unlike Kinzer's Reset, McCarthy does not offer a precise way to solve what he states as a serious and significant threat, but instead, calls the readers' attention to the problem itself for America and its future, in a well-researched, but strongly biased and polemical fashion.

Nonetheless, because of its potential sensationalism, it is likely to attract a very large American readership of individuals fearful about the future of America, either because of what such authors provide as "the Iran" or "the China threat," especially since his earlier, Willful Blindness, was very quickly a best seller after its publication.

Reilly, in his thoughtfully philosophical, historical, and political book, believes that many Middle Easterners and intelligent Muslims have created the modern Islamic crisis, because a millennium ago, the Muslim mind became closed, without the ability of future generations to reopen it in order for modernizing trends to reemerge. Both McCarthy and Reilly spend considerable effort in discussing the sometimes dualistic Muslim view of the nature of God, and the highly negative role of the Islamists, McCarthy writing in a sensational, alarmist narrative, and Reilly as a more thoughtful scholar of Islam.

Among the three books, all of them make important contributions to an understanding of the Middle East, Kinzer in relation especially to Turkey and Iran; McCarthy in his overview of the Islamists' emphasis on Jihad against America and the enabling feature of the Left and the Obama presidency; and Reilly's historical, philosophical, and political analysis of the opening and later closing of the Muslim mind by its rejection of reason versus dogma. Each, in its own way provides a valuable perspective on the current Middle East and its relationship to other Middle Eastern states, as well as to the United States, and each stresses the importance of Islamic theological tenets on its potential for modernization on its own terms.

References

Agarwala, R. (2002). The Rise of China; Threat Or Opportunity? New Delhi, India: Bookwell.

Baru S. Cordesman, A.H. & Kleiber, M. (2007). Iran's Military Forces and War Fighting Capabilities: The Threat in the Northern Gulf. Washington, DC: Westport.

Cordesman, A.H.& Al-Rodhan, K.R. (2006). Iran's Weapons of Mass Destruction: The Real and Potential Threat. Washington, D.C. CSIS,

Elwell, C.K., Labonte, M,& Morrison, W.M.(2008). Is China a Threat to the U.S .Economy? Washington, D.C.: CRS Report for Congress.

Fuller, G.E.(2007). New Turkish Republic: Turkey as a Pivotal State in the Muslim World. Washington, D.C.: United States Institute of Peace Research. Pivotal State series.

Geertz, B. (2002). How the People's Republic Targets America. Washington, D.C. :Regery Company.

Hitchcock, M.(2006). Iran: The Coming Crisis: Radical Islam, Oil, and the Nuclear Threat. New York, NY: The Doubleday Religious Publishing Group.

Huntington, S. (1996). The Clash of Civilizations and the Remaking of World Order. NewYork, NY: Simon and Schuster.

Jafarzadeh, A. (2008). The Iran Threat: President Ahmadinejad and the Coming Nuclear Crisis. New York, NY: Palgrave Macmillan.

Kiesbye, S.(2010). Is Iran a Threat to Global Security? Farmington Hills, MI: Greenhaven Press. At Issues series.

Kinzer, S. (2010). Reset: Iran, Turkey and America's Future. New York, NY: Times Books, Henry Holt and Company.

Mango, A. (2002). Ataturk: The Biography of the Founder of Modern Turkey. New York, NY: Penguin Group.

Jacques, M. (2009). When China Rules the World: The End of the Western World and the Birth of a New Global Order. New York, NY: The Penguin Press.

McCarthy, A.C.(2010). The Grand Jihad: How Islam and the Left Sabotage America. New York,, NY: Encounter Books.

Menges, C.C.(2005). China: The Gathering Threat. Nashville, TN: Nelson Current.

Morris, C.(2006). The New Turkey: The Quiet Revolution on the Edge of Europe. London, England: Granta Books.

Peerenboom ,R.P.(2008). China Mmodernizes: Threat to the West or Model for the Rest? Oxford: Oxford University Press.

Prosser, M.H. (2009: September). Obama's Culturally Transformational Identitiesand Accommodations toward the Middle East and Islam. Journal of Middle Eastern and Islamic Studies (in Asia). Vol.3. No. 3. pp. 1-13).

Reilly, R.R. (2010). The Closing of the Muslim Mind: How Intellectual Suicide Created the Modern Islamic Crisis. Wilmington, DE: ISI Books.

Said, E.W. (1979) Orientalism. New York, NY: Vintage Books.

Said, E.W. (1981). Covering Islam: How the Media and the Experts Determine How We See the Rest of the World. New York, NY: Pantheon Books.

Storey, I. (2009). The China Threat: Perceptions, Myths and Reality. London, England: Taylor and Francis Group.

Timberlake, E. (2002). Red Dragon Rising: Communist China's Military Threat to America. Washington, D.C.: Regery.

Yee, H.S. (2010). China's Rise; Threat or Opportunity? Houston,TX: Questia. Routledge Security in Asia series.

Yee, H. & Storey, I.(2004). China threat: Perceptions, myths. London, England: Routledge.

Yu, Y. & Fan, P. (2009: September). Five keys to the Middle East issue: A review of Middle East Politics and Society. Journal of Middle Eastern and Islamic Studies (in Asia). Vol. 3.

Zhu, W.(2009). Prologue. In L. Wang, Middle East politics and society. Beijing, China: Peking Publishing House.

Acknowledgements

Zhang Shengyong's essay, "The Perception of China and Its Influence on Sino-US Relations" was initially published in Intercultural Communication Studies (2011).

Michael H. Prosser's essay, "Personal Reflections on Reading Discourse on the Middle East for New Intercultural Understandings," was initially published in The Journal of Middle Eastern and Islamic Studies (in Asia) 2012: January).

The following essays were published initially in Li Mengyu and Michael H. Prosser's Communicating Interculturally (2012), Beijing, China: Higher Education Press:

Part I:
Michael H. Prosser, "The American Millennials,"
Daniel F. Alonso, "Argentinian and Latin American Youth,"
Helene Dislaire, "Belgian Youth,"
Sergei A. Samoilinki, "Youth in Modern Russia,"
Anya Klyukanova, "A Russian Girl, Lovely Parents, and a Russian Passport,"
Yves Assidou, "Togo: Corridor of Western Africa,"

Part II:
Li Mengyu, "Harmony as a Major Value,"
Joanna, Liu "A Glimpse of the Life of Contemporary Chinese Women"
Judy Yeonoka, "Japanese Youth Today: The Glocal Generation,"
Li Mengyu, "China's Contemporary Youth: The Post 1980s Generation,"
William Zhu, "My Cultural Background,"
Jacky Zhang, "The Story of My 30+ Years,"
Zing Zhang, "From the Mini-UN to the Real UN,"

Part III:
Aliaa A. Khidr, "Growing Up in Egypt"
Edmaad M.O. Abdel Rahman, "Egyptian Youth Nowadays Is a Mystery,"
Ali E. Abdel-Rahman, "Life as a Teenager in Egypt."

All essays have previously appeared in www.michaelprosser.com .

We are very grateful for the wise direction and design of the book by Dr. Uli Spalthoff, director of operations at Dignity Press, Evelin Lindner, the founder of the Human Dignity and Humiliation Studies Network, and Linda Hartling, Director of the Network as well as managing director of Dignity Press.

Contributors

Page numbers indicate contributions.

Ali E. Abdel-Rahman, Montecello High School, Charlottesville, Virginia 479

Edmaad M. O. Abdel Rahman, University of Virginia, Charlottesville, Virginia 477

Tyrone L. Adams 59

Daniel F. Alonso, Universidad Austral, Argentina 84

Yves Assidou, Togo, Shanghai University of Finance and Economics, Shanghai, China 96

Cui Litang, Xiamen University, Tan Kha Kee College, Xiamen, China 273

Cui Wu, Beijing, China 224

Helene Dislaire, Malmedy, Belgium 87

Jean-Louis Dislaire, Belgium 87

Ray T. Donahue, Nagoya Gakuin University, Nagoya, Japan 175

Mary Finocchario, Kansas City, Kansas 57

He Daokuan, Shenzhen University, Shenzhen, China 243

D. Ray Heisey (d. May 20, 2011) 358, 421

Jing Zhang, The United Nations, New York City, New York 308, 310

Kelly Ni 224

Aliaa A. Khidr, University of Virginia, Charlottesville, Virginia 473

Anya Klyukanova, University of Oregon, Eugene, Oregon 94

Grace Liang Xiaoxue, Shanghai International Studies University, Shanghai, China 312

Li Mengyu, Ocean University of China, Qingdao, China 216, 287

Evelin G. Lindner 100

Joanna Liu (pseudonym), Beijing Language and Culture University, Beijing, China 238

Rebeccah Kinnamon Neff 71

Elizabeth Marie Prosser 82

Biographies of the Editors

Michael H. Prosser, Ph.D. (University of Illinois), a founder of the academic field of intercultural communication, has taught full-time at the University of Buffalo, Indiana University, the University of Virginia, University of Swaziland, Rochester Institute of Technology, Yangzhou University, Beijing Language and Culture University, Shanghai International Studies University, and Ocean University of China, and as a visiting faculty member at several other universities.

He has edited/coedited, authored/coauthored fifteen earlier books, including most recently with Steve J. Kulich, Intercultural Perspectives on Chinese Communication (2007); Values Frameworks at the Theoretical Cross Roads of Culture, Intercultural Research, Vol. 4 (2012); and Values Dimensions and Their Contextual Dynamics across Cultures, Intercultural Research, Vol. 5 (in press); and Li Mengyu and his book Communicating Interculturally (2012). Cui Litang's and Michael H. Prosser's Social Media in Asia is forthcoming from Dignity Press. Michael H. Prosser was the series editor for seventeen books in his series "Civic Discourse for the Third Millennum" for Ablex, Praeger, and Greenwood Publishers.

Past President of SIETAR International, he has been honored by Ball State University, the International Communication Association, SIETAR International, and the Chinese Association for Intercultural Communication. He is a Fellow of the International Academy for Intercultural Research, and is listed in the Marquis Who's Who in American Education, Who's Who in America, Who's Who in Asia, and Who's Who in the World. He has three children and nine grandchildren.

Mansoureh Sharifzadeh (B. A. Damavand College, Tehran-Iran), has been an English language teacher at public and private pre-university centers of Tehran since 1978. Translating books from English to Persian, she was awarded honors by President Seyyed Mohammed Khatami in 2004. She is a writer of English and Persian published articles and a frequent contributor to the www.michaelprosser.com blog.

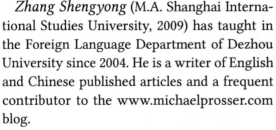

Her connection with the second last president of Damavand College, Professor D. Ray Heisey in 2008, caused her to face fundamental changes in her perspectives about global communication and writing papers.

She has two sons.

Zhang Shengyong (M.A. Shanghai International Studies University, 2009) has taught in the Foreign Language Department of Dezhou University since 2004. He is a writer of English and Chinese published articles and a frequent contributor to the www.michaelprosser.com blog.

His academic life became involved with international relations and intercultural communication in 2006 at Shanghai International Studies University. Particularly, he was a faculty member there of the First Buddhism English Training of China This special experience helped him research Buddhism and China's traditional culture.

Zhang Shengyong has attended several International Association for Intercultural Communication Studies conferences, including the most recent one in Taiwan in 2012, and also the International Communication Association 2010 conference in Singapore, all of which totally opened his mind to global values and knowledge. Through his international travels to 12 countries and regions of the world, he began to think deeply about China's image in the world, on China's youth, their role in spreading Chinese culture, and improving China's image more broadly.

In 2011, he published his first book with Ms. Xu Jun, Research on China's Global Image which has developed his deep interests in intercultural and international communication.

Index

H

I

Other books from Dignity Press:

Arctic Queen
The Pearl

Evelin Lindner
A Dignity Economy

Howard Richards
The Nurturing of Time Future

Howard Richards and Joanna Swanger
Gandhi and the Future of Economics

Ada Aharoni
Rare Flower

Pierre-Amal Kana
Afghanistan – Le rêve pashtoun et la voie de la paix

Victoria Fontan
Decolonizing Peace

Deepak Tripathi
A Journey Through Turbulence

More about these at www.dignitypress.org

Dignity Press
World Dignity University Press

Printed in the USA
CPSIA information can be obtained
at www.ICGtesting.com
LVHW021614310124
770340LV00009B/158